Hiking Marin

141 Great Hikes in Marin County

Don and Kay Martin

Bob Johnson, illustrator

Disclaimer - Notice of Liability

The information in this book is distributed on an "As is" basis, without warranty. We can not accept responsibility for trail conditions or for trail information. When it comes to trail safety, there are several reasons why you can't rely on this book. First, nature and the park agencies are not static. Hillsides erode, trees fall down, signs change and trails change. Second, the map is not the trail. No matter how descriptive the map or text is, it can't describe each and every junction or feature, root or rut. Third, the book contains errors, not on purpose, but there are errors just the same.

This is our disclaimer that we do not accept liability or legal responsibility for any injuries, damage, loss of direction or time allegedly associated with using this book. For the best information, check the local ranger stations.

Contact Information

Inquiries should be addressed to:
Martin Press LLC
P.O. Box 2109
San Anselmo, CA 94979
or email: book@marintrails.com

Cover Photo Locations

Chimney Rock, Muir Woods, Tennessee Valley, Cataract Creek and Bon Tempe Lake

Photo Credits

22   *S.S. Tennessee*: National Maritime Museum, San Francisco
44   Gravity Car: A.C. Graves-Ted Wurm Collection
48   Muir Woods Inn: Muir Woods National Monument
80   Tamalpais Tavern: photo courtesy of Joseph A. Baird, Jr.
138 Papermill: Samuel P. Taylor State Park
140 Hotel: Samuel P. Taylor State Park
194 Bear Valley Country Club: Anne T. Kent California Room, Marin County Library
202 The Oaks: Jack Mason Museum
246 Schooner *Point Reyes*: Point Reyes National Seashore
260 Tule Elk: photo by John Aho, Point Reyes National Seashore
All other photos by the authors.

Acknowledgments

This book includes material from two other books, *MT TAM* and *Point Reyes National Seashore*. We are extremely grateful to everyone who has helped us in producing these books. We are especially thankful to Ron Angier, Greg Archbald, Sue Baty, Janet Bowman, Chris Bramham, John Del'Osso, Lincoln Fairley, Wilma Follette, Tom Gaman, Dave Gould, Geoff Geupel, Rand Knox, Dewey Livingston, Jim Locke, Jennifer Matkin, Casey May, Eric McGuire, Bill Michaels, Ron Miska, Al Molina, Mia Monroe, Eric Mohr, Joe Mueller, Don Neubacher, Chuck Oldenburg, Jerry Olmsted, Jeff Price, Leonard Page, Larry Perkins, Steven Petterle, Ron Paolini, Pat Robards, Solange Russek, Nicholas Salcedo, Fred Sandrock, Bob Stewart, Meryl Sundove, Ted Wurm, Lanny Waggoner and Jack Williams.

We would also like to thank our hiking and running friends who have shared many enjoyable times on the trails with us: Dick and Sharon Shlegeris, Bill and Dixie James, Charles James, Steve and Marge Paradis, Shel and Joy Siewert, Phil and Mary Neff, Mike and Lynn Spurlock, Steve and Ruth Nash, Arlene Hansen, Mary Lou Grossberg, Sue Steele, John and Greg Hart and the Bovine Bakery Brunch Bunch.

We especially want to thank the members of our family, Jennifer Martin and Daryl Odnert, Theresa Martin and Brian Simon, Susan Martin and Greg Martin, for their enthusiastic and valuable support.

Although these people have helped us in many ways, we are responsible for all errors that have occurred.

Notes about Previous Editions

The first edition of this book contained 121 hikes spread throughout seven regions in Marin, labeled A-G. The 2nd edition kept these 121 hikes with some changes and added 12 new hikes in Region H. Likewise, this 3rd edition has kept the 133 hikes from previous editions and added 9 new hikes in Region J (there is no Region I).*

Thus, we have maintained continuity in hike numbers. For example, Hike A11, in all 3 editions, climbs Ring Mountain. Hike G5, in all 3 editions, hikes the Bayview - Muddy Hollow area in Point Reyes.

However, some hikes from the 1st and 2nd edition have been changed, either because trails have changed, or to improve the hike. These changes are listed on pages 264 and 290.

*There are actually more hikes than these numbers indicate, since some pages have multiple hikes on them. Counting every hike, this third edition has 168 total hikes with 15 new hikes in Region J.

Table of Contents

This book is dedicated

To the citizens of Marin County, past and present, who have had the foresight, energy and perseverance to protect the natural beauty of Marin and thus create the finest urban park system in the world.

To the park rangers and volunteer associations who love and maintain this park system for our education and enjoyment.

Public lands visited in this book include

Golden Gate National Recreation Area
Muir Woods National Monument
Point Reyes National Seashore
Angel Island State Park
China Camp State Park
Mt. Tamalpais State Park
Olompali State Park
Samuel P. Taylor State Park
Tomales Bay State Park
Alto Bowl - Camino Alto Open Space Preserves
Baltimore Canyon - King Mountain Open Space Preserves
Blithedale Ridge Open Space
Bolinas Lagoon Open Space
Cascade Canyon - White Hill Open Space Preserves
Deer Island Open Space
Gary Giacomini Open Space
Ignacio Valley Open Space
Indian Tree - Little Mountain Open Space Preserves
Indian Valley Open Space
Loma Alta Open Space
Loma Verde Open Space
Lucas Valley Open Space
Mt. Burdell Open Space
Old St. Hilary Open Space - Tiburon Ridge
Pacheco Valle Open Space
Ring Mountain Open Space
Roy's Redwoods - French Ranch Open Space Preserves
Rush Creek Open Space
San Pedro Mountain Open Space
Terra Linda-Sleepy Hollow Divide Open Space
Audubon Canyon Ranch
Las Gallinas Sanitary Wildlife Ponds
Marin Municipal Water District
Marinwood Community Services District
McInnis County Park
Stafford Lake County Park

How to Use this Book

Choosing a Hike

Not sure where to go? We usually plan our hikes around the season and weather. In the winter, we look for creeks, waterfalls and views. In spring, green-covered hills and wildflowers are the main attraction. In the fall, we head out to the coast. Check out Appendices 1 and 2 for many more ideas.

Hike Descriptions

Here is a sample entry of a hike description with a brief explanation.

Distance: 6.9 miles   Shaded: 60%
Elevation Change: 1300'   Occasionally steep.
Rating: Hiking - 10   Difficulty - 7   Some poison oak.
When to Go: Excellent anytime, best from March to June.

Distance and Shade

Distance measurements refer to the total hike distance. Shaded refers to the percent of tree cover. Shaded 60% means that the total distance is shaded about 60% by trees or tall shrubs.

Elevation Change

Elevation change helps determine how strenuous the hike is. A 1300' change means the hike climbs 1300' and descends 1300'.

Hiking and Difficulty

The Hiking Rating depends on aesthetics. How interesting is the hike? For example, the Bear Valley-Old Pine-Sky trails, Hike F3, has a variety of flora, rolling terrain and good views. We consider it interesting 90-100% of the time and so, rated it a 10.

Hiking Rating
8	Interesting 70-80% of the time
9	Interesting 80-90% of the time
10	Interesting 90-100% of the time

Obviously, this rating system is subjective and depends on what we like. Also, our rating of hikes is based on the best possible conditions, the best season, views, wildflowers, and especially weather. Hikes that are great in good weather, can be miserable when foggy and windy.

The Difficulty Rating ranges from 1 to 10 depending primarily on footing and steepness. For example, Hike D3, above Cascade Canyon, has a short 30' section of trail that is very steep and slippery. It has been given a difficulty rating of 9.

Difficulty Rating
1-2   Easy
3-5   Moderate
6-8   Difficult
9-10   Very difficult

Note that Easy and Moderate hikes can develop poor trail conditions. For example, during the El Nino storms of 1998, dozens of trails were closed due to fallen trees, slides and washouts.

When To Go

The When to Go rating is based on flora and fauna, weather, season, views, trail and road conditions. Since winter provides rainfall and water runoff, and late winter and spring produce wildflowers, these two seasons are the best times to go on most hikes.

Using The Maps

The lower 3-dimensional map contains "3-D slices" as shown in the figure below. Scales shown on the map are approximate, since elevations are exaggerated and maps are viewed at a camera angle of 25-40°.

Jurisdiction

Directions to Start

Hike Location

Note that behind the 3D slice, it is empty and black

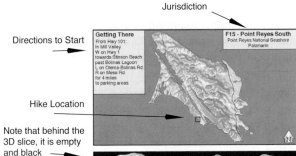

Map Symbols

`------`   Hikers Only

`-- >>> --`   Very Steep-Arrow Points Uphill

`--- ·`   Bicycles Allowed

`———`   Roads and Cars

Ranger Station

Trailhead

Pickup Cars for Shuttle Hike

4   Junction Number

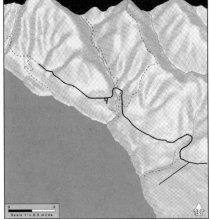

Suggestions and Precautions

As hiking becomes more popular, it attracts a wider variety of people with different levels of hiking experience. We offer the following suggestions and precautions, especially for beginning hikers.

What to Take on a Hike

Some of the hikes in this book, like those on open space lands, are short and often in full view of civilization. The most essential items to take on these hikes are fluids and clothes for protection from sun, fog or wind. However, when hiking in more remote areas, such as Mt. Tamalpais or Point Reyes, it is best to be prepared. Here is a sample checklist of things to take.

Adequate Fluids	First Aid Kit
Light Jacket	Extra Food
Poncho in Winter	Hat
Suncreen in Summer	Knife
Book or Map	Flashlight
Binoculars	Compass
Whistle	

Hiking Boots

Most of the trails described in this book are uneven, rocky or rutted. Hiking boots are preferred. They protect the feet and provide stable support. They reduce the chance of injuries, such as sprained ankles.

Hiking Alone

Hiking alone is not recommended. However, if you do go out alone, tell someone where you are going and when you will return or leave a note in your car at the trailhead with this information.

Fluids

Fluids are essential when hiking or staying outdoors. Often, people go hiking or go to the beach and wind up the day with a mild headache. Usually, this is attributed to too much exposure, too much sun or too much wind. Many times, the problem is too little fluids. Hiking requires about 1/2 quart of fluid per hour, or more, depending on the temperature and elevation change.

It is always a good idea to carry water on a hike and to drink it regularly whether you feel thirsty or not. Do not drink water from streams or lakes. It may contain giardia, which causes severe stomach problems until medically treated.

Hikers and Bicyclists

Where possible, hikes have been routed off bike roads and onto trails. All bike roads are marked on the maps. Hiking on weekdays, if possible, is the best way to avoid bicycles.

Poison Oak

Poison oak for some is a minor irritation, for many, a major irritation and for a few, a medical emergency. The best advice is to learn to identify the plant by its leaves and avoid touching it. An old saying is,

"Leaves of three, leave it be."

In fall, poison oak leaves turn crimson red and drop off. In winter, the bare branches are difficult to identify, yet still retain their toxic oils. It helps to stay on designated trails and to watch out for branches that lean out onto the trail. If you are allergic to it, carry small individually packaged Handi-wipes and wash an affected area within minutes.

Ticks and Lyme Disease

Ticks are common in Marin and are especially noticeable during the rainy season from November to May. Recent studies have shown that 1-2% of the western black-legged ticks in Marin County carry Lyme disease.

Poison Oak

The best way to avoid ticks is to stay on trails. It also helps to wear light clothing so that ticks can be seen. Be sure to brush yourself frequently, especially after passing through tall grass or shrubs. After a hike, check yourself completely. Ticks anesthetize the skin before biting so you'll seldom feel the original bite.

Early removal of a tick reduces the risk of infection. Use tweezers. Grab the tick mouth parts as close to the skin as possible and pull straight out. Wash hands and clean the bite with an antiseptic. Monitor the bite area for a month for symptoms.

The first recognizable symptom of Lyme disease is usually a disk or ringlike rash that occurs 3-30 days after the tick bite. One or more rashes may occur and not always at the bite. A rash only appears 60-80% of the time. Other symptoms may include flulike fever, chills, fatigue, headaches and a stiff neck. Since early diagnosis of Lyme disease is crucial, see a doctor if you think you have it.

Western Black-Legged Tick - enlarged 8 times

Parking

When parking on narrow streets, please respect local neighborhoods. Most cities require a 12' pavement clearance for emergency vehicles. Also, remember to lock your car and don't leave valuables in view. Vandalism and theft at trailheads in Marin is not common, but it does happen. You might check with park rangers about problem areas.

Rattlesnakes and Mountain Lions
Both are present and dangerous, but rarely seen in Marin. Rattlesnakes will often sun themselves in open areas in the spring. The best way to avoid rattlesnakes is to stay on the trail and avoid climbing over loose rocky areas.

If you do see a mountain lion, don't run. Stand your ground, keep eye contact, make yourself look bigger, perhaps using your jacket or daypack. Then, slowly back away. If attacked, fight back.

Wildfires
Wildfires are part of the natural history of Marin. These fires can be deadly. During periods of extreme fire danger, called "Red Flag Days," public lands may be closed. In late summer and fall, avoid hilltops and ridges during hot, dry or windy days.

Getting Lost
It is surprisingly easy to get lost on hikes, even when using an up-to-date book with good maps. There are four major reasons for this: there are lots of deer trails, which can be confusing, a few trails are overgrown, some junctions lack signs, and people take short-cuts.

Note that some trail signs give trail names, while other trail signs give trail destinations. If you are in a new area, our advice is to follow the book carefully and note each junction on the map. You can use a stopwatch and restart it at each junction to help estimate distance traveled. Most important, stay on trails and don't take shortcuts.

Maintained and Unmaintained Trails
Most maintained trails require periodic "brushing," the cutting or mowing of shrubs and grasses. The average trail gets brushed every 3-5 years. Often, the hike description will mention that trails "may be overgrown in places," but this depends on when it was last brushed.

There are many unmaintained or unofficial trails in Marin. These are old trails fallen out of use, trails too difficult to maintain, trails through sensitive areas, and social trails created by people taking short cuts or just exploring.

Park agencies prefer that you do not use unmaintained trails, although in most cases it is not illegal. We have removed most of these trails from our hikes and maps for safety reasons, but have kept a few of them to clarify junctions and to provide options for better or more adventurous routes.

Copying or Downloading Hikes
We recommend carrying the book in your daypack in case you modify or change hikes. However, for convenience, you can copy or download a hike on a single piece of paper to carry in your hand or pocket. See each region's Table of Contents for downloading details.

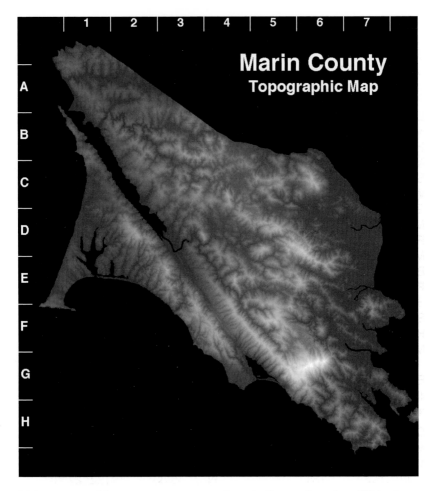

Marin County
Topographic Map

This topographic map uses grey scale to indicate elevation. White is 2600' elevation and black is 0' elevation. The map was created by taking USGS digital elevation data and converting it to shades of grey.

Because the eye is very sensitive to changes in grey, the map clearly shows the main geological features of Marin. The most prominent feature is the Point Reyes peninsula, which is separated from the rest of Marin by the Olema Valley or San Andreas Fault Zone.

Mt. Tamalpais is the highest (whitest point on the map) mountain in Marin County and the mountain crest can be seen running down to Rock Spring, then turning northwest and following Bolinas Ridge, which parallels Olema Valley. Just to the north of Bolinas Ridge, Lagunitas Creek drains into Tomales Bay.

Selected Mountains in Marin with GPS Coordinates
Location refers to the Topographic Map.

Summit		Location	Latitude	Longitude
Mt. Tamalpais	2571'	G6	N37° 55.75'	W122° 34.68'
Big Rock*	1887'	D5	N38° 03.55'	W122° 36.27'
Pine Mountain*	**1762'**	**F5**	**N37° 58.63'**	**W122° 39.13'**
Loma Alta*	1592'	E6	N38° 01.47'	W122° 36.74'
Mt. Burdell*	1558'	C6	N38° 08.78'	W122° 35.50'
Hicks Mountain	**1532'**	**C4**	**N38° 07.77'**	**W122° 43.57'**
Mt. Barnabe*	1466'	E4	N38° 01.61'	W122° 42.98'
Shroyer Mtn.	1458'	D5	N38° 03.93'	W122° 40.24'
White Hill	**1430'**	**F5**	**N37° 59.73'**	**W122° 37.67'**
Green Hill	1418'	F5	N37° 59.85'	W122° 40.32'
Mt. Wittenberg*	1407'	E3	N38° 02.36'	W122° 49.29'
Firtop	**1324'**	**F3**	**N37° 59.57'**	**W122° 46.58'**
Mt. Vision	1282'	D2	N38° 05.33'	W122° 52.44'
Black Mountain	1280'	D3	N38° 04.85'	W122° 45.95'
Pilot Knob*	**1187'**	**F6**	**N37° 56.90'**	**W122° 35.31'**
Bald Hill*	1141'	F6	N37° 57.90'	W122° 34.88'
San Pedro Mtn.	1058'	E7	N37° 59.59'	W122° 30.08'
Hill 88*	**960'**	**H7**	**N37° 50.56'**	**W122° 32.37'**
Mt. Livermore	796'	H8	N38° 05.69'	W122° 25.86'

Note that Mt. Tamalpais includes an entire ridgeline running from East Peak at 2571' through West Peak at 2560' to Rock Spring at 1970' (located at G5 on the Topographic Map), all points higher than any other mountain in Marin.

Other Locations outside Marin

Mt. Diablo	3849'		N37° 52.90'	W121° 54.89'
Mt. St. Helena	4339'		N38° 40.16'	W122° 38.02'
Sutro Tower	1811'		N37° 45.33'	W122° 27.15'

Notes about GPS coordinates

These coordinates were taken from 4 sources, www.wayhoo.com, topo maps from TOPO™, aerial photos from www.terraserver.com and from a handheld WAAS enabled GPS unit by the authors (summit marked by an asterisk *). All data uses the reference grid NAD83. Not all readings agreed, with the typical maximum difference being 0.02'. This could be due to map errors, GPS errors, atmospheric conditions or differences in locating the summit (most common source of large differences). When the summit is clearly defined, readings were much closer.

In Marin, 0.01' of latitude equals about 60 feet on land, while 0.01' of longitude equals about 48 feet on land. Most modern GPS units claim an accuracy of 20 feet.

A - Southern Marin - 15 Hikes

Starting from East Fort Baker at 60'
A1   Bay Trail and Fire Road   1.6 and 1.2

Starting from along Conzelman Road
A2   Kirby Cove and Hawk Hill Trails   1.8 and 0.5
A3   Coastal - SCA - Bobcat Trails   7.1

Starting from Rodeo Beach at 20'
A4   Rodeo Beach to Point Bonita   3.7
A5   Coastal - Wolf Ridge - Miwok Trails   5.2

Starting from Tennessee Valley
A6   Oakwood Valley - Wolf Ridge Trails   7.7
A7   Tennessee Valley Trail   3.8
A8   Miwok - Coyote Ridge - Coastal Trails   5.1

Starting from Panoramic Hwy at 660'
A9   Diaz Ridge - Redwood Creek Trails   6.8

Starting from Muir Beach at 20'
A10 Coastal - Coyote Ridge - Green Gulch Trails   5.0

Starting from Tiburon Peninsula at 20'
A11 Ring Mountain Open Space   2.6

Starting from Angel Island at 5'
A12 North Ridge Trail to Mt. Livermore   4.9
A13 Angel Island Perimeter Trail   5.2

Starting from Mill Valley at 200'
A14 Glen - Warner Cyn. - Blithedale Ridge FR   4.6

Starting from Larkspur at 170'
A15 Baltimore Canyon to Blithedale Ridge   5.3

Notes
Dogs allowed on hikes A5, A14 and A15.
To download a hike, go to www.marintrails.com
The password for this region is a5bj2gr

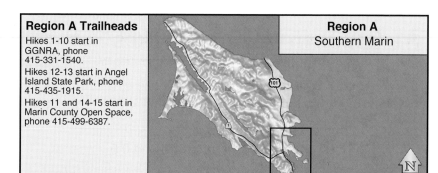

Region A Trailheads

Hikes 1-10 start in GGNRA, phone 415-331-1540.

Hikes 12-13 start in Angel Island State Park, phone 415-435-1915.

Hikes 11 and 14-15 start in Marin County Open Space, phone 415-499-6387.

Region A
Southern Marin

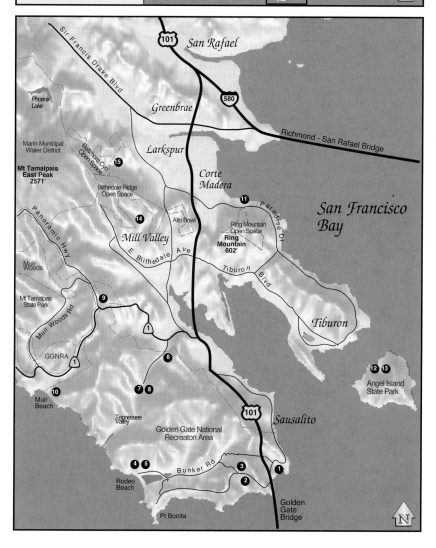

9

A1 Bay Trail and Fire Road in Fort Baker

Distance: 1.6 and 1.2 miles   Shaded: 0% and 40%
Elevation Change: See below   Some auto traffic along route.
Rating: Hiking - 8   Difficulty - 2 and 3
When to Go: Best when calm and clear. Bring binoculars.

One hike explores the shoreline in East Fort Baker. The other hike climbs up a ridge to offer a classic view of the Golden Gate Bridge.

To the Fishing Pier and back - 1.6 miles and 30' Change
0.0 From the Bay trail parking area, head downhill 70 yds. to pick up the Bay trail that starts down a flight of stairs. At the bottom of the stairs, head along the fence, bordering the Discovery Museum.

0.1 Bay Area Discovery Museum and junction. For information about the children's museum, call 339-3900. Head left along the first gravel road (the Bay trail) and follow it towards Battery Yates.

0.2 Junction and bunker. Head left to explore the cliff and area around Battery Yates, which was built in 1906. Then return here to continue along the road.

0.6 Cavallo Pt. and boat dock. Next to the breakwater, look for a gun platform beyond the large rock. Then head inland. **Option**: You can walk out along the breakwater to view the sailboats and small craft.

0.7 At the end of the parking area, go left across the gangplank in front of the Yacht Club building. Continue west along the beach.

0.9 Coast Guard Station. Continue around the beach area.

1.0 Fishing pier and turnaround point ❶. The end of the pier offers great views of the bridge and also of Lime Pt., which is directly under the bridge. Lime Pt. is named after a 20-ton schooner that shipwrecked there in 1878. To complete the hike, head back to the car.

Fire Road - Murray Circle - 1.2 miles and 200' Change
0.0 From the Bay trail parking area, head downhill 80 yds. and take the Drown FR that heads up to the right. The road offers classic views of the GG Bridge and of Fort Baker. East Fort Baker was constructed in 1897 as a harbor defense site. It is named after Colonel Edward Baker, a civil war hero, lawyer, U.S. Senator and friend of Abraham Lincoln.

0.6 Junction ❷. Take the Murray trail down to Murray Circle, then go left out to Fort Baker Rd. (aka East Rd.). Cross the road and circle around the museum to take the stairs back up to the parking area.

1.2 Back at the parking area. No facitlities here.

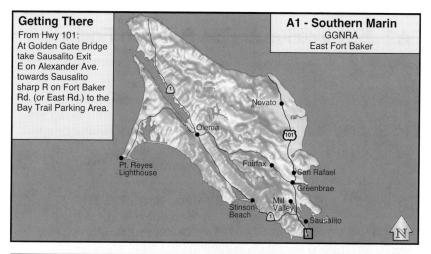

Getting There

From Hwy 101:
At Golden Gate Bridge take Sausalito Exit E on Alexander Ave. towards Sausalito sharp R on Fort Baker Rd. (or East Rd.) to the Bay Trail Parking Area.

A1 - Southern Marin
GGNRA
East Fort Baker

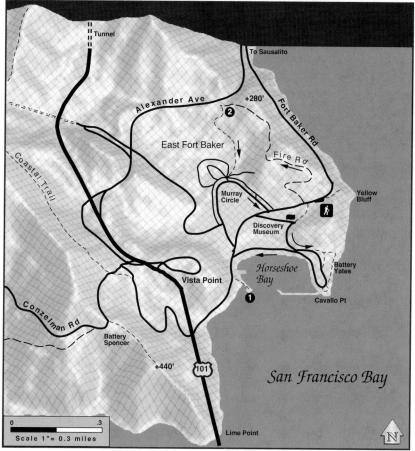

A2 Kirby Cove and Hawk Hill Trails

Distance: 1.8 and 0.5 miles   Shaded: 30% and 10%
Elevation Change: See below.   Can be windy.
Rating: Hiking - 9   Difficulty - 4 and 3   Moderately steep hills.
When to Go: Best when calm and clear in September and October.

These two out-and-back hikes explore the southern Marin Headlands offering unparalleled views. Observe fall raptor migration at Hawk Hill.

To Kirby Cove and back - 1.8 miles and 400' Change
0.0 Park at Battery Spencer on Conzelman Rd. right above the Golden Gate Bridge. Be sure to lock your car and take any valuables with you. **Option**: Take a short stroll out the ridge to a lookout point above the Golden Gate Bridge. The hike to Kirby Cove starts on the right by passing through a gate and heading down a paved road.

0.7 Junction. At a Y in the road, head left through the group camping area located under the pine trees.

0.9 Bunker and beach at Kirby Cove and turnaround point ❶. There are trails to the beach at both ends of the beach.

To Hawk Hill and back - 0.5 miles and 50' Change
0.0 Park at the top of Conzelman Rd. just before it becomes a one-way road. Take the upper tunnel through to the other side. An information sign at the start of the tunnel describes Battery 129.

At the other end of the tunnel, there is a great view of Pt. Bonita and the lighthouse. From here, follow the trail signs right.

0.1 Gun emplacement. The lower tunnel leads out to an enormous gun mount, built to house a 16" naval gun. The gun was brought to the site in 1943, but was never mounted because the war had shifted to the western Pacific. Over one million cubic yds. of concrete were poured into this battery with walls and floors eight to twelve feet thick. The hike continues to the right, up the stairs.

Red-tailed Hawk

0.2 Junction. Head left to explore the hilltop.

0.3 Hawk Hill and turnaround point ❷. During the peak season, over 2000 hawks a day have been counted passing overhead. These hawks concentrate here to catch the rising wind currents necessary to cross the waters of the Golden Gate. When ready to continue, return to the junction and take the paved road left downhill.

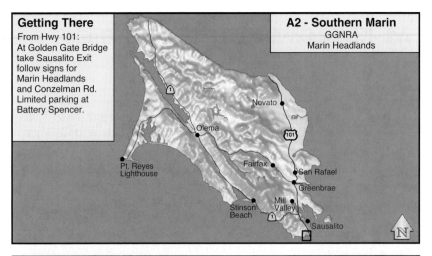

Getting There

From Hwy 101:
At Golden Gate Bridge take Sausalito Exit follow signs for Marin Headlands and Conzelman Rd. Limited parking at Battery Spencer.

A2 - Southern Marin
GGNRA
Marin Headlands

Novato

1

Olema

Pt. Reyes
Lighthouse

Fairfax

San Rafael

Greenbrae

Stinson
Beach

Mill
Valley

1

Sausalito

N

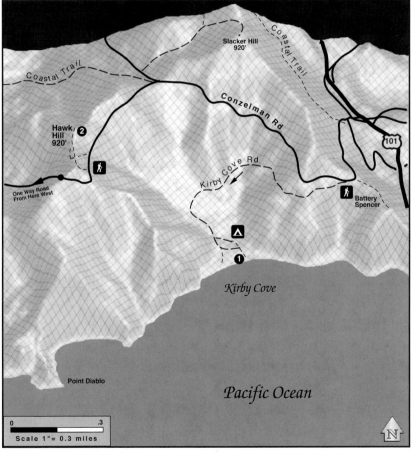

Coastal Trail

Slacker Hill
920'

Coastal Trail

Coastal Trail

Conzelman Rd

Hawk
Hill
920'

2

101

Kirby Cove Rd

One Way Road
From Here West

Battery
Spencer

Kirby Cove

1

Point Diablo

Pacific Ocean

0   .3
Scale 1"= 0.3 miles

N

13

A3 Coastal - SCA - Bobcat Trails

Distance: 7.1 miles   Shaded: 10%
Elevation Change: 1000'   Heavy bicycle traffic on weekends.
Rating: Hiking - 9   Difficulty - 6   Some poison oak.
When to Go: Good when calm and clear. Best in March for flowers.

This is a great hike that travels up Rodeo Valley, then down Gerbode Valley. It offers sweeping views and beautiful wildflowers in spring.

0.0 From the grassy parking area, cross Bunker Rd. and take the signed Coastal trail into the meadow. Ahead at the gate, continue straight. Spring wildflowers include poppies, blue lupine, Indian paintbrush and yellow mimulus. As you head uphill, stay right. Watch for bicycles and more great flowers.

1.6 Junction ❶ with McCullough Rd. Walk down McCullough Rd. 50 yds. to the trail gate. Take the Coastal trail uphill into dense coastal scrub that includes coyote bush, cow parsley, blackberries, sage, poison oak, bracken fern and wild cucumber.

1.9 Junction ❷. Take the short spur trail right to Slacker Hill.

2.2 Slacker Hill at 920'. Incomparable views. Return to junction ❷.

2.5 Junction ❷. Go right. On the north side of Slacker Hill, look for the small wooden blind, used to help trap hawks.

2.8 Junction and wind funnel. Stay on the ridge on the SCA trail. In the fall, afternoon winds are funneled up Rodeo Valley to roar over this low spot in the ridgeline. Ahead, watch for poison oak.

3.8 Junction ❸ with the Rodeo Valley trail. Head straight, then right, then left towards the eucalyptus trees. Pass through the gate and enter a small rain forest created by the tall trees and heavy fog drip. Notice the growth of ivy 50' up the trunks of the eucalyptus.

4.0 Junction. Continue past the Morning Sun trail, then take a short spur trail right to a viewpoint. Return to the road and go right.

4.5 Two junctions ❹. Go left, then left again onto the Bobcat trail.

4.6 Junction. In April, a carpet of yellow lotus marks this junction. Stay right on the Bobcat trail to make a long downhill descent. On weekends, stay to the right and watch for bicycles.

6.6 Junction ❺. Take the Rodeo Valley trail left.

7.0 Junction. Go right to cross a small bridge that leads to a paved road and the parking area.

7.1 Back at the parking area. No facilities.

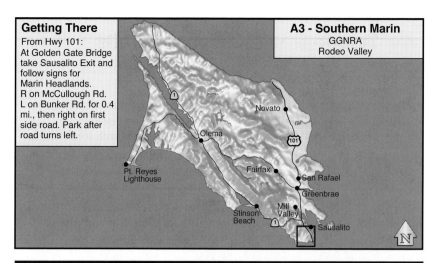

Getting There

From Hwy 101:
At Golden Gate Bridge take Sausalito Exit and follow signs for Marin Headlands.
R on McCullough Rd. L on Bunker Rd. for 0.4 mi., then right on first side road. Park after road turns left.

A3 - Southern Marin
GGNRA
Rodeo Valley

Novato

101

Olema

Pt. Reyes
Lighthouse

Fairfax

San Rafael

Greenbrae

Stinson
Beach

Mill
Valley

Sausalito

N

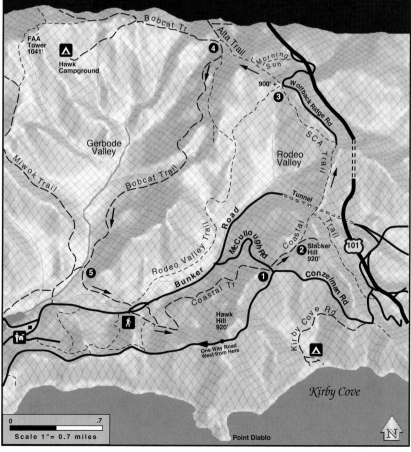

Bobcat Tr

Alta Trail

Morning Sun

FAA
Tower
1041'

Hawk
Campground

4

900' +

3

Wolfback Ridge Rd

Gerbode
Valley

SCA Trail

Rodeo
Valley

Miwok Trail

Bobcat Trail

Tunnel

Bunker

Rodeo Valley Trail

Road

McCullough Rd

Coastal Trail

101

5

Coastal Tr

2

Slacker
Hill
920'

Conzelman Rd

Hawk
Hill
920'

Kirby Cove Rd

One Way Road
West from Here

Kirby Cove

0   .7

Scale 1"= 0.7 miles

Point Diablo

N

15

A4 Rodeo Beach to Point Bonita

Distance: 3.7 miles   Shaded: 10%
Elevation Change: 350'   Hike uses the road for 1.5 miles.
Rating: Hiking - 9   Difficulty - 5   Can be very windy.
When to Go: Good anytime. Often great weather in fall and winter.

This hike explores the beach, coastal area and old military forts from Rodeo Beach to Pt. Bonita. Great ocean views.

0.0 From the Rodeo Beach parking area, head south along the beach. Up ahead, notice Bird Rock extending from the shoreline. To the west of Bird Rock lies the "Potato Patch," a dangerously shallow sandbar that can increase the height of northerly swells.

0.3 Junction ❶. Follow the unofficial trail up through the iceplant.

0.5 Junction. Take the old road right towards the YMCA building.

0.8 Junction. Follow the paved road around the YMCA area.

1.0 Junction ❷ with the Lighthouse trail. Take the paved road right past Battery Mendell. Be sure to follow the road counterclockwise to get the best views. Watch for car traffic along here.

1.2 Bird Rock overlook. Great views of the coast north and south. To continue the hike, take the trail along the cliff past the two "pillboxes."

1.4 Far end of Battery Mendell. Continue along the clifftop another 70 yds. to a sign and a view down to small remains of a wrecked ship. Then backtrack and take the trail towards the lighthouse. **Option**: An unofficial trail continues along the unstable cliffs towards the radar tower. If you take it, be sure to loop around the tower to an easy trail back, rather than try to go down the steep, dangerous cliff.

1.6 Junction ❷. Take the road right towards the Pt. Bonita lighthouse. Ahead, at the low point on the trail, you can see remains of the Life Saving Station established in 1899. More than 20 shipwrecks occurred on the nearby Marin coast. The lighthouse is open 12:30-3:30 on Sat., Sun. and Mon. The hike returns to the entrance road.

1.9 Junction ❷ with the entrance road. Take the main road right.

2.0 Junction. Head right uphill towards Battery Wallace and picnic area.

2.3 Junction ❸. Follow the road sign that says "Beach" past the old Nike missile site. Call 331-1453 for hours that the missile site is open.

2.8 Junction ❹ and Visitor Center. It's worth a stop at the Visitor Center to see the displays. Then, take the Lagoon trail left.

3.7 Back at the parking area with water, tables and restrooms.

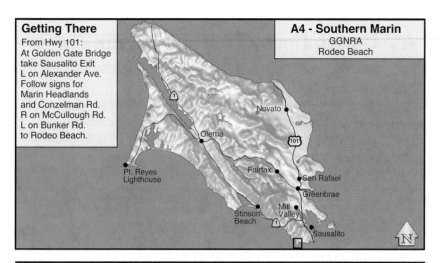

Getting There

From Hwy 101:
At Golden Gate Bridge
take Sausalito Exit
L on Alexander Ave.
Follow signs for
Marin Headlands
and Conzelman Rd.
R on McCullough Rd.
L on Bunker Rd.
to Rodeo Beach.

A4 - Southern Marin
GGNRA
Rodeo Beach

Novato

Olema

Pt. Reyes
Lighthouse

Fairfax

San Rafael

Greenbrae

Stinson
Beach

Mill
Valley

Sausalito

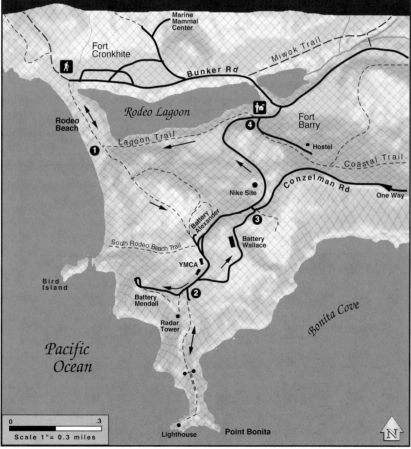

Marine
Mammal
Center

Fort
Cronkhite

Miwok Trail

Bunker Rd

Rodeo Lagoon

Fort
Barry

Rodeo
Beach

❶

Lagoon Trail

❹

Hostel

Coastal Trail

Nike Site

Conzelman Rd

One Way

❸

South Rodeo Beach Trail

Battery
Alexander

Battery
Wallace

YMCA

Bird
Island

❷

Battery
Mendell

Bonita Cove

Radar
Tower

Pacific
Ocean

0   .3
Scale 1"= 0.3 miles

Lighthouse   Point Bonita

17

A5 Coastal - Wolf Ridge - Miwok Trails

Distance: 5.2 miles   Shaded: 0%
Elevation Change: 1000'   Some poison oak. Bicycles on weekends.
Rating: Hiking - 9   Difficulty - 7   Two steep, rocky sections.
When to Go: Good when clear, calm. Best March-May for flowers.

This is one of the best ridge hikes in the Marin Headlands offering great coastal views, many old bunkers and hills of wildflowers.

0.0 From the parking area, go past the gate and up the paved road.

0.1 Junction. Take the trail left towards the ocean and a fortified lookout point. At the bunker, continue uphill and parallel the road.

0.2 Steep cliffs. The trail skirts a steep cliff that drops off dramatically to a small ocean cove. There are alternate trails here. This hike follows the main trail, a dirt road, up to a Y-junction.

0.4 Y-junction ❶. Take the trail right. The road left ends at a fence.

0.5 Junction. The trail joins the paved road and heads inland. Up ahead, the road passes Battery Townsley, an underground bunker system that held two 16-inch naval guns. After the bombing of Pearl Harbor in 1941, this battery housed 150 men on 15 minute alert.

0.7 Junction. The road right heads downhill. Continue left. Ahead, part of the road is closed due to major slides. Take the path, which turns into stairs near the top. Watch for poison oak.

1.1 Junction. The trail joins the paved road again, but only for 100'.

1.2 Junction ❷. The Coastal trail goes right to pick up the paved road. **Option**: For a more interesting, but steeper route, take the red gravel road left towards a bunker and great views north to Tennessee Valley. Continue up the road, which gets steep and rocky. At the top, walk carefully around the collapsing bunkers.

1.5 Junction. The trail joins the road. Continue east.

1.6 Junction ❸ with Wolf Ridge trail. Continue up the road to Hill 88.

1.8 Hill 88. This was once a Nike missile radar station. Now, it is a group camp site. Great 360 degree views. Return to junction ❸.

2.0 Junction ❸. Take the Wolf Ridge trail right. Be careful on the steep sections. Small rocks can cause sliding. Good flowers ahead.

2.7 Junction ❹. Take the Miwok trail right. Bicycles likely.

4.1 Junction ❺ with Bobcat trail. Continue right on the Miwok trail.

4.5 Warehouse. Cross Bunker Road and take the Lagoon trail west.

5.2 Back at the parking area with water and restrooms.

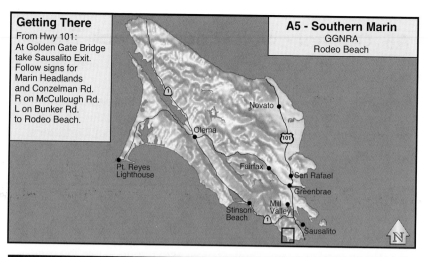

Getting There

From Hwy 101:
At Golden Gate Bridge take Sausalito Exit. Follow signs for Marin Headlands and Conzelman Rd. R on McCullough Rd. L on Bunker Rd. to Rodeo Beach.

A5 - Southern Marin
GGNRA
Rodeo Beach

Novato

Olema

101

Pt. Reyes
Lighthouse

Fairfax

San Rafael

Greenbrae

Stinson
Beach

Mill
Valley

Sausalito

N

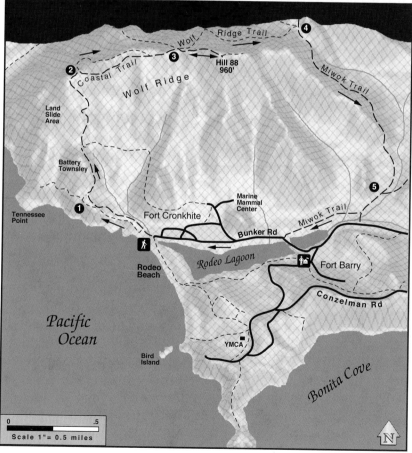

Wolf   Ridge Trail   **4**

Coastal Trail   **3**   **Hill 88**
960'

2   Miwok Trail

Wolf Ridge

Land
Slide
Area

Battery
Townsley

5

Marine
Mammal
Center

Tennessee
Point   **1**   Fort Cronkhite

Miwok Trail

Bunker Rd

Fort Barry

Rodeo
Beach   Rodeo Lagoon

Pacific
Ocean   Conzelman Rd

Bird
Island   YMCA

Bonita Cove

0   .5
Scale 1"= 0.5 miles

N

A6 Oakwood Valley - Wolf Ridge Trails

Distance: 7.7 miles   Shaded: 20%
Elevation Change: 1400'   Some poison oak. May be windy.
Rating: Hiking - 7   Difficulty - 8   Some steep ups and downs.
When to Go: Good when clear and calm. Best in April for flowers.

This hike climbs out of Oakwood Valley to the second highest point in the Marin Headlands, then returns via Tennessee Valley.

0.0 There are two parallel routes up Oakwood Valley. It's best to take the road just before the GGNRA sign if the ground is very wet. This hike describes a trail that starts at the sign and heads into a meadow.

0.7 Bridge and junction. The trail crosses a bridge to join the road.

1.0 Junction ❶. Ahead, the road deadends. Take the trail to the right.

1.4 Ridgetop and junction. Good views east. Head right up the road.

1.8 Junction, knoll and viewpoint. Stay on the road to the right.

1.9 Two junctions ❷. Go right, then right again to take the signed Bobcat trail, which heads north towards power lines. This "trail" was once a 60' wide road that was part of Marincello, a proposed city of 20,000 planned for the headlands in the 1960s. The development was blocked in court and the land sold to the Nature Conservancy for $6.5 million. Later, it was given to the GGNRA.

2.7 Junction ❸. Continue on the Bobcat trail towards the antenna.

3.0 Double junction and FAA antenna. Just past the Miwok trail (north), take the left-most trail around the FAA transmitter for good views south. Continue west on this trail to rejoin the Miwok trail, which now makes a long descent that is steep in places.

3.6 Junction with Old Spring trail. Continue on the Miwok trail.

3.7 Junction. Leave the road and take the trail right, which becomes the Wolf Ridge trail heading for Hill 88.

4.5 Junction ❹. Take the Coastal trail right downhill, which gets steep in places. Watch for coyotes which have been seen here. **Option**: Go left for 0.2 miles to the top of Hill 88 and good views in all directions.

5.7 Bridge and junction. Take Tennessee Valley trail (seasonal) right.

7.0 Parking lot. Continue 100 yds. and take the Miwok trail left. Then leave the Miwok trail and go right on a narrow trail. **Option**: If you're concerned about poison oak, take the Tennessee Valley Rd.

7.7 The trail crosses the creek to return to the parking area.

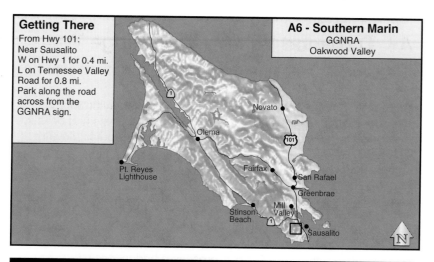

Getting There

From Hwy 101:
Near Sausalito
W on Hwy 1 for 0.4 mi.
L on Tennessee Valley
Road for 0.8 mi.
Park along the road
across from the
GGNRA sign.

A6 - Southern Marin
GGNRA
Oakwood Valley

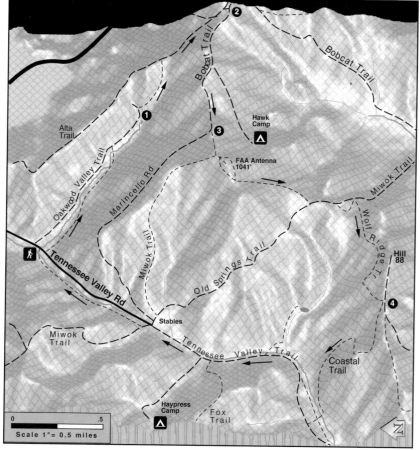

A7 Tennessee Valley Trail

Distance: 3.8 miles   Shaded: 0%
Elevation Change: 200'   Crowded on weekends. Bicycles likely.
Rating: Hiking - 8   Difficulty - 2   Can be very windy.
When to Go: Best when clear, calm and low tide.

This is one of the most popular hikes in Marin as it offers easy, level access to the beach and ocean. Good flowers on cliffs by the beach.

0.0 From the parking area, head west past the gate on the road.

0.7 Junction and ranch house. Continue straight on the dirt road.

1.0 Junction ❶. If open, take the trail left. You may notice scat on the trail, most likely from bobcat, fox or skunks. In the 1840s, this valley, also known as "Elk Valley," was abundant with mammals. Historian Jack Mason writes that, "the ground was white with the bones of deer, elk and wild cattle killed for their hides."

1.7 Lagoon and dam. The old stock pond invites a variety of shorebirds, mallard ducks, coots, sea gulls and occasionally pelicans.

1.8 Beach and junction ❷. Head down to the south end of the beach.

1.9 Wreck of the *S.S. Tennessee*. During certain times of the year, when the sand is lowered by wave action, it is possible to see remains of the *Tennessee* (usually the engine), which beached here on a foggy March 6, 1853. The *Tennessee* was a side-paddle steamer that carried 551 passengers bound for San Francisco and the gold rush. Eventually, they all made it, as did much of the cargo. Two smaller vessels also wrecked here, the *Tagus* in 1851 and the *Fourth of July* in 1878. The only casualty was

*S.S. Tennessee
Shipwrecked here in 1853*

the captain of the fifty-ton *Fourth of July* who was killed when enormous waves tossed his ship end over end onto the sand.

Option: At low tide, it may be possible to get around the southern rocks to another small, sandy beach with interesting rock formations.

2.0 Junction ❷. **Option**: A small trail makes a moderately steep climb to a bunker and great view point. Otherwise, retrace your steps.

3.8 Back at the parking area with restroom and picnic tables.

22

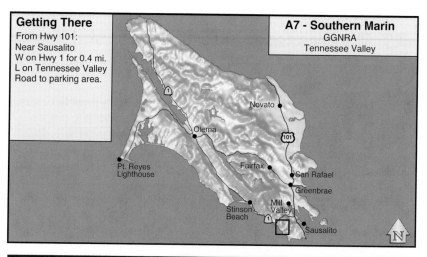

Getting There

From Hwy 101:
Near Sausalito
W on Hwy 1 for 0.4 mi.
L on Tennessee Valley
Road to parking area.

A7 - Southern Marin
GGNRA
Tennessee Valley

Novato

Olema

Pt. Reyes
Lighthouse

Fairfax

San Rafael

Greenbrae

Stinson
Beach

Mill
Valley

Sausalito

N

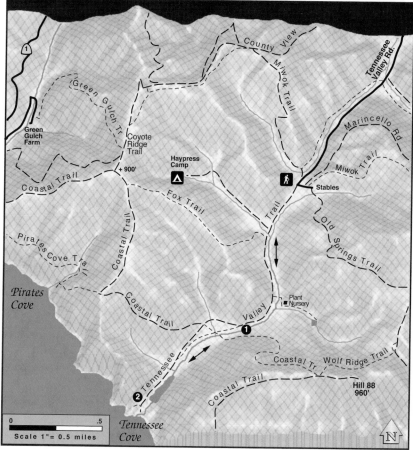

County View

Miwok Trail

Green Gulch Tr.

Tennessee Valley Rd.

Green
Gulch
Farm

Coyote
Ridge
Trail

Marincello Rd.

Coastal Trail

+ 900'

Haypress
Camp

Miwok Trail

Stables

Fox Trail

Coastal Trail

Pirates Cove Trail

Valley Trail

Old Springs Trail

Pirates
Cove

Coastal Trail

Plant
Nursery

1

Tennessee

Coastal Tr.

Wolf Ridge Trail

Coastal Trail

Hill 88
960'

2

| 0 | .5 |
Scale 1"= 0.5 miles

Tennessee
Cove

N

23

A8 Miwok - Coyote Ridge - Coastal Trails

Distance: 5.1 miles   Shaded: 0%
Elevation Change: 1000'   Bicycles likely. May be overgrown.
Rating: Hiking - 7   Difficulty - 5   Moderately steep in places.
When to Go: Good when clear. Best weather often in fall and winter.

This hike climbs out of Tennessee Valley to Coyote Ridge, then returns down the Coastal trail. Great views of the ocean and valleys.

0.0 From the east end of the Tennessee Valley parking lot, take the signed Miwok trail, which starts out paralleling the road downhill.

0.1 Bridge and junction. Continue left, uphill on the Miwok trail.

0.9 Double junction ❶. Go left, then left again to head across the top of the ravine. Good views down to the valley. Tennessee Valley, also known as "Elk Valley," was once part of the 19,000 acre Rancho Saucelito granted to William Richardson in 1838. Captain Richardson was the first port captain for San Francisco Bay. His all-Indian crew used a tule raft to meet incoming ships and guide them into the bay.

1.2 Ridgetop and junction. The Miwok trail is straight ahead with good views to Mt. Tamalpais. Continue left. **Note**: There are two, then three parallel routes on the ridgetop. Generally, this hike follows the trail farthest south, which is also the narrowest trail.

1.5 Rocky outcrops. Two rocky outcrops lie 150' apart, both offering good views south down the valley. Caution: Rattlesnakes often like to sun on rocks, especially in the spring. Always watch where you walk. The hike continues on a narrow, overgrown trail to a 3rd rock outcrop.

1.7 Junction with an abandoned road. Head right uphill. At the top, check your clothes for ticks if grasses crowded the trail.

1.8 Junction ❷ with Coyote Ridge trail. Head left uphill on the road.

1.9 High point at 1031'. Wonderful views in all directions.

2.1 Junction with the Green Gulch trail. Continue left.

2.3 Junction. Go left on the Coastal trail.

2.4 Junction with the Fox trail. Continue straight on the Coastal trail.

3.1 Junction ❸. Before heading left down the Coastal trail, take the small trail west for 50 yds. to a bluff overlooking the ocean.

3.8 Junction. Take the Tennessee Valley trail left. **Option**: Go right if you want to visit the beach at Tennessee Cove.

5.1 Back at the parking area with restroom and tables.

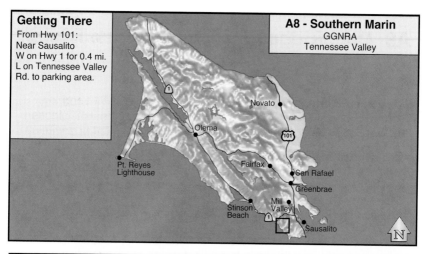

Getting There

From Hwy 101:
Near Sausalito
W on Hwy 1 for 0.4 mi.
L on Tennessee Valley
Rd. to parking area.

A8 - Southern Marin
GGNRA
Tennessee Valley

Novato

Olema

Pt. Reyes
Lighthouse

Fairfax

San Rafael

Greenbrae

Stinson
Beach

Mill
Valley

Sausalito

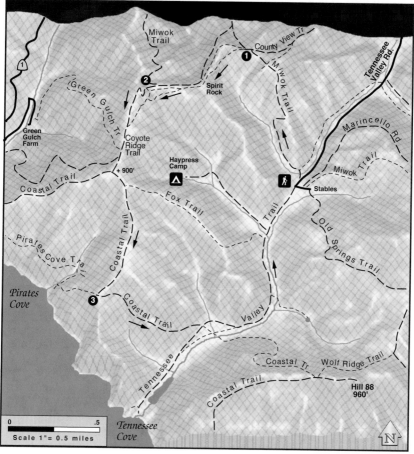

Miwok
Trail

County View Tr

Miwok
Trail

Spirit
Rock

Tennessee Valley Rd.

Green Gulch Tr

Coyote
Ridge
Trail

Green
Gulch
Farm

Marincello Rd.

Miwok Trail

Coastal Trail

+ 900'

Haypress
Camp

Fox Trail

Stables

Coastal Trail

Pirates Cove Tr

Old Springs Trail

Pirates
Cove

Coastal Trail

Valley

Tennessee

Coastal Tr

Wolf Ridge Trail

Hill 88
960'

Coastal Trail

Tennessee
Cove

0   .5
Scale 1"= 0.5 miles

A9 Diaz Ridge - Redwood Creek Trails

Distance: 6.8 miles   Shaded: 40%
Elevation Change: 1100'   Some poison oak. Can be muddy.
Rating: Hiking - 8   Difficulty - 7   Short steep downhill section.
When to Go: Good in spring. Best weather often in fall and winter.

This hike follows Diaz Ridge down to Muir Beach, then circles back through Franks Valley before making a gradual climb to the ridge.

0.0 Park about 0.1 mile past the switchback on Panoramic Hwy. Go through the gate and take the Diaz Ridge trail southwest through grasslands. This ridge is named after George Diaz who operated a ranch here and the Sausalito Creamery in the early 1900s.

0.4 Two junctions with the Miwok trail. Continue straight on the ridge.

1.2 Junction ❶ and gate. Go through the chained gate and take the trail downhill. Be sure to refasten the chain. This pastureland is often used to graze horses. Ahead, great views to Muir Beach. **Note**: Just past the gate, the old trail down has become severely eroded and an unofficial bypass trail has been created to the left.

1.9 Junction and rock. The trail levels out on a knoll with a large rock outcrop. Head right downhill on one of an assortment of trails carved out by the horses. Aim for the front of the stables.

2.1 Junction ❷ with Hwy 1. Cross the highway and take the paved road past the Pelican Inn to Muir Beach. This grove of Monterey pines along the road

Monarch Butterfly

is winter home to thousands of Monarch butterflies that migrate here in the fall.

2.2 Junction. Take the fire lane to bypass the road.

2.5 Junction, bridge and beach. Follow the creek out to Muir Beach. Retrace steps back to junction ❷ when ready to continue.

3.1 Junction ❷. Carefully walk along the left shoulder of the highway.

3.3 Highway intersection and junction. Go up the Muir Woods Road for 50' to pick up the Redwood Creek trail.

4.8 Junction ❸. Take the signed Miwok trail right to begin a long, gradual climb into a bay-filled canyon. Look for shooting star, trillium and hounds tongue in early March. Poison oak may crowd the trail.

6.4 Junction. Take the Diaz Ridge trail left.

6.8 Back at the parking area. No facilities.

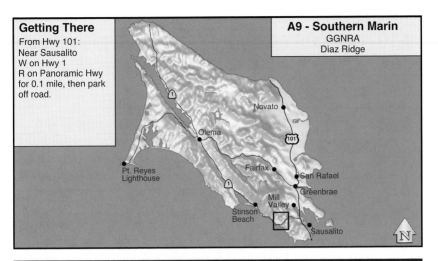

Getting There

From Hwy 101:
Near Sausalito
W on Hwy 1
R on Panoramic Hwy
for 0.1 mile, then park
off road.

Novato

Olema

Pt. Reyes
Lighthouse

Fairfax

San Rafael

Greenbrae

Mill
Valley

Stinson
Beach

Sausalito

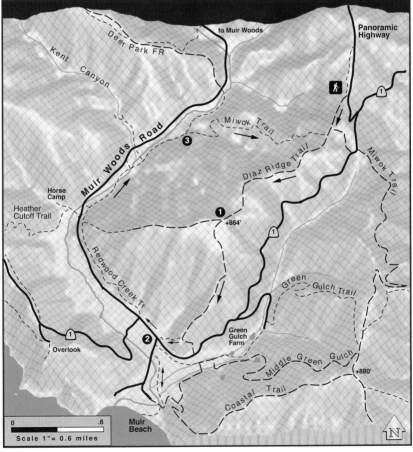

to Muir Woods

Panoramic
Highway

Deer Park FR

Kent Canyon

Miwok Trail

Muir Woods Road

Diaz Ridge Trail

Miwok Trail

❸

Horse
Camp

Heather
Cutoff Trail

❶
+864'

Redwood Creek Tr

Green Gulch Trail

Green

❷

Overlook

Green
Gulch
Farm

Middle Green Gulch
+880'

Coastal Trail

Muir
Beach

0 _____ .6
Scale 1" = 0.6 miles

27

A10 Coastal - Coyote Ridge - Green Gulch

Distance: 5.0 miles   Shaded: 10%
Elevation Change: 1300'   Can be muddy in winter.
Rating: Hiking - 9   Difficulty - 6   Steep and rutted in places.
When to Go: Great whenever clear and not windy.

This hike out of Muir Beach passes through wild and remote coastal hills offering striking views of the ocean. Good wildflowers in spring.

0.0 From the end of the parking lot, head west towards the ocean, then cross the footbridge over Redwood Creek. After the first heavy rains, salmon pass here on the way to spawn in Muir Woods. On the other side of the bridge, go left to pick up the Coastal trail.

0.1 Junction with Middle Green Gulch trail. Head right on the Coastal trail, which climbs gradually uphill with good views back to Muir Beach. Near the top of the hill, take the spur trail right to a knoll that offers great views and once was a peregrine falcon nest site.

0.5 Junction ❶. Take the Pirates Cove trail (may be signed Coastal Trail) right, with spectacular views down plunging cliffs to the ocean.

1.4 Junction. At the bottom of a large ravine, a short spur trail drops steeply 100' to a small plateau and a superb view of the coast and rugged cliffs. From here, the next section of trail is steep uphill.

1.7 Junction ❷. After reaching a plateau, head left on the Coastal trail, which climbs more gradually.

2.4 Junction. The Fox trail joins from the right. Continue left.

2.5 Junction. Head right on the Coyote Ridge trail.

2.6 Two junctions ❸. Take the second left, the Green Gulch trail downhill. Look for spring flowers here including tidy tips and poppies.

2.9 Junction with a crossing trail. Continue straight downhill.

3.0 Hope Cottage. A small rock-wall cottage, originally built in 1888, is being restored by volunteers from Green Gulch Farm.

4.0 Junction ❹ with road. Go right 50', then take the stairs down to the paved road. Continue left to pass through Green Gulch Farm, a non-profit farm and Zen center. Follow the main road past the plant nursery, down the center of the valley and through the crop fields.

4.8 Junction and gate. Head left along the tall deer-fence, then right towards the ocean and wooden bridge.

5.0 Back at the parking area with picnic tables and restrooms.

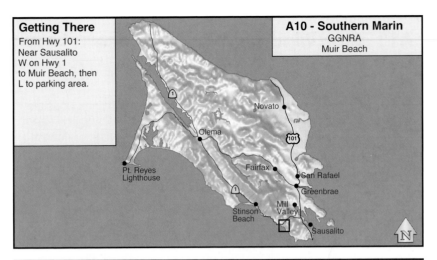

Getting There

From Hwy 101:
Near Sausalito
W on Hwy 1
to Muir Beach, then
L to parking area.

A10 - Southern Marin
GGNRA
Muir Beach

Novato

Olema

Pt. Reyes
Lighthouse

Fairfax

San Rafael

Greenbrae

Mill
Valley

Stinson
Beach

Sausalito

N

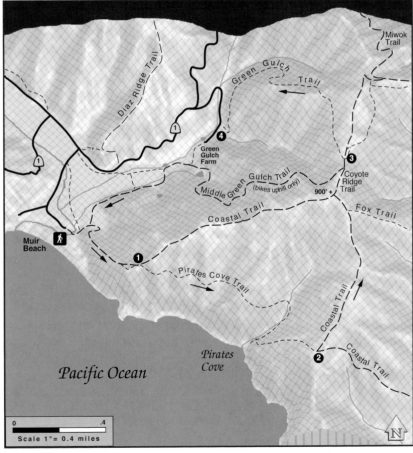

Miwok
Trail

Diaz Ridge Trail

Green Gulch Trail

Green
Gulch
Farm

Middle Green Gulch Trail
(bikes uphill only)

Coyote
Ridge
Trail

900' +

Fox Trail

Coastal Trail

Muir
Beach

Pirates Cove Trail

Coastal Trail

Coastal Trail

Pacific Ocean

Pirates
Cove

| 0 | .4 |

Scale 1"= 0.4 miles

N

A11 Ring Mountain Open Space

Distance: 2.6 miles   Shaded: 10%
Elevation Change: 600'   Can be muddy. Strong winds possible.
Rating: Hiking - 10   Difficulty - 7   Very rocky downhill areas.
When to Go: Best on clear, calm days in March to May for flowers.

This climb up the grassy slopes of Ring Mountain provides some of the best views and wildflower displays in the Bay area.

0.0 Park on Paradise Drive just past Westward Drive. Look for the Nature Preserve sign and gate. The trail crosses a small bridge to an information display. Pick up a nature guide if it's available.

0.2 Junction ❶. Head left on the Loop Trail. Up ahead, the trail crosses a small creek. Look for the white Oakland star tulip.

0.3 Post 4 and junction. There are several unofficial crossing trails. Continue right on the main trail. Numbered posts mark the way.

0.9 Knoll, road and junction ❷. After climbing a knoll offering grand views south, the trail drops down to a road. Continue across the road to Turtle Rock. From the south side of the rock, take the footpath uphill to the east, aiming to the right of the water tank.

1.0 Junction. Continue across the road and head uphill on the unofficial trail, which soon passes over a serpentine outcrop.

1.2 Junction ❸. The trail meets the road, but again, leave the road and head right, up towards the highest point.

1.3 Ring Mountain at 602'. The summit of Ring Mountain was flattened to house anti-aircraft guns after World War II. The broad hilltop is worth exploring for its magnificent views and wildflowers. The hike continues by taking the paved road back towards the west.

1.5 Junction. Leave the paved road and head west towards Mt. Tam.

1.6 Junction ❷ again. Go back to Turtle Rock and now take the path to the right, west down a rocky outcrop towards another large rock.

1.7 Petroglyph Rock. A sign shows some of the art on the rock. When ready to continue, go back 100 yds. to the road, then left uphill.

1.8 Junction ❹. Take the Phyllis Ellman trail downhill. At post 13, bear left to look for the rare Tiburon Mariposa lily, a tan-colored flower that grows only on Ring Mountain and flowers in late May. **Option:** You can add another two miles to this hike by taking the dirt road left uphill to go out and back along the ridge. This extension offers good views west.

2.6 Back at the parking area with no facilities.

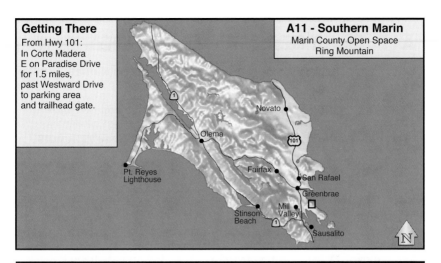

Getting There

From Hwy 101:
In Corte Madera
E on Paradise Drive
for 1.5 miles,
past Westward Drive
to parking area
and trailhead gate.

Novato

Olema

1

101

Pt. Reyes
Lighthouse

Fairfax

San Rafael

Greenbrae

Stinson
Beach

Mill
Valley

1

Sausalito

N

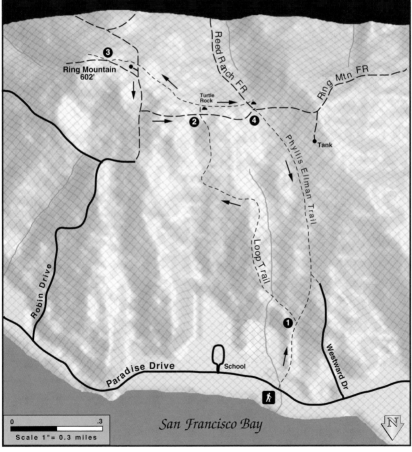

Reed Ranch FR

Ring Mtn FR

❸

Ring Mountain
602'

Turtle
Rock

❷

❹

Tank

Phyllis Ellman Trail

Loop Trail

Robin Drive

❶

Westward Dr

Paradise Drive

School

San Francisco Bay

0   .3

Scale 1" = 0.3 miles

N

31

A12 North Ridge Trail to Mt. Livermore

Distance: 4.9 miles   Shaded: 50%
Elevation Change: 800'   For ferry info from Marin, call 435-2131.
Rating: Hiking - 9   Difficulty - 6   Afternoons can be windy.
When to Go: Best anytime when clear. Good early spring flowers.

Bring binoculars and camera to climb to the highest point on Angel Island with one of the most spectacular views in the world.

0.0 When you get off the ferry, immediately head left and take the signed North Ridge trail uphill. The trail starts out under oaks and pines, passes a small picnic area, then climbs a series of stairs.

0.2 Junction ❶ with Perimeter Rd. Go right 50' and continue uphill on the North Ridge trail which is much less steep. Good views down to Ayala Cove and north to Tiburon and Mt. Tamalpais. Wherever the trail enters the northeast side of the island, vegetation is dense.

1.0 Junction with Fire Rd. Go left 50' and continue up the trail.

1.9 Junction ❷ with the Sunset trail. Great views south to Alcatraz Island and San Francisco. Take the Sunset trail right uphill.

2.2 Mt. Livermore at 796' and picnic benches. Spectacular views in all directions. Note that there are 3 picnic areas on concrete pads just

View from the Sunset trail

below the summit. This is the level of the old summit at 781', which was leveled by the military for a Nike missile radar site. In 2002, 15' was added to the summit restoring it to its original height.

2.5 Junction ❷ again. Continue right on the Sunset trail.

Originally, Angel Island was covered with trees and known as Wood Island. Most of the trees were cut to supply fuel for steamships entering the bay. Later, non-native trees invaded the area. In the 1990s, groves of eucalyptus trees were cut along the Sunset trail and removed by helicopter. Now, the Sunset trail is open offering spectacular views.

3.4 Junction ❸. Go right 50' on the Fire Rd., and continue downhill. In the spring, look for brilliant blue patches of forget-me-nots.

4.6 Junction ❹. Cross the Perimeter Rd. and head down to the cove.

4.9 Ayala Cove, Visitor Center, snackbar and ferry dock.

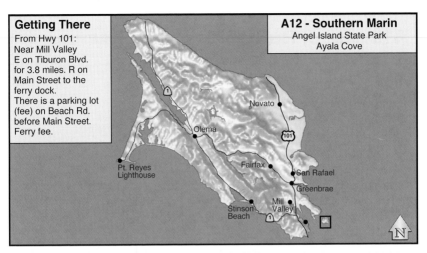

Getting There

From Hwy 101:
Near Mill Valley
E on Tiburon Blvd.
for 3.8 miles. R on
Main Street to the
ferry dock.
There is a parking lot
(fee) on Beach Rd.
before Main Street.
Ferry fee.

A12 - Southern Marin
Angel Island State Park
Ayala Cove

Novato

Olema

Pt. Reyes
Lighthouse

Fairfax

San Rafael

Greenbrae

Stinson
Beach

Mill
Valley

San Francisco Bay

Pt. Blunt

No Access

Perimeter Rd

Nike
Missile
Site

Service Rd Only

Perimeter Rd

Perles
Beach

Battery
Ledyard

Fire Rd

Camp Reynolds
(West Garrison)

Sunset Trail

Fort McDowell
(East Garrison)

Quarry
Beach

❷

**Mt. Livermore
796'**

Fire Rd

Perimeter Rd

Quarry
Point

North
Ridge
Trail

❸

❹

Perimeter Rd

❶

*Ayala
Cove*

Immigration Station
(North Garrison)

**Tiburon
Ferry**

0   .4

Scale 1"= 0.4 miles

33

A13 Angel Island Perimeter Trail

Distance: 5.2 miles   Shaded: 30%
Elevation Change: 300'
Rating: Hiking - 9   Difficulty - 3   Lots of bicycles.
When to Go: Best when clear. Afternoons can be windy.

This hike on the main road around Angel Island visits all the historical areas including the Immigration Station. Great views and picnic sites.

0.0 From the dock, walk to the picnic area and Visitor Center. Take the road behind the Visitor Center to the right and head west.

0.3 Junction ❶. Take Perimeter Rd to the right to circle the island counterclockwise. Stay to the right and watch for bicycles.

0.7 Junction ❷ with Camp Reynolds. The artillery batteries near here were part of the defense system of San Francisco Bay that included the Presidio in San Francisco, Alcatraz Island and the Marin Headlands. The various gun emplacements started with Spanish cannons at Fort Point in 1776 and ended in 1974 with the closing of a Nike missile site at Fort Barry in Marin. The local batteries started in the 1860s and were replaced in the 1900s.

1.2 Battery Ledyard with spectacular views of the Golden Gate.

2.7 Nike missile site, active from 1954 to 1962.

2.9 Junction ❸ with Fort McDowell. Just above the ballfield and group picnic area, take the concrete stairs downhill. Then go left to pass in front of the large grey building, barracks that housed almost 700 men.

3.2 Junction with road to the dock at Quarry Point. Continue straight. Up ahead you can explore the yellow hospital building on the left. **Option 1**: Explore the area down by the dock. **Option 2**: Near the dock, take the East Bay View Trail to the Immigration Station.

4.1 Junction ❹. Take the road downhill to the Immigration Station.

4.3 Immigration Station, museum and China Cove. The museum is open weekends. This station, built in 1910, was designed as an "Ellis Island West" to handle the expected arrival of Europeans when the Panama Canal opened. As a result of World War I, that never happened and the station wound up handling mostly Chinese immigrants. The station closed in 1940 after 175,000 Chinese had passed through. When ready, go back up to junction ❹ with Perimeter Rd. Head right.

4.9 Junction ❺. Take the trail or the road down to Ayala Cove.

5.2 Back at the ferry dock. Snackbar, bicycle rentals and restrooms.

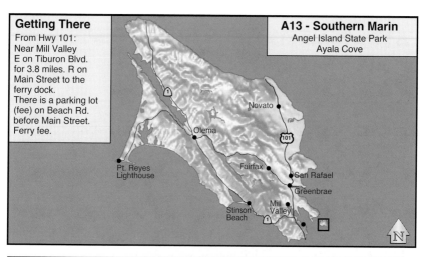

Getting There

From Hwy 101:
Near Mill Valley
E on Tiburon Blvd.
for 3.8 miles. R on
Main Street to the
ferry dock.
There is a parking lot
(fee) on Beach Rd.
before Main Street.
Ferry fee.

A13 - Southern Marin
Angel Island State Park
Ayala Cove

A14 Warner Cyn. FR - Blithedale Ridge

Distance: 4.6 miles   Shaded: 50%
Elevation Change: 900'   May have standing water.
Rating: Hiking - 9   Difficulty - 6   Moderately steep and rocky.
When to Go: Best in winter for falls and early March for trillium.

This hike circles Warner Canyon to visit the small winter falls, then climbs to Blithedale Ridge to offer great views of Mt. Tamalpais.

0.0 Start at the Open Space gate at the end of Glen Drive and take the Glen FR uphill. Ahead, you can get a good feel for Warner Canyon which has mostly redwoods on the north-facing slopes and oaks and chaparral along the south-facing Glen FR.

0.4 Junction ❶. Take the Elinor FR left. The road crosses the head of the canyon and a creek, then heads gradually downhill.

1.3 Junction ❷. Take the signed Warner Canyon trail left (The sign should read Warner Falls trail.) The trail may be overgrown.

1.8 Warner Falls. Since the canyon is fairly small, water runoff and the series of cascades are best seen after heavy rains. Look for trillium in late winter. The trail ends here at the falls. Various paths up along the falls are very steep and unsafe. Retrace your steps.

2.3 Junction ❷ again. Take the Elinor FR right uphill.

2.4 Junction. At a sharp bend in the road, a small trail heads left into the redwoods. This is a new trail that zig-zags up to the ridge. Ignore smaller trails that lead off into the ravine.

2.8 Junction with the Maytag trail. Head left 100' to the ridge.

2.8+ Junction ❸. Take the Blithedale Ridge FR right. (On hot days, you can backtrack and follow the Maytag trail as it parallels the ridge.) Up ahead, look for great views across Blithedale Canyon to Mt. Tam. **Option:** Head left on the ridge for 200 yds. to a knoll with good views south to Belvedere, Angel Island, Alcatraz Island and San Francisco.

3.6 Junction ❹. Take the Corte Madera Ridge FR right. About 100' ahead, the road offers a classic view down Warner Canyon and out across Richardson Bay to San Francisco. Warner Canyon was named after Alexander Warner, a San Francisco physician who bought a summer home here in 1885.

3.7 Junction. At the saddle, take the Glen FR downhill to the right.

4.2 Junction ❶ again. Continue left down the Glen FR.

4.6 Back at the parking area. No facilities.

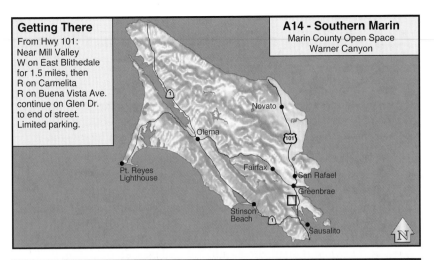

Getting There

From Hwy 101:
Near Mill Valley
W on East Blithedale
for 1.5 miles, then
R on Carmelita
R on Buena Vista Ave.
continue on Glen Dr.
to end of street.
Limited parking.

Novato

Olema

Pt. Reyes
Lighthouse

Fairfax

San Rafael

Greenbrae

Stinson
Beach

Sausalito

N

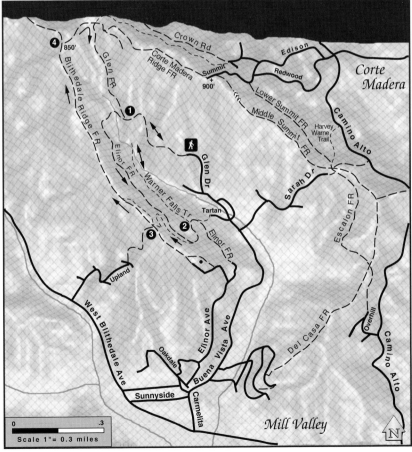

4   850'

Crown Rd

Edison

Corte Madera
Ridge FR

Summit
900'

Redwood

Corte
Madera

Blithedale Ridge FR

Glen FR

Lower Summit FR

Middle Summit FR

Harvey
Warne
Trail

Camino Alto

1

Elinor FR

Glen Dr

Warner Falls Tr

Tartan

2

3

Sarah Dr

Escalon FR

Elinor FR

Upland

West Blithedale Ave

Oakdale

Elinor Ave

Buena Vista Ave

Del Casa FR

Overhill

Camino Alto

Sunnyside

Carmelita

Mill Valley

0   .3
Scale 1"= 0.3 miles

N

A15 Baltimore Cyn. to Blithedale Ridge

Distance: 5.3 miles   Shaded: 60%
Elevation Change: 700'   Can be flooded during heavy runoff.
Rating: Hiking - 9   Difficulty - 9   Some rocks, roots and ruts.
When to Go: Best in winter for falls and early March for trillium.

This hike passes through beautiful Baltimore Canyon with redwoods and Dawn Falls, then climbs to Blithedale Ridge for great views.

0.0 Be sure to park in a designated space. Go to the end of the street and take the trail across the bridge and bear right. Take the Dawn Falls trail into a magnificent redwood forest dotted with occasional bays and big-leaf maple. Up ahead, the trail passes by a dam that once supplied water to the town of Larkspur.

0.5 Junction with Ladybug trail across the creek. Continue straight. During heavy water runoff, sections of the trail can be flooded, which may require a detour. In early March, look for trillium with its 3 green leaves and 3 white petals.

1.0 Dawn Falls. After a short climb, the trail skirts lovely Dawn Falls.

1.2 Junction ❶. Go left on Crown Rd., which is also called Southern Marin Line FR. The road was built by the water district to pipe water from the Bon Tempe treatment plant to southern Marin. Notice the "suspension system" used to carry the water pipe across the ravine. It is also known as the "Little Golden Gate."

2.1 Junction ❷. At the exposed pipes, take the H-Line Rd. right uphill.

2.4 Junction. Take the Blithedale Ridge FR to the right. Up ahead, rewards for the steep climb are apparent with great views west to Mt. Tamalpais and east to the bay and Mt. Diablo. In recent years, vegetation along the ridgetop has been thinned to create fuel breaks that will help fire fighters contain wildfires.

2.9 Junction ❸. Take the signed Hoo-Koo-E-Koo trail to the right. The hike now passes through dense chaparral: manzanita and chamise with occasional oak, bay and madrone trees. More great views down Baltimore Canyon.

3.3 Junction with Dawn Falls trail. Continue straight.

3.8 Junction ❹. Take Crown Rd. to the right.

4.1 Junction ❶ again. Take the Dawn Falls trail downhill to the left and return back through Baltimore Canyon.

5.3 Back at the parking area with no facilities.

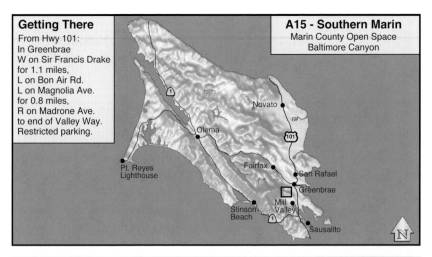

Getting There

From Hwy 101:
In Greenbrae
W on Sir Francis Drake
for 1.1 miles,
L on Bon Air Rd.
L on Magnolia Ave.
for 0.8 miles,
R on Madrone Ave.
to end of Valley Way.
Restricted parking.

A15 - Southern Marin
Marin County Open Space
Baltimore Canyon

Novato

101

Olema

Pt. Reyes
Lighthouse

Fairfax

San Rafael

Greenbrae

Stinson
Beach

Mill
Valley

Sausalito

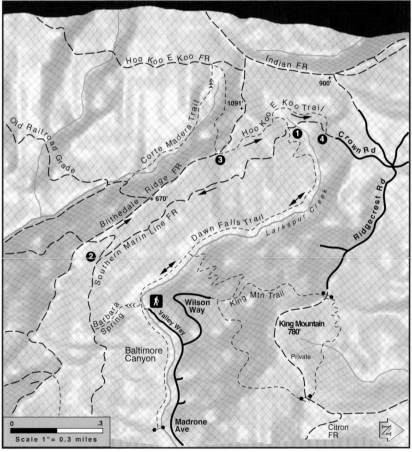

Hoo Koo E Koo FR

Indian FR

+
900'

Old Railroad Grade

Corte Madera Trail

1091'
+

Hoo Koo E Koo Trail

Hoo Koo E

❶

❹

Crown Rd

❸

Blithedale Ridge FR

+ 670'

Southern Marin Line FR

Dawn Falls Trail

Larkspur Creek

Ridgecrest Rd

❷

Barbara Spring

Valley Way

Wilson Way

King Mtn Trail

King Mountain
780'

Private

Baltimore
Canyon

Madrone
Ave

Citron
FR

0 .3
Scale 1"= 0.3 miles

39

B - Mt. Tamalpais South - 21 Hikes

Starting from West Blithedale Ave at 240'
B1   Blithedale Ridge - Corte Madera Trails 6.6
B2   Old Railroad Grade - Hoo-Koo-E-Koo FR 6.7

Starting from Muir Woods at 150'
B3   Muir Woods - Hillside Trails 1.9
B4   Muir Woods - Fern Creek Trails 3.6
B5   Ocean View - Redwood - Sun Trails 4.2
B6   Muir Woods - TCC - Dipsea Trails 6.3

Starting from Mtn. Home Inn at 920'
B7   Panoramic - Lost - Sierra Trails 3.9
B8   Mountain Home Inn to East Peak 4.7
B9   Matt Davis - Troop 80 Trails 5.1
B10 Old RR Grade to West Point Inn 5.3

Starting from Bootjack at 1350'
B11 TCC - Alpine Trails 3.7
B12 Bootjack - Rock Spring Trails 4.2

Starting from Pantoll Ranger Station at 1500'
B13 Easy Grade to Mountain Theater 3.4
B14 Dipsea - Steep Ravine Trails 3.6
B15 Matt Davis - Coastal - Cataract Trails 6.6
B16 Matt Davis Trail to Stinson Beach 7.2

Starting from Rock Spring at 1970'
B17 Simmons - Potrero - Arturo Trails 5.4
B18 Benstein - International Trails 5.4
B19 Cataract - High Marsh - Kent Trails 6.0

Starting from East Peak at 2300'
B20 East Peak Loop and Plankwalk Trails 0.7 and 0.6
B21 Northside - Colier - Lakeview Trails 5.0

Notes
Dogs allowed on hikes B1, B2, B10, B17 and B19
To download a hike, go to www.marintrails.com
The password for this region is b1pn2gp

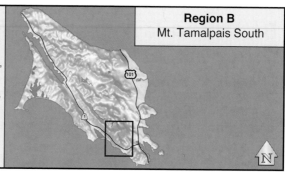

Region B Trailheads

Hikes 1-2 start in Marin Co. Open Space, phone 415-499-6387.

Hikes 3-6 start in Muir Woods, phone 415-388-2595.

Hikes 7-10 and 17-19 start in Marin Municipal Water Dist., phone 415-945-1181.

Hikes 11-16 and 20-21 start Mt. Tamalpais State Park, phone 415-388-2070.

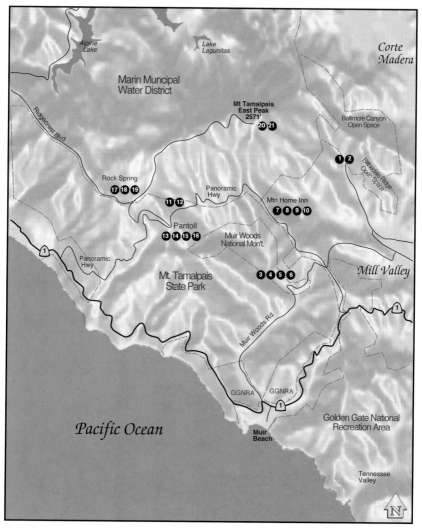

B1 Blithedale Ridge - Corte Madera Trails

Distance: 6.6 miles   Shaded: 40%
Elevation Change: 1500'   Lots of hills. Some bicycles.
Rating: Hiking - 9   Difficulty - 9   One steep downhill.
When to Go: Save this hike for cool, clear winter days.

Bring binoculars and camera for this roller-coaster hike along Blithedale Ridge offering stunning views of Mt. Tam and Marin.

0.0 Start near the Old Railroad Grade trailhead located near the end of West Blithedale Ave. Go through the gate and head uphill on the dirt road. Stay to the right and watch for bicycles.

0.1 Junction. Turn right and take the H-Line FR as it starts a moderately steep climb out of the canyon and into open chaparral.

0.7 Two junctions ❶. Go right on Blithedale Ridge to climb to a spectacular viewpoint of Mt. Tamalpais.

1.2 Junction ❷ with the Corte Madera Ridge FR. There are two great view spots near here. First, go left 50' for a great view down Warner Canyon and out towards San Francisco. Then return to this junction and continue on the road up to the next knoll.

1.3 Knoll and view spot. This picture-taking spot offers a striking profile of the East Peak of Mt. Tamalpais. Return to junction ❶.

1.9 Back at junctions ❶. Continue straight, then right down H-Line FR.

2.5 Junction. Take Crown Rd. left, the only level part of this hike. This road is also called the Southern Marin Line FR, and provides access to water pipes from Bon Tempe Lake to Southern Marin.

3.6 Junction. Take the Hoo-Koo-E-Koo trail left uphill.

4.5 Junction ❸ with Blithedale Ridge FR. It's worth a short detour up the steep hill for great views of Bill Williams Canyon and points north.

4.7 Knoll and viewpoint. King Mtn. is close on the right. Then comes San Pedro Mtn. further on the left, with Big Rock Ridge to the north.

4.9 Junction ❸ again. Go right on the Hoo-Koo-E-Koo trail.

5.5 Two junctions ❹. Take the Corte Madera trail left as it descends steeply alongside the creek. The trail crosses the creek four times, so if you lose the trail, look for it on the other side of the creek.

5.9 Junction with Horseshoe FR. Head right downhill.

6.0 Junction with the Old Railroad Grade. Continue left downhill.

6.6 Back at the trailhead. No facilities.

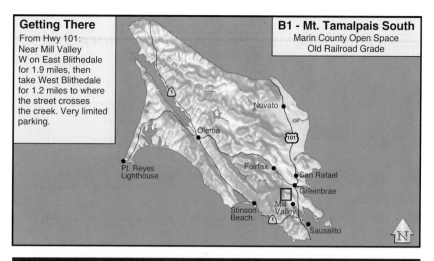

Getting There

From Hwy 101:
Near Mill Valley
W on East Blithedale
for 1.9 miles, then
take West Blithedale
for 1.2 miles to where
the street crosses
the creek. Very limited
parking.

B1 - Mt. Tamalpais South
Marin County Open Space
Old Railroad Grade

Novato

101

Olema

Pt. Reyes
Lighthouse

Fairfax

San Rafael

Greenbrae

Stinson
Beach

Mill
Valley

Sausalito

N

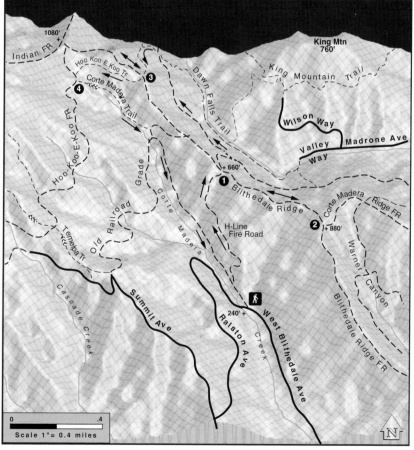

1080'

Indian FR

King Mtn
760'

Hoo Koo E Koo Tr

King Mountain Trail

Corte Madera Trail

❸

Dawn Falls Trail

❹

Hoo-Koo-E-Koo FR

Wilson Way

Corte Madera Trail

Valley Way

Madrone Ave

+ 660'

❶

Blithedale Ridge

Corte Madera

Corte Madera Ridge FR

❷ + 880'

Old Railroad Grade

H-Line
Fire Road

Temelpa Tr

Warner Canyon

Cascade Creek

Summit Ave

Ralston Ave

240' +

West Blithedale Ave

Creek

Blithedale Ridge FR

0   .4
Scale 1" = 0.4 miles

N

43

B2 Old Railroad Grade - Hoo-Koo-E-Koo

Distance: 6.7 miles   Shaded: 50%
Elevation Change: 900'   Heavy bicycle traffic on weekends.
Rating: Hiking - 7   Difficulty - 6   Some rocky sections.
When to Go: Best on cool, clear weekdays.

This hike follows the historic Old Railroad Grade as it gradually climbs up the mountain. Open chaparral areas provide great views.

0.0 Start at the Old Railroad Grade trailhead near the end of West Blithedale Ave. Go through the gate and start a long gradual uphill.

1.8 Junction ❶ with Summit Ave and Fern Canyon Rd. The hike continues uphill on the paved road for 0.6 miles. Great views.

2.9 Two junctions and the Double Bowknot. Two roads separated by 100' head left and join to form Gravity Car Grade, which leads to the Mtn. Home Inn and Muir Woods.

Gravity Car

Continue right to pass the concrete landing, Mesa Station, where passengers could transfer to gravity cars and coast down Gravity Car Grade. This road section is part of the famous Double Bowknot where tracks made a series of switchbacks and ran parallel to each other five times. From 1896 to 1930, the Mt. Tamalpais & Muir Woods Railway, better known as the "Crookedest Railroad in the World," attracted bay area residents and tourists to outings on the mountain.

3.2 Junction ❷. Go right on Hoo-Koo-E-Koo FR. Good views ahead.

4.9 Two junctions ❸. Take the Corte Madera trail downhill for 10', then left on the Hoo-Koo-E-Koo trail. Up ahead, the trail passes Echo Rock, where you can sometimes hear sounds from down the canyon.

5.5 Junction. Take Blithedale Ridge FR downhill to the right.

5.7 Junction. Take Horseshoe FR right downhill.

5.9 Junction. Head downhill on the Corte Madera trail. **Option**: Stay on the Horseshoe FR. They both travel parallel downhill for 0.1 mile.

6.0 Junction with the Old Railroad Grade. This hairpin curve in the old RR Grade was known as Horseshoe Curve. Continue left downhill.

6.7 Back at the trailhead. No Facilities.

Getting There

From Hwy 101:
Near Mill Valley
W on East Blithedale
for 1.9 miles, then
take West Blithedale
for 1.2 miles to where
the street crosses
the creek. Very limited
parking.

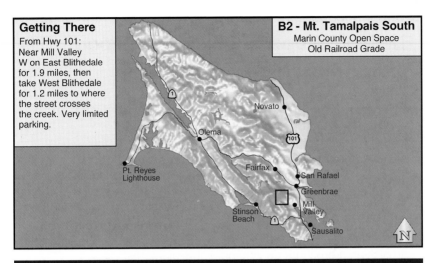

Novato

Olema

Pt. Reyes
Lighthouse

Fairfax

San Rafael

Greenbrae

Mill
Valley

Stinson
Beach

Sausalito

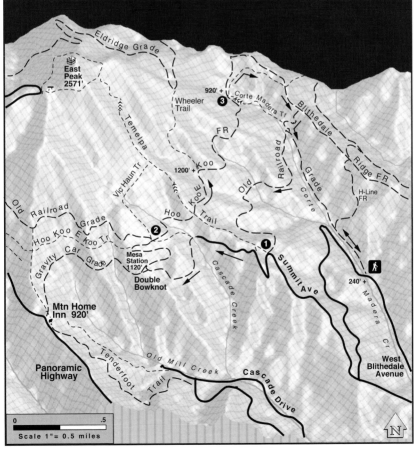

Eldridge Grade

East
Peak
2571'

Temelpa Tr

Vic Haun Tr

Wheeler
Trail

920' +

③

Corte Madera Tr

FR

1200' +

Koo E Koo Trail

Hoo

Old

Railroad Grade

Corte

Blithedale

Ridge FR

H-Line
FR

Old   Railroad

Hoo Koo E Koo Tr

Gravity   Car   Grade

②

Mesa
Station
1120'

Double
Bowknot

Cascade Creek

①

Summit Ave

240' +

Madera Ct

Mtn Home
Inn 920'

Tenderfoot   Trail

Old Mill Creek

Cascade Drive

Panoramic
Highway

West
Blithedale
Avenue

0   .5

Scale 1"= 0.5 miles

B3 Muir Woods - Hillside Trails

Distance: 1.9 miles   Shaded: 100%
Elevation Change: 200'   Some rocks, roots and stairs on Hillside.
Rating: Hiking - 10   Difficulty - 3   Can be crowded.
When to Go: Excellent anytime, best in spring for trillium.

This Muir Woods hike takes the most heavily traveled trail on Mt. Tamalpais. It winds along the floor of a beautiful, virgin redwood forest.

0.0 Start at the Muir Woods entrance (pay fee). Follow the Main trail along the right side of Redwood Creek. The trail has several nature information signs describing the redwood forest. At the entrance, you can pick up a brochure describing points of interest.

0.5 Cathedral Grove. A beautiful redwood grove dedicated to the founding of the United Nations in San Francisco in 1945. Tanoak and western sword fern are the dominant shrublike growth under the redwood canopy, while redwood sorrel provides most of the ground cover. Ahead, the light green leaves of western azalea, hazel and big leaf maple stand out against the dark green, redwood background.

0.6 Junction with Fern Creek. Continue left. Notice how some redwoods have an enormous number of sprouts growing out of the base, while others have grey-green lichens growing on the bark.

0.7 Junction with Camp Eastwood trail. Continue left.

0.9 Two junctions ❶. Bear left, cross Bridge 4 and head uphill. Go left again up the Hillside trail.

Trillium

1.1 Ravine. The first of three small, picturesque ravines. Ferns, mosses, pink trillium, sorrel and the striking clintonia grow along the bank. Notice the large Douglas fir just past the stream bed. Its bark differs from nearby redwoods in texture and in the moss covering. Redwoods often have lichens growing on them, but seldom mosses.

1.6 Junction. The Hillside trail gently descends to the canyon floor. Stay right to enter Bohemian Grove with some of the tallest trees in the park, nearly 260'. Ahead at Bridge 1, look for spawning silver salmon and steelhead trout in wintertime.

1.8 Snack shop, gift shop and restroom facilities.

1.9 Parking lot. Continue walking along the creek to see several large red alders in a riparian setting. Further downstream, across from the highway entrance, notice the incredibly tangled buckeye trees with moss-covered trunks criss-crossing every which way.

46

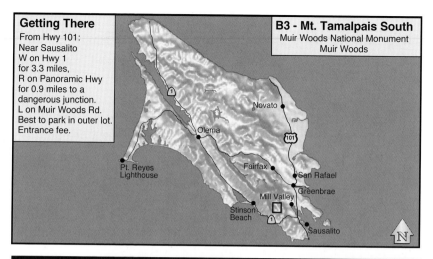

Getting There

From Hwy 101:
Near Sausalito
W on Hwy 1
for 3.3 miles,
R on Panoramic Hwy
for 0.9 miles to a
dangerous junction.
L on Muir Woods Rd.
Best to park in outer lot.
Entrance fee.

B3 - Mt. Tamalpais South
Muir Woods National Monument
Muir Woods

Novato

Olema

Pt. Reyes
Lighthouse

Fairfax

San Rafael

Greenbrae

Mill Valley

Stinson
Beach

Sausalito

N

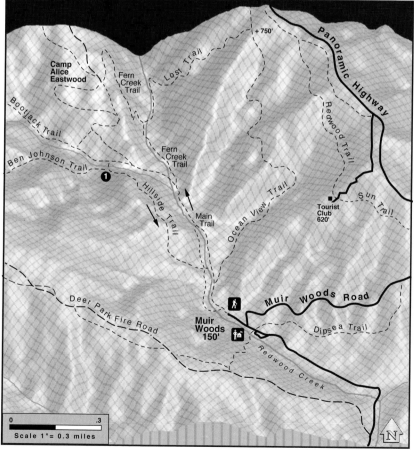

Camp
Alice
Eastwood

Fern
Creek
Trail

Lost Trail

+ 750'

Panoramic Highway

Bootjack Trail

Ben Johnson Trail

Redwood Trail

Fern
Creek
Trail

Ocean View Trail

Sun Trail

Hillside Trail

Tourist
Club
620'

Main
Trail

Deer Park Fire Road

Muir Woods Road

Dipsea Trail

Muir
Woods
150'

Redwood Creek

0   .3

Scale 1"= 0.3 miles

N

B4 Muir Woods - Fern Creek Trails

Distance: 3.6 miles   Shaded: 100%
Elevation Change: 300'
Rating: Hiking - 9   Difficulty - 4   Moderately steep.
When to Go: Excellent anytime, best in February and March.

This is a great redwood forest hike that leaves the crowded Muir Woods floor to explore Fern Canyon and Camp Alice Eastwood.

Note: The bridge at mile 1.1 was destroyed in 2002 by a fallen redwood. In summer, it may be possible to ford the creek about 100' upstream on an unofficial trail. If not, it's still worth doing an out and back hike.

0.0 Start at the Muir Woods entrance (fee). Follow the Main trail along the right side of Redwood Creek.

0.7 Junction. Take the Fern Creek trail right along the small creek. Watch for white trillium in March and the striking pink clintonia in April.

1.1 Junction ❶ with Lost trail. Cross the creek. Continue upstream on the west bank past the stairs, then loop back on the trail.

1.8 Plevin Cut and Camp Alice Eastwood junctions ❷. At the first junction, continue right to the parking area. The camp, named for Alice Eastwood, avid botanist, writer and hiker, was dedicated in 1949 on her 90th birthday.

Muir Woods Inn 1908

This was also the location of the Muir Woods Inn, which served visitors who coasted down on gravity cars in the early 1900s.

From the camp, cross the paved parking circle to Camp Eastwood Rd. signed to Muir Woods. The road starts downhill passing through madrone, manzanita, oak, yerba santa and non-native broom.

2.5 Junction ❸. Take the signed Bootjack Spur trail right down to Redwood Creek, then go left and head downstream.

2.7 Junction and park boundary. Continue left along the creek.

3.1 Bridge and Cathedral Grove. Cross Bridge 3 to return down the right side of Redwood Creek. Look for redwood burls. Further ahead lies Bohemian Grove with some of the tallest trees in the park at 260'.

3.6 Snack shop, gift shop, restroom facilities and parking lot.

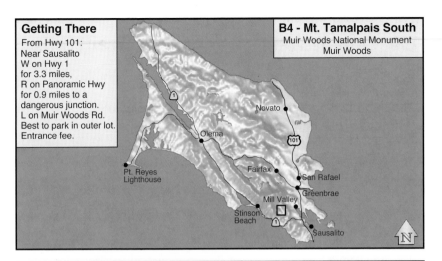

Getting There

From Hwy 101:
Near Sausalito
W on Hwy 1
for 3.3 miles,
R on Panoramic Hwy
for 0.9 miles to a
dangerous junction.
L on Muir Woods Rd.
Best to park in outer lot.
Entrance fee.

B4 - Mt. Tamalpais South
Muir Woods National Monument
Muir Woods

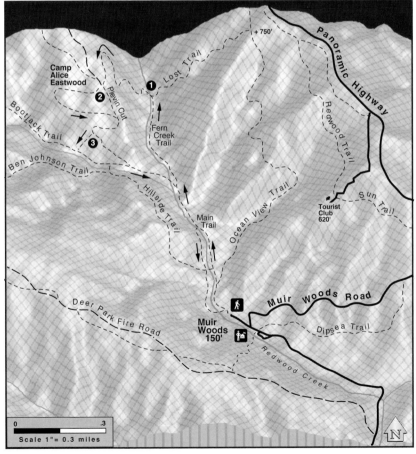

49

B5 Ocean View - Redwood - Sun Trails

Distance: 4.2 miles   Shaded: 60%
Elevation Change: 900'   Some ruts, rocks and roots.
Rating: Hiking - 9   Difficulty - 6   Mud possible.
When to Go: Best February to April for flowers.

This is a great hike out of Muir Woods into mixed conifers, then on to the Sun trail where wildflowers start in February.

0.0 At the Muir Woods entrance (fee), take the Main trail up the right side of Redwood Creek past magnificent redwoods. Look for the cross-cut section of a redwood trunk and historical information.

0.2 Junction ❶. Take the signed Ocean View trail right for a long steady climb. In February, look for pink trillium and blue hound's tongue among the ferns, tanoak and redwoods.

1.5 Junction with Lost trail. Stay right and continue uphill. Look for chaparral being overgrown by taller trees: bay, fir and redwood.

1.8 Junction and highway. Take the Panoramic trail right. From here, you can get long-range views of the ocean, which is about 3 miles away.

2.1 Junction ❷. Bear right, downhill on the signed Redwood trail.

2.4 Old bench. What's left of an old bench once provided a good spot to enjoy the views across Muir Woods to the ocean. Rocky ahead.

2.8 Junction with Tourist Club. This club was founded in 1912 as a branch of a European hiking club. The club is private, but often sells refreshments on weekend afternoons. The trail passes above the club to a road and then heads left 100' to the signed Sun trail.

Indian Paintbrush

2.9 Junction ❸. Head right on the Sun trail which earns its name by skirting the south-facing hillside overlooking Muir Woods. Wildflowers begin in February, building to a peak in April. In the past, sections of the Sun trail have been overgrown with French and Spanish broom and was impassable. Hopefully, the broom, a non-native shrub that crowds out natives, can be kept under control.

3.5 Junction. Follow the signed Dipsea trail right as it drops steeply down the hillside and crosses the highway into a bay-filled ravine.

4.1 Service area and site of a dance pavilion in the 1920s and 30s.

4.2 Parking lots, snack shop, gift shop and restroom facilities.

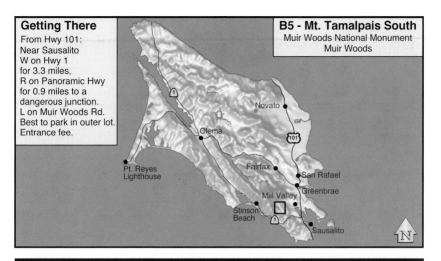

Getting There

From Hwy 101:
Near Sausalito
W on Hwy 1
for 3.3 miles,
R on Panoramic Hwy
for 0.9 miles to a
dangerous junction.
L on Muir Woods Rd.
Best to park in outer lot.
Entrance fee.

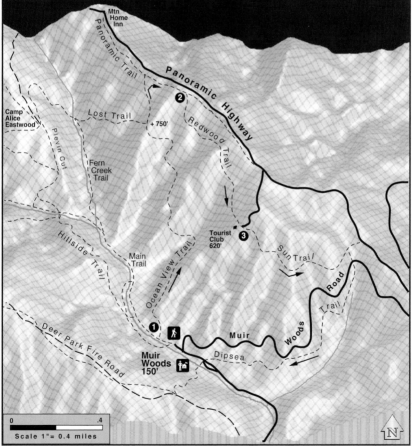

Scale 1"= 0.4 miles

51

B6 Muir Woods - TCC - Dipsea Trails

Distance: 6.3 miles   Shaded: 70%
Elevation Change: 1300'   Some ruts, rocks and roots.
Rating: Hiking - 9   Difficulty - 7   Lots of stairs.
When to Go: Good anytime, best in April after the bridge opens.

A dramatic hike into dense redwood forest with plunging creek, then down an open ridge with views and flowers, and into a lush canyon.

Note: During high water runoff, the bridge on the Dipsea trail, which crosses Redwood Creek, may be flooded or removed. If in doubt, check before starting. The bridge is 100' west of the outer parking area.

0.0 Start at the Muir Woods parking lot. Follow the Main trail along the right side of Redwood Creek. Look for nature signs along the way.

0.9 Junction ❶. Take the signed Bootjack trail, continuing along the right side of Redwood Creek. The Bootjack trail makes an almost straight climb from Muir Woods to the Mtn. Theater, climbing 1800' in 3 miles. It is also one of Tam's oldest trails, dating to before 1900.

1.3 Slides and debris. Downed trees and large boulders testify to the power of fast-moving water in the creek.

2.3 Van Wyck Meadow and double junction ❷. This meadow with its large picturesque rock and "population sign" has often served as a gathering and resting spot. Continue past the first trail and take the signed TCC trail left over the creek.

3.7 Double junction ❸ with the Stapelveldt trail. First go left, then right to take the signed TCC trail towards the Dipsea trail.

4.1 Junction ❹. Eventually, we'll take the Dipsea trail left down to Muir Woods. However, now go right, uphill 200' to the hilltop for great views and wildflowers. This hill is known as "Cardiac Hill" to the 1500 Dipsea runners who struggle up from Muir Woods each June. When ready, backtrack down the trail and follow the Dipsea trail to the road.

4.5 Junction. Leave the road and go right down the Dipsea trail. The trail and the road (Deer Park FR) intersect several times.

4.7 Open hillside. This grassy ridge is called "Hogsback" by Dipsea runners. It is said to be where the Dipsea race is won or lost.

5.9 Junction ❺. Take the trail left, down into a moist canyon filled with bay, hazel, berries and ferns. If the bridge is flooded, take the road.

6.2 Bridge. Cross the creek under red alders and head left.

6.3 Back at Muir Woods with full facilities.

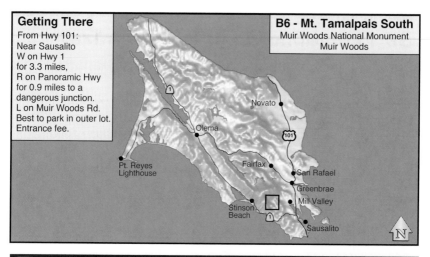

Getting There

From Hwy 101:
Near Sausalito
W on Hwy 1
for 3.3 miles,
R on Panoramic Hwy
for 0.9 miles to a
dangerous junction.
L on Muir Woods Rd.
Best to park in outer lot.
Entrance fee.

Novato

Olema

Pt. Reyes
Lighthouse

Fairfax

San Rafael

Greenbrae

Mill Valley

Stinson
Beach

Sausalito

N

Rock Spring Trail

Spike Buck Cr.

Old Railroad Grade

West Point Inn
1785'

Hoo-Koo-E-Koo Tr.

Rattlesnake Cr.

Old Stage Rd

Matt

Davis

Trail

Gravity Car Grade

Panoramic Highway

Bootjack
1350'

Troop 80 Trail

Van Wyck
Meadow
1040'
2

Mtn Home
Inn 920'

Camp Eastwood Rd.

Fern Creek

Pantoll
1500'
3

Bootjack Trail

Sierra
Trail

TCC
Trail

Lost Tr.

4

Stapelveldt Tr.

Fern Creek

Ocean
View
Trail

+
1400
Cardiac
Hill

Ben Johnson Trail

Redwood Creek

Fern
Creek
Trail

1

Dipsea Trail

Deer Park Fire Road

Main
Trail

Coast View Trail

Kent Creek

Muir Woods
150'

Dipsea Tr.

5

0   .5
Scale 1" = 0.5 miles

N

B7 Panoramic - Lost - Sierra Trails

Distance: 3.9 miles   Shaded: 70%
Elevation Change: 800'   Lots of stairs.
Rating: Hiking - 9   Difficulty - 6   Some rocks and roots.
When to Go: Good anytime, best December to March.

This is a great hike that descends into magnificent Fern Canyon, then gradually climbs back through chaparral and redwoods.

0.0 From the north end of the parking lot opposite the Mtn. Home Inn, take the Trestle trail down the stairs. At the paved road, head left.

0.1 Gate and junction. Take the signed Panoramic trail right. Grasses may crowd the trail in summer. Good views towards the ocean.

0.2 Junction ❶. Take the Ocean View trail right towards Muir Woods. This area has been repeatedly burned to control French broom.

0.5 Junction. At the redwood grove, take the Lost trail right. This trail was constructed in 1914 by members of the Tourist Club. It is steep in places and was blocked (hence "lost") for a long time after a massive slide in the1930s. New stairs make the descent easier. At the bottom, the trail ends in a magnificent redwood canyon, Fern Canyon.

1.1 Junction with Fern Creek. Head left towards Muir Woods. **Option:** The old Fern Creek bridge crossed here (destroyed in 2002). In summer, you may be able to ford the creek on an unofficial trail (about 100' upstream) and take the Fern Creek trail towards junction ❷.

1.4 Kent Tree. Look for a nature sign that explains this fallen, landmark tree.

1.5 Junction. Take the main Muir Woods trail right.

1.6 Junction. Take the Camp Eastwood trail right.

1.9 Junction. Take the Plevin Cut trail (narrow trail heading uphill) up through the redwood trees.

Huckleberry

2.1 Plevin Cut and Camp Eastwood junctions ❷. Go left up to Camp Eastwood, then across the paved area and take the signed Sierra trail. **Note:** See Hike B4 for historical information about Camp Eastwood.

2.2 Picnic table and bench. The road abruptly ends and, up ahead, the trail swings in and out of the transition zone between two unlikely bedfellows, redwood and chaparral.

3.1 Junction ❸. Head right on Troop 80 trail towards Mtn. Home Inn.

3.5 Junction and creek. Go left on the paved Camp Eastwood Rd.

3.9 Junction. Take the stairs to the parking lot with water and restrooms.

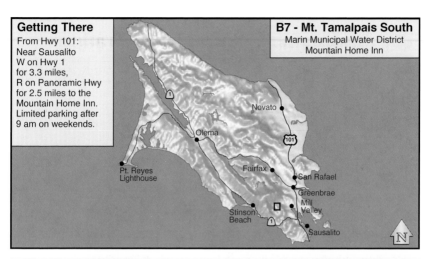

Getting There

From Hwy 101:
Near Sausalito
W on Hwy 1
for 3.3 miles,
R on Panoramic Hwy
for 2.5 miles to the
Mountain Home Inn.
Limited parking after
9 am on weekends.

B7 - Mt. Tamalpais South
Marin Municipal Water District
Mountain Home Inn

Novato

Olema

Fairfax

San Rafael

Greenbrae

Mill Valley

Pt. Reyes
Lighthouse

Stinson
Beach

Sausalito

N

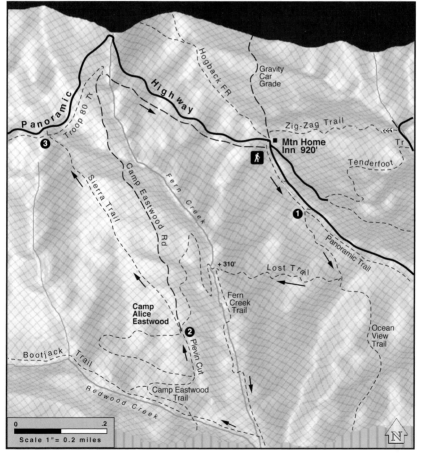

Panoramic

Highway

Hogback FR

Gravity
Car
Grade

Zig-Zag Trail

Troop 80 Tr

Mtn Home
Inn 920'

Tenderfoot

Tr

Sierra Trail

Camp Eastwood Rd

Fern Creek

Panoramic Trail

+310'

Lost Trail

Fern
Creek
Trail

Camp
Alice
Eastwood

Plevin Cut

Ocean
View
Trail

Bootjack Trail

Redwood Creek

Camp Eastwood
Trail

0   .2
Scale 1"= 0.2 miles

N

55

B8 Mountain Home Inn to East Peak

Distance: 4.7 miles   Shaded: 30%
Elevation Change: 1600'   Lots of stairs.
Rating: Hiking - 9   Difficulty - 9   Steep and rocky.
When to Go: Best on cool, clear, calm winter days.

This is the shortest and quickest hike to the top of Mt. Tamalpais. It offers strenuous exercise and spectacular views in all directions.

0.0 Start at the Mountain Home Inn and head north across the highway and up the paved road towards the fire station. Take the Hogback FR past the fire station and up past a new water tank.

0.3 Junction with the Matt Davis trail. Continue up Hogback, which gets steeper as it passes manzanita, oak, madrone, bay and fir.

0.6 Junction ❶. Take the Old Railroad Grade left for a more gradual climb. The trail provides sweeping views in chaparral areas, then enters Fern Canyon with redwoods and occasional madrones.

1.0 Junction. Take the signed Fern Creek trail on the right and start a steep climb up the right side of the creek. New stairs make it easier.

1.2 Creek crossing and then junction ❷. Tall chain ferns and a new bridge mark the creek crossing. The trail leaves the creek to enter a dense stand of bay trees, then veers right to pass a water tank and the Tavern Pump trail. Continue on the Fern Creek trail. This water source has been supplying water to the East Peak for over 100 years.

1.7 Junction with paved road. Take the old automobile road, now a trail, right towards the picnic area and East Peak.

1.8 Parking area, Visitor Center and snack bar. See Hike B20 for hours and for historical information about East Peak. When ready, take the signed Plankwalk trail up the north side of Mt. Tam.

2.0 East Peak and fire lookout station at 2571'. Stunning views! On clear winter days, look for the snow-covered Sierra Nevada to the east.

2.2 East Peak parking lot. Take the paved trail to the west.

2.4 Two junctions ❸. At the 2nd jct., take the Old Railroad Grade left.

3.1 Junction ❹. Take the signed Miller trail left. Ahead, the rock stairs can be steep and slippery. Once the trail enters an oak-bay forest, the going is easier. Watch for the rocky creek crossing ahead.

3.6 Junction. Take the Old Railroad Grade left.

4.1 Junction ❶. Take the Hogback FR right for a steep descent.

4.7 Mountain Home parking area with restrooms and water.

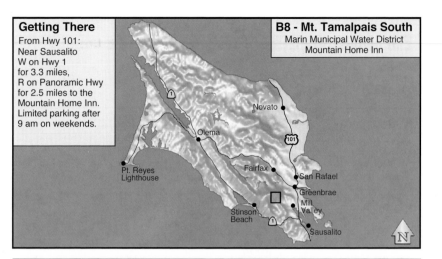

Getting There

From Hwy 101:
Near Sausalito
W on Hwy 1
for 3.3 miles,
R on Panoramic Hwy
for 2.5 miles to the
Mountain Home Inn.
Limited parking after
9 am on weekends.

B8 - Mt. Tamalpais South
Marin Municipal Water District
Mountain Home Inn

Novato

Olema

101

Fairfax

San Rafael

Greenbrae

Mill Valley

Stinson Beach

Sausalito

Pt. Reyes Lighthouse

N

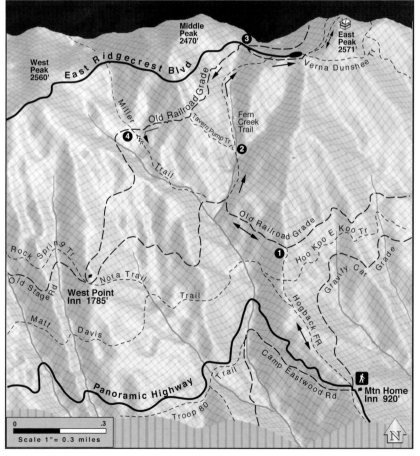

57

B9 Matt Davis - Troop 80 Trails

Distance: 5.1 miles   Shaded: 60%
Elevation Change: 550'   Some traffic noise.
Rating: Hiking - 9   Difficulty - 6   Rocky in places.
When to Go: Good in winter and spring for views, sun and creeks.

This is a great hike along south-facing ridges, into redwood canyons and over cascading creeks, offering views to the city and coast.

0.0 From the north end of the parking lot opposite the Mountain Home Inn, cross the highway and take the paved road up past the fire station.

0.3 Water tank and junction ❶. Just past the new water tank, take the signed Matt Davis trail left towards the west. Good views south. Matt Davis, known as the "dean of trail workers," lived in a small cabin he built above Bootjack Camp. He was paid by the Tamalpais Conservation Club to work on trails; he built this trail in the 1920s.

0.6 Fern Creek. The concrete weir above the bridge was part of a water intake system that is no longer used. Are the densely-packed, skinny redwoods young trees or stunted growth? Old-timers report similar groves 50 years ago.

1.3 Junction with the Nora trail. Cross the bridge and continue west.

2.6 Bootjack picnic area and junction ❷. Follow the paved path through the picnic area down to the parking lot. Cross Panoramic Hwy and take the signed Bootjack trail downhill.

2.8 Junction with the Alpine trail. Continue downhill under redwoods.

3.1 Van Wyck Meadow and junction ❸. The meadow, originally called Lower Rattlesnake Camp, was renamed for Sidney M. Van Wyck, president of the TCC in 1920-21. At "Council Rock," once a meeting place in the center of the meadow, take a spur trail left, east towards the Troop 80 trail and Mountain Home Inn.

3.2 Junction and plaque. At the bottom of some steps, a plaque dedicates a Douglas fir tree to World War I veterans. Continue straight on the Troop 80 trail, built by the Ingleside Boy Scout Troop.

3.7 Water pipeline. This steel water pipeline, started in 1904, was used to bring water from Rattlesnake Creek, Spike Buck Creek and other nearby creeks to a reservoir in Mill Valley and then on to the growing communites of Tiburon and Belvedere.

4.7 Junction with the paved Camp Eastwood Road. Head left uphill.

5.1 Junction. Take the stairs to the parking lot with water and restrooms.

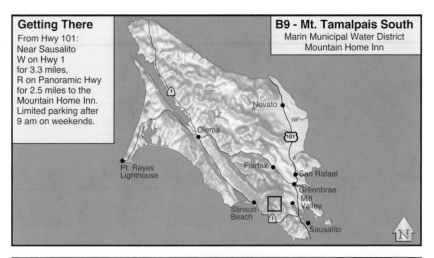

Getting There

From Hwy 101:
Near Sausalito
W on Hwy 1
for 3.3 miles,
R on Panoramic Hwy
for 2.5 miles to the
Mountain Home Inn.
Limited parking after
9 am on weekends.

B9 - Mt. Tamalpais South
Marin Municipal Water District
Mountain Home Inn

Novato

Olema

Pt. Reyes
Lighthouse

Fairfax

San Rafael

Greenbrae
Mill
Valley

Stinson
Beach

Sausalito

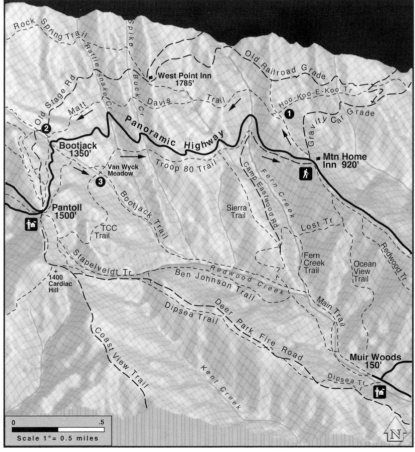

Rock Spring Trail

Spike

Old Stage Rd

Rattlesnake Cr

Buck Cr

West Point Inn
1785'

Davis   Trail

Old Railroad Grade

Hoo-Koo-E-Koo Tr

Gravity Car Grade

Matt

❶

Panoramic Highway

❷

Bootjack
1350'

Van Wyck
Meadow

Troop 80 Trail

Mtn Home
Inn 920'

❸

Camp Eastwood Rd

Fern Creek

Pantoll
1500'

Bootjack Trail

TCC
Trail

Sierra
Trail

Lost Tr

Redwood Tr

Stapelveldt Tr

1400
Cardiac
Hill

Redwood Creek

Ben Johnson Trail

Fern
Creek
Trail

Ocean
View
Trail

Dipsea Trail

Deer Park Fire Road

Main Trail

Coast View Trail

Kent Creek

Muir Woods
150'

Dipsea Tr

0   .5

Scale 1"= 0.5 miles

B10 Old RR Grade to West Point Inn

Distance: 5.3 miles   Shaded: 60%
Elevation Change: 800'   Heavy bicycle traffic on weekends.
Rating: Hiking - 8   Difficulty - 6   Steep uphill on Hogback FR.
When to Go: Best on a clear day in fall, winter or spring.

This figure-8 hike takes the Old Railroad Grade to West Point Inn, then returns via trails and Gravity Car Grade to the Mountain Home Inn.

0.0 From the parking lot, cross the highway and take the paved road up towards the fire station. The road turns into Hogback FR, also called Throckmorton FR, which once led hikers all the way to East Peak, but is now closed for erosion control beyond the Old Railroad Grade.

0.3 Water tank and junction. Continue up Hogback, which gets steeper here, providing an opportunity to stop and enjoy the view.

0.6 Junction ❶. Turn left on the Old Railroad Grade which climbs gradually; the grade is never more than 7%. The entire 8.1 miles of road and railroad track from downtown Mill Valley to East Peak took just six months to build in 1896.

1.0 Junction with Fern Creek trail. Just past the main ravine, a small spring supports graceful chain ferns.

2. 1 Junction ❷ and West Point Inn. This historic railroad tavern, built in 1904, was a restaurant and stopover point for passengers taking the stage to Bolinas and Willow Camp (later Stinson Beach).

West Point Inn

The inn was called West Point Inn because this is the western-most point of the Old Railroad Grade.

To continue the hike, take the signed Nora trail located in front of the inn. This well-maintained trail descends under a canopy of tall chaparral, then enters a grove of skinny redwoods.

2.6 Junction ❸. Take the signed Matt Davis trail left.

3.3 Junction. Take the Hoo-Koo-E-Koo trail left, across a stream and past a leaning redwood tree. Ahead, continue across Hogback FR.

4.1 Junction ❹. Go right on the Old Railroad Grade past Mesa Station.

4.3 Junction. Take Gravity Car Grade to the right.

5.3 Back at the parking lot with water and restrooms.

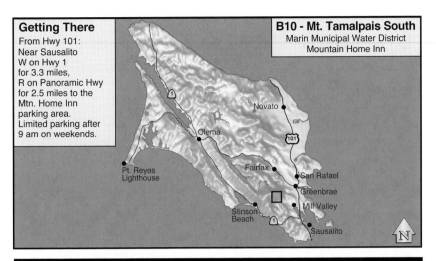

Getting There

From Hwy 101:
Near Sausalito
W on Hwy 1
for 3.3 miles,
R on Panoramic Hwy
for 2.5 miles to the
Mtn. Home Inn
parking area.
Limited parking after
9 am on weekends.

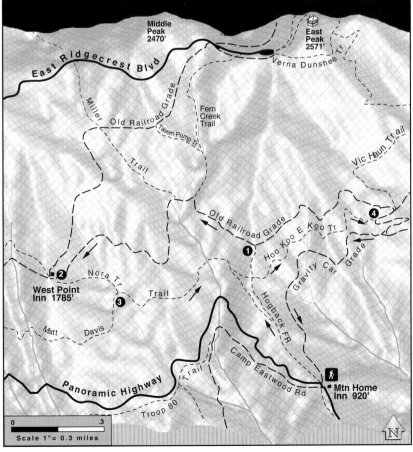

B11 TCC - Alpine Trails

Distance: 3.7 miles   Shaded: 90%
Elevation Change: 500'
Rating: Hiking - 9   Difficulty - 6   Moderately steep downhill.
When to Go: Good anytime, best in early spring.

This is a good hike exploring the dense woods east of Pantoll.
Cardiac Hill on the Dipsea trail provides vistas and wildflowers.

0.0 Start at the Bootjack parking lot. Cross the highway and take the
signed Bootjack trail towards Van Wyck Meadow. The trail zig-zags
down past Douglas fir and bay and into a redwood forest. In early
spring, look for white milkmaids and blue hound's tongue.

0.2 Junction with Alpine trail. Continue straight down the ravine. Fire
scars on the redwoods are most likely from the fire of 1929, which
burned much of the south side of Mt. Tamalpais.

0.4 Junction ❶. Just past the bench and western azalea shrubs,
continue right on the Bootjack trail. The trail goes alongside moss-
covered boulders, then down past a large, brown sandstone slab.

0.5 Junction and Van Wyck Meadow. Take the signed TCC trail right,
across the creek and into redwoods. The TCC trail was built in 1918
and named for the Tamalpais Conservation Club, often called the
"Guardians of the Mountain" for their conservation activities.

2.0 Junction ❷ with the Stapelveldt and Ben Johnson trails. Go left,
then right to take the TCC trail towards the Dipsea trail. **Option**: Take
the Stapelveldt trail downhill to enter a redwood ravine. At a junction at
960', take the Ben Johnson trail to the Deer Park FR and Dipsea trail.

2.4 Junction. Take the Dipsea trail right uphill.

2.5 Junction ❸ and hill. Congratulations! You have just climbed
"Cardiac," as it's called by the throng of Dipsea runners who run from
Mill Valley to Stinson Beach each June. Go right on the road.

2.6 Junction with Coastal FR. Bear right into Douglas fir and bay.

2.8 Junction. Take the Old Mine trail right. Up ahead, an 1863 mining
claim was staked out in search of gold and silver.

3.1 Pantoll and junction ❹. Water, tables and restrooms. Continue
past the ranger station and take the signed Alpine trail just before the
highway. The trail follows the road downhill.

3.5 Junction. Take the signed Bootjack trail left.

3.7 Back at Bootjack with water, tables and restrooms.

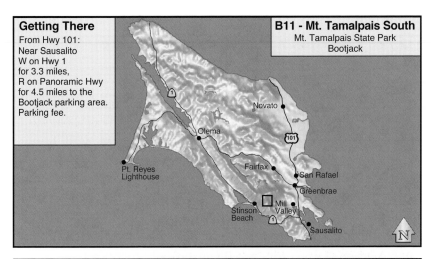

Getting There

From Hwy 101:
Near Sausalito
W on Hwy 1
for 3.3 miles,
R on Panoramic Hwy
for 4.5 miles to the
Bootjack parking area.
Parking fee.

B11 - Mt. Tamalpais South
Mt. Tamalpais State Park
Bootjack

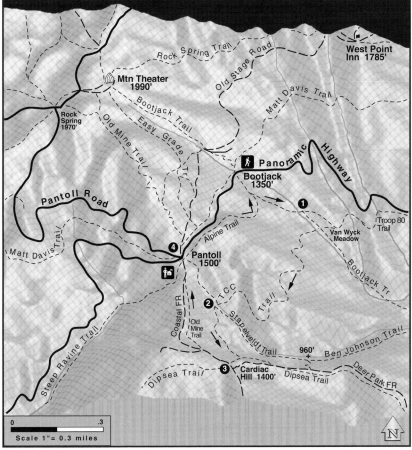

63

B12 Bootjack - Rock Spring Trails

Distance: 4.2 miles   Shaded: 70%
Elevation Change: 600'   Rocky and rutted in places.
Rating: Hiking - 9   Difficulty - 6   Moderately steep uphill.
When to Go: Good any cool, clear day, best February to April.
This hike visits two of Mt. Tam's most treasured landmarks, the Mtn.
Theater and West Point Inn. Good views and small waterfalls.

0.0 Start at the Bootjack parking lot. Head up towards the right side of the bathroom. At a signed junction with the Matt Davis trail, continue on the Bootjack trail, which switchbacks up towards the Mtn. Theater.

0.2 Junction ❶ with Old Stage Rd. In the early 1900s, a stage coach made a daily run from West Point Inn to Stinson Beach. Our hike just crosses the road. Go left on the paved road 20', then right 20', then left to continue on the winding, uphill Bootjack trail. In early spring, look for blue hound's tongue, white milkmaids and purple iris.

0.8 Junction and Mtn. Theater. Turn right at the junction and head towards the theater. Go up to the top of the theater to enjoy a unique setting and view. This natural amphitheater has been the site of summer plays since 1913. To continue the hike, go across the top to the northeast corner of the theater. See map inset, Hike B13.

0.9 Junction ❷. Take the Rock Spring trail towards West Point Inn. This south-facing trail immediately passes a large greenstone rock, dedicated to Austin Pohli, who was the first business manager of the Mountain Play, and died at age 20 while climbing in Yosemite.

1.5 Rocky knoll. Great views to San Francisco and the East Bay.

2.4 West Point Inn. No water, but restrooms and beverages are available on most weekends. A pancake breakfast is served once a month from May to September in this glorious setting. To continue the hike, take the signed Nora trail in front of the picnic area downhill.

2.9 Junction ❸. Take the Matt Davis trail right over the bridge, out of the redwoods, and into a mixture of oak, huckleberry, manzanita and chamise with occasional Douglas fir and bay trees.

3.4 Controlled burn area. The last major fire on the south side of the mountain was in 1929, burning 2500 acres, most of the railroad track and 117 homes in Mill Valley. Now, controlled burns are necessary to reduce the fire danger. This area was burned in 1984.

4.2 Back at Bootjack picnic area with restrooms, tables and water.

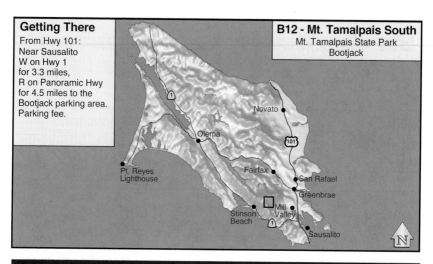

Getting There

From Hwy 101:
Near Sausalito
W on Hwy 1
for 3.3 miles,
R on Panoramic Hwy
for 4.5 miles to the
Bootjack parking area.
Parking fee.

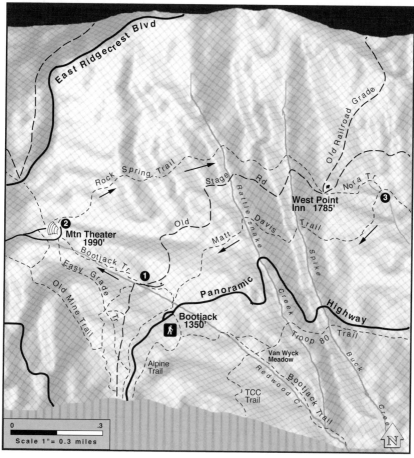

Scale 1" = 0.3 miles

B13 Easy Grade to Mtn. Theater

Distance: 3.4 miles   Shaded: 50%
Elevation Change: 600'   Moderately steep.
Rating: Hiking - 10   Difficulty - 6   Some rocky patches,
When to Go: Good any clear day, best in spring.

This short hike climbs from Pantoll to the Mtn. Theater, then over open hills to O'Rourke's Bench with magnificent views of the coast.

0.0 Start at the Pantoll parking lot. Cross the highway, bear right and go along the paved section of Old Stage Rd. signed to West Point Inn.

0.1 Junction. Take the signed Easy Grade trail left towards the Mtn. Theater. The trail climbs up wooded hills with occasional views east.

0.3 Junction with Easy Grade Spur trail. Continue uphill.

0.8 Mtn. Theater and junction. Head up the right side of the theater, then back across the top and admire the views. This natural amphitheater has been the site of plays since 1913. The present theater was built in 1934 using over 40,000 stones, some weighing 4000 lbs. Each stone is buried so that only a fraction is visible. Head west on the paved road.

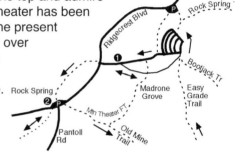

Map of Mtn. Theater Area

1.0 Junction ❶. Head left on the signed road to Madrone Grove and explore the hilltop covered with large madrone, oak and Douglas fir trees. Then, backtrack to the paved road and go left (west) through the gate, cross the highway and pick up the signed trail towards Rock Spring.

1.2 Rock Spring and junction ❷. From the parking area, cross the highway, bear right and take the trail to the ridgetop. Pass through the serpentine outcrop, staying on the ridgetop. Continue over a hilltop.

1.6 O'Rourke's Bench. The stone bench, under a bay tree, is dedicated to one of the mountain's pioneers. Continue west on the ridge.

1.8 Viewpoint ❸. Great views west to Stinson Beach. Now backtrack.

2.4 Junction ❷ again. Cross the parking lot and take the signed Mtn. Theater FT, here a dirt road, uphill heading southeast.

2.5 Junction with Old Mine trail. Bear right along the open hillside.

3.4 Back at Pantoll ranger station. Full facilities.

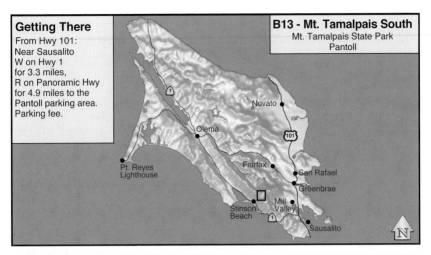

Getting There

From Hwy 101:
Near Sausalito
W on Hwy 1
for 3.3 miles,
R on Panoramic Hwy
for 4.9 miles to the
Pantoll parking area.
Parking fee.

Novato

Olema

Pt. Reyes
Lighthouse

Fairfax

San Rafael

Greenbrae

Stinson
Beach

Mill
Valley

Sausalito

N

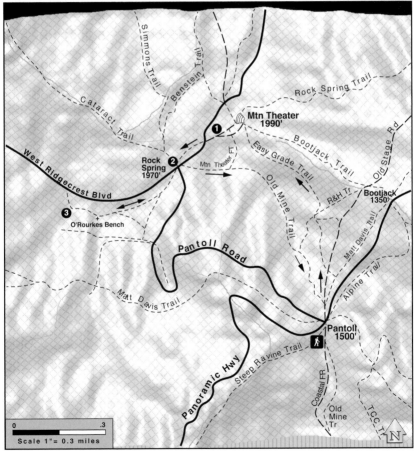

Simmons Trail

Benstein Trail

Rock Spring Trail

Cataract Trail

Mtn Theater
1990'

❶

West Ridgecrest Blvd

❷ **Rock**
Spring
1970'

Mtn Theater

Bootjack Trail

Easy Grade Trail

Old Stage Rd

❸

O'Rourkes Bench

R&H Tr

Bootjack
1350'

Old Mine Trail

Matt Davis Trail

Pantoll Road

Matt Davis Trail

Alpine Trail

Pantoll
1500'

Steep Ravine Trail

Panoramic Hwy

Coastal FR

Old
Mine
Tr

TCC Tr

0   .3
Scale 1"= 0.3 miles

N

67

B14 Dipsea - Steep Ravine Trails

Distance: 3.6 miles   Shaded: 70%
Elevation Change: 1100'   Lots of stairs and one ladder.
Rating: Hiking - 10   Difficulty - 8   Steep in places.
When to Go: Good in winter and spring, best on a clear April day.

This is a breathtaking hike through forest, along coastal hills, then up spectacular Steep Ravine. Good wildflowers and good views.

0.0 Start at the Pantoll parking lot. Take the paved road next to the ranger station south 200' to the signed Old Mine trail. Go left into Douglas fir forest with some oak and bay. In March, look for white zigadene, yellow buttercup, blue hound's tongue and purple iris.

0.2 Mining claim. In 1863, prospectors dug for gold and silver.

0.3 Junction. Continue south on the Coastal FR.

0.5 Junction with the old Lone Tree FR. Stay on the Coastal FR.

0.6 Junction ❶. Follow the Dipsea trail right. This trail is thought to be one of the oldest on the mountain. In 1905, it became part of the famous Dipsea race that covers 7.1 miles from downtown Mill Valley to Stinson Beach.

1.3 Point ❷. The trail leaves the ridge (and the old Lone Tree FR).

1.4 Fence. Bear right. The trail drops down through Douglas fir, redwood, then bay trees kept moist by winter rain and summer fog. Ahead, the trail drops so steeply that it's hard to believe that 1500 Dipsea runners plunge through here at full speed each June.

Dipsea Race - June 1993

2.0 Junction ❸ and bridge. Cross the bridge, go right on the Steep Ravine trail and enjoy the finest scenery on Mt. Tam. Steep Ravine offers spectacular redwoods, ferns, mosses, berries, tumbled trees, wooden bridges, quiet pools and cascading waterfalls.

2.4 Notched redwood. A large redwood lying across the trail is notched to allow passage. As you duck, look for white fairy bells.

2.8 Ladder. Webb Creek is squeezed by large boulders. The only way up is to climb a 10' ladder, which can be slippery when wet.

3.6 Back at Pantoll with camping, restrooms, tables and water.

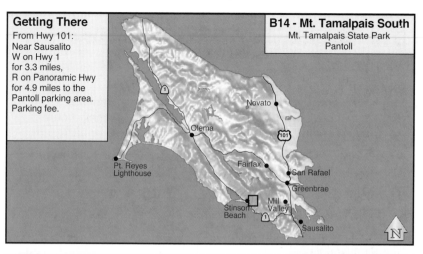

Getting There

From Hwy 101:
Near Sausalito
W on Hwy 1
for 3.3 miles,
R on Panoramic Hwy
for 4.9 miles to the
Pantoll parking area.
Parking fee.

Novato

Olema

Pt. Reyes
Lighthouse

Fairfax

San Rafael

Greenbrae

Stinson
Beach

Mill
Valley

Sausalito

N

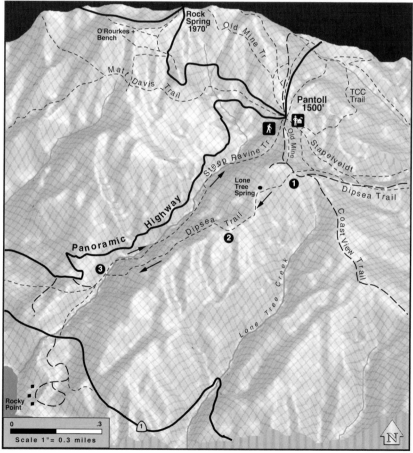

Rock
Spring
1970'

O'Rourkes
Bench

Old Mine Tr

Mat Davis Trail

TCC
Trail

Pantoll
1500'

Old Mine

Stapelveldt

Steep Ravine Tr

Lone
Tree
Spring

❶

Dipsea Trail

Panoramic   Highway

Dipsea Trail

❷

Coast View Trail

❸

Lone Tree Creek

Rocky
Point

1

0   .3

Scale 1" = 0.3 miles

N

69

B15 Matt Davis - Coastal - Cataract

Distance: 6.6 miles   Shaded: 50%
Elevation Change: 900'   May be overgrown in summer.
Rating: Hiking - 10   Difficulty - 6   One short, steep uphill.
When to Go: Best on a clear day in March or April.

Here is a magnificent hike through dense forest, past flowering hillsides, then along a refreshing creek. Spectacular views.

0.0 From the Pantoll parking lot, cross Panoramic Hwy and take the paved Pantoll Rd. 200' uphill to the Matt Davis trail signed to Stinson Beach. The trail starts out along open hillside, but soon enters dense woods of Douglas fir, oak and bay. Spring wildflowers along the trail include white zigadene, yellow poppy, blue hound's tongue, blue-eyed grass, blue dicks and iris.

1.3 Junction. Unofficial trails cross here. To the left, short spur trails lead to a lookout point offering better views of the coast. On the right, a trail climbs up to join a higher trail on the hillside.

1.6 Junction ❶. The Matt Davis trail heads downhill. Stay right to climb gently on the Coastal trail. In summer, grasses crowd the trail.

2.4 Rock outcroppings. Green-grey lichens enjoy the cool and moist coastal climate on these small rocky patches.

3.3 Junction ❷. Turn right and take the Willow Camp FR steeply up to the first knoll, then take the short trail left to Ridgecrest Blvd.

3.5 Highway junction. Continue on the dirt road to Laurel Dell.

3.8 Junction ❸. Take the short connector trail right over the bridge on Cataract Creek. Then, go left on the Cataract trail to Laurel Dell.

4.1 Laurel Dell picnic area. Continue north on the Cataract trail.

4.2 Waterfalls and turnaround point. Beneath a big-leaf maple, moss-covered rocks and ferns, Cataract Creek starts its vigorous plunge to Alpine Lake. To continue the hike, backtrack south along the left side of Cataract Creek towards Rock Spring.

4.6 Junction and airplane engine. About 100' past junction ❸, down in the middle of the creek, look for a Navy Corsair airplane engine, the result of a mid-air plane collision October 4, 1945.

5.6 Rock Spring. Cross the highway, bear left and take the signed Mtn. Theater fire trail uphill, then right on the Old Mine trail.

5.9 Rocky knoll and spectacular views. Continue downhill.

6.6 Back at Pantoll Ranger Station. Full facilities.

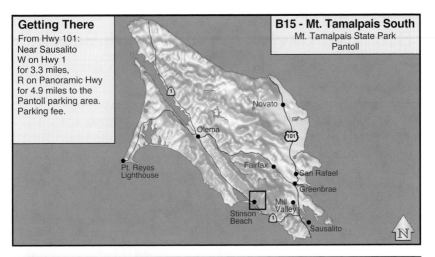

Getting There

From Hwy 101:
Near Sausalito
W on Hwy 1
for 3.3 miles,
R on Panoramic Hwy
for 4.9 miles to the
Pantoll parking area.
Parking fee.

Novato

Olema

101

Pt. Reyes
Lighthouse

Fairfax

San Rafael

Greenbrae

Mill
Valley

Stinson
Beach

Sausalito

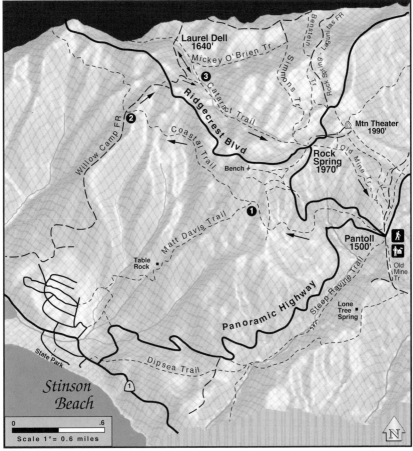

Laurel Dell
1640'

Mickey O'Brien Tr

Berstein

Rock Spring Lagunitas FR

Simmons Tr

Cataract Trail

Ridgecrest Blvd

Mtn Theater
1990'

Willow Camp FR

Coastal Trail

Bench

Old Mine Tr

Rock
Spring
1970'

Matt Davis Trail

Pantoll
1500'

Table
Rock

Old
Mine
Tr

Steep Ravine Trail

Panoramic Highway

Lone
Tree
Spring

State Park

Dipsea Trail

1

Stinson
Beach

0 .6
Scale 1" = 0.6 miles

B16 Matt Davis Trail to Stinson Beach

Distance: 7.2 miles   Shaded: 60%
Elevation Change: 1600'   Many stairs. Some poison oak.
Rating: Hiking - 10   Difficulty - 8   Steep in places.
When to Go: Good anytime, best in winter and spring.

This strenuous, but spectacular hike, starts out on coastal hills, then descends to Stinson Beach and returns along scenic Steep Ravine.

0.0 From the Pantoll parking lot, cross Panoramic Hwy and take the paved Pantoll Rd. 200' uphill to the signed Matt Davis trail heading west towards Stinson Beach.

0.4 Webb Creek. Mosses, chain ferns, bays and Douglas fir provide a woodsy setting next to bedrock carved by Webb Creek.

1.2 Open hillsides. Great views to Stinson Beach and Bolinas Mesa. Look for checkerbloom and lupine among the spring wildflowers.

1.6 Junction ❶. Take the signed Matt Davis trail left towards Stinson Beach. The trail makes a gradual descent until it enters a Douglas fir forest where it drops more quickly. Lots of stairs.

3.5 Table Rock. At a fencepost under buckeye trees, take a spur trail 10' to the right to Table Rock. Great views of Stinson Beach.

3.9 Junction ❷. Go left across the creek and bridge. Up ahead, bear to the right at the Y-junction.

4.0 Paved street. The trail emerges on Belvedere Street. Continue west towards Shoreline Hwy. At the Hwy, go right 200 yds., then go left on Calle del Mar past the Parkside Cafe to the beach entrance.

4.3 Stinson Beach. The park has complete amenities: grass, trees and shade, beach, swimming, water, food and restrooms. It offers a great place for resting and picnicking, although it may be crowded on summer weekends. After enjoying the beach, retrace your steps to the Parkside Cafe, go right on Arenal to Shoreline Hwy (Hwy 1).

4.6 Shoreline Hwy. Crosss the highway and take the new spur trail to Panoramic Hwy to start the famed Dipsea trail towards Pantoll.

5.0 Open hillsides. Take the most prominent trail across the "moors" up towards the steps and fire road. Continue across the fire road.

5.6 Bridge and junction ❸. Take the signed Steep Ravine trail left. This is a magnificent area offering an inspiring setting of redwoods, ferns, mosses, creeks and waterfalls.

7.2 Back at the Pantoll parking area with water and restrooms.

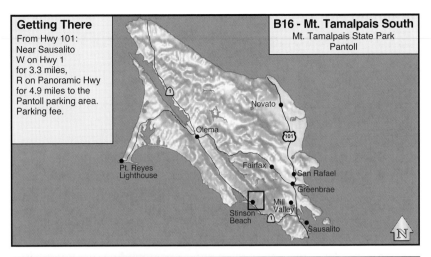

Getting There

From Hwy 101:
Near Sausalito
W on Hwy 1
for 3.3 miles,
R on Panoramic Hwy
for 4.9 miles to the
Pantoll parking area.
Parking fee.

B16 - Mt. Tamalpais South
Mt. Tamalpais State Park
Pantoll

Novato

Olema

Pt. Reyes
Lighthouse

Fairfax

San Rafael

Greenbrae

Mill
Valley

Stinson
Beach

Sausalito

N

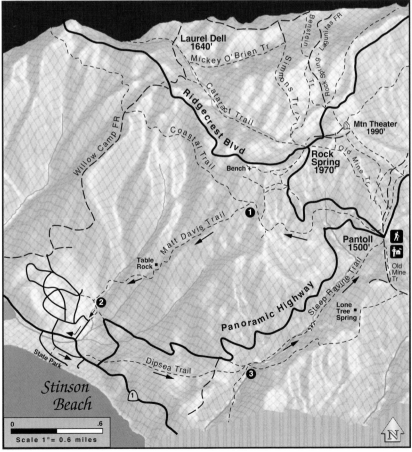

Laurel Dell
1640'

Mickey O'Brien Tr

Simmons Tr

Benstein Tr

Rock Spring-Lagunitas FR

Cataract Trail

Ridgecrest Blvd

Willow Camp FR

Coastal Trail

Mtn Theater
1990'

Old Mine Tr

Rock
Spring
1970'

Bench +

1

Matt Davis Trail

Table
Rock

Pantoll
1500'

Old
Mine
Tr

2

Steep Ravine Trail

Lone
Tree
Spring

Panoramic Highway

State Park

3

Dipsea Trail

1

*Stinson
Beach*

0   .6
Scale 1" = 0.6 miles

N

B17 Simmons - Potrero - Arturo Trails

Distance: 5.4 miles   Shaded: 70%
Elevation Change: 1200'   Simmons trail very rocky in places.
Rating: Hiking - 10   Difficulty - 8   Some stairs.
When to Go: Best in winter and spring after rain.

This is a great hike through woods and chaparral that visits 3 of Mt. Tam's favorite picnic areas, then climbs to the old Air Force Base.

0.0 Start at the Rock Spring parking area and take the signed Cataract trail into the meadow. Just ahead, continue straight on the Simmons trail towards the signed Benstein trail.

0.2 Junction ❶. Bear left on the signed Simmons trail and head downhill towards Ziesche Creek. Look for the coral root orchid in May.

1.2 Barth's Retreat and junction ❷. The trail drops down to Barth's Retreat. Emil Barth, pianist and avid hiker, built his camp in the 1920s. To continue, take the Mickey O'Brien trail, which stays on the south side of Barth's Creek, downhill towards Laurel Dell.

1.9 Junction with Cataract trail. Head right towards Laurel Dell.

2.0 Junction ❸. Take the Laurel Dell FR right. **Option:** If the creeks are full, take the Cataract trail down to check out the falls. Ahead, at the large bend in the road, take the Old Stove trail to parallel the road.

3.0 Junction with trail to Barth's Retreat. Continue straight. **Note:** An unofficial trail (not on the map) goes left down towards Music Camp.

3.1 Junction ❹. Take the fire road connector left to Potrero Camp.

3.2 Potrero Camp, picnic area and junction. Cross the small bridge and continue into the first of two meadows, Potrero Meadows.

3.6 Double junction. Take the Rock Spring-Lagunitas FR left 60 yds., then go through the Rifle Camp picnic area to take the Arturo trail uphill.

4.2 Junction ❺. Go right up the road to explore the old Air Force base and enjoy the views. At the west end of the broad flat area, take the paved road (heading towards a communication tower) for 100'.

4.5 Junction. Take the Mountain Top trail downhill past old fence posts. The trail is narrow and steep at first, but soon widens out.

5.0 Junction, gate and road. Cross Ridgecrest Blvd. and take the trail past the dirt parking lot to the Mountain Theater.

5.1 Mountain Theater. Circle the top of the theater, then take the paved path to the road. Cross the road and take the trail to Rock Spring.

5.4 Rock Spring parking area. Ocean view, tables and restrooms.

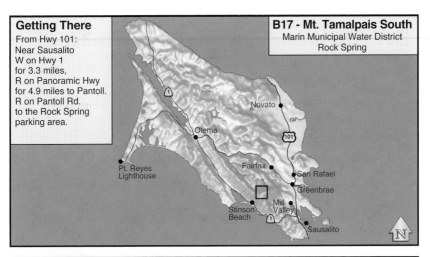

Getting There

From Hwy 101:
Near Sausalito
W on Hwy 1
for 3.3 miles,
R on Panoramic Hwy
for 4.9 miles to Pantoll.
R on Pantoll Rd.
to the Rock Spring
parking area.

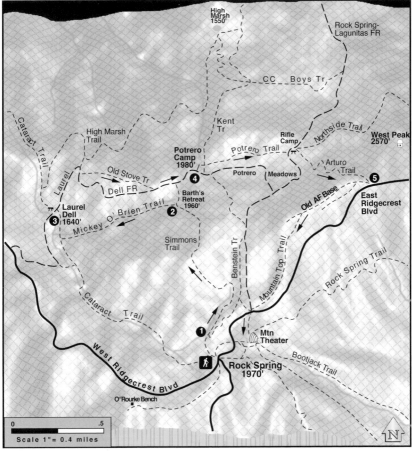

Scale 1"= 0.4 miles

75

B18 Benstein - International Trails

Distance: 5.4 miles   Shaded: 60%
Elevation Change: 800'   Some rocky patches. Lots of stairs.
Rating: Hiking - 9   Difficulty - 6   Some bicycle traffic.
When to Go: Best when clear for views, and March-April for orchids.

This is a great hike that explores the highest trails on both sides of the mountain offering tremendous views and good wildflowers in season.

0.0 Take the Cataract trail into the meadow. Up ahead, continue straight on the Simmons trail towards the Benstein trail.

0.2 Junction. Take the signed Benstein trail right past lichen-covered Douglas fir and moss-covered rocks. In late March, look for the delicate and beautiful calypso orchid usually found under Douglas fir. It has a bright pink flower with a lower scoop-like petal colored to attract insects for pollination. The plant, also called "fairy slipper," is common in the Pacific northwest, but rare here.

Calypso Orchid

0.4 Junction with trail to the Mountain Theater. Continue left towards signed Potrero Meadows.

0.7 Junction ❶. Go left on the Rock Spring-Lagunitas Rd.

1.3 Junction ❷ and Rifle Camp. Go down through the picnic area, cross the creek and take the signed Northside trail heading east.

1.8 Rocky ridgeline, great views. Look for Mt. St. Helena, which lies exactly behind the two towers on Big Rock Ridge, both within 1° of true north. The nearby Sargent cypress trees are mostly found on rocky serpentine soil, which is deficient in calcium, but high in magnesium.

1.9 Junction ❸. Take the signed International trail right. Rocky ahead.

2.4 Junction with Ridgecrest Blvd. Cross the road and take the signed Miller trail down the stairs. This trail was named for John Miller, who worked on trails for over 30 years starting in 1921.

2.7 Junction ❹. Turn right and take the Old RR Grade downhill.

3.4 Junction and West Point Inn. Restroom, tables and view. To continue the hike, take the Rock Spring trail west of the inn.

5.1 Mountain Theater. Water, restroom and picnic area. Continue right, around the top of the theater, and along the paved path to Ridgecrest Blvd. Cross the road and take the trail to Rock Spring.

5.4 Rock Spring parking area. Ocean view, tables and restrooms.

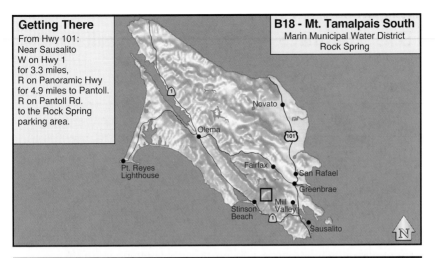

Getting There

From Hwy 101:
Near Sausalito
W on Hwy 1
for 3.3 miles,
R on Panoramic Hwy
for 4.9 miles to Pantoll.
R on Pantoll Rd.
to the Rock Spring
parking area.

B18 - Mt. Tamalpais South
Marin Municipal Water District
Rock Spring

Novato

Olema

Pt. Reyes
Lighthouse

Fairfax

San Rafael

Greenbrae

Stinson
Beach

Mill
Valley

Sausalito

N

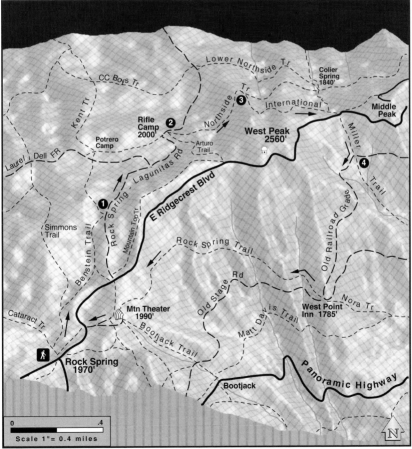

Lower Northside Tr

CC Boys Tr

Colier
Spring
1840'

Kent Tr

Northside Tr

3

International

Middle
Peak

Rifle
Camp
2000'

2

West Peak
2560'

Potrero
Camp

Arturo
Trail

Miller Trail

4

Laurel Dell FR

Lagunitas Rd

E Ridgecrest Blvd

Rock Spring

1

Old Railroad Grade

Simmons
Trail

Mountain Top Tr

Rock Spring Trail

Benstein Trail

Old Stage Rd

Nora Tr

Cataract Tr

Mtn Theater
1990'

West Point
Inn 1785'

Bootjack Trail

Matt Davis Trail

Rock Spring
1970'

Bootjack

Panoramic Highway

0 .4
Scale 1"= 0.4 miles

N

77

B19 Cataract - High Marsh - Kent Trails

Distance: 6.0 miles   Shaded: 90%
Elevation Change: 1100'   Can have standing water in winter.
Rating: Hiking - 10   Difficulty - 8   Steep and rocky in places.
When to Go: Good anytime, great in winter and spring.

This is a magnificent hike that features creeks, forests, views and flowers in some of the most remote areas on the mountain.

0.0 Start at the Rock Spring parking area and take the Cataract trail down the left side of the meadow towards Cataract Creek. The Cataract trail offers some of the finest hiking on Mt. Tam with pools, waterfalls, small meadows, wildflowers and Douglas fir forest.

1.2 Junction with Mickey O'Brien trail. Continue straight.

1.3 Restroom, junction and Laurel Dell picnic area. From the picnic area, take the signed Cataract trail downstream.

1.5 Junction ❶, bench and waterfalls. Here, Cataract Creek starts its dramatic plunge towards Alpine Lake. **Option**: For slightly better views of Cataract Falls, head downhill 100'. Take the High Marsh trail right. Up ahead, the trail skirts an open hillside with great views north of the Kent Lake drainage and a glimpse of Kent Lake.

2.3 Junction with spur trail to Laurel Dell FR. Continue on the High Marsh trail, which mostly follows a roller-coaster pattern, downhill into forested ravines, then uphill to ridges covered with chaparral.

3.0 Creek and junction. A large 10' boulder in the stream bed marks the unofficial trail right to Music Camp. Continue straight.

3.3 Junction. The unofficial Willow trail heads downhill left. Continue straight and slightly uphill, then past a small grove of madrone trees.

3.5 High Marsh and junction. The Cross Country Boys trail heads right. Continue straight as the trail skirts the marsh. The marsh, which is slowly filling in, was created by a large landslide.

3.6 Junction ❷. Take the signed Kent trail right.

4.2 Junction. The CC Boys trail crosses here. Continue straight.

4.6 Potrero Camp and junction ❸. Take the dirt road south to Laurel Dell FR, then go left 100' and take the signed Benstein trail uphill. The trail climbs past a serpentine outcrop and Sargent cypress trees.

5.3 Junction ❹. Take the Rock Spring-Lagunitas FR right 100 yds., then head downhill on the signed Benstein trail.

6.0 Back at the Rock Spring parking area with restrooms.

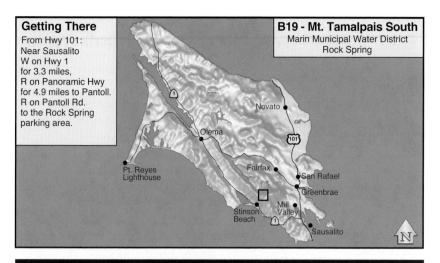

Getting There

From Hwy 101:
Near Sausalito
W on Hwy 1
for 3.3 miles,
R on Panoramic Hwy
for 4.9 miles to Pantoll.
R on Pantoll Rd.
to the Rock Spring
parking area.

Novato

Olema

Pt. Reyes
Lighthouse

Fairfax

San Rafael

Greenbrae

Mill
Valley

Stinson
Beach

Sausalito

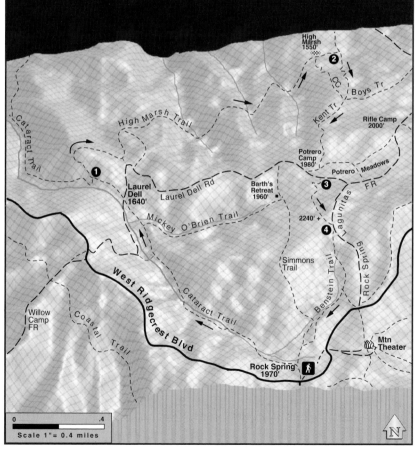

High
Marsh
1550'

Boys Tr

Kent Tr

Rifle Camp
2000'

High Marsh Trail

Cataract Trail

Potrero
Camp
1980'

Potrero   Meadows

Laurel
Dell
1640'

Laurel Dell Rd

Barth's
Retreat
1960'

Mickey O'Brien Trail

2240' +

Lagunitas   FR

Simmons
Trail

Benstein Trail

Rock Spring

West Ridgecrest Blvd

Cataract Trail

Willow
Camp
FR

Coastal   Trail

Mtn
Theater

Rock Spring
1970'

0   .4

Scale 1"= 0.4 miles

79

B20 East Peak Loop and Plankwalk Trails

Distance: 0.7 and 0.6 miles   Shaded: 20%
Elevation Change: See below.   The Plankwalk trail is steep.
Rating: Hiking - 10   Difficulty - 1 and 8
When to Go: Great anytime on a clear, windless day.

One hike loops around the East Peak on a paved path. The other hike climbs to the top of Mt. Tamalpais. Both offer incomparable views.

Verna Dunshee Trail - 0.7 miles and 50' Change
0.0 From the parking lot, go east and take the signed Verna Dunshee trail to circle the peak counterclockwise. The concrete picnic area is all that remains of the Tamalpais Tavern, a restaurant and inn built by the railroad in the 1890s. It suffered serious damage in a forest fire in 1913 and again in a kitchen fire in 1923. Each time, it was quickly rebuilt and, because of its remote location, thrived during prohibition. In 1942, the tavern was leased to the army for barracks. After the war, it fell into disrepair and was destroyed.

Tamalpais Tavern 1922

0.1 View. Look down at Mesa Junction. Here you can see the Old Railroad Grade make its famous Double Bowknot, laying claim to the "Crookedest Railroad in the World."

0.2 Sunrise Point. On a clear day, this point offers one of the finest views in the world!

0.7 Parking area with tables, water and restrooms. A small visitor museum and snack bar are usually open on weekends from 12-4 pm (during the summer, the refreshment stand is open daily). Both are closed during bad weather. A Gravity Car Barn, with a working replica of a gravity car, is being planned for the area next to the museum.

Plankwalk Trail - 0.6 miles and 300' Change
0.0 From the East Peak snack bar, head east and left to take the signed Plankwalk trail uphill. Beyond the wooden planks, the trail becomes rocky and steep.

0.3 East Peak and the Gardner Lookout Station at 2571'. You can scramble around the rocks to find panoramic views in all directions. Landmarks include Mt. St. Helena 51 miles north, Mt. Diablo 37 miles east, San Bruno Mtn. 18 miles south and Pt. Reyes 25 miles west.

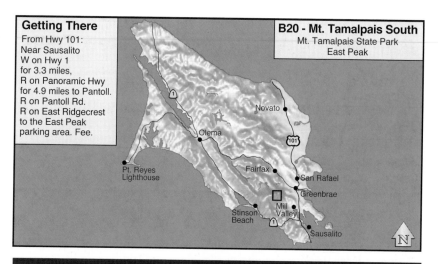

Getting There

From Hwy 101:
Near Sausalito
W on Hwy 1
for 3.3 miles,
R on Panoramic Hwy
for 4.9 miles to Pantoll.
R on Pantoll Rd.
R on East Ridgecrest
to the East Peak
parking area. Fee.

Novato

101

Olema

Fairfax

Pt. Reyes
Lighthouse

San Rafael

Greenbrae

Mill
Valley

Stinson
Beach

Sausalito

N

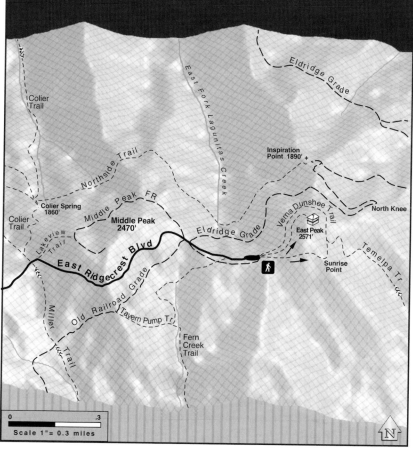

Colier
Trail

East Fork Lagunitas Creek

Eldridge Grade

Northside Trail

Inspiration
Point 1890' +

Colier Spring
1860'

Middle Peak FR

Colier
Trail

Middle Peak
2470'

Lakeview Trail

Eldridge Grade

Verna Dunshee Trail

North Knee

East Peak
2571'

East Ridgecrest Blvd

Old Railroad Grade

Sunrise
Point

Temelpa Tr

Miller Trail

Tavern Pump Tr.

Fern
Creek
Trail

0 .3

Scale 1"= 0.3 miles

N

B21 Northside - Colier - Lakeview Trails

Distance: 5.0 miles   Shaded: 80%
Elevation Change: 600'   One steep uphill.
Rating: Hiking - 8   Difficulty - 7   Very rocky in places.
When to Go: Good anytime, best March to May after rain.

Wear sturdy boots to hike the rocky north slopes below East Peak.
Good chaparral, some redwoods and lots of oak and nutmeg.

0.0 From the East Peak parking lot, take paved trail west, away from
the restrooms, and along the south side of the mountain.

0.3 Junction ❶ with Eldridge Grade. This upper section of Eldridge
Grade, built in 1884 for wagon traffic, is very rocky.

0.8 Junction and viewpoint. A large flat rock lies 30' to the left of the
road, offering commanding views of the Marin watershed and hills to
the north. The rocky, steep East Peak FT (unmaintained) descends
from here to Inspiration Point directly below on the ridgeline.

1.3 Junction ❷. Take the Northside trail, which starts out as a road,
left toward Colier Spring.

1.4 Inspiration Point and more great views. The hike leaves the road
here and follows the narrow Northside trail, which starts out level and
heads southwest into the steep canyon below East Peak. Look for
California nutmeg, a California endemic with flat, one-inch, sharp,
green needles. This 20' evergreen tree is common on this trail.

3.1 Colier Spring. Pause at the bench just below the spring to enjoy
the large redwood grove. Alice Eastwood called this area "Butterfly
Spring" because of the many specimens she found here. From here,
take the signed (Upper) Northside trail towards the west.

3.6 Open area and junction ❸. The trail breaks out onto a rocky
serpentine area. Take the signed International trail left uphill.

4.1 Two junctions ❹. Continue up to Ridgecrest Blvd., then head east
100' to pick up the Lakeview trail which climbs toward Middle Peak.

4.3 Junction. Continue downhill on the Middle Peak FR. **Option:**
Head uphill for 200 yds. to explore part of Middle Peak. Back in 1905,
two 300' wooden towers on Middle Peak were reported to be the
tallest, wireless telegraph towers in the world. That winter, they blew
over in a storm and were not replaced.

4.7 Junction ❶ again. Cross the road and return up the paved trail.

5.0 Back at the East Peak parking area with water, tables and
restrooms. See Hike B20 for historical information about East Peak.

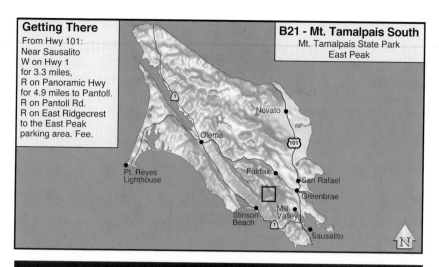

Getting There

From Hwy 101:
Near Sausalito
W on Hwy 1
for 3.3 miles,
R on Panoramic Hwy
for 4.9 miles to Pantoll.
R on Pantoll Rd.
R on East Ridgecrest
to the East Peak
parking area. Fee.

B21 - Mt. Tamalpais South
Mt. Tamalpais State Park
East Peak

Novato

101

Olema

Pt. Reyes
Lighthouse

Fairfax

San Rafael

Greenbrae

Stinson
Beach

Mill
Valley

Sausalito

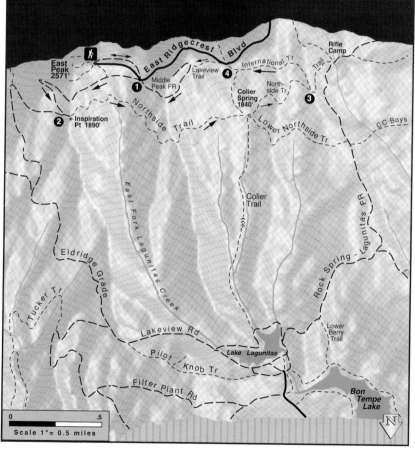

East Ridgecrest Blvd

Rifle
Camp

East
Peak
2571'

Lakeview
Trail

International Tr

Trail

Middle
Peak FR

Colier
Spring
1840'

North-
side Tr

Northside Trail

② + Inspiration
Pt 1890'

Lower Northside Tr

CC Boys

Colier
Trail

Rock Spring - Lagunitas FR

East Fork Lagunitas Creek

Eldridge Grade

Tucker Tr

Lakeview Rd

Lower
Berry
Trail

Pilot Knob Tr

Lake Lagunitas

Filter Plant Rd

Bon
Tempe
Lake

0   .5
Scale 1"= 0.5 miles

C - Mt. Tamalpais North - 19 Hikes

Starting from below Phoenix Lake in Ross at 80'
C1   Phoenix Lake Trail 2.8
C2   Tucker - Bill Williams Trails 3.1
C3   Worn Springs FR to Bald Hill 5.4
C4   Hidden Meadow - Yolanda Trails 3.9

Starting from Crown Road in Kent Woodlands at 450'
C5   Eldridge Grade - Tucker Trails 5.5

Starting from Deer Park in Fairfax at 200'
C6   Deer Park FR- Yolanda Trail 3.3
C7   Deer Park FR- Canyon - Six Points Trail 3.7

Starting from along Fairfax-Bolinas Rd.
C8   Azalea Hill and Pine Mountain Trails 0.4 and 4.4
C9   Carson Falls and Oat Hill FR 4.0 and 7.4
C10 Old Sled - Old Vee - Carson Falls 6.0
C11 Cataract - High Marsh - Kent Trails 7.8

Starting from Sky Oaks Road at 700'
C12 Taylor - Concrete Pipe - Bullfrog FR 3.2

Starting from below Bon Tempe Lake at 660'
C13 Bon Tempe Lake Trail 4.1
C14 Kent Trail - Rocky Ridge FR 5.2

Starting from below Lake Lagunitas at 730'
C15 Lake Lagunitas FR 1.8
C16 Lakeview Road to Pilot Knob 2.2
C17 Pumpkin Ridge - Bon Tempe Trails 3.3
C18 Colier Spring - Northside - Kent - Stocking 6.7
C19 Lake Lagunitas to East Peak 10.2

Notes
Dogs allowed on all hikes except C19.
To download a hike, go to www.marintrails.com
The password for this region is c9dm2hw

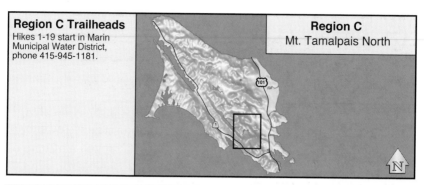

Region C Trailheads

Hikes 1-19 start in Marin Municipal Water District, phone 415-945-1181.

Region C
Mt. Tamalpais North

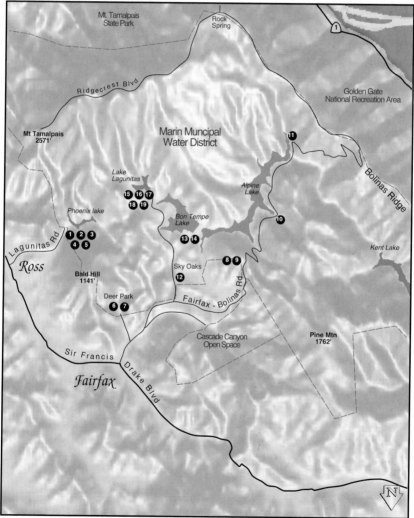

C1 Phoenix Lake Trail

Distance: 2.8 miles   Shaded: 70%
Elevation Change: 200'   Bicycle traffic on roads.
Rating: Hiking - 8   Difficulty - 4   One moderately steep area.
When to Go: Best in March and April for water runoff and flowers.

This heavily traveled trail around the lake passes through a mixture of oak, bay and redwood trees with wildflowers and good views.

0.0 Start at Natalie Greene Park in Ross. Notice the massive slide that occurred in 1986. Slide debris has raised this area by as much as 3 feet. Take the trail up the left side of the creek to the dam.

0.2 Dam. Go left to circle the lake clockwise. The milky-green color of the water is due to algae and sediment, which are removed when the water is treated. However, this lake is so small that its water is only used for drinking during drought years.

0.8 Junction ❶. Turn right and take the signed Gertrude Ord trail up the stairs. The trail passes through a mixture of tall oak, bay, Douglas fir and madrone trees shading low-growing tanoak and fuzzy-leaved hazel. Pink trillium, white milkmaids and blue hound's tongue are the first wildflowers in February and March.

1.3 Junction. The stairs down to the right can be used as a shortcut in dry times. For a more interesting route, follow the trail left into the redwood ravine. The storm of 1986 scoured the creek bottom lowering the channel by 3 feet. Upstream, previous mudslides have left much debris, including several large trees.

2.0 Junction ❷. Turn right to take the Phoenix Lake FR east towards the dam. This road was once part of a stage route connecting San Rafael to Bolinas. Up ahead, Phoenix Log Cabin, built in 1893 for the Porteous Ranch foreman, has been restored. Notice the octagonal turret and natural window frames. The cabin is not open to the public. Please do not enter the area, as it is also a ranger residence.

*Phoenix Log Cabin
Originally Built in 1893*

2.5 Dam. Go left down the road.

2.8 Parking area with water, tables and restroom facilities.

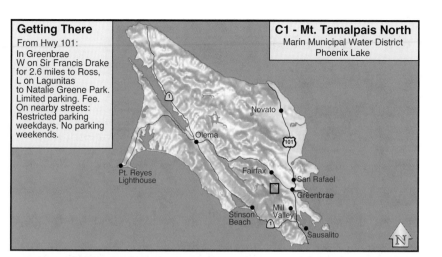

Getting There

From Hwy 101:

In Greenbrae
W on Sir Francis Drake
for 2.6 miles to Ross,
L on Lagunitas
to Natalie Greene Park.
Limited parking. Fee.
On nearby streets:
Restricted parking
weekdays. No parking
weekends.

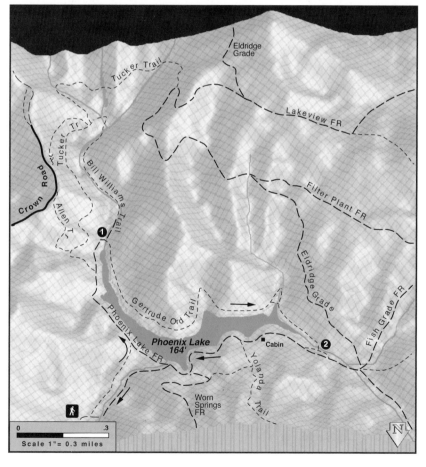

Scale 1"= 0.3 miles

87

C2 Tucker - Bill Williams Trails

Distance: 3.1 miles   Shaded: 80%
Elevation Change: 400'   Creek not fordable during heavy runoff.
Rating: Hiking - 8   Difficulty - 6   Short steep section.
When to Go: Good anytime, best after rain.

This is a fine hike that explores two small canyons offering enchanting oak-bay woods, redwoods, ferns and mosses in a creekside setting.

0.0 Start at Natalie Greene Park in Ross. From the parking lot, take the trail up the left side of the creek to the stairs and dam.

0.2 Dam. Go left to circle the lake clockwise.

0.6 Junction ❶. Turn left on the signed Harry Allen trail and head into a small ravine with oak, bay and buckeye trees. This trail was originally part of a longer trail built by Allen in the 1920s connecting Baltimore Canyon to Phoenix Lake. Early flowers include pink shooting star, blue hound's tongue, and lots of white zigadene.

0.8 Junction. The Harry Allen trail goes left uphill. Stay right and follow the Tucker trail past mosses, lichens and maidenhair ferns.

1.1 Main canyon. Redwoods grow along the north slope of Bill Williams canyon. Oaks and bays grow here along the south side. Up ahead, a small dam is just visible down the steep hillside.

Maidenhair Fern

1.5 Two junctions ❷. The Tucker Cutoff trail comes down from the left. At the second junction, 100' ahead, turn right and take the Bill Williams trail down two sets of stairs to the creek. Bill Williams lived in a cabin near here and legend has it that he was a civil war deserter who absconded with gold that is still buried in the canyon.

1.6 Two bridges. Cross the small bridges, then go uphill 100' to a Y- junction. An unmaintained trail goes left uphill. Go right down to the creek to cross over rocks. (The creek may not be fordable in high water.) Continue along the creek past the dam to another bridge. This dam was built in 1886 as part of a local water supply before Phoenix Lake was created in 1906. Cross the creek and continue through the redwoods.

2.3 Phoenix Lake FR. Continue along the lake to the dam.

2.8 Dam and junction. Cross the dam and take the road downhill.

3.1 Back at the parking area with water, tables and restrooms.

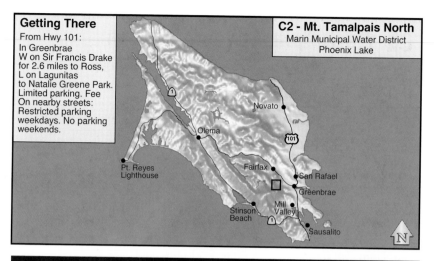

Getting There
From Hwy 101:
In Greenbrae
W on Sir Francis Drake
for 2.6 miles to Ross,
L on Lagunitas
to Natalie Greene Park.
Limited parking. Fee
On nearby streets:
Restricted parking
weekdays. No parking
weekends.

C2 - Mt. Tamalpais North
Marin Municipal Water District
Phoenix Lake

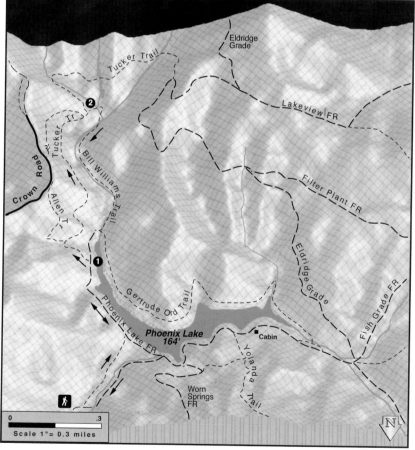

C3 Worn Springs FR to Bald Hill

Distance: 5.4 miles   Shaded: 40%
Elevation Change: 1200'   Bicycles possible.
Rating: Hiking - 8   Difficulty - 7   Moderately steep in places.
When to Go: Good any cool, clear, calm day; best in spring.

Take binoculars and water to make the long climb up the road to Bald Hill. Spectacular views and lovely wildflowers in spring.

0.0 Start at Natalie Greene Park in Ross. From the parking lot, take the road uphill past oak, bay and madrone. Look for white wild onion and iris along the road in spring.

0.3 Dam. Take the Phoenix Lake FR to the right.

0.4 Junction ❶. Take the signed Worn Springs FR right toward Bald Hill. This road was named after George Austin Worn, descendant of the family that founded the town of Ross.

0.7 Reservoir and junction. The small Ross Reservoir can hold one million gallons and is used only during drought. Take the left road and climb steeply. Up ahead, the road levels out briefly. The spring of Worn Spring is located in the grove of oak, bay and madrone trees.

1.4 Views. Good views south and east. Yellow buttercup, poppy, white popcorn flower, blue-eyed grass, blue dicks, lupine, and pink checkerbloom grow along the road from March to May.

2.1 Junction ❷. The road left is the way down. For now, turn right and walk 150' to the top of the hill.

2.2 Bald Hill. Spectacular 360 degree views. Explore the hilltop to discover the best wildflower display, often yellow gold fields. To continue the hike, backtrack to junction ❷ and bear right.

2.4 Junction with private dirt road to Upper Road in Ross. Stay left to continue on Worn Springs FR, which gets steep in places.

2.7 Junction ❸. Take the Yolanda (North) trail to the left, which skirts the hillside above the old Deer Park school.

3.6 Junction ❹ at Six Points. Take the first left to continue on the Yolanda (South) trail. This is a spectacular section of trail that skirts the south side of Bald Hill offering stunning views of Mt. Tamalpais.

4.7 Y-junction. Take the spur trail left past the "No Horses" sign.

4.9 Junction. Go right on Worn Springs FR and retrace your steps to the dam and the parking area.

5.4 Back at Natalie Greene Park with water, tables and restrooms.

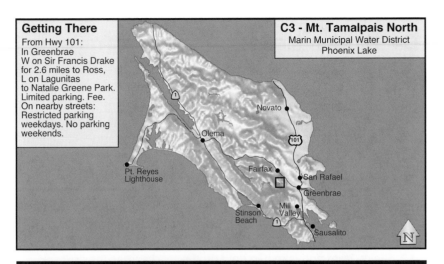

Getting There

From Hwy 101:
In Greenbrae
W on Sir Francis Drake
for 2.6 miles to Ross,
L on Lagunitas
to Natalie Greene Park.
Limited parking. Fee.
On nearby streets:
Restricted parking
weekdays. No parking
weekends.

Novato

Olema

Fairfax

San Rafael

Greenbrae

Pt. Reyes
Lighthouse

Stinson
Beach

Mill
Valley

Sausalito

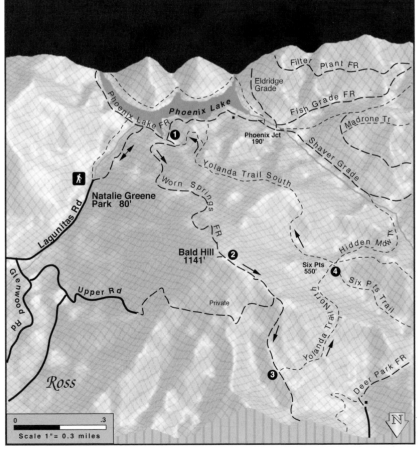

Filter Plant FR

Eldridge
Grade

Fish Grade FR

Madrone Tr

Phoenix Lake FR

Phoenix Lake

Phoenix Jct
190'

Shaver Grade

❶

Yolanda Trail South

Worn Springs FR

Natalie Greene
Park 80'

Lagunitas Rd

Hidden Mdw

Bald Hill
1141'

❷

Six Pts
550'

❹

Six Pts Trail

Glenwood Rd

Upper Rd

Private

Yolanda Trail North

❸

Deer Park FR

Ross

0 .3
Scale 1" = 0.3 miles

C4 Hidden Meadow - Yolanda Trails

Distance: 3.9 miles   Shaded: 70%
Elevation Change: 600'
Rating: Hiking - 9   Difficulty - 6   A few rocks and roots.
When to Go: Good in spring, best in April and May.

The hike explores a small hidden meadow, then climbs to skirt a south-facing hillside with great views and fine wildflowers.

0.0 From the Natalie Greene Park in Ross, start out on the left side of the creek. The trail passes through the picnic area, then climbs steeply up to the dam under a dense canopy of bay trees.

0.2 Stairs, dam and lake. Go right on the road across the spillway. Watch for osprey, cormorants and ducks. The cormorants are skillful fish catchers and are unwelcome by fishermen.

0.6 Junction and cabin. Continue around the lake. Two hundred feet ahead, Phoenix Log Cabin, built in 1893, has been restored.

0.9 Phoenix Jct ❶. Take signed Shaver Grade to the right up towards Five Corners. Shaver Grade was originally a logging road built by Isaac Shaver in the 1890s to haul lumber from near Alpine Dam to Ross Landing (now the site of College of Marin, Kentfield).

1.2 Junction ❷. Take the Hidden Meadow trail right along the creek.

1.4 Creek bed, junction and meadow. A large oak, backed by a buckeye welcomes visitors to Hidden Meadow. Stay to the right and continue along a small seasonal creek. Ahead, the trail climbs more steeply on the grassy hillside. Look for yellow buttercups, blue dicks and white popcorn flower in April.

1.9 Six Points Jct ❸. Take the signed Yolanda (South) trail towards Phoenix Lake. Colorful wildflowers and spectacular views lie ahead as the trail winds along the south-facing, canyon hillside.

2.3 Rock slide. A small rock slide was started by one of many winter storms. Two hundred feet above the slide is Rocky View Point.

2.4 Wildflowers. Pink shooting stars, blue dicks, yellow poppies, red larkspur and iris stand guard on small rocky outcroppings.

2.7 Spectacular views of Mt. Tamalpais!

3.0 Downhill. The trail tumbles downhill past several fallen trees. Stay right at the small Y-junction ahead.

3.2 Junction. Go left on Phoenix Lake FR towards the dam.

3.9 Back at the parking lot with tables, water and restrooms.

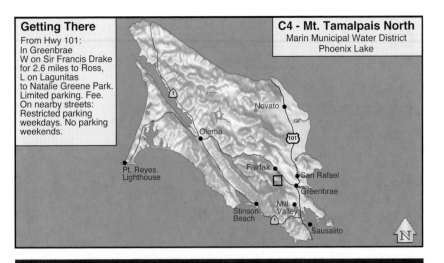

Getting There

From Hwy 101:
In Greenbrae
W on Sir Francis Drake
for 2.6 miles to Ross,
L on Lagunitas
to Natalie Greene Park.
Limited parking. Fee.
On nearby streets:
Restricted parking
weekdays. No parking
weekends.

C4 - Mt. Tamalpais North
Marin Municipal Water District
Phoenix Lake

Novato

Olema

Pt. Reyes
Lighthouse

Fairfax

San Rafael

Greenbrae

Stinson
Beach

Mill
Valley

Sausalito

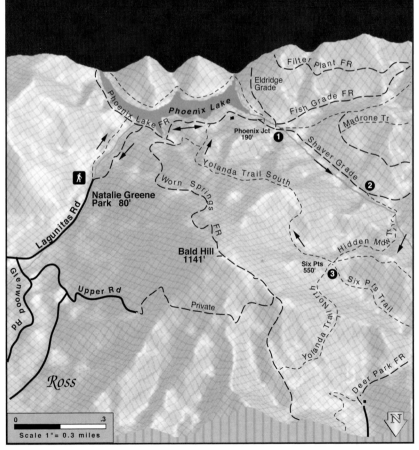

Filter Plant FR

Eldridge
Grade

Phoenix Lake

Fish Grade FR

Phoenix Lake FR

Madrone Tr

Phoenix Jct
190'   **1**

Shaver Grade

Yolanda Trail South

2

Natalie Greene
Park 80'

Worn Springs FR

Lagunitas Rd

Hidden Mdw Tr

Bald Hill
1141'

Six Pts
550'   **3**

Six Pts Trail

Glenwood Rd

Upper Rd

Private

Yolanda Trail North

Deer Park FR

Ross

0   .3

Scale 1"= 0.3 miles

C5 Eldridge Grade - Tucker Trails

Distance: 5.5 miles   Shaded: 70%
Elevation Change: 900'   Bicycles on weekends.
Rating: Hiking - 9   Difficulty - 8   Steep downhill in places.
When to Go: Best in late winter and early spring.

Lots of water, views and wildflowers make this a great hike on the steep north slope of Mt. Tam. May be impassable after heavy rain.

0.0 Be sure to park along Crown Rd. where it is wide enough, with at least 12' clearance. Walk south along the road towards house #123.

0.2 Junction. Pass through the guard rail and take the Allen trail right downhill. The trail gets steep and rocky near the bottom.

0.5 Junction ❶ with Tucker trail. Continue right on the Allen trail.

0.7 Junction with the lake. Head right on Phoenix Lake FR. Ahead, continue across the dam to circle the lake counter-clockwise.

1.7 Phoenix Jct ❷. Take the first left road, signed Eldridge Grade, for a steady climb through an interesting combination of redwood, big-leaf maple, oak, bay and madrone. This road was built as a toll road by John C. Eldridge in the 1880s as the first wagon road to the summit. It has suffered many slides and is now being maintained as a trail. It is also a heavily traveled bicycle route.

2.5 Junction with Filter Plant FR. Continue left uphill.

2.9 Hairpin junction. Take either road as they merge ahead.

3.3 Junction ❸ with the Tucker trail. As the road curves right, take the signed Tucker trail left towards Phoenix Lake.

3.5 Creek and waterfall. A trail sign marks the spot of the old Tucker cabin site, which dated from the late 1800s. There is a waterfall above the site, but it's hard to get a good view.

From here, the trail makes a steep descent down the north slope of Mt. Tam past tumbling creeks, cascading waterfalls, western azalea, redwood and iris. This is a magnificent section of trail.

4.2 Bill Williams Creek. Cross the creek to head uphill.

4.3 Junction ❹ with the Bill Williams trail. Continue straight on the Tucker trail. At a Y-junction 100' ahead, stay left.

5.0 Junction ❶ again. Take the Allen trail right uphill.

5.3 Crown Rd. Head left along the road to the parking area.

5.5 Back at the parking area. No facilities.

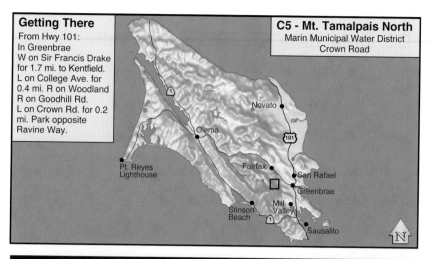

Getting There

From Hwy 101:
In Greenbrae
W on Sir Francis Drake
for 1.7 mi. to Kentfield.
L on College Ave. for
0.4 mi. R on Woodland
R on Goodhill Rd.
L on Crown Rd. for 0.2
mi. Park opposite
Ravine Way.

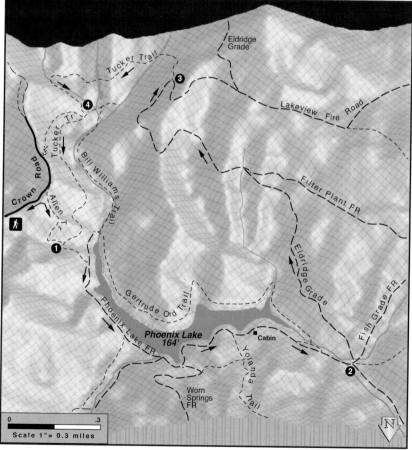

Scale 1" = 0.3 miles

95

C6 Deer Park FR - Yolanda Trail

Distance: 3.3 miles   Shaded: 70%
Elevation Change: 400'   Some bicycle traffic.
Rating: Hiking - 9   Difficulty - 6   Moderately steep in places.
When to Go: Good November to May, best in April for iris.

This is a good wildflower hike that begins in a canyon, then climbs the north slopes of Bald Hill. Great views of Mt. Tam and Bolinas Ridge.

0.0 Start at Deer Park in Fairfax. From the parking area, go left around the school and cross the field. Deer Park FR begins at the gate just past a magnificent bay tree and heads into a canyon.

0.5 Oak Tree Jct ❶. Take the narrow Junction trail right past French broom. Then cross a small bridge and climb up an open hillside. Look for blue dicks, buttercup, filaree, paintbrush, clover, lupine, monkeyflower and popcorn flower scattered on the hillside in spring.

0.9 Boy Scout Jct. Take the Bald Hill trail which starts up a steep path. About 100' up from the junction, look for a view west, framed by trees, to Bolinas Ridge. Below the ridge, you can see the Bolinas-Fairfax Rd. In 1884, it was a stagecoach road to Bolinas, once Marin's largest town as loggers provided lumber for San Francisco.

1.3 Junction. Continue left on the Bald Hill trail. Up ahead, the trail skirts above Hidden Meadow and offers great views to Mt. Tam.

1.6 Six Points Jct ❷. Take the signed Yolanda trail (Yolanda North), towards Worn Springs FR. The narrow trail follows the hillside contour through wooded stands of oak, bay and madrone.

2.1 Knoll. A spur trail heads 100' onto an oak-covered knoll. Lots of lichen on the trunks.

2.3 Wildflowers. Another open hillside displays spring flowers including white woodland star, baby blue-eyes and in late April, Chinese houses.

2.5 Junction with Worn Springs FR. Turn left and head downhill. Good views east to the bay.

Chinese Houses

2.6 Junction. **Option.** Take the Buckeye trail left to skip a steep climb.

2.9 Junction ❸. Follow the signed Deer Park trail left as it descends in switchbacks down the hillside. Lots of wildflowers bloom here in early spring, followed later by the sweet-smelling buckeye tree in May. At the bottom of the hill, bear right towards the schoolyard.

3.3 Parking area with water, picnic tables and restrooms.

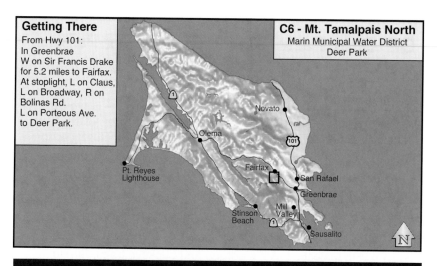

Getting There

From Hwy 101:
In Greenbrae
W on Sir Francis Drake
for 5.2 miles to Fairfax.
At stoplight, L on Claus,
L on Broadway, R on
Bolinas Rd.
L on Porteous Ave.
to Deer Park.

C6 - Mt. Tamalpais North
Marin Municipal Water District
Deer Park

Novato

Olema

Pt. Reyes
Lighthouse

Fairfax

San Rafael

Greenbrae

Mill
Valley

Stinson
Beach

Sausalito

N

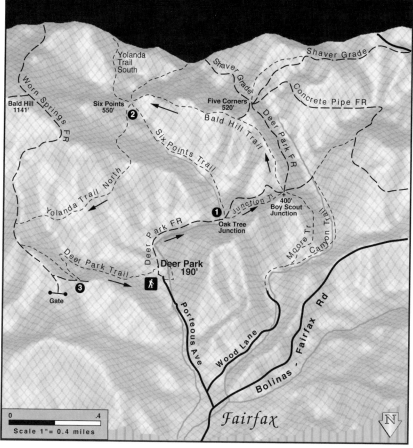

Yolanda
Trail
South

Shaver Grade

Shaver Grade

Worn Springs FR

Bald Hill
1141'

Six Points
550'

❷

Five Corners
520'

Concrete Pipe FR

Six Points Trail

Bald Hill Trail

Deer Park FR

Yolanda Trail North

400'
Boy Scout
Junction

Junction Tl.

❶

Oak Tree
Junction

Moore Tr.

Canyon Tl.

Deer Park FR

Deer Park Trail

Deer Park
190'

❸

Gate

Porteous Ave.

Wood Lane

Bolinas - Fairfax Rd

Fairfax

0   .4

Scale 1" = 0.4 miles

N

C7 Deer Park FR - Canyon - Six Points

Distance: 3.7 miles   Shaded: 90%
Elevation Change: 550'   Can be muddy or dusty. Bicycle traffic.
Rating: Hiking - 9   Difficulty - 6   Steep in places.
When to Go: Good November to May, best February through April.

This hike along roads and trails explores the hills and canyons west of Bald Hill offering great views, dark forests and lovely wildflowers.

0.0 Start at Deer Park in Fairfax. From the parking area, go left around the school and through the field. Deer Park FR begins at the gate just past a large bay tree and heads into a broad, shaded canyon with majestic oaks, madrone and buckeye trees. Spring wildflowers along the road include white milkmaids, Solomon's seal, yellow buttercup, blue hound's tongue, forget-me-nots, lupine and iris.

0.5 Oak Tree Jct. ❶. Just before the road heads uphill, take the Junction trail right past a large oak and cross a small bridge. The trail climbs above a ravine on an open hillside. In late April, look for a small, white flower called jewel flower, Streptanthus.

0.9 Boy Scout Jct. Take the spur road downhill to the right towards the signed Canyon trail. The road can be muddy in winter.

1.0 Junction. At the bottom of the hill, cross the creek and go left on the Canyon trail. The trail enters a dark forest of mostly bay trees covered with moss. Up ahead, the trail makes a steep zig-zag climb.

1.3 Junction ❷. Take the Concrete Pipe FR left. This road was originally a service road for a concrete water pipe built in 1918 to carry water from Alpine Lake to a pump station. A steel pipe was added in 1926. The concrete pipe can be seen at the bend up the road. There is an excellent display of wildflowers along the roadbank in April, including iris, blue larkspur, Chinese houses and woodland star.

Blue Larkspur

2.0 Five Corners Jct. Take the second left, a spur road, that climbs steeply up towards Six Points. At the top of the hill, the trail levels out and provides great views southeast to Mt. Tam. Look for iris in April.

2.6 Six Points Jct ❸. Take the first left, Six Points trail, down a narrow path marked by wooden erosion barriers. This trail is also known as the "dark trail," as it descends into a forest of bay trees.

3.2 Oak Tree Jct. ❶. Turn right and backtrack along Deer Park FR.

3.7 Parking area with water, tables and restroom facilities.

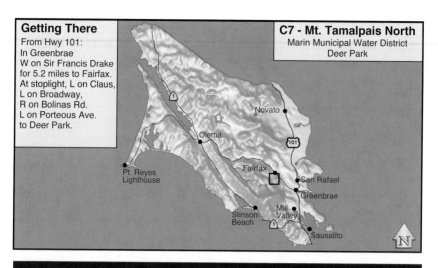

Getting There

From Hwy 101:
In Greenbrae
W on Sir Francis Drake
for 5.2 miles to Fairfax.
At stoplight, L on Claus,
L on Broadway,
R on Bolinas Rd.
L on Porteous Ave.
to Deer Park.

C7 - Mt. Tamalpais North
Marin Municipal Water District
Deer Park

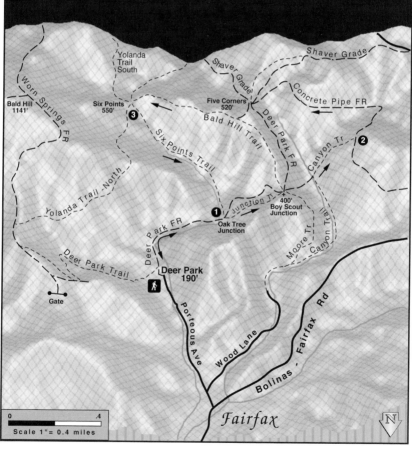

C8 Azalea Hill and Pine Mountain Trails

Distance: 0.4 and 4.4 miles   Shaded: 0%
Elevation Change: See below.   Lots of bicycles likely.
Rating: Hiking - 7   Difficulty - 4 and 5   Rocky in places.
When to Go: Save these hikes for clear, cool winter days.

These two out-and-back hikes explore the Pine Mountain area south of Fairfax. They offer interesting chaparral and great views.

To Azalea Hill at 1180' and Back - 0.4 miles and 150' Change
0.0 From the parking area, head east up the trail. Ahead, several unofficial trails take off to explore viewpoints and picnic areas.

0.2 Turnaround point ❶. A knoll offers great views of Bon Tempe Lake with Mt. Tamalpais in the background. **Option**: You can continue downhill, which gets steep in places, to reach Bullfrog FR (See map C14). Eventually, MMWD will designate the official trail down.

To Pine Mtn. at 1762' and Back - 4.4 miles and 700' Change
0.0 From the parking area, head west through the gate on Pine Mtn. FR. Over the next 2 miles, this road clearly shows the relationship between soil and plants. Along the rocky, light blue-grey serpentine areas, there is low-growing chaparral, mostly manzanita.

When the road turns brown with soil from sedimentary rocks, the plants are taller and include grasses, coyote bush, chemise and Douglas fir.

1.0 Ridgetop and two junctions. Bear right at both junctions. As you head downhill, look for the jutting profile of Mt. St. Helena 45 miles due north in

*Pine Mountain
as seen from Azalea Hill trail*

Sonoma County. It lies beyond a saddle on Big Rock Ridge, easily identified by the two tall antennas.

1.4 Junction. Take the signed Pine Mountain FR left. Up ahead, notice the Sargent cypress trees growing on serpentine soil.

2.2 Pine Mtn. and turnaround point ❷. The road doesn't quite reach the top, which is marked by a small metal pole sticking out of a rock. A 50 yd. trail takes you there for more great views. Before heading back, go down the road another 50 yds. to a viewpoint south to Kent Lake with Bolinas Ridge in the background. When ready, retrace your steps.

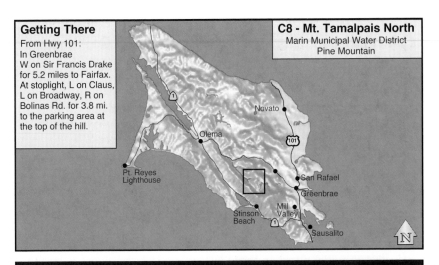

Getting There

From Hwy 101:
In Greenbrae:
W on Sir Francis Drake
for 5.2 miles to Fairfax.
At stoplight, L on Claus,
L on Broadway, R on
Bolinas Rd. for 3.8 mi.
to the parking area at
the top of the hill.

C8 - Mt. Tamalpais North
Marin Municipal Water District
Pine Mountain

Novato

Olema

Pt. Reyes
Lighthouse

San Rafael

Greenbrae

Stinson
Beach

Mill
Valley

Sausalito

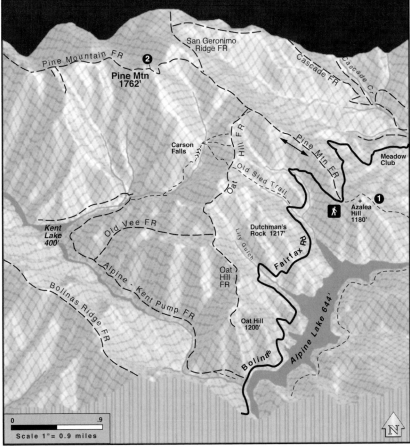

Pine Mountain FR

San Geronimo
Ridge FR

Pine Mtn
1762'

Cascade FR

Cascade Cr

Carson
Falls

Oat Hill FR

Old Sled Trail

Pine Mtn FR

Meadow
Club

Azalea
Hill
1180'

Kent
Lake
400'

Old Vee FR

Dutchman's
Rock 1217'

Lily Gulch

Fairfax Rd

Alpine - Kent Pump FR

Oat
Hill
FR

Bolinas Ridge FR

Oat Hill
1200'

Bolinas

Alpine Lake 644'

0   .9
Scale 1"= 0.9 miles

C9 Carson Falls and Oat Hill FR

Distance: 4.0 and 7.4 miles   Shaded: 0% and 20%
Elevation Change: 800' and 1100'   Rocky in places.
Rating: Hiking - 9   Difficulty - 6   Many bicycles on weekends.
When to Go: Best during winter rain runoff and in spring.

Both of these out-and-back hikes offer great views. The first hike visits the tallest waterfall in Marin, the second hike explores the ridges.

To Carson Falls at 1000' and Back - 4.0 miles and 800' Change
0.0 From the parking area at 1070', head west on Pine Mtn. FR. The trail starts out in serpentine soil that stunts the chaparral vegetation.

1.0 Ridgetop and junction. Head left on Oat Hill FR.

1.6 Junction. Take the Old Spool trail downhill right all the way to the falls. The trail can be rocky and muddy in places.

2.0 Top of Carson Falls and turnaround point ❶. The main viewpoint of the falls is on the left. The trail right crosses the creek, then drops steeply down loose rock to a viewpoint at the middle of the falls. **Note**: The Foothill Yellow-legged Frog lives and breeds in this creek and is a "species of special concern." Consequently, it is illegal for people or dogs to enter the water. The frog is 1.5-2.5" in size, appears brown or reddish, often mottled. The rear legs have yellow undersides.

To End of Oat Hill FR at 1150' and Back - 7.4 miles and 1100' Change
0.0 From the parking area, head west on Pine Mtn. FR. This trailhead and road is a major mountain bike area, especially busy on weekends.

1.0 Ridgetop and junction. Head left on the signed Oat Hill FR.

2.7 Junction with Old Vee FR. Continue straight. The vegetation makes a dramatic change here with small, lush groves of chinquapin, bay, Douglas fir and redwood trees. Just ahead, good views east.

Carson Creek drainage area

3.3 Junction. The road left deadends at the base of Oat Hill, where an unofficial trail makes a very steep ascent to the top. Head right.

3.7 Hilltop and turnaround point ❷. The grassy hilltop offers great views of the Kent Lake watershed. The road ends downhill 0.1 miles further, where 3 posts block the road. When ready, head back.

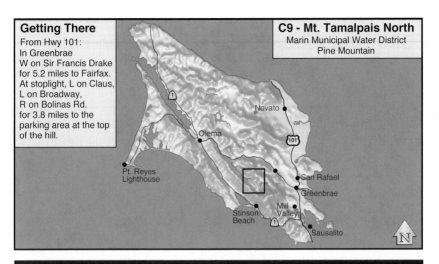

Getting There

From Hwy 101:
In Greenbrae
W on Sir Francis Drake
for 5.2 miles to Fairfax.
At stoplight, L on Claus,
L on Broadway,
R on Bolinas Rd.
for 3.8 miles to the
parking area at the top
of the hill.

C9 - Mt. Tamalpais North
Marin Municipal Water District
Pine Mountain

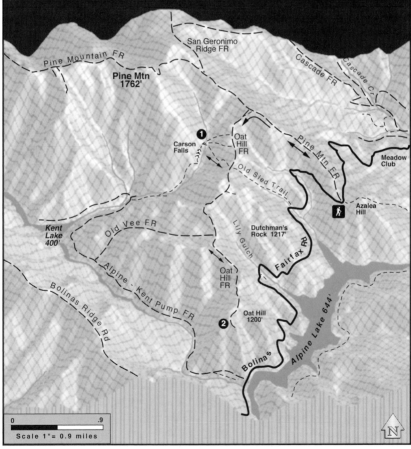

C10 Old Sled - Old Vee - Carson Falls

Distance: 6.0 miles   Shaded: 50%
Elevation Change: 1400'   Very steep along Little Carson Falls.
Rating: Hiking - 9   Difficulty - 9   Muddy, very rocky in places.
When to Go: Best late winter and early spring for water runoff.

This hike involves steep climbing, but offers great views and lots of creeks and waterfalls, including Little Carson Falls, the tallest in Marin.

0.0 From the parking area at milemarker 4.83, take the trail farthest right. The Old Sled trail starts by paralleling the road for 30', then heads inland to climb the right side of the ravine. This trail was once used to deliver dairy products from Liberty Ranch to San Rafael. It is well worn, rocky and easy to follow.

0.6 Junction ❶. Head left on Oat Hill FR. Good views to Bolinas Ridge.

1.7 Junction ❷. Take Old Vee FR right. Watch for bicycles.

2.8 Junction ❸. Take the level Kent Pump FR right.

4.1 Junction ❹ and pump house. Take the 2nd right 200' to see a small falls and the start of the Pine Mtn. Tunnel, which runs 1.6 miles under Pine Mtn. When ready, backtrack to take the 1st right uphill.

4.4 Meadow and redwood grove. The trail crosses a small meadow and enters into a beautiful redwood grove, once the location of the Big Trees hunting camp, a private lease on public land until 1971.

Bear to the left and cross the main creek on a redwood log. The Little Carson Falls trail follows the left side of the main creek uphill. It crosses a small tributary, with a 10' waterfall on the left, then climbs very steeply. Up ahead, the trail temporalily leaves the main creek to circle up to a viewpoint in the middle of the 100' falls.

4.8 Little Carson Falls "middle viewpoint." From the viewpoint, backtrack 50', and continue on the trail uphill to a grassy meadow. Follow the trail to ford the main creek (difficult during heavy runoff).

4.9 Little Carson Falls "top viewpoint." A short spur trail leads to the east side of the falls. **Caution**: Loose rocks. Continue the hike by taking the Old Spool trail right across the serpentine rock outcropping.

5.4 Junction ❶ again with Oat Hill FR. Cross the road and take the Old Sled trail downhill to the start. Originally, the trail continued all the way down to, what is now, the bottom of Alpine Lake, where it met the San Rafael-Bolinas stage route.

6.0 Back at the parking area. No facilities.

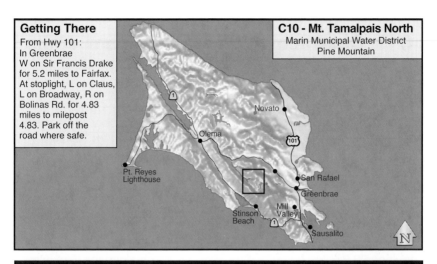

Getting There

From Hwy 101:
In Greenbrae
W on Sir Francis Drake
for 5.2 miles to Fairfax.
At stoplight, L on Claus,
L on Broadway, R on
Bolinas Rd. for 4.83
miles to milepost
4.83. Park off the
road where safe.

C10 - Mt. Tamalpais North
Marin Municipal Water District
Pine Mountain

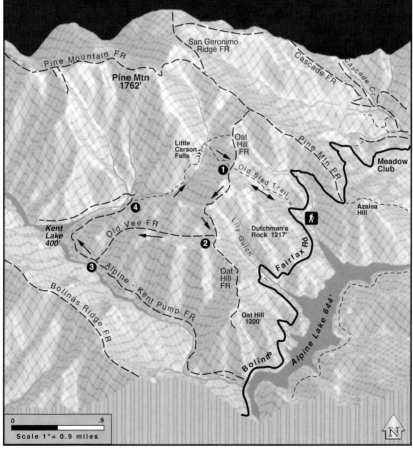

Scale 1"= 0.9 miles

C11 Cataract - High Marsh - Kent Trails

Distance: 7.8 miles   Shaded: 90%
Elevation Change: 2100'   Very steep in places.
Rating: Hiking - 10   Difficulty - 8   Can be slippery when wet.
When to Go: Best during rainy season and in spring for flowers.

This is a strenuous, but spectacular, hike in the most remote section of Mt. Tamalpais. Wonderful pools, waterfalls and conifer forests.

Note: Many people just do an up and down hike along Cataract Creek. The section up to junction ❶ is the most scenic and the steepest.

0.0 Park anywhere south of Alpine Dam and walk to the signed trailhead 0.2 miles from the dam. The trail starts along the lake in a conifer forest, then begins a steep climb along cascading waterfalls.

0.6 Bridge, then junction ❶ with the Helen Markt trail. Continue uphill along the creek. Ahead, the trail levels somewhat.

1.3 Junction. A short spur trail goes right for views of Cataract Falls.

1.4 Bench and junction ❷ with the signed High Marsh trail. A bench provides a welcome rest stop. Continue uphill along the creek.

1.6 Laurel Dell picnic area. Tables and restrooms. Backtrack down the trail to junction ❷ and take High Marsh trail right, which skirts the hillside. Up ahead, on the open hillside, look for woodland star, popcorn flower, fiddleneck, poppy and blue dicks in the spring.

3.6 Creek and two junctions. After crossing Swede George Creek, an unofficial trail comes down from the right, and 100 yds. further, descends to the left. Continue straight on the High Marsh trail.

3.8 Junction and High Marsh. The CC Boys trail heads right. Stay left along the marsh, which is a drainage pond created by a landslide.

4.0 Junction ❸. Take the signed Kent trail left downhill. After crossing a bridge, continue straight, away from the creek.

4.2 Junction near Serpentine Knoll. Bear left and head downhill.

4.6 Junction ❹ with the Stocking trail. Go left 20', then right down towards Alpine Lake. The Kent trail descends through an enchanting redwood forest, then past a slide on a fork of Swede George Creek.

5.4 Junction ❺ with the Helen Markt trail and Alpine Lake. Go left, as the trail leaves the lake to traverse several ridges. Ahead, the trail crosses a creek on a bridge built from lumber floated across the lake.

7.2 Junction ❶ again. Go right, back down Cataract Creek.

7.8 Back at the trailhead. No facilities.

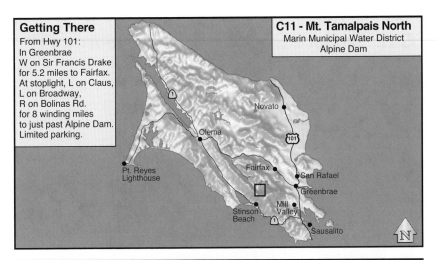

Getting There

From Hwy 101:
In Greenbrae
W on Sir Francis Drake
for 5.2 miles to Fairfax.
At stoplight, L on Claus,
L on Broadway,
R on Bolinas Rd.
for 8 winding miles
to just past Alpine Dam.
Limited parking.

C11 - Mt. Tamalpais North
Marin Municipal Water District
Alpine Dam

Novato

Olema

Pt. Reyes
Lighthouse

Fairfax

San Rafael

Greenbrae

Stinson
Beach

Mill
Valley

Sausalito

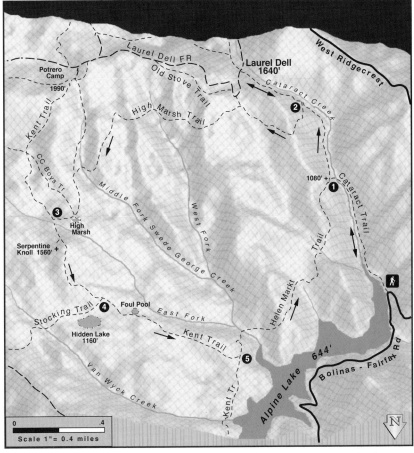

West Ridgecrest

Laurel Dell FR

Laurel Dell
1640'

Old Stove Trail

Cataract Creek

Potrero
Camp
1990'

High Marsh Trail

Kent Trail

CC Boys Tr.

Middle Fork Swede George Creek

West Fork

1080' +

Cataract Trail

High
Marsh

Serpentine
Knoll 1560' +

Helen Markt Trail

Stocking Trail

Foul Pool

East Fork

Kent Trail

Hidden Lake
1160'

Kent Tr.

Alpine Lake 644'

Van Wyck Creek

Bolinas - Fairfax Rd.

0   .4
Scale 1"= 0.4 miles

C12 Taylor - Concrete Pipe - Bullfrog FR

Distance: 3.2 miles   Shaded: 60%
Elevation Change: 250'   Bikes likely on some fire roads.
Rating: Hiking - 7   Difficulty - 5   One moderately steep section.
When to Go: Good mosses when wet, flowers in April.

This is a pleasant hike, mostly along fire roads, through open and wooded areas offering a wide selection of wildflowers and local views.

0.0 Start at the parking area just past the Sky Oaks toll booth and walk back towards the toll booth. Notice the large oaks on the right. In the early morning, look for grey foxes that have a den nearby.

Grey Fox

0.1 Junction. The Taylor trail begins at a gate to the left (north) of the ranger station and starts down parallel to the main road.

0.6 Junction ❶ with Concrete Pipe FR. Bear right and watch for some great spring wildflowers, including iris, modesty, blue dicks, Chinese houses, baby-blue eyes, lupine, blue larkspur and pink shooting star. The best display is in late April.

1.3 Five Corners Jct. Take the Elliott trail right to climb the steps and parallel Shaver Grade. The trail gets steep here.

1.6 Junction ❷. Go left on Shaver Grade. Watch for bicycles.

1.9 Junction. Go straight across Sky Oaks Rd. and take the trail.

2.0 Junction. Take either the dirt road or the parallel trail down towards Alpine Lake. This road was part of the Bolinas-Fairfax-San Rafael stage route that started service in the 1880s. Look for deer on the open hillside to the right.

2.4 Junction ❸ with the road to Bon Tempe dam. Continue right.

2.5 Alpine Lake and picnic spot. When full, the scenic lake lives up to its name. To continue the hike, go past the gate along Bullfrog FR.

2.9 Rock quarry. Red-brown sandstone and blue-green serpentine mark the site of an old quarry along the road. Rock from the quarry was used to build Bon Tempe dam in 1949.

3.0 Golf course. The road skirts by the Meadow Club. Look for moss and lichen growing on the serpentine rocks breaking through the thin hillside soil. The trail now veers left on a boardwalk through a low part of the meadow. Up ahead, bear right to return to the parking area.

3.2 Parking area with restrooms and water near the ranger station.

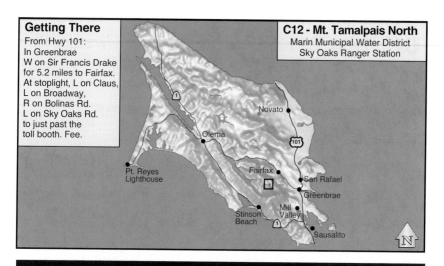

Getting There

From Hwy 101:
In Greenbrae
W on Sir Francis Drake
for 5.2 miles to Fairfax.
At stoplight, L on Claus,
L on Broadway,
R on Bolinas Rd.
L on Sky Oaks Rd.
to just past the
toll booth. Fee.

C12 - Mt. Tamalpais North
Marin Municipal Water District
Sky Oaks Ranger Station

Novato

Olema

101

Pt. Reyes
Lighthouse

Fairfax

San Rafael

Greenbrae

Stinson
Beach

Mill
Valley

1

Sausalito

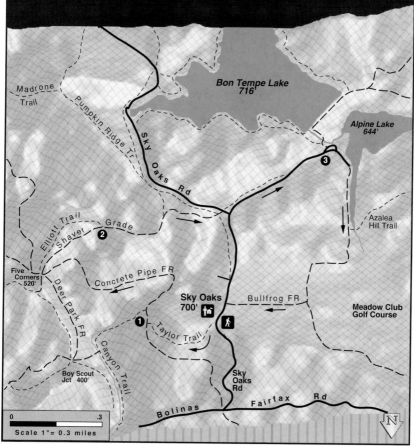

Madrone
Trail

Bon Tempe Lake
716'

Pumpkin Ridge Tr.

Sky Oaks Rd

Alpine Lake
644'

3

Elliott Trail

Shaver Grade

2

Azalea
Hill Trail

Five
Corners
520'

Deer Park FR

Concrete Pipe FR

1

Sky Oaks
700'

Bullfrog FR

Meadow Club
Golf Course

Taylor Trail

Canyon Trail

Boy Scout
Jct 400'

Sky
Oaks
Rd

Bolinas   Fairfax   Rd

0   .3

Scale 1"= 0.3 miles

C13 Bon Tempe Lake Trail

Distance: 4.1 miles   Shaded: 50%
Elevation Change: 50'   Some mud after heavy rains.
Rating: Hiking - 9   Difficulty - 3
When to Go: Good anytime, best in spring.

This is the best of the three lake hikes. It passes through wooded and open hillsides that provide good wildflowers and great views.

0.0 From the parking area below Bon Tempe dam, head up the dirt road towards the dam, which was built in 1949. At the dam, go right to circle the lake counter-clockwise. Stop and enjoy some great views across the lake to Mt. Tamalpais and also down to Alpine Lake.

0.3 Junction ❶ and restroom. At dam's end, take the signed Bon Tempe trail into oak-bay woodland. March flowers include white milkmaids, woodland star, blue hound's tongue and iris.

0.8 Bridge. The first of 3 bridges along the "Shadyside" of Bon Tempe. Up ahead, many of the taller trees are black oak, too tall to clearly see their distinctive leaves, which are 4-6 inches long with deep lobes. Look for fallen leaves on the path.

1.3 Grassland. Yellow gold fields, buttercup, sun cups, blue lupine and pink shooting star grow among the grasses here.

1.6 Junction ❷ and Lagunitas picnic area. Just past the redwood grove, go left across the bridge into the picnic area. Skirt the Lagunitas parking area and continue left on around the lake. The large set of valves is used to send water from the lake to a treatment plant.

2.0 Junction ❸. A road (to be closed) goes inland. Stay along the lake.

2.5 Large Douglas fir stand majestically on Pine Point peninsula overlooking the lake. Occasionally, osprey and great blue heron are seen here. Cormorants, gulls and wintering ducks are common. Pileated woodpeckers and red-shouldered hawks nest in the trees.

2.8 Junction with the paved Sky Oaks Road. Go left. Ahead, the paved ramp provides fishing access for the disabled.

3.1 Junction ❹. Leave the paved road to follow the trail around the "Sunnyside" of the lake. Watch for yellow sun cups, buttercup, poppy, white popcorn flower, iris and blue lupine in spring.

3.9 Pumphouse. Follow the road past the pumphouse and up the hill, then head downhill towards the parking area.

4.1 Back at the parking area. Restrooms only.

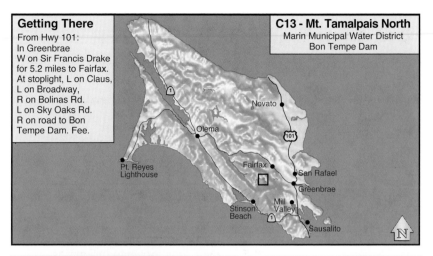

Getting There

From Hwy 101:
In Greenbrae:
W on Sir Francis Drake
for 5.2 miles to Fairfax.
At stoplight, L on Claus,
L on Broadway,
R on Bolinas Rd.
L on Sky Oaks Rd.
R on road to Bon
Tempe Dam. Fee.

C13 - Mt. Tamalpais North
Marin Municipal Water District
Bon Tempe Dam

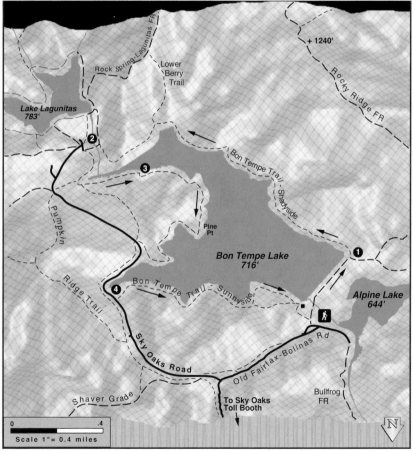

111

C14 Kent Trail - Rocky Ridge FR

Distance: 5.2 miles   Shaded: 70%
Elevation Change: 800'   May be overgrown with huckleberries.
Rating: Hiking - 10   Difficulty - 7   Rocky, rutted in places.
When to Go: Good anytime, best in spring.

This is an exhilarating hike along the conifer shores of Alpine Lake, up through a redwood forest, emerging onto a ridge with good views.

0.0 Start at the parking area below Bon Tempe dam and head uphill, bearing right, to the spillway. Go across the dam and enjoy the views.

0.3 Junction ❶. At dam's end, continue right along Alpine Lake and past lichen-covered oaks. In February, look for white milkmaids, yellow buttercup, pink shooting star and blue hound's tongue among the ferns and mosses along the road bank.

0.8 Pumphouse and Kent trail. The road ends at a pumphouse where water from Alpine Lake is pumped to Bon Tempe Lake and on to a treatment plant. Follow the narrow trail as it winds along the lake. An old 6" water pipeline lies along much of the trail here.

1.8 Views. The trail offers great views of conifer forest across the lake, just like the high Sierra Nevada. Just ahead, the trail enters Van Wyck canyon with small seasonal waterfalls and a bridge.

2.1 Big fir. A giant Douglas fir stands on a small knoll watching over skinny madrones; its side trunk is as big as the main trunk.

2.3 Junction ❷. Take the signed Kent trail left. This trail was originally called the Swede George trail after an oldtimer who had a cabin in the area around 1870. Huckleberries can be picked here in early fall.

2.6 Canyon and forest. The trail enters a large canyon of tall oaks, bay and redwood. Up past a slide, the trail skirts Foul Pool, crosses a small stream, and climbs through a magnificent redwood forest.

3.1 Junction ❸. The Kent trail goes right uphill. Take the signed Stocking trail straight. The trail soon heads downhill 200 yds., skirting secluded Hidden Lake, then uphill along a creek bed.

3.5 Bridge across Van Wyck creek. There are several unmaintained trails on this hike, especially along creeks, that are not on the map.

3.7 Junction ❹. Take the signed Rocky Ridge FR left. Ahead, look for views to San Pedro Mtn. lying between Bald Hill and Pilot Knob.

4.9 Junction. Go right and cross the dam.

5.2 Back at the parking area. Restroom facilities only.

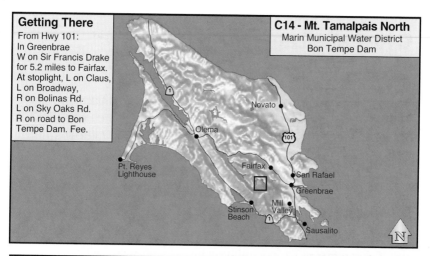

Getting There
From Hwy 101:
In Greenbrae
W on Sir Francis Drake
for 5.2 miles to Fairfax.
At stoplight, L on Claus,
L on Broadway,
R on Bolinas Rd.
L on Sky Oaks Rd.
R on road to Bon
Tempe Dam. Fee.

Novato

Olema

Pt. Reyes
Lighthouse

Fairfax

San Rafael

Greenbrae

Stinson
Beach

Mill
Valley

Sausalito

N

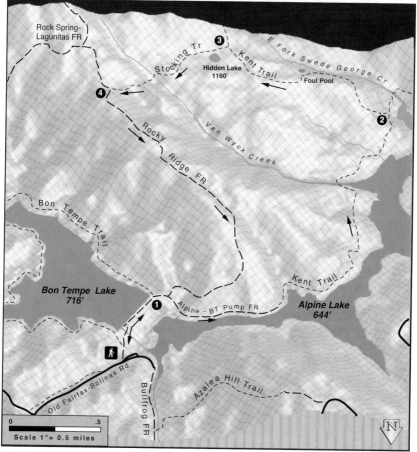

Rock Spring-
Lagunitas FR

Stocking Tr

3

Hidden Lake
1160'

Kent Trail

E Fork Swede George Cr

Foul Pool

4

2

Rocky

Ridge FR

Van Wyck Creek

Bon Tempe Trail

Bon Tempe Lake
716'

1

Alpine - BT Pump FR

Kent Trail

Alpine Lake
644'

Old Fairfax-Bolinas Rd

Bullfrog FR

Azalea Hill Trail

0   .5
Scale 1" = 0.5 miles

N

C15 Lake Lagunitas FR

Distance: 1.8 miles   Shaded: 70%
Elevation Change: 50'   Some standing water after heavy rains.
Rating: Hiking - 9   Difficulty - 2   Bicycle traffic on weekends.
When to Go: Good November to May, best February to April.

This is a level hike on roads around the lake with mosses, redwoods, oaks and great views across the lake to Mt. Tamalpais. Good birding.

0.0 Start at the Lagunitas parking lot. If you're fortunate, you might hear or see a pileated woodpecker nearby. It is a large 15" woodpecker with a black body, partly white neck and red tufted head. There are many other birds around the lake area, including wintering water birds. Often, you can see osprey flying over the treetops. To start the hike, go into the picnic area and pick up the trail next to the spillway. Climb up to the dam, which was built in 1873.

0.1 Dam. See if you can spot the rare Pacific pond turtles sunning on the floating logs by the dam. Go right over the spillway to circle the lake counter-clockwise. In February, look for white milkmaids, red Indian warrior and blue hound's tongue.

0.3 Junction ❶ with Rock Spring-Lagunitas FR. Continue left.

0.5 Bridge and redwoods. This first of 3 bridges crosses a creek that

Lake Lagunitas

provides water for a grove of redwoods. You rarely see moss on redwoods, but often can find a grey-green lichen on the bark.

0.9 Mosses. In winter, look for a fine display of mosses, lichens, ferns, succulents and other moisture lovers along the rocky bank.

1.2 Bridge and junction ❷. Under a canopy of tall oaks and madrones, the road crosses the East Fork of Lagunitas Creek. Go straight after the bridge and left on Lakeview FR. **Option**: Go right on Lakeview FR and visit Pilot Knob. See Hike C16.

1.4 Junction with road uphill. Continue left.

1.5 Junction. The road veers right up to the ranger's residence. Stay left on the trail as it passes through French broom and down the stairs to the dam. Cross the dam to head down the stairs to the picnic area.

1.8 Parking area. Water, picnic tables and restroom facilities.

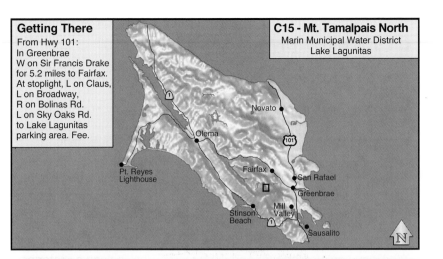

Getting There

From Hwy 101:
In Greenbrae
W on Sir Francis Drake
for 5.2 miles to Fairfax.
At stoplight, L on Claus,
L on Broadway,
R on Bolinas Rd.
L on Sky Oaks Rd.
to Lake Lagunitas
parking area. Fee.

C15 - Mt. Tamalpais North
Marin Municipal Water District
Lake Lagunitas

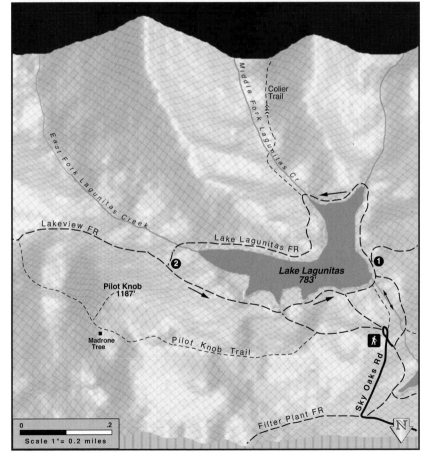

115

C16 Lakeview FR to Pilot Knob

Distance: 2.2 miles   Shaded: 70%
Elevation Change: 500'   Some bicycles.
Rating: Hiking - 8   Difficulty - 5   Moderately steep.
When to Go: Good November to May, best February to April.

This is a good hike through mixed forest, climbing to Pilot Knob for great views, then passing the largest madrone tree seen anywhere.

0.0 Start at the Lagunitas parking lot. Take the road overlooking the picnic area up to the dam. February flowers include white milkmaids and blue hound's tongue under the oak, bay and madrone trees.

0.2 Dam. Look for the rare and endangered Pacific pond turtles that often sun themselves on the floating logs by the dam. Go left up the stairs past the ranger residence and on to Lakeview FR.

0.6 Junction ❶. The road right goes around the lake. Stay left and enjoy great views to Mt. Tam on the right and Pilot Knob on the left.

1.1 Junction ❷. Take the signed trail to Pilot Knob left up the hill. The trail climbs steeply through tall madrone, oak, Douglas fir and redwood trees with an understory of tanoak and huckleberry.

1.4 Junction ❸. At a knoll, next to a large bay tree, take the spur trail left uphill to Pilot Knob. Ahead, notice the grove of young redwoods that will someday overgrow the tall madrones nearby.

1.5 Pilot Knob at 1187'. Enjoy great views south to Mt. Tam, west to Bon Tempe lake, and to Mt. Diablo in the east bay. To continue the hike, return down the spur trail and bear left along the main trail.

1.8 Madrone. The grandfather of madrones! An incredible madrone tree with six main trunks, each the size of a single madrone. The tree has limited foliage and may not live many more years. The trail continues along the ridgetop past lichen-covered oaks and more normal-sized madrone trees.

Giant Madrone Tree

2.1 Junction. The road left returns along the lake. Head right past redwood, Douglas fir, oak and madrone trees and follow the steep downhill road back to the parking lot.

2.2 Parking lot. Water, tables, barbecue and restrooms.

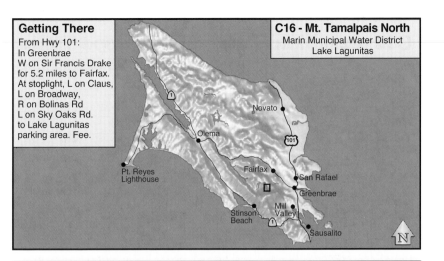

Getting There

From Hwy 101:
In Greenbrae
W on Sir Francis Drake
for 5.2 miles to Fairfax.
At stoplight, L on Claus,
L on Broadway,
R on Bolinas Rd
L on Sky Oaks Rd.
to Lake Lagunitas
parking area. Fee.

C16 - Mt. Tamalpais North
Marin Municipal Water District
Lake Lagunitas

Novato

Olema

Pt. Reyes
Lighthouse

Fairfax

San Rafael

Greenbrae

Stinson
Beach

Mill
Valley

Sausalito

N

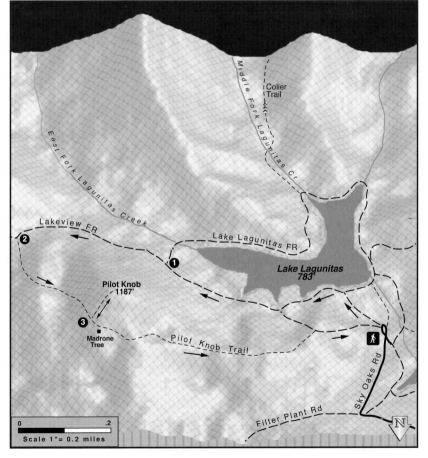

Middle Fork Lagunitas Cr

Colier
Trail

East Fork Lagunitas Creek

Lakeview FR

2

Lake Lagunitas FR

1

Lake Lagunitas
783'

Pilot Knob
1187'

3

Madrone
Tree

Pilot Knob Trail

Sky Oaks Rd

Filter Plant Rd

N

0	.2

Scale 1"= 0.2 miles

117

C17 Pumpkin Ridge - Bon Tempe Trails

Distance: 3.3 miles   Shaded: 50%
Elevation Change: 400'   Trail can be crowded with grasses.
Rating: Hiking - 9   Difficulty - 4   Some stairs.
When to Go: Best around mid-April for spectacular iris.

This hike explores the rolling hills north of Bon Tempe Lake. Good views, oaks and wildflowers along the wooded ridges and lake.

0.0 Start at the Lagunitas parking lot and head west to the edge of Bon Tempe Lake. Follow the dirt road past the large valves out to Sky Oaks Rd. In spring, look for yellow sun cups, buttercups and a pale purple lily, Calochortus, in the meadow along the road.

0.2 Junction ❶ with Sky Oaks Rd. Cross the paved road and head up the open hillside dotted with lichen-covered oaks. This is classic oak-woodland country with occasional madrones and firs mixed in. However, now there is evidence of sudden oak death, both in the oaks and madrones.

The Pumpkin Ridge trail follows the ridgetop providing fine vistas of Mt. Tam. In April, the ridgetop displays a nice selection of iris with delicate hues of cream, gold, violet and blue.

Douglas Iris

0.9 Junction ❷. Just before the Sky Oaks Rd., take the Sky Oaks-Lagunitas trail right as it parallels the road heading north.

1.2 Junction with Shaver Grade and Sky Oaks Rd. Continue on the trail directly across the paved road.

1.3 Junction ❸ with the road to Bon Tempe dam. Go down the road a few feet, then take the trail that parallels the road for a while.

1.6 Parking area. Go through the gate and then bear left 200' ahead to climb up to the lake. Continue around the "Sunnyside" of the lake.

2.6 Junction with Sky Oaks Rd. Cross the road and take the trail right.

2.9 Junction ❹. with Sky Oaks Rd. Cross the road and take the left trail uphill. The lakes area has recently been cleared of non-native Coulter pines, which were planted in the 1930s. More than 600 pines have been removed; some trunks can be seen lying along this trail.

3.2 Junction with Bon Tempe lake trail. Go left around the valves and back towards the parking area.

3.3 Parking area with water, tables, barbecue and restrooms.

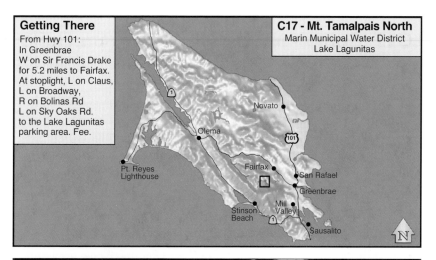

Getting There

From Hwy 101:
In Greenbrae
W on Sir Francis Drake
for 5.2 miles to Fairfax.
At stoplight, L on Claus,
L on Broadway,
R on Bolinas Rd
L on Sky Oaks Rd.
to the Lake Lagunitas
parking area. Fee.

C17 - Mt. Tamalpais North
Marin Municipal Water District
Lake Lagunitas

Novato

Olema

Pt. Reyes
Lighthouse

Fairfax

San Rafael

Greenbrae

Stinson
Beach

Mill
Valley

Sausalito

N

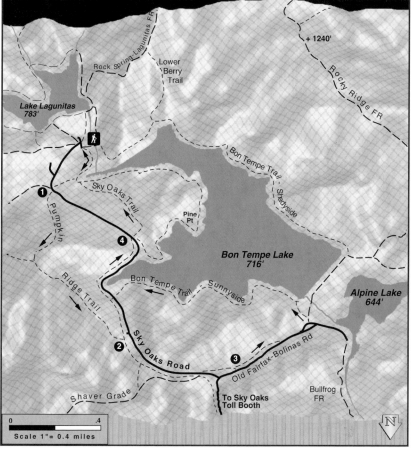

+ 1240'

Rock Spring-Lagunitas FR

Lower
Berry
Trail

Rocky Ridge FR

Lake Lagunitas
783'

Bon Tempe Trail - Shadyside

❶

Sky Oaks Trail

Pumpkin

Pine
Pt

❹

Bon Tempe Lake
716'

Alpine Lake
644'

Ridge Trail

Bon Tempe Trail

Sunnyside

❷

Sky Oaks Road

Old Fairfax-Bolinas Rd

❸

Shaver Grade

To Sky Oaks
Toll Booth

Bullfrog
FR

N

0   .4

Scale 1" = 0.4 miles

C18 Colier - Northside - Kent - Stocking

Distance: 6.7 miles   Shaded: 80%
Elevation Change: 1500'   Very steep, rocky in places.
Rating: Hiking - 9   Difficulty - 10   Requires creek crossing.
When to Go: Good anytime, except during heavy water runoff.

This strenuous hike, best for experienced hikers, offers cascading creeks, redwoods, views north and a challenge not to get lost.

Note: MMWD have closed 4 trails along this hike: Upper Berry, Azalea Meadow, Lagoon FR and a connector trail. The trails are no longer on our maps, which may create confusion if the junctions still exist.

0.0 Start at the Lagunitas parking lot. Head into the picnic area and up along the spillway to the dam. Head right, to circle the lake.

0.5 Bridge and junction ❶. Turn right and follow the signed Colier trail up the left side of the creek. Ahead, the trail crosses the creek twice?

1.6 Colier Spring, resting bench and junction ❷. To continue the hike, take the first trail on the right, the Lower Northside trail.

2.5 Two junctions and viewpoint. At a chaparral clearing, the Rocky Ridge FT crosses. Continue straight for another 50 yds. to the Rock Spring-Lagunitas FR, then go right downhill.

2.6 Junction ❸. Go left on the Cross Country Boys trail (may still be signed Upper Berry). Ahead 200 yds., just past a bridge, stay right.

2.8 Junction with the old Lagoon FR. Continue on the CC Boys trail.

3.0 Two junctions. Go right, then left on the signed CC Boys trail.

3.3 Junction ❹. Take the signed Kent trail right downhill.

3.9 Junction with High Marsh trail. Continue straight on the Kent trail, which soon crosses Swede George creek and then goes uphill. Watch for two unofficial trails that cross Kent, just past the bridge.

4.1 Junction. Head right 50 yds. up through chaparral to a viewpoint on Serpentine Knoll, then return and continue downhill on Kent trail.

4.5 Junction ❺. Head right on Stocking trail, then past Hidden Lake.

5.1 Junction. Take the Rocky Ridge FR right uphill.

5.5 Junction ❻ with the Rock Spring-Lagunitas FR. Head left downhill. Watch for bicycles along here, especially on weekends.

6.0 Junction. Take the signed Lower Berry trail left.

6.4 Junction with Bon Tempe Lake. Head right along the lake.

6.7 Parking area. Water, picnic tables and restroom facilities.

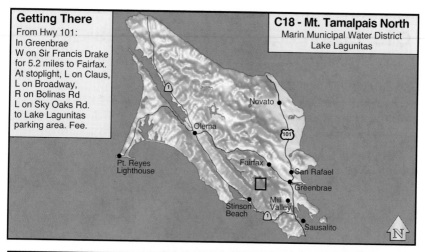

Getting There
From Hwy 101:
In Greenbrae
W on Sir Francis Drake
for 5.2 miles to Fairfax.
At stoplight, L on Claus,
L on Broadway,
R on Bolinas Rd
L on Sky Oaks Rd.
to Lake Lagunitas
parking area. Fee.

C18 - Mt. Tamalpais North
Marin Municipal Water District
Lake Lagunitas

Novato

Olema

Pt. Reyes
Lighthouse

Fairfax

San Rafael

Greenbrae

Stinson
Beach

Mill
Valley

Sausalito

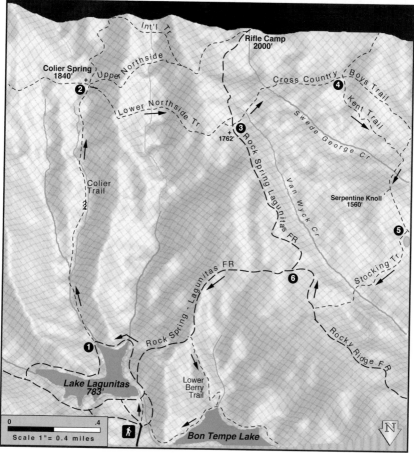

Int'l Tr.

Rifle Camp
2000'

Colier Spring
1840'

Upper Northside

Cross Country

Boys Trail

Lower Northside Tr.

Kent Trail

Swede George Cr.

Colier
Trail

1762'

Rock Spring Lagunitas FR

Van Wyck Cr.

Serpentine Knoll
1560'

Rock Spring - Lagunitas FR

Stocking Tr.

Rock Spring - Lagunitas FR

Lake Lagunitas
783'

Lower
Berry
Trail

Rocky Ridge FR

Scale 1" = 0.4 miles

0   .4

Bon Tempe Lake

C19 Lake Lagunitas to East Peak

Distance: 10.2 miles   Shaded: 60%
Elevation Change: 1800'   Lots of bicycle traffic on weekends.
Rating: Hiking - 7   Difficulty - 7   Rocky in places.
When to Go: Best when cool and clear on weekdays.

This hike climbs to the top of Mt. Tamalpais for great views, then loops back to Lake Lagunitas past streams and secluded forests.

0.0 Start at the Lake Lagunitas parking lot. Take the road overlooking the picnic area up to the dam. Then head left up the stairs.

0.5 Junction with Lake Lagunitas FR, which goes right to circle Lake Lagunitas. Continue straight on Lakeview FR.

1.3 Junction ❶. Take Eldridge Grade straight. This road, built for wagon traffic in the late 1880s, makes a long gradual climb up Mt. Tam.

2.4 Junction with Indian FR. Continue uphill on Eldridge Grade.

3.6 Junction. Take the Northside trail right 100 yds. to Inspiration Point for great views north, then return to continue up Eldridge.

4.8 Junction ❷. Cross Ridgecrest Blvd. and take the paved trail east.

5.1 East Peak viewpoint, Visitor Center and snackbar. These are usually only open on weekends (during the summer, the refreshment stand is open daily). Both are closed during bad weather. **Option**: Take the Plankwalk trail to climb to the top of Tam (see Hike B20).

5.4 Junction ❷ again. Go 200' past Eldridge Grade to take the Middle Peak FR right. The road circles the peak, heading for the antennas.

6.0 Junction. At a hairpin turn, take the Lakeview trail right which heads east, tunneling through low-growing oaks and tall manzanita. **Option**: Continue uphill 200 yds. to explore parts of Middle Peak.

6.7 Junction ❸ with road. Head 100' along E. Ridgecrest Blvd., then take the International trail right. About 200' downhill at the junction to the Colier trail, continue straight on the International trail.

7.2 Junction. Take the Northside trail left. Ahead, continue across the broad, serpentine ridge past the Rocky Ridge FT. Good views north.

7.8 Junction ❹ at Rifle Camp. Head down the Rock Spring-Lagunitas FR.

8.9 Junction with the Rocky Ridge FR. Continue straight, downhill.

9.4 Junction ❺. Take the signed Lower Berry trail left downhill.

9.9 Junction. Head right along the Bon Tempe Lake trail.

10.2 Back at the parking area with restrooms, tables and water.

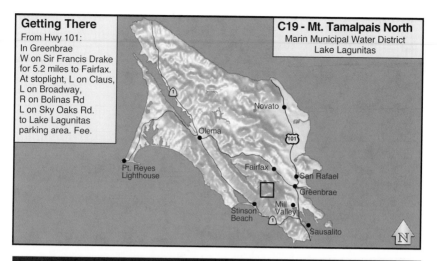

Novato

Olema

101

Fairfax   San Rafael

Greenbrae

Pt. Reyes
Lighthouse

Stinson
Beach

Mill
Valley

Sausalito

N

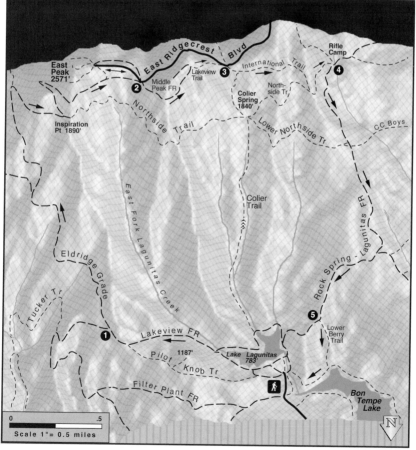

East Ridgecrest Blvd

Rifle
Camp

East
Peak
2571'

Middle
Peak FR

Lakeview
Trail

International Trail

4

3

Northside Trail

Colier
Spring
1840'

North-
side Tr

Inspiration
Pt. 1890'

Lower Northside Tr

CC Boys

East Fork Lagunitas Creek

Colier
Trail

Rock Spring - Lagunitas FR

Eldridge Grade

5

Tucker Tr

Lower
Berry
Trail

Lakeview FR

1187'

Pilot Knob Tr

Lake Lagunitas
783'

Filter Plant FR

Bon
Tempe
Lake

N

0   .5

Scale 1"= 0.5 miles

D - Central Marin - 15 Hikes

Starting from Kent Woodlands at 640'
D1   King Mountain Loop Trail 3.6

Starting from Cascade Canyon in Fairfax
D2   Cascade FR - Cascade Falls Trail 1.7
D3   Cascade Canyon to White Hill 8.6
D4   Toyon Fire Road to Cascade Peak 4.5

Starting from Fairfax at 240'
D5   Loma Alta Open Space Loop 6.3

Starting from Woodacre at 200'
D6   Roy's Redwoods Trails 2.8

Starting from Samuel P. Taylor State Park
D7   Creek - Ox Trails History Loop 2.6
D8   Pioneer Tree - Barnabe Creek Trails 3.3
D9   Mt. Barnabe FR Loop 5.6
D10 Devil's Gulch - Stairstep Falls Trails 4.1
D11 Devil's Gulch to Mt. Barnabe 6.7

Starting from near the Marin Civic Center at 100'
D12 Marin Civic Center to China Camp 5.7*

Starting from China Camp State Park at 20'
D13 Miwok - Oak Ridge - Shoreline Trails 5.5
D14 Bayview Trail - Miwok FT 5.7
D15 Shoreline - Turtle Back Island Trails 3.8

Notes
* Shuttle Hike
Dogs allowed on hikes D1-D6.
To download a hike, go to www.marintrails.com
The password for this region is d5sp2fm

Region D Trailheads

Hikes 1-6 and 12 start in Marin County Open Space, phone 415-499-6387.

Hikes 7-11 start in Samuel P. Taylor State Park, phone 415-488-9897.

Hikes 13-15 start in China Camp State Park, phone 415-456-0766.

Region D
Central Marin

GGNRA

Samuel P. Taylor State Park

GGNRA

French Ranch Open Space

Bolinas Lagoon

Kent Lake

Nicasio Valley Rd

Audubon Canyon Ranch

Bolinas Ridge

Marin Muncipal Water District

Pine Mtn 1762'

Giacomini Open Space

Roy's Redwoods Open Space

Fairfax-Bolinas Rd

Alpine Lake

Cascade Cyn Open Space

Sir Francis Drake Blvd

Loma Alta Open Space

Bon Tempe Lake

Lake Lagunitas

Big Rock 1887'

Mt Tamalpais 2571'

Bald Hill 1141'

Fairfax

Lucas Valley Rd

Lucas Valley Open Space

Ignacio Valley Open Space

Terra Linda Ridge Open Space

Marinwood Comm. Services District

Pacheco Vale Open Space

Ignacio Blvd

San Anselmo

Blithedale Ridge Open Space

King Mtn Open Space

San Rafael

Marinwood

101

Corte Madera

Greenbrae

101

San Pedro Mtn Open Space

Barbier Park

Las Gallinas County Park

China Camp State Park

580

D1 King Mountain Loop Trail

Distance: 3.6 miles   Shaded: 60%
Elevation Change: 700'   Moderately steep.
Rating: Hiking - 7   Difficulty - 6   Can be rocky or muddy.
When to Go: Best when clear and cool. Good flowers in spring.

This hike explores the loop trail around King Mountain, which passes through oak-bay woodland, then redwood groves. Good local views.

0.0 Head up the Citron FR that starts with an easy climb past non-native acacia, and eucalyptus trees, and French broom. This hike demonstrates the struggle to eliminate non-native plants. Volunteers have worked long hours on King Mountain, but much still needs to be done.

0.5 Junction. A road heads uphill, right towards private property. Continue straight towards the fence. It can be muddy here.

0.6 Gate, fence and paved road. Head left up the dirt road.

0.8 Junction ❶. Leave the road and take the signed Loop trail left. Portions of this trail pass through easements on private land, part of the agreement that allows four luxury homes on top of the mountain. However, it appears that only one, very large, home will be built.

1.6 Junction with the trail to Wilson Way. Continue straight.

1.7 Junction ❷ with the Ladybug trail to Dawn Falls. **Option**: For a longer hike, head downhill to Baltimore Canyon and the Dawn Falls trail. This trail requires fording Larkspur Creek, which can be a foot deep or more during heavy runoff. There are plans to build a bridge across the creek.

2.2 Junction ❸ with Ridgecrest Rd. Go right 20', then left to pick up the trail, which zig-zags down several flights of stairs into small groves of tall, second generation redwoods.

2.4 Bridge. The trail levels out here. Look for nutmeg trees ahead under the bay and redwood trees. Nutmeg needles look like redwood needles, but they are twice as long and have very sharp points.

2.8 Junction ❶ again. Go left down the road. Ahead, you can see a water tank and beyond that, a ball field at the College of Marin. Corte Madera Creek, to the right of the ball field, used to be called Ross Landing (now Kentfield). From the 1850s to the 1870s, small schooners used the landing to haul redwood logs, firewood and bricks to San Francisco. Over 15,000 board feet of lumber was shipped daily, much of it coming down Shaver Grade from Lagunitas mill.

3.6 Back at the parking area. No facilities.

126

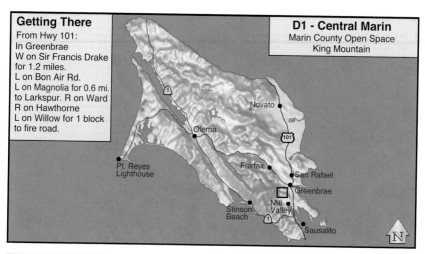

Getting There

From Hwy 101:
In Greenbrae
W on Sir Francis Drake
for 1.2 miles.
L on Bon Air Rd.
L on Magnolia for 0.6 mi.
to Larkspur. R on Ward
R on Hawthorne
L on Willow for 1 block
to fire road.

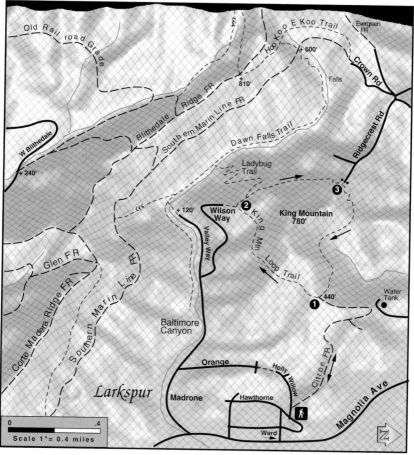

127

D2 Cascade FR - Cascade Falls Trail

Distance: 1.7 miles   Shaded: 70%
Elevation Change: 400'   Cascade Creek may be impassable.
Rating: Hiking - 9   Difficulty - 6   One short steep section.
When to Go: Good a few weeks after heavy rains. Best in March.

This hike explores Cascade Canyon and Cascade Falls west of Fairfax. Most of the hike is along creeks. Great flowers in spring.

Note: Fairfax requires 12' of pavement clearance when parking.

0.0 Start at the open space gate at the end of Cascade Dr. Head through the gate and stay right on the High Water trail all the way to the road. Look for wildflowers: milkmaid, shooting star, hound's tongue, Indian warrior and mission bells, starting in late February.

0.2 Junction ❶. The trail joins a road and both head right uphill.

0.3 Bridge and junction ❷. Cross the bridge and head up the left side of the creek. Look for trillium hidden along the bank in March.

0.5 Refreshing Cascade Falls. Continue by retracing your steps. **Note**: A very poor unofficial trail continues up past the falls eventually reaching another falls about a half mile upstream. It is not recommended.

0.9 Junction ❶ again. Leave the trail and, if possible, follow the road across Cascade Creek. In winter, it takes two to three weeks after heavy rain for the creek to subside enough to ford. Continue downstream on the other side. (If the creek is too deep to cross, retrace your steps.)

1.0 Bridge and junction ❸. Just before the bridge, take the trail up the right edge of a side creek. Up ahead at a Y, stay along the creek.

1.1 Spur trail. About 50' uphill, take a short spur trail upstream to a dramatic setting of moss-covered rocks. Return to the main trail to continue the hike, which moves away from the creek slightly and climbs uphill. Ahead at a Y-junction with a trail signed to the right, stay left. After crossing a knoll, the trail drops back down to the creek passing through abundant spring wildflowers.

1.5 Viewpoint. The trail reaches the highest point on this hike offering views out through the trees. You can see Cascade Canyon with the grassy slopes of the top of White Hill directly behind the canyon.

1.5+ Two bridges and junction ❹. Continue downhill.

1.6 Junction with Cascade Creek. Ford the creek and head right.

1.7 Back at the parking area. No facilities.

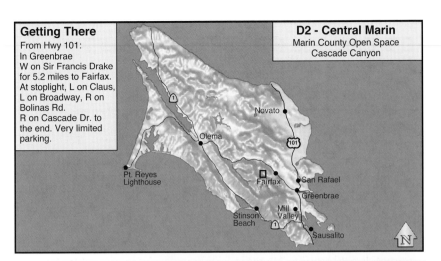

Getting There

From Hwy 101:
In Greenbrae
W on Sir Francis Drake
for 5.2 miles to Fairfax.
At stoplight, L on Claus,
L on Broadway, R on
Bolinas Rd.
R on Cascade Dr. to
the end. Very limited
parking.

D2 - Central Marin
Marin County Open Space
Cascade Canyon

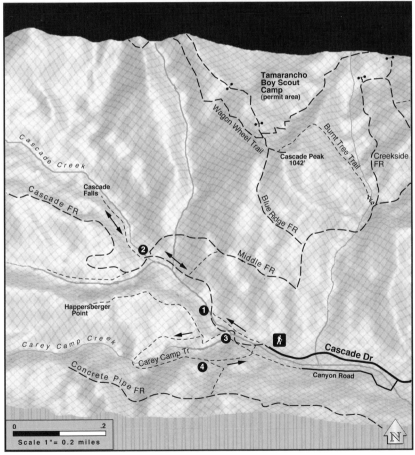

129

D3 Cascade Canyon to White Hill

Distance: 8.6 miles   Shaded: 30%
Elevation Change: 1900'   Lots of bicycle traffic on weekends.
Rating: Hiking - 8   Difficulty - 9   Steep in places.
When to Go: Good anytime when cool. Best in spring.

This hike explores the upper reaches of Cascade Canyon and White Hill. It offers spectacular views, and abundant spring wildflowers.

0.0 Start at the Cascade Open Space gate at the end of Cascade Drive. Head through the gate and stay right on the trail. March wildflowers include milkmaids, buttercup, shooting star, hound's tongue, Indian warrior, iris and mission bells.

0.3 Bridge and junction ❶. Cross the bridge. Go right along the creek.

0.5 Cascade Falls. After visiting the falls, backtrack to junction ❶.

0.7 Junction ❶ again. Take the Cascade FR right (called Repack by bicyclists. In the late 1970s, bicyclists raced their old Schwinn bikes down here, vaporizing the grease on the coaster brakes, which required repacking them). Continue past a trail along the creek and head uphill. Watch for bicycles.

2.7 Junction ❷. Go right on San Geronimo Ridge Rd.

3.7 Junction ❸. Go right on White Hill FR. Stay right on the main FR at each junction ahead.

4.7 Junction. Head right on Blue Ridge FR to climb White Hill.

5.2 White Hill at 1430' where open grassland allows spectacular 360° views. The hike continues over White Hill to drop steeply down.

5.7 Junction ❹. At the low saddle, take the Wagon Wheel trail right. Watch for bicycles. This trail was originally built by the Bicycle Trails Council of Marin when the land belonged to the Boy Scouts. Marin County Open Space bought the land and left the trail open to bikes.

7.0 Two junctions ❺. Take the road right for 100 yds., past a FR on the right and then take the trail left downhill. The trail follows a ridge, then veers right under dense tree cover. The end of the trail is quite steep. **Option**: Continue uphill for a short climb to Cascade Peak.

7.5 Creek and junction. Cross the creek and take the FR right.

7.8 Junction. Continue downhill on the road, which can get steep. Stay on the road all the way to the bottom of Cascade Canyon.

8.3 Junction. Take the trail left along the creek.

8.6 Back at the trailhead. No facilities.

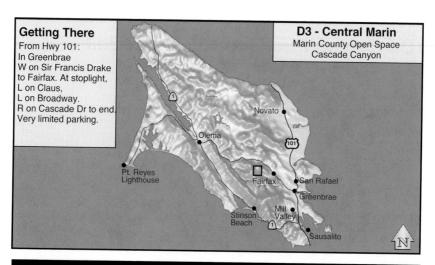

Getting There

From Hwy 101:
In Greenbrae
W on Sir Francis Drake
to Fairfax. At stoplight,
L on Claus,
L on Broadway.
R on Cascade Dr to end.
Very limited parking.

Novato

Olema

Pt. Reyes
Lighthouse

101

Fairfax

San Rafael

Greenbrae

Stinson
Beach

Mill
Valley

Sausalito

N

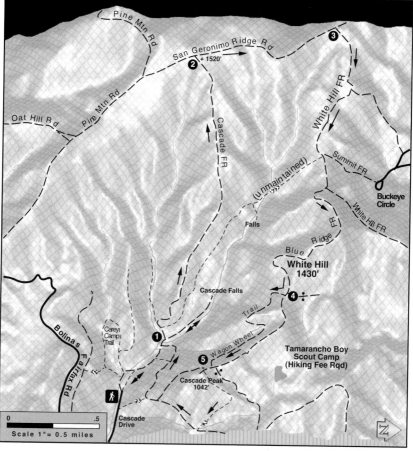

Pine Mtn Rd

San Geronimo Ridge Rd

2 + 1520'

3

White Hill FR

Oat Hill Rd

Pine Mtn Rd

Cascade FR

Summit FR

Buckeye
Circle

White Hill FR

(unmaintained)

Falls

FR

Blue   Ridge

White Hill
1430'

Cascade Falls

4 ⚴

Bolinas

Fairfax Rd

Careyl
Camp
Trail

Trail

1

Wagon Wheel

5

Tamarancho Boy
Scout Camp
(Hiking Fee Rqd)

🚶

Cascade Peak
1042'

Cascade
Drive

0		.5

Scale 1" = 0.5 miles

N

131

D4 Toyon Fire Road to Cascade Peak

Distance: 4.5 miles   Shaded: 70%
Elevation Change: 1400'   Some poison oak. Bicycles likely.
Rating: Hiking - 9   Difficulty - 9   Mud possible. Steep in places.
When to Go: Good on clear, cool days, best in March.

This difficult hike explores the hills and ridges above Fairfax. It offers interesting rock formations, an oak-bay-madrone forest and great views.

Note: Fairfax requires 12' of pavement clearance when parking.

0.0 From Toyon Dr., go through the open space gate heading uphill.

0.5 Junction ❶. Head right uphill on the Cul-de-Sac FR.

0.7 Knoll. The road ends on a small knoll. Continue downhill on the Cul-de-Sac trail. In spring, look for milkmaids, hound's tongue, iris and lots of Indian warrior under the oak and madrone trees. Broom and poison oak crowd the trail in several places here.

1.0 Junction ❷. The trail joins the Toyon FR. Go right on the road.

1.1 Junction. The hike heads left here. However, it's worth a short 100 yd. detour on the road right to view the open hills, most of which are part of the Tamarancho Boy Scout Camp.

1.5 Creek and junction ❸. Cross the creek and take the signed trail uphill to the right to start a long steep climb through dense vegetation.

2.0 Junction ❹ with the Burnt Tree FR. Head left for a short climb.

2.1 Cascade Peak at 1042'. Great views. Notice that there are two peaks, both of which are worth exploring.

2.2 Junction ❹ again. Continue straight down the road.

2.3 Junction. Go left on the Blue Ridge FR, which gets steep in places. The southern exposure offers good views across the canyon.

2.8 Junction ❺. The Middle FR heads left back up into the canyon.

3.1 Junction ❸ again. Stay right to head uphill.

3.2 Junction ❶ again. Head right to visit two points of interest.

3.4 Junction. It's worth taking both trails 0.1 miles from here, then returning. The lower trail leads to an open mine. The upper trail leads to a small plaque commemorating Pam Ettinger, who died in an accident in 1974. This ridge was named for her after her family purchased the ridge and donated it to open space.

4.0 Junction ❶ again. Head right down the Toyon FR.

4.5 Back at the parking area on Toyon Dr. No facilities.

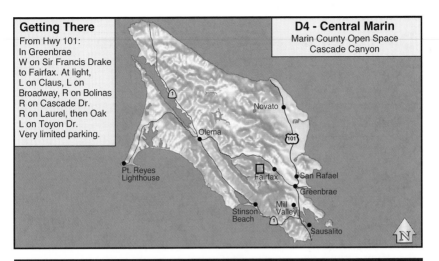

Getting There

From Hwy 101:
In Greenbrae
W on Sir Francis Drake
to Fairfax. At light,
L on Claus, L on
Broadway, R on Bolinas
R on Cascade Dr.
R on Laurel, then Oak
L on Toyon Dr.
Very limited parking.

D4 - Central Marin
Marin County Open Space
Cascade Canyon

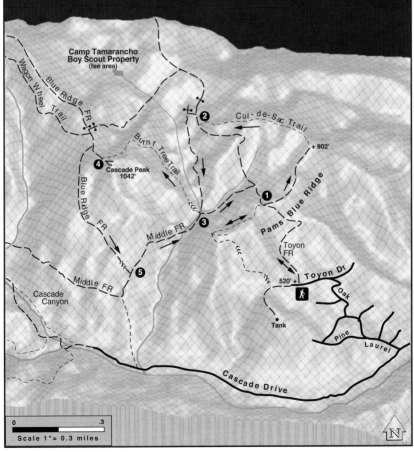

133

D5 Loma Alta Open Space Loop

Distance: 6.3 miles   Shaded: 20%
Elevation Change: 1400'   Can be muddy. Bicycle traffic possible.
Rating: Hiking - 7   Difficulty - 7   Steep in places.
When to Go: Best on clear, cool days in winter and spring.

This hike explores the Loma Alta open space just west of Fairfax. It offers great views and an unexpected 30' waterfall.

0.0 Park at the end of Glen Drive just past White Hill School in Fairfax. The hike starts by passing through an open space gate along Glen FR, then enters a woodsy canyon filled with bay trees.

0.5 Water tanks and junction ❶. Go left on Smith Ridge FR.

1.8 Junction ❷ with Gunshot FR. Continue uphill to a viewpoint and gate.

2.2 Gate and junction ❸. Go through the gate and continue uphill to the right. A public easement on private land allows access to the road.

2.7 Loma Alta at 1592' with outstanding views north to Big Rock Ridge, west to Mt. Barnabe, east to Mt. Diablo and south to Mt. Tamalpais. This vantage point also offers a good view of the profile of the "sleeping maiden" along the ridge of Mt. Tamalpais. Legend has it that a young Miwok maiden was saved from the devil Diablo tribe by a great shuddering of the mountain. Afterwards, her profile could be seen on the ridgetop. When ready, head back down the road.

3.2 Junction ❸ again. Retrace your steps and close all gates.

3.6 Junction ❷. Head right down Gunshot FR which is steep in places.

4.3 Gate and junction ❹. Turn sharp left and continue downhill.

4.7 Junction with overgrown road. Stay left and head downhill to a hidden waterfall. It's surprising to find this picturesque 30' waterfall here.

5.0 The road narrows to a trail and drops down steeply into a ravine. Continue straight uphill out of the ravine. Ahead, the trail enters a narrow pass that can be wet and muddy after rains. Also, watch out for poison oak on the banks. This road was once the railroad route over White Hill to West Marin. After the pass, continue straight.

5.5 Junction with road to school. Continue left into the canyon.

6.0 Bridge, fence and junction ❺. At the end of the fence, take a sharp right down into a bay-filled canyon on the Fox Hollow trail. Ahead, the trail crosses the creek. **Note**: If the creek is too high to cross, backtrack to junction ❺ and continue up to the Glen FR.

6.3 Back at the parking area. No facilities.

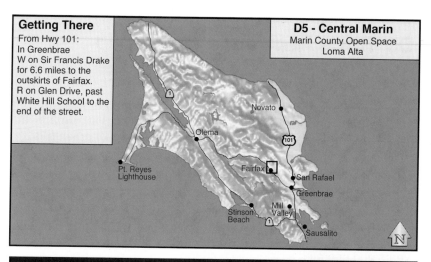

Getting There

From Hwy 101:
In Greenbrae
W on Sir Francis Drake
for 6.6 miles to the
outskirts of Fairfax.
R on Glen Drive, past
White Hill School to the
end of the street.

D5 - Central Marin
Marin County Open Space
Loma Alta

Novato

101

Pt. Reyes
Lighthouse

Olema

Fairfax

San Rafael

Greenbrae

Stinson
Beach

Mill
Valley

Sausalito

N

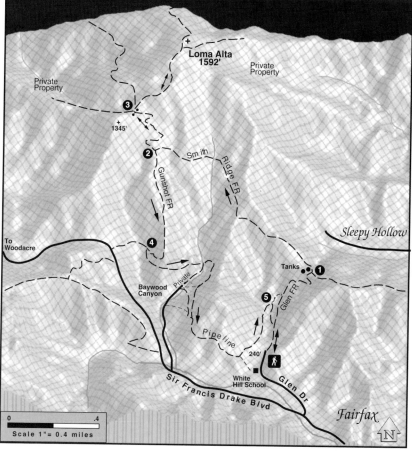

Loma Alta
1592'

Private
Property

Private
Property

❸

+
1345'

❷

Smith

Ridge FR

Gunshot FR

Private
Property

Sleepy Hollow

To
Woodacre

❹

Tanks

❶

Private

Baywood
Canyon

❺

Glen FR

Pipe line

240'

White
Hill School

Glen Dr.

Sir Francis Drake Blvd

Fairfax

0 .4
Scale 1" = 0.4 miles

N

135

D6 Roy's Redwoods Trails

Distance: 2.8 miles   Shaded: 90%
Elevation Change: 650'   Can be muddy. Some poison oak.
Rating: Hiking - 9   Difficulty - 7   Steep downhill at mile 2.3.
When to Go: Good in fall and winter. Best in spring for green hills.

This short hike explores the hill area around a magnificent grove of redwoods. Good wildflowers in spring and local views.

0.0 Pass through the open space gate and at the junction, head into a picturesque meadow ringed by tall bays and stately redwoods. This area is named after the Roy brothers who owned the property for 80 years and operated a dairy ranch nearby.

0.1 At the far end of the meadow, angle to the right to pass between two small redwood groves. The right grove consists of a large 30' diameter ring of second generation redwoods. The original tree must have been huge. Continue up the trail into an open area.

0.3 Junction ❶. Take the Roy's Redwoods Loop trail to the right.

0.5 Saddle and junction ❷. Take the trail to the left for about 100' just past a notched rock for good views east. Return to junction ❷ and continue left. The trail winds down off the hill passing through a large ravine darkened by dense stands of oaks, bays and redwoods.

1.0 Junction ❸ at a post at the bottom of the hill. **Option 1**: You can continue towards Sir Francis Drake Blvd. to loop back to the starting point. However, the route can be noisy, windy and overgrown. Otherwise, retrace your steps back up the hill. **Option 2**: For an alternate, but steeper loop back to junction ❷, head left along the creek, then uphill on the unmaintained trail, which may be rutted and overgrown.

1.5 Junction ❷. Take the Roy's Redwoods Nature trail left uphill.

1.8 Loop junction. Take the trail left which climbs the hill, then loops back to this point. Up ahead, the trail crests the hilltop and offers glimpses south to the golf course, Pine Mountain and Mt. Tamalpais.

2.2 Junction ❷ again. Head left. Watch closely for the next junction.

2.3 Junction. Take the trail left, a short steep downhill section, past the sign (No Horses). Watch out for poison oak. At the bottom of the hill, keep left and look for the trail which follows the creek and skirts the hillside. This main redwood grove is a great area to just wander about and explore. The trail, which may be overgrown or blocked in places, stays to the left near the hillside.

2.8 Trailhead with restroom. **Option**: For more hiking here, see Hike J4.

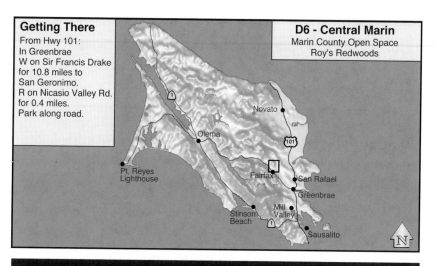

Getting There

From Hwy 101:
In Greenbrae
W on Sir Francis Drake
for 10.8 miles to
San Geronimo.
R on Nicasio Valley Rd.
for 0.4 miles.
Park along road.

D6 - Central Marin
Marin County Open Space
Roy's Redwoods

Novato

Olema

101

Pt. Reyes
Lighthouse

Fairfax

San Rafael

Greenbrae

Stinson
Beach

Mill
Valley

1

Sausalito

N

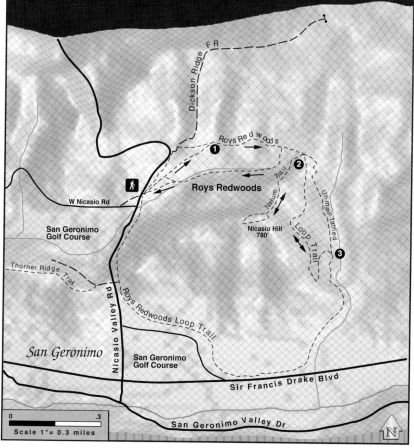

Dickson Ridge FR

Roys Redwoods

① ②

Roys Redwoods

Nature Trail

Unmaintained

W Nicasio Rd

San Geronimo
Golf Course

Nicasio Hill
780'

Loop Trail

③

Thorner Ridge Trail

Nicasio Valley Rd

Roys Redwoods Loop Trail

San Geronimo

San Geronimo
Golf Course

Sir Francis Drake Blvd

0   .3

Scale 1"= 0.3 miles

San Geronimo Valley Dr

N

137

D7 Creek - Ox Trails History Loop

Distance: 2.6 miles   Shaded: 80%
Elevation Change: 200'   Bicycles likely. Some traffic noise.
Rating: Hiking - 9   Difficulty - 2   Can be muddy in places.
When to Go: Best in summer for weather and winter for quiet.

This is an easy hike along Papermill Creek featuring redwoods, a riparian setting, and a glimpse into the history of Samuel P. Taylor Park.

0.0 Park in the main picnic area. The hike starts at the museum and ranger station where you can pick up a brochure that describes the history of the park at numbered posts. At the large redwood stump, take the paved road left through the picnic area.

0.1 Post 2. A billboard displays historical photos. Continue along the road and across the bridge, then take a right on the bike path. This path is part of the old railroad bed that ran from Sausalito to the coast and north to the Russian River town of Cazadero.

0.3 Junction ❶. Leave the bike path and take the signed Creek trail right. The trail passes by a large redwood, then bays and alders.

0.6 Junction. The trail climbs back up to the bike path for 200 yds. then drops back down towards the creek. By taking the Creek trail, you'll miss historical posts 5, 6 and 7, but you can still read the brochure.

0.7 Junction. At the Y in the trail, a wooden post points the way to the right.

0.8 Creek junction ❷. A large boulder stands opposite the creek at Devil's Gulch. Head uphill into a storage area and continue right.

1.2 Junction. A rock and plaque mark the site of the first papermill built on the west coast by Samuel P. Taylor. Continue on the trail.

Artist Sketch of the New Papermill

1.3 Bridge, swimming hole and restroom. After exploring the area, head back along the bike path.

1.4 Junction ❸. Take the Ox trail right uphill. This was the original trail used to bring supplies to the mill by oxen.

2.3 Junction. The trail ends on the camp road. Head left downhill.

2.6 Back at the picnic area with full facilities.

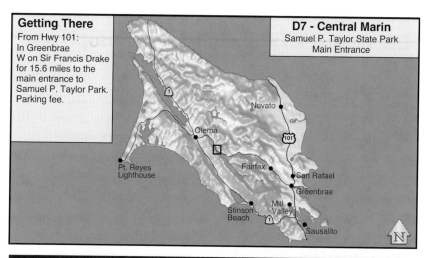

Getting There

From Hwy 101:
In Greenbrae
W on Sir Francis Drake
for 15.6 miles to the
main entrance to
Samuel P. Taylor Park.
Parking fee.

D7 - Central Marin
Samuel P. Taylor State Park
Main Entrance

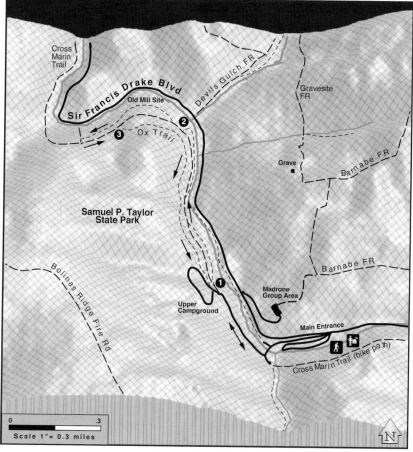

139

D8 Pioneer Tree - Barnabe Creek Trails

Distance: 3.3 miles   Shaded: 90%
Elevation Change: 400'   Some poison oak, traffic noise.
Rating: Hiking - 9   Difficulty - 5   Can be muddy and overgrown.
When to Go: Best in February for trillium and late fall for colors.

This is a relatively easy hike that features the magnificent redwood forest of Samuel P. Taylor State Park with the Pioneer Tree.

0.0 Park in the main picnic area near the Visitor Center. This area was the site of the Camp Taylor Hotel, which began as a one story hotel in 1874. Two stories were added later as shown in the picture. Passenger service on the North Pacific Coast Railroad began in 1875; by 1890 up to 3000 people came to Camp Taylor on weekends to picnic, swim, camp and hike.

Camp Taylor Hotel 1908

To start the hike, follow the road across the bridge on Lagunitas Creek, then bear left to go past the group picnic area.

0.2 Junction ❶. Take the signed Pioneer Tree trail right up Wildcat Canyon. This is a beautiful redwood forest with many lovely ferns.

1.6 Pioneer Tree. A bench provides a place to rest and contemplate the large gnarled Pioneer Tree. Notice the ring of redwoods around the main trunk. Redwoods sprout new growth from roots and burls, especially after a tree has been damaged. If possible, look inside the hollowed-out section of the tree. It has a double cavity.

1.8 Viewpoint. Go right 50' on a spur trail to a rocky outcropping.

2.2 Junction ❷. Take the bike path right across the bridge.

2.3 Junction. Take the Barnabe Creek trail (once called Riding and Hiking trail) left uphill.

2.6 Creek. The trail drops down a ravine alongside Barnabe Creek towards the main road, then heads up a moderately steep fire road.

2.9 Junction ❸. Take the road left down towards Madrone Camp.

3.0 Madrone Group Camp. Continue down the paved road.

3.1 Highway. Carefully cross the road and take the trail left.

3.3 Back at the parking area with full facilities.

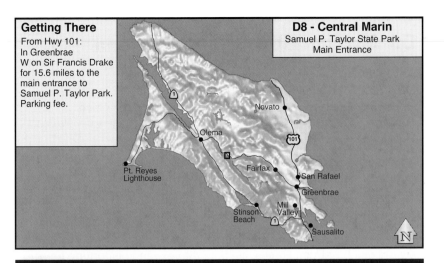

Getting There

From Hwy 101:
In Greenbrae
W on Sir Francis Drake
for 15.6 miles to the
main entrance to
Samuel P. Taylor Park.
Parking fee.

D8 - Central Marin
Samuel P. Taylor State Park
Main Entrance

Novato

Olema

Pt. Reyes
Lighthouse

Fairfax

San Rafael

Greenbrae

Stinson
Beach

Mill
Valley

Sausalito

N

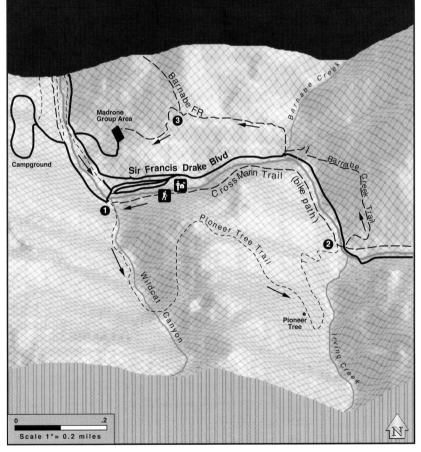

Barnabe FR

Barnabe Creek

Madrone
Group Area

❸

Barnabe Creek Trail

Campground

Sir Francis Drake Blvd

Cross Marin Trail (bike path)

❶

Pioneer Tree Trail

❷

Wildcat Canyon

Pioneer
Tree

Irving Creek

0   .2

Scale 1"= 0.2 miles

N

141

D9 Mt. Barnabe FR Loop

Distance: 5.6 miles   Shaded: 40%
Elevation Change: 1400'   Some bicycles. Traffic noise.
Rating: Hiking - 7   Difficulty - 7   Fire road is steep in places.
When to Go: Best on clear, cool, calm days.

This hike climbs out of the redwoods of Taylor park and up along the southern ridge of Mt. Barnabe to offer great views of central Marin.

0.0 From the main picnic area, take the road along the creek across the bridge. The go left again along the old railroad bed. The North Pacific Coast Railroad was built in 1874 by James Shafter, who owned much of Point Reyes. He hoped to expand his fortune hauling lumber from the Russian River to Sausalito, then by ferry to San Francisco. The railroad also brought tourists in the other direction. This service ended when the 1250' tunnel through White Hill collapsed in the big earthquake of 1906. The coast section of the railroad continued operating until 1938, when it was abandoned.

0.7 Bridge and junction. Continue on the Cross Marin Trail, which has also been known as the Old Railroad Grade or the Taylor Bike Path.

1.5 Junction ❶. Take the signed Barnabe FR uphill. This road is a long, moderately steep climb that starts out in a deep forest and ends on a grass-covered mountain top. Good views along the way.

2.4 Junction ❷. The Ridge trail heads to the left to parallel the fire road. If the trail is overgrown with grasses, it's better to stay on the road. There are lots of ticks in these hills, so it's not a good idea to hike through grass, especially in winter and spring. **Note**: There may be alternative trails on the left that parallel the Ridge trail and the FR.

3.4 Mt. Barnabe, fire lookout station and junction ❸. This peak offers one of the great viewing spots of West Marin. On a clear day you can see Tomales Bay to the northwest, Mt. Diablo to the east and the jutting profile of Mt. St. Helena to the north. Also, Mt. Barnabe sits in a unique central position relative to the ridgeline running from the East Peak of Mt. Tamalpais to Bolinas Ridge. This ridgeline spans a full 180 degrees from southwest to northeast. When ready to continue, take the Barnabe FR downhill, which can be steep in places.

4.6 Junction ❹. The FR right goes by the Taylor grave. Head left.

5.0 Junction. Go right downhill through the Madrone Group Area.

5.3 Junction. Cross the highway and take the North Creek trail left.

5.6 Back at the main picnic area. Water, tables and restrooms.

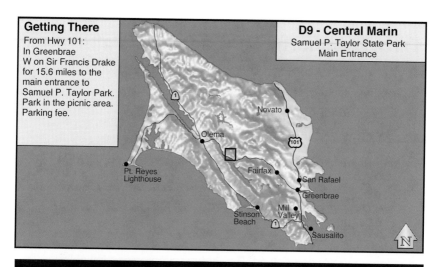

Getting There

From Hwy 101:
In Greenbrae
W on Sir Francis Drake
for 15.6 miles to the
main entrance to
Samuel P. Taylor Park.
Park in the picnic area.
Parking fee.

D9 - Central Marin
Samuel P. Taylor State Park
Main Entrance

Novato

Olema

101

Pt. Reyes
Lighthouse

Fairfax

San Rafael

Greenbrae

Stinson
Beach

Mill
Valley

Sausalito

N

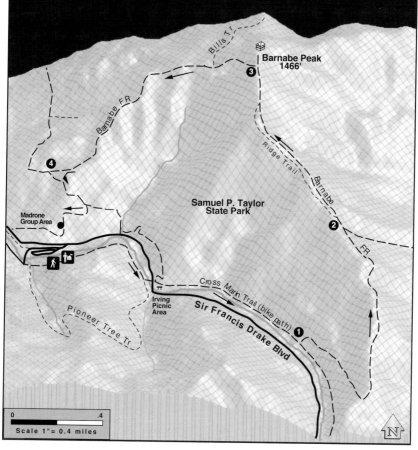

Bills Tr

Barnabe Peak
1466'

❸

Barnabe FR

Ridge Trail

Barnabe

❹

Samuel P. Taylor
State Park

❷

FR

Madrone
Group Area

Cross Marn Trail (bike path)

Pioneer Tree Tr

Irving
Picnic
Area

Sir Francis Drake Blvd

❶

0   .4
Scale 1"= 0.4 miles

N

143

D10 Devil's Gulch - Stairstep Falls

Distance: 4.1 miles   Shaded: 80%
Elevation Change: 400'
Rating: Hiking - 9   Difficulty - 4   Can be muddy.
When to Go: Best 2-3 weeks after the first heavy rains.

In winter, this hike offers fall colors, a picturesque waterfall and spawning salmon. Wait a few days after rain for the water to clear.

0.0 Park off the highway near milepost 18.05. Carefully cross the highway and hike up the paved road into Devil's Gulch.

0.1 Junction. Take the trail along the creek. Bay trees and sword fern dominate the riparian setting. Big-leaf maple provides fall color.

In early winter, watch for coho salmon in the creek. It takes about 5" of rain before the salmon will enter Tomales Bay and head up Papermill Creek to spawn. Once in the creek, they stay in deep pools during low water flow and move upstream after rains and runoff. Spawning salmon are three years old and undergo major changes as they end their life cycle. Males turn brick red and their upper jaws distort forming a hooklike shape. Females often turn a dull bronze.

Later, starting in February, look for steelhead trout that also spawn here. They are smaller than the coho and may return to the sea.

0.2 Junction ❶ and bridge. Cross the bridge and head left to take Bills trail towards Mt. Barnabe.

0.8 Junction ❷. Take the left trail which heads down into a ravine.

1.0 Stairstep Falls. The trail ends here with great views of the 50' picturesque falls. The hike now backtracks to the bridge.

1.8 Bridge and junction ❶ again. Cross the bridge and head right up the narrow trail along the creek. Notice the magnificent redwood here. There are lots of redwoods in SP Taylor Park, but very few in Devil's Gulch, which is probably why this one survived the loggers.

2.1 Y-junction. At a deep ravine, take the easier trail left up the hillside.

2.2 Junction ❸ with road. Head right to explore the upper reaches of Devil's Gulch. This road was first built as a toll road to Nicasio Valley.

2.8 Gate. This is the turn-around point. **Option**: Continue 0.3 miles to explore the next canyon located on GGNRA property. Gate at right.

3.4 Junction ❸ again with the creek trail. Continue along the road.

3.8 Paved road and horse camps. Restrooms and water nearby.

4.1 Highway and parking area. No facilities.

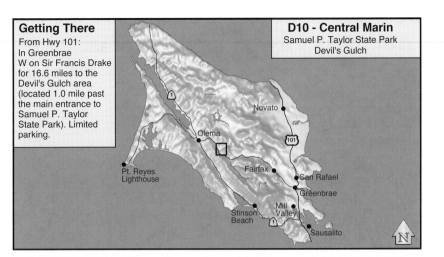

Getting There

From Hwy 101:
In Greenbrae
W on Sir Francis
Drake for 16.6 miles to the
Devil's Gulch area
(located 1.0 mile past
the main entrance to
Samuel P. Taylor
State Park). Limited
parking.

D10 - Central Marin
Samuel P. Taylor State Park
Devil's Gulch

Novato

Olema

101

Pt. Reyes
Lighthouse

Fairfax

San Rafael

Greenbrae

Stinson
Beach

Mill
Valley

Sausalito

N

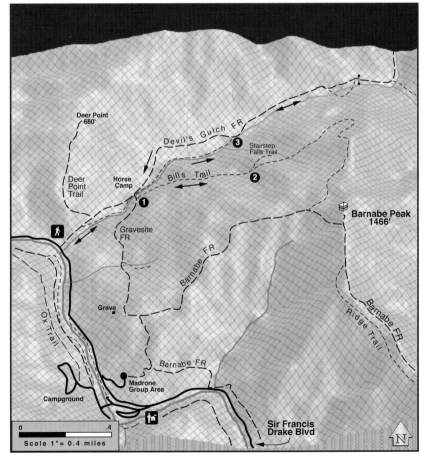

Deer Point
680'

Devil's Gulch FR

Stairstep
Falls Trail ❸

Deer
Point
Trail

Horse
Camp

Bill's Trail ❷

❶

Barnabe Peak
1466'

Gravesite
FR

Barnabe FR

Grave

Ox Trail

Barnabe
Ridge Trail

Barnabe FR

Madrone
Group Area

Campground

Sir Francis
Drake Blvd

0 .4

Scale 1"= 0.4 miles

N

145

D11 Devil's Gulch to Mt. Barnabe

Distance: 6.7 miles   Shaded: 70%
Elevation Change: 1400'   Bicycle traffic possible.
Rating: Hiking - 8   Difficulty - 7   Moderately steep downhill.
When to Go: Best in spring for views of green hills.

This hike climbs through forest up the backside of Mt. Barnabe, then descends the south-facing open hillsides. Great views.

0.0 Park off the highway near milepost 18.05. Carefully cross the highway and hike up the paved road into Devil's Gulch.

0.1 Junction. Take the trail along the creek.

0.2 Junction ❶ and bridge. Cross the bridge and head left to take Bills trail towards Mt. Barnabe.

0.8 Junction ❷. Take the left trail for a short sidetrip.

1.0 Stairstep Falls. The trail ends here with great views of the 50' picturesque waterfalls. The hike now backtracks to Bills trail.

1.2 Junction ❷ again. Head left and continue uphill. This trail, built to state requirements of 5% incline or less, provides a long, easy climb through a magnificent forest of bay, fir and big-leaf maple.

4.2 Junction ❸. Head left up the Barnabe FR.

4.4 Mt. Barnabe and junction ❹. This peak was named after an old white mule purchased by Taylor from the army. "Barnabe" was the Taylor children's favorite pet. He often escaped from his corral and could be found grazing on these hillsides. The fire lookout station is run by the county. The hike now backtracks down the Barnabe FR.

4.6 Junction ❸ again. Continue downhill on the Barnabe FR.

5.8 Junction. Take the Gravesite FR right.

5.9 Junction ❺ and grave site. The white picket fence encloses the grave site of Samuel Taylor and his wife. Taylor, scouting for lumber, entered this area on horseback over Indian trails in 1854. He purchased 100 acres from Rafael Garcia and, two years later, he constructed the first papermill on the Pacific Coast.

From the grave site, take the Gravesite FR north.

6.2 Creek and junction. Cross the creek, then take the trail left. The road right heads up to a water storage area.

6.5 Junction ❶ again and bridge. Head left.

6.7 Back at the parking area. No facilities.

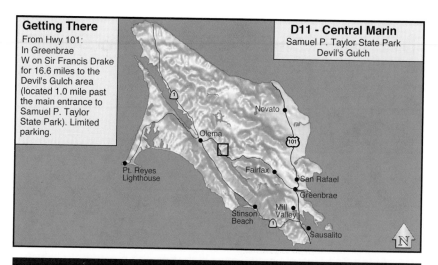

Getting There

From Hwy 101:
In Greenbrae
W on Sir Francis Drake
for 16.6 miles to the
Devil's Gulch area
(located 1.0 mile past
the main entrance to
Samuel P. Taylor
State Park). Limited
parking.

D11 - Central Marin
Samuel P. Taylor State Park
Devil's Gulch

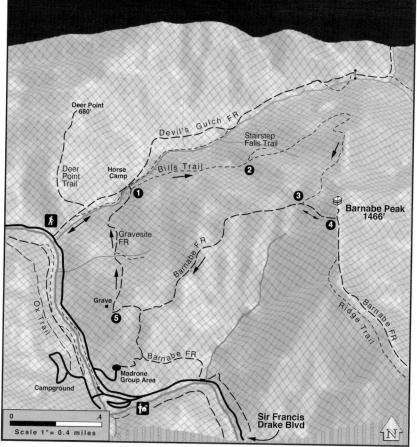

147

D12 Marin Civic Center to China Camp*

Distance: 5.7 miles   Shaded: 70%
Elevation Change: 1200'   On weekends, bicycles likely.
Rating: Hiking - 8   Difficulty - 8   Steep in places.
When to Go: Good anytime, best when clear.

This one-way hike climbs to the Nike site on San Pedro Mountain to offer breathtaking views east, then winds down to China Camp.

*Shuttle Hike. Leave pickup cars along the road near Back Ranch campground. Shuttle hikers back on N. San Pedro Rd. to San Pablo Ave, then go left for one block and park near the trailhead.

0.0 At the San Rafael Open Space sign, take the paved path, which starts out in grassland with some manzanita and oaks nearby. Ahead, the path turns to dirt and is rutted in places.

0.1 Junction. Take the Scettrini FR right uphill.

0.4 Junction ❶. Continue left on the Scettrini FR as it heads into an oak, bay, madrone woodland that has suffered some Sudden Oak Death fungus. On weekends, keep right and watch for bicycles.

0.9 Junction with Aquinas FR. Stay left on what is now San Pedro Ridge FR. Good views down the steep canyon south to the Dominican area and ahead, views north to the Civic Center.

1.3 More views! A "bald spot" in the road opens up 300° views.

2.1 Junction ❷. At the gate, take the paved road right to the Nike missile site (radar portion only), park and picnic area. Be sure to visit the concrete platform farthest east. It offers tremendous views down to China Camp and the mudflats, and east across San Pablo Bay.

This hike passes through three jurisdictions. It starts on San Pedro Mtn. Open Space, then enters San Rafael's Harry Barbier Memorial Park, and ends in China Camp State Park. Over 700 acres of the open space land was donated by Frank Sinatra in the 1970s.

2.4 Junction ❸. Take the Ridge FR left downhill into the state park.

2.7 Junction under powerlines. Head downhill to the left.

2.9 Junction. Continue down to the left on the Back Ranch FT.

3.1 Junction ❹. Take the Bay View trail left for a long gradual descent. **Option**: For a faster trip downhill, stay on the Back Ranch FT.

4.2 Wooden fence and junction. Take the switchback to the right. Down below, cross the road and continue on the Bay View trail.

5.7 Gate and parking area. Restrooms at campground.

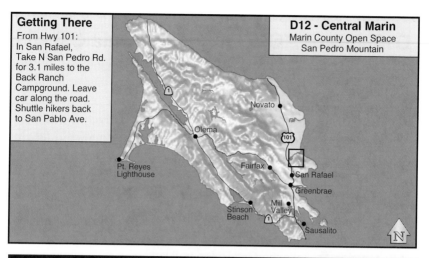

Getting There

From Hwy 101:
In San Rafael,
Take N San Pedro Rd.
for 3.1 miles to the
Back Ranch
Campground. Leave
car along the road.
Shuttle hikers back
to San Pablo Ave.

D12 - Central Marin
Marin County Open Space
San Pedro Mountain

Novato

Olema

Pt. Reyes
Lighthouse

Fairfax

San Rafael

Greenbrae

Mill
Valley

Stinson
Beach

Sausalito

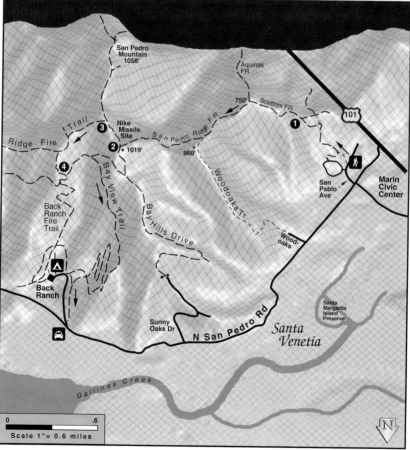

San Pedro
Mountain
1058'

Aquinas
FR

750'   Scettrini FR

1

Ridge Fire   **3**   Nike
Missile
Site   San Pedro Ridge FR

2   + 1019'   960'

4

Bay View Trail

Back
Ranch
Fire
Trail

Bay Hills Drive

Woodoaks Tr

Wood-
oaks

San
Pablo
Ave

Marin
Civic
Center

Back
Ranch

Sunny
Oaks Dr   N San Pedro Rd   *Santa
Venetia*

Santa
Margarita
Island
Preserve

Gallinas Creek

0 _____ .6
Scale 1"= 0.6 miles

D13 Miwok - Oak Ridge - Shoreline Trails

Distance: 5.5 miles   Shaded: 70%
Elevation Change: 500'   Bicycles likely.
Rating: Hiking - 9   Difficulty - 4   Moderately steep uphill start.
When to Go: Good anytime. Best early morning in winter and spring.

This is the best hike for exploring China Camp State Park and the historic village area. It also provides good views and spring flowers.

0.0 Park along the main road near the gate to Miwok Meadows. Head through the gate 100 yds. and take the Miwok FT uphill. Spring flowers include iris, suncups, buttercups and blue-eyed grass.

0.6 Junction ❶. Take the Oak Ridge trail left.

0.9 Junction with McNears FT. Head down the road 50', then go right.

1.1 Viewpoint! A grassy hillside overlooking a MMWD water tank provides views south. The view is unusual because Pt. San Pablo in the east bay lies much closer than many familiar Marin landmarks.

1.5 Junction ❷. Cross the McNears FT and take the trail downhill.

2.1 Junction. The trail right goes to Peacock Gap. Continue straight.

2.2 Junction. Take the Shoreline trail right.

2.4 Ranger Station. Continue across the road on the Shoreline trail.

2.7 Junction ❸. Take the Village trail left, which passes through a ravine. Down below, cross N. San Pedro Rd. and continue on the trail. Then take the paved road down to China Camp Village.

3.0 China Camp Village and Museum. During the 1880s, nearly 500 people, Chinese fishermen and their families, lived in this village. Many originally came for the gold rush, then stayed to fish for grass shrimp. At one time, there were three general stores, a boat store and a barber shop here. Part of their story is described in the museum.

To continue the hike, head back up the paved road.

3.2 Junction. Take the signed Rat Rock Cove trail to the right which parallels the main road. If the trail is overgrown, check yourself for ticks on the other side. Stay on the trail until it ends at the road.

3.5 Junction with N. San Pedro Rd. Walk along the side of the road.

3.6 Junction ❹. Head left towards the Ranger Station.

3.7 Junction. Take the signed Shoreline trail right and stay on it to the start. There's lots more evidence of Sudden Oak Death on this trail.

5.5 Junction with Miwok Fire trail and the parking area. No facilities.

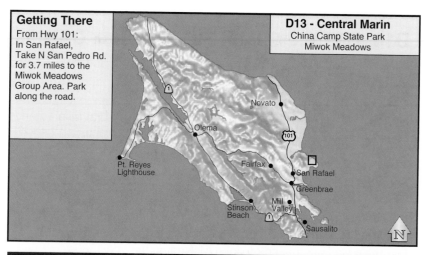

Getting There

From Hwy 101:
In San Rafael,
Take N San Pedro Rd.
for 3.7 miles to the
Miwok Meadows
Group Area. Park
along the road.

D13 - Central Marin
China Camp State Park
Miwok Meadows

Novato

Olema

Pt. Reyes
Lighthouse

Fairfax

San Rafael

Greenbrae

Stinson
Beach

Mill
Valley

Sausalito

N

Peacock Gap
Golf Course

McNears
Drive

Biscayne Drive

Ridge Fire Trail

Shoreline Tr.

2

Oak Ridge Trail

McNears Fire Trail

1

+400'

**China Camp
Historic Area**

3

Miwok Fire Trail

4

Rat Rock
Cove

Bullhead
Flat

Shoreline Trail

Weber Pt.

N San Pedro Rd

Buckeye Pt.

Chicken Coop
Hill

San Francisco Bay

0   .3

Scale 1"= 0.3 miles

N

D14 Bay View Trail - Miwok Fire Trail

Distance: 5.7 miles   Shaded: 70%
Elevation Change: 750'   Heavy bicycle traffic likely weekends.
Rating: Hiking - 9   Difficulty - 6   Steep downhill at mile 4.5.
When to Go: Good anytime. Best early winter mornings.

This pleasant hike circles above the campground and picnic area in China Camp visiting small forested ravines. Good views.

0.0 Park along the road near the Back Ranch Meadows campground. At the kiosk, take the signed Shoreline trail right as it parallels the road into the campground. China Camp and all of San Pedro Mountain was purchased by John McNear in the late 1860s.

0.2 Junction. Take the signed Bay View trail right. This area provides an opportunity to compare madrones and manzanitas. Both have dense, smooth trunks. The madrone, a tree, is larger with big, light-green glossy leaves and orange-brown peeling bark, while the manzanita, a shrub, has smaller leaves and deep red bark. The manzanita has profuse blooms starting in January.

0.4 Junction ❶. Head uphill on the Powerline FT for 50', then take the Bay View trail left to continue the gradual climb.

1.0 Wooden fence and junction ❷. Continue straight for a short detour.

1.1 Junction. The Powerline FT comes up from the right. Take the trail left out to a small knoll with two power towers and views north. When done, retrace your steps. Look for lots of red Indian warrior here and up ahead in March.

1.2 Junction ❷ again. Continue straight.

2.6 Powerline and junction ❸. Take the Back Ranch FT left downhill for 100 yds., then continue on the Bay View trail to the right. This section of the Bay View trail was built in 1995.

Indian Warrior

3.9 Saddle and jct ❹. At a large intersection, take the Ridge FT left.

4.2 Junction. Take the signed Miwok Fire trail left downhill.

4.7 Junction with Shoreline trail. Head north along N. San Pedro Rd. **Option**: To avoid the road and for a longer hike, take the Shoreline trail.

4.8 Junction. Cross the road and take a small trail to Bullet Hill for nice views of the salt marsh and bay. Continue down the other side of the hill.

5.1 Junction. Take the nature trail around Turtle Back Island.

5.7 Back at the parking area. No facilities here.

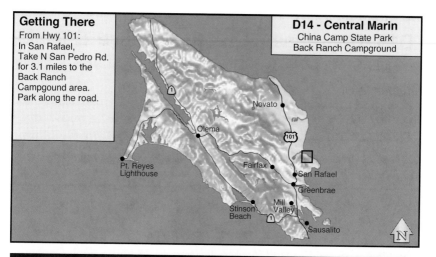

Getting There

From Hwy 101:
In San Rafael,
Take N San Pedro Rd.
for 3.1 miles to the
Back Ranch
Campgound area.
Park along the road.

D14 - Central Marin
China Camp State Park
Back Ranch Campground

Novato

Olema

Pt. Reyes
Lighthouse

Fairfax

San Rafael

Greenbrae

Stinson
Beach

Mill
Valley

Sausalito

Knight
Drive

Ridge Fire Trail

Nike
Missile
Site

Bay View Trail

740' +

+ 1019'

Bay View Trail

McNears FT

China Camp
State Park

Back
Ranch
Fire
Trail

Bay Hills Drive

400'

Miwok Fire Trail

Shoreline Trail

Group
Area

Miwok
Meadows

Shoreline Trail

Back Ranch
Meadows
Campground

Chicken
Coop Hill

Bullet
Hill

Turtle
Back
Island

N San Pedro Road

Duck
Blinds

Duck
Blinds

Jake's
Island

San Francisco Bay

Gallinas Creek

0   .4
Scale 1"= 0.4 miles

D15 Shoreline - Turtle Back Island Trails

Distance: 3.8 miles   Shaded: 50%
Elevation Change: 200'   Part of hike is along the road. Some ruts.
Rating: Hiking - 8   Difficulty - 4   Bicycles likely on weekends.
When to Go: Good anytime. Best early winter and spring mornings.

This mostly level hike explores the northern part of China Camp, including Turtle Back Island. Good wildflowers from February-May.

0.0 Park along the road near the Back Ranch Meadows campground. At the kiosk, take the signed Shoreline trail right as it parallels the road into the campground.

0.2 Junction ❶. The Bay View trail climbs uphill to the right. Continue left. Notice the 10-15' manzanita shrubs along the way. Ahead, the trail crosses the overflow camping area, then enters into an oak-bay canyon. Look for evidence of "Sudden Oak Death" or SOD along here. One of the first major discoveries of this fungal disease was in China Camp, where up to 80% of the oak trees are now infected.

0.6 Bridge. An unofficial trail heads up the canyon. Keep to the left.

0.8 Junction ❷. Continue straight across the broad Back Ranch FT.

1.3 Junction with North San Pedro Rd. Stay on the Shoreline trail.

1.5 Junction. Continue on the new upper trail across the open meadow. Much of the grass in the park is rattlesnake grass, a non-native introduced from Europe.

2.4 Group area and junction ❸. The trail follows a split-rail fence to enter the group picnic area. Continue along the dirt road.

2.7 North San Pedro Rd. Head left to go north along the paved road.

2.8 Bullet Hill. Take the short path to the top of the hill for great views east out to the bay. The hike continues down the other side of the hill.

2.9 Main road again. Continue north along the road. Pickleweed is the primary plant in the salt marsh, which also harbors the rare salt marsh harvest mouse and the clapper rail, a shy, brown 15" henlike bird.

3.1 Turtle Back Island and junction ❹. Take the dirt road through the gate and on around the island. Nature signs describe the area. Up ahead, the trail to Jake's Island is now closed because too many people have been trapped on the island by high tide. Jake was a notorious poacher who built a cabin and lived on the island from the 1920s to the 1940s.

3.8 Back at the parking area. No facilities here.

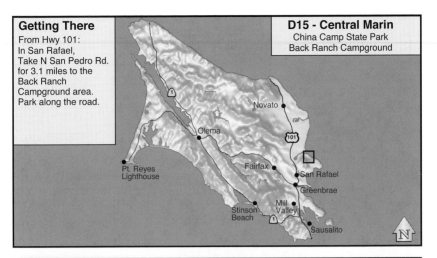

E - North Marin - 14 Hikes

Starting from Terra Linda at 280'
E1   Terra Linda - Sleepy Hollow Ridge Trails 3.3*

Starting from Smith Ranch Road at 10'
E2   McInnis Park - Las Gallinas Wildlife Ponds 3.0

Starting from Marinwood
E3   Blackstone Canyon and Queenstone FR 2.2 and 4.7
E4   Big Rock Ridge - Luiz Fire Roads 4.2

Starting from Pacheco Valle at 120'
E5   Loma Verde - Pacheco Valle Ridge Trails 4.7

Starting from Indian Valley College at 200'
E6   Indian Valley FR - Waterfall Trail 2.6
E7   Schwindt - Wildcat Trails 3.8

Starting from Deer Island at 20'
E8   Deer Island Loop Trail 3.1

Starting from Vineyard Road in Novato at 280'
E9   Deer Camp - Big Trees Trails 7.2

Starting from Stafford Lake County Park at 200'
E10 Stafford Lake County Park 2.0

Starting from Mt. Burdell
E11 Fieldstone - Simmons Trails 2.7
E12 West Flank of Mt. Burdell 4.7
E13 Old Quarry Trail to Mt. Burdell 5.5

Starting from Olompali State Park at 40'
E14 Two Hikes at Olompali State Park 2.7 and 10.3

Notes
* Shuttle Hike
Dogs allowed on all hikes except E10, E14.
To download a hike, go to www.marintrails.com
The password for this region is e4ds2ty

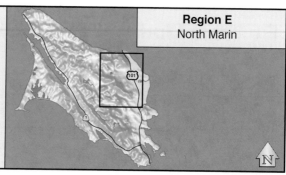

Region E Trailheads

Hikes 1-2 and 4-13 start in Marin County Open Space, phone 415-499-6387.

Hike 3 starts in Marinwood Community Services District, phone 415-479-7751.

Hike 14 starts in Olompali State Park, phone 415-892-3383.

Region E
North Marin

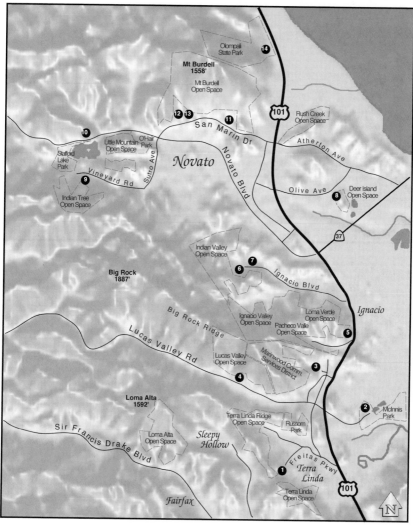

Olompali State Park
14

Mt Burdell 1558'
Mt Burdell Open Space

12 13   11   San Marin Dr
10   101   Rush Creek Open Space

Little Mountain Open Space   O'Hair Park   Atherton Ave
Stafford Lake Park   Sutro Ave   *Novato*

Vineyard Rd   Novato Blvd
9
Indian Tree Open Space   Olive Ave   Deer Island Open Space
                                                                     8
                                                                          37

Big Rock 1887'   Indian Valley Open Space
                            6 7   Ignacio Blvd

Big Rock Ridge   Ignacio Valley Open Space   Loma Verde Open Space   *Ignacio*
Lucas Valley Rd   Pacheco Valle Open Space   5

                            Lucas Valley Open Space   Marinwood Comm. Services District   3
                            4

Loma Alta 1592'
                            Terra Linda Ridge Open Space   Russom Park   2   McInnis Park
Sir Francis Drake Blvd   Loma Alta Open Space   *Sleepy Hollow*

                                               Freitas Pkwy
                            1   *Terra Linda*
                                               101
                            Terra Linda Open Space
Fairfax

E1 Terra Linda - Sleepy Hollow Ridge*

Distance: 3.3 miles   Shaded: 10%
Elevation Change: 700'   Can be muddy. Dogs likely.
Rating: Hiking - 7   Difficulty - 6   Moderately steep in places.
When to Go: Best in winter and early spring before the grasses dry.

This one-way hike follows a U-shaped ridge around Terra Linda and the Santa Margarita Valley. It offers lovely views of surrounding hills.

*Shuttle Hike. Leave pickup cars at the end of Wintergreen Terrace. Shuttle all hikers to the very end of Freitas Parkway. **Option**: The shuttle distance is only 1.1 miles and can easily be walked.

0.0 Go through the open space gate and uphill on the paved path.

0.1 Junction and saddle. Take a sharp right and continue climbing. Good views west to Sleepy Hollow and Loma Alta. During the 1970s, a road was planned here to connect Sleepy Hollow with Terra Linda.

0.2 Plateau. Continue on around to the right and follow the ridge.

0.6 Junction ❶. Take the right road which offers shade and a change in vegetation from grass to trees. Ahead, great views down the valley.

This valley and hills were once part of a 22,000 acre rancho, an 1844 land grant to Timothy Murphy, a 300-pound Irishman. According to historian Jack Mason, Murphy, known as Don Timoteo, was well-liked and was the most legendary figure in early Marin. One day his horse threw him to the ground in front of a brown bear. He had no choice but to wrestle with the bear until both agreed to separate. When he died in 1853, much of his property went to his nephew, John Lucas.

1.4 Junction ❷. Head downhill to the right. **Option**: The Luiz Ranch FR left goes uphill on open space land for about a mile.

1.8 Junction and saddle. Continue downhill to the right.

1.9 Junction ❸. Before reaching the street, head left on the trail.

2.1 Junction. Under a power line, take the trail left uphill.

2.2 Fence and junction. Head right on an unofficial trail, which may be overgrown. The fence is part of a private residence on a narrow strip of land that juts into county open space.

2.8 Junction. A road comes up from the left. Continue straight.

3.2 Junction ❹. At a small saddle, take the signed trail right downhill. **Note**: The ridge ends 200 yds. ahead. All trails off the ridge are steep.

3.3 Back at the shuttle parking area. No facilities.

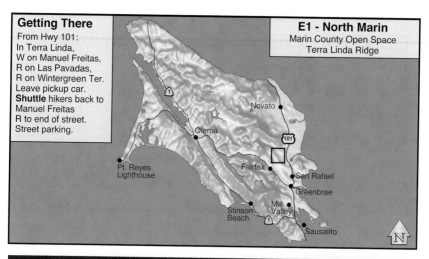

Getting There

From Hwy 101:
In Terra Linda,
W on Manuel Freitas,
R on Las Pavadas,
R on Wintergreen Ter.
Leave pickup car.
Shuttle hikers back to
Manuel Freitas
R to end of street.
Street parking.

E1 - North Marin
Marin County Open Space
Terra Linda Ridge

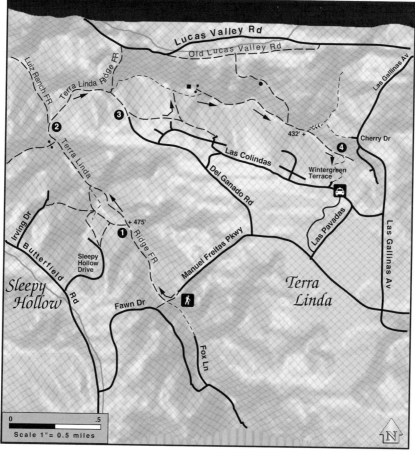

Scale 1" = 0.5 miles

159

E2 McInnis Park - Las Gallinas Ponds

Distance: 3.0 miles   Shaded: 0%
Elevation Change: 120'   Bring binoculars.
Rating: Hiking - 7   Difficulty - 2   Mostly levees.
When to Go: Best on winter mornings for shorebirds.

This hike climbs a small hill in McInnis Park for great views, then skirts wildlife ponds in Las Gallinas Sanitary District. Good birding.

0.0 From the skateboard parking area, take the dirt road southwest and circle above the tennis courts. Continue east on the paved path.

0.1 Junction. As you enter the Nike missile site, take the signed trail right, then stay left and skirt the hillside just above the golf course. At the paved road, go downhill, then left past the treatment plant.

0.2 Junction ❶. Cross the bridge, then head left to circle the inner pond clockwise. This 20 acre freshwater marsh holds treated water on its way to the bay. The small islands have been created to shelter birds. All of the ponds are required during summer months when treated water can not be dumped into the bay.

White Pelicans with St. Vincents Church in the background

0.8 Junction ❷. Head left.

1.4 Power tower, viewpoint and junction ❸. One rare and endangered bird you might see is the California clapper rail, a drab-brown, henlike bird that is found in bay area salt marshes. During twilight in the spring mating season, you can listen for pairs of birds exchanging a rapid clattering call.

1.7 Turnaround point ❹. The gravel road changes to dirt, which can be muddy in winter. You can continue on the road which ends next to the old airbase at Hamilton Field. Eventually, about 1000 acres of the old runway area will be returned to wetlands.

2.8 Junction ❶. Go past the treatment plant and follow the paved road uphill to the missile site, which dates to the 1950s. Hippies occupied the underground storage areas in the 1960s until authorities flooded the holes. Now, the relined storage areas hold fresh water.
Option: You can add 2.5 miles by taking the levee loop, which starts 100 yds. from the bridge. Parts of the levees are overgrown in summer.

3.0 Back at the parking area. Restrooms and water.

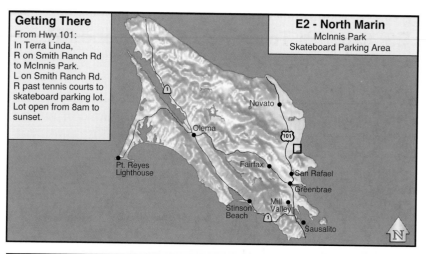

Getting There

From Hwy 101:
In Terra Linda,
R on Smith Ranch Rd
to McInnis Park.
L on Smith Ranch Rd.
R past tennis courts to
skateboard parking lot.
Lot open from 8am to
sunset.

E2 - North Marin
McInnis Park
Skateboard Parking Area

Novato

Olema

Pt. Reyes
Lighthouse

Fairfax

San Rafael

Greenbrae

Mill
Valley

Stinson
Beach

Sausalito

N

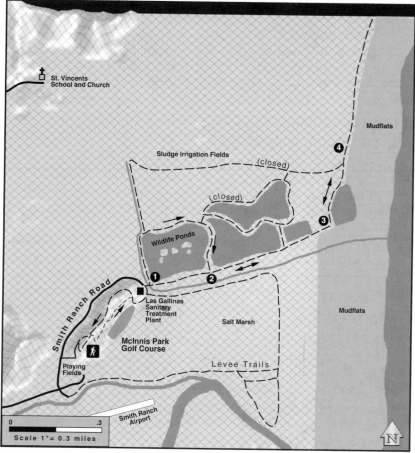

St. Vincents
School and Church

Mudflats

Sludge Irrigation Fields

(closed)

❹

(closed)

❸

Wildlife Ponds

❶

❷

Las Gallinas
Sanitary
Treatment
Plant

Salt Marsh

Mudflats

McInnis Park
Golf Course

Levee Trails

Playing
Fields

Smith Ranch Road

Smith Ranch
Airport

0   .3

Scale 1"= 0.3 miles

N

E3 Canyon Trail and Queenstone FR

Distance: 2.2 and 4.7 miles   Shaded: 80% and 40%
Elevation Change: See below.   Longer hike extremely steep.
Rating: Hiking - 10 and 7   Difficulty - 7 and 10   Rocky in places.
When to Go: Good when cool and clear. Best in spring.

These two hikes start out in small, lovely Blackstone Canyon. The longer hike climbs to a FR on Big Rock Ridge offering great views.

Blackstone Canyon Trail - 2.2 miles and 200' Change

0.0 At the end of the street, follow the trail up the left side of the creek. This delightful narrow canyon is shaded by oaks and bays.

0.9 False junction. A trail goes left 30' into a ravine and ends. Continue on the trail along the main creek. Up ahead, look for several small waterfalls, one of them 8' tall.

1.0 Junction ❶ at a small ravine. Continue uphill 100 yds. to a dam, about 10' wide and 8' high, then return here. **Note**: Be sure to visit the dam to verify the exact location of junction ❶.

1.1 Dam and turnaround point. The trail ends 20 yds. ahead.

1.2 Junction ❶ again. Head back or continue the hike below.

2.2 Back at the start. No facilities.

Queenstone FR and streets - 4.7 miles and 1300' Change

Note: The trail is extremely steep and hard to follow in places.

1.2 Junction ❶, take the small trail right into the ravine. The trail quickly turns right, out of the ravine, and onto a small narrow ridge to begin a long, very steep climb. Watch out for poison oak.

1.5 Plateau and oak tree. The trail levels out briefly at 940'. Ahead, the trail may be difficult to follow. It veers slightly left to pass next to a small rock outcrop, then left a little more to cross below a small mine with tailings. The trail continues climbing, entering a U-shaped ravine, then veers left to the road. If tall grass crowds the trail, check yourself for ticks once you're at the road.

1.7 Junction ❷ with the Queenstone FR. Cross the road and take a short spur trail out onto a ridge to a great viewpoint. (Or go left 100 yds. to the spur trail, depending where you came onto the FR.) When ready, head down the Queenstone FR.

3.7 Junction ❸ and gate. Head down the street and go left on Miller Creek, left on Las Gallinas, left on Blackstone, left on Valleystone.

4.7 Back at the parking area on Valleystone. No facilities.

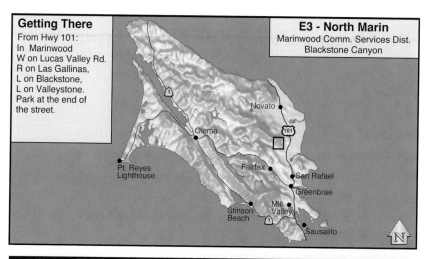

Getting There

From Hwy 101:
In Marinwood
W on Lucas Valley Rd.
R on Las Gallinas,
L on Blackstone,
L on Valleystone.
Park at the end of
the street.

E3 - North Marin
Marinwood Comm. Services Dist.
Blackstone Canyon

Novato

Olema

Pt. Reyes
Lighthouse

Fairfax

San Rafael

Greenbrae

Stinson
Beach

Mill
Valley

Sausalito

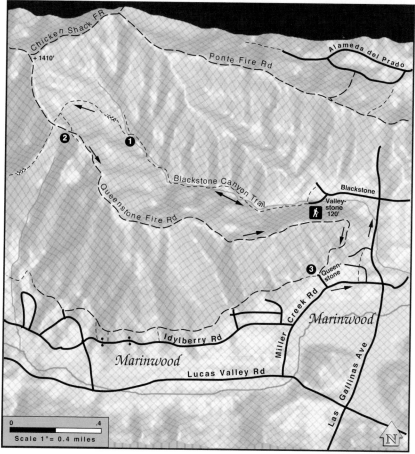

Chicken Shack FR

+ 1410'

Ponte Fire Rd

Alameda del Prado

❷

❶

Blackstone Canyon Trail

Queenstone Fire Rd

Blackstone

Valley-
stone
120'

❸ Queen-
stone

Marinwood

Idylberry Rd

Miller Creek Rd

Marinwood

Lucas Valley Rd

Las Gallinas Ave

0   .4

Scale 1" = 0.4 miles

163

E4 Big Rock Ridge - Luiz Fire Roads

Distance: 4.2 miles   Shaded: 20%
Elevation Change: 1500'   Can be windy. Some poison oak.
Rating: Hiking - 7   Difficulty - 8   Long steep uphill and down.
When to Go: Save for winter and early spring, when cool.

Bring binoculars and climb up the south-facing slope of Big Rock Ridge to a hilltop offering magnificent views in all directions.

0.0 Start at the fire road at the end of Rubicon Dr. One hundred yds. in, at a junction, continue straight to pass through a creek bed.

0.3 Junction ❶. Stay along the creek for a short detour to a small landing where three creeks join together, then return to junction ❶.

0.5 Junction ❶ again. Head left to begin a steep climb to the ridge.

0.9 Falls and ferns. A 10' waterfall carved from bedrock and surrounded by chain ferns creates a pleasant grotto.

1.2 Junction ❷. Take the Big Rock Ridge FR left.

1.6 Junction ❸ with Luiz FR. Continue uphill to a viewpoint.

1.7 Junction. Continue uphill to great views and a gate, which is the turnaround point. **Option 1**: Take the small trail right to the hilltop for some great views. The most prominent landmark north is Mt. Burdell with Novato at its base. To the south, Loma Alta rises above Lucas Valley Rd. Big Rock Ridge gets its name from a large 30' boulder located at the upper end of Lucas Valley next to Lucas Valley Rd. It can just be seen from here. The highest point on Big Rock Ridge, the second tallest mountain in Marin, is its antenna-covered peak at 1895'. **Option 2**: Continue on the Big Rock Ridge FR past the gate to the top. The FR passes over an easement on private land.

2.0 Junction ❸ again. Take the Luiz FR road right for a long descent.

3.6 Junction ❹. Cross the street. Take the footpath along the creek.

3.9 Bridge and street. Go left on Bridgegate Drive.

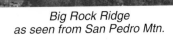

Big Rock Ridge
as seen from San Pedro Mtn.

4.1 Junction. Just opposite Golden Iris Terrace, take the fire road right down past the gate.

4.2 Back at the parking area on Rubicon Drive. No facilities.

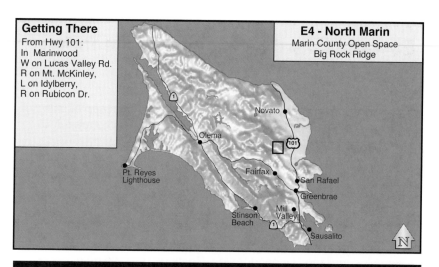

Getting There

From Hwy 101:
In Marinwood
W on Lucas Valley Rd.
R on Mt. McKinley,
L on Idylberry,
R on Rubicon Dr.

E4 - North Marin
Marin County Open Space
Big Rock Ridge

Novato

Olema

Pt. Reyes
Lighthouse

Fairfax

San Rafael

Greenbrae

Stinson
Beach

Mill
Valley

Sausalito

N

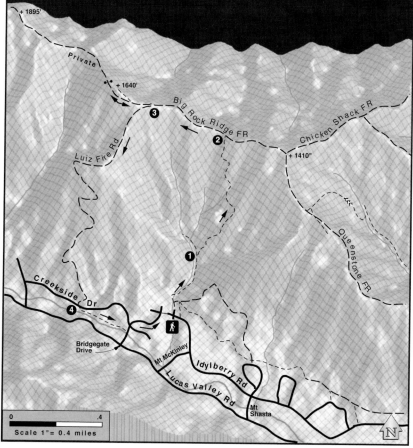

+ 1895'

Private

+ 1640'

3

Big Rock Ridge FR

2

Chicken Shack FR

Luiz Fire Rd

+ 1410"

1

Queenstone FR

Creekside Dr

4

Bridgegate
Drive

Mt McKinley

Idylberry Rd

Lucas Valley Rd

Mt
Shasta

0		.4

Scale 1" = 0.4 miles

N

E5 Loma Verde - Pacheco Valle Ridge

Distance: 4.7 miles   Shaded: 50%
Elevation Change: 1400'   Steep in places. Very steep at mile 3.8.
Rating: Hiking - 7   Difficulty - 9   Part of hike on streets.
When to Go: Good when cool. Best when clear.

This hike climbs a ridge to circle above Pacheco Valle. It offers oak woodland hills and great views north, south and east.

0.0 Park along Clay Ct. or in the Park and Ride lot across the street. Go through the open space gate and head uphill on the paved road.

0.3 Tennis court and gate. The tennis court sits atop a water reservoir supplying Pacheco Valley. Continue past the gate.

0.9 Junction. Take the small unofficial trail right to a hilltop with good views east to Hamilton Field and across the bay. From World War II to the early 1970s, the Air Force operated Hamilton Field and often, you could see bomber and fighter planes taking off and landing.

The area directly below is part of the original 6,600 acre historic Pacheco Ranch granted to Ignacio Pacheco in 1840. The ranch is still owned by descendants of the Pacheco family. About a half-mile north of the trailhead on Alameda del Prado, you can see a white Victorian house built by Ignacio's son in 1881. Continue on the unofficial trail.

1.0 Double junction ❶. Go left on the Via Escondido FR, then right on the Chicken Shack FR. **Option**: Take the unofficial trail, which parallels the Chicken Shack FR. It offers good views north.

1.5 Junction with Little Cat FR. Continue straight uphill.

2.3 Viewpoint. A clearing offers views north to Big Rock Ridge.

2.7 Junction ❷ and viewpoint. Continue 50' past the Ponte FR to a rock and resting point with views of Big Rock Ridge. When ready, head down the Ponte FR. **Option**: Take the unofficial trail which parallels the Ponte FR. It is more difficult, but has better views, especially to the south.

3.7 Junction. The FR left goes down to the street. Continue straight, slightly uphill. **Option**: Go left here for a much easier route.

3.8 Junction. The road ahead is very steep! Take the bypass trail (also very steep) right downhill, then continue straight across a road.

4.2 Junction ❸ and water tank. Head left down the trail to the street.

4.4 Junction with the street. Head right to Alameda del Prado. Ahead, cross the divided street to pick up a paved trail on the other side.

4.7 Back at the parking area. No facilities.

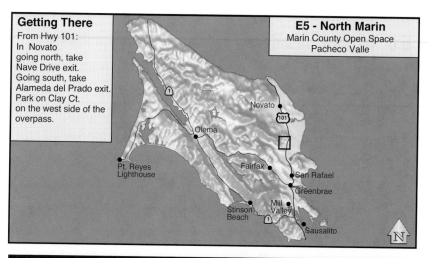

Getting There

From Hwy 101:
In Novato
going north, take
Nave Drive exit.
Going south, take
Alameda del Prado exit.
Park on Clay Ct.
on the west side of the
overpass.

E5 - North Marin
Marin County Open Space
Pacheco Valle

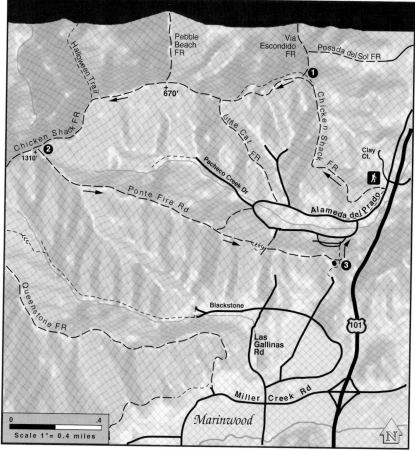

E6 Indian Valley FR - Waterfall Trail

Distance: 2.6 miles   Shaded: 70%
Elevation Change: 200'
Rating: Hiking - 7   Difficulty - 6   Some rocky sections.
When to Go: Good winter and spring. Best in March for flowers.

This is a pleasant hike that explores north-facing slopes near Indian Valley College. It offers oak-bay woods and spring wildflowers.

0.0 From the parking area, head west on the street toward the turnaround circle, then right past the IVC corporation yard. Up in the large meadow, continue straight on the Indian Valley FR.

0.5 Bridge and junction ❶. Take the Waterfall trail left across the bridge into oak-bay woodland and up the right side of the creek. This hike follows the largest trail, which winds up the ravine crossing the creek several times. March wildflowers include milkmaids, shooting star, mission bells and buttercups. Iris in the ravine bloom in April.

0.7 Waterfall and junction. A 15' seasonal waterfall provides a refreshing sight during heavy runoff. Continue straight up the canyon.

1.5 Junction ❷. The Burgi trail heads left up to a knoll and an unofficial trail heads right up to private property on Big Rock Ridge. Continue straight and head downhill into a canyon. Good views.

Waterfall Trail

2.1 Pacheco Pond and junction. Head right to skirt the reservoir, which was built for the Pacheco ranch in 1948. This valley was a land grant to Ignacio Pacheco, a sergeant in the Mexican army, in 1840.

2.2 Junction. At the far right corner of the reservoir, the unofficial High Meadow trail heads uphill to the right. Continue straight, downhill, where the trail joins the Pacheco Pond FR. **Option**: For a longer and more strenuous hike, take the High Meadow trail steeply uphill to the Montura FR. Then go left 0.1 mile and take the FR steeply down to IVC. This option adds a half-mile and 400' to the hike and offers excellent views out to the bay.

2.5 Ball fields. Take the trail right to pass next to the ball field.

2.6 Back at the parking area. Restrooms near the ball field.

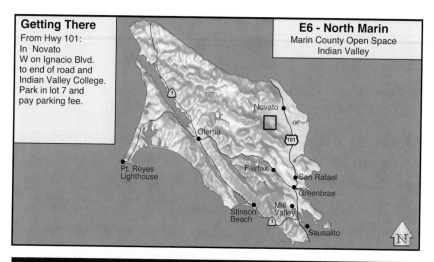

Getting There

From Hwy 101:
In Novato
W on Ignacio Blvd.
to end of road and
Indian Valley College.
Park in lot 7 and
pay parking fee.

E6 - North Marin
Marin County Open Space
Indian Valley

Novato

Olema

Pt. Reyes
Lighthouse

Fairfax

San Rafael

Greenbrae

Stinson
Beach

Mill
Valley

Sausalito

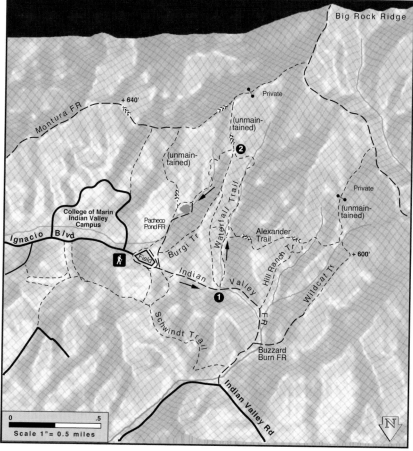

Big Rock Ridge

Montura FR

+ 640'

Private

(unmain-
tained)

(unmain-
tained)

2

Private

(unmain-
tained)

College of Marin
Indian Valley
Campus

Pacheco
Pond FR

Burgi Tr

Waterfall Trail

Alexander
Trail

Ignacio Blvd

Field

Indian

Valley

Hill Ranch Tr

Wildcat Tr

+ 600'

1

Schwindt Trail

FR

Buzzard
Burn FR

Indian Valley Rd

0   .5

Scale 1" = 0.5 miles

E7 Schwindt - Wildcat Trails

Distance: 3.8 miles   Shaded: 70%
Elevation Change: 550'   Horseback riders likely.
Rating: Hiking - 8   Difficulty - 7   Can be boggy.
When to Go: Good in fall and winter. Best in early spring for flowers.

This woodsy hike tours the oak-bay hills around Indian Valley College and open space areas. Many unofficial trails for exploring.

0.0 After entering Indian Valley College, take the 2nd left to park in lot #2. From the parking lot, cross Ignacio Blvd, head left on the sidewalk 70 yds. and then take the trail right into the parcourse. **Note**: If the low area before junction ❶ is too wet, take the trail right under the trees to the upper end of the small valley and loop back around.

0.2 Junction ❶. Go left up through the beautiful rolling hills. Up ahead, the trail joins an old road and continues west. Look for a large, stately oak tree that is missing a major branch.

0.4 Saddle. Good views southwest to Big Rock Ridge. Head downhill, and at each Y bear right towards the open space gate.

0.6 Open space gate. Take the Ad and Gloria Schwindt trail, which makes a moderately steep descent through a grove of bay trees.

0.8 Junction. The road right leads to stables. Bear left.

1.1 Junction. The trail joins a gravel road. Head left on the road.

1.2 Junction ❷. Take the Buzzard Burn FR right down into a creek bed, then steeply up a ridge. Ahead, notice the large manzanita shrubs struggling for sun under the taller oaks. Many are dying out.

1.5 Hilltop. The trail crests a small hill, where you can go left 100' to get a view out to the bay.

1.9 Junction ❸. The Wildcat trail ends here. Take the Hill Ranch trail left. Ahead, at a wood fence and the next junction, bear left again.

2.1 Junction ❹ with the signed Alexander trail, which climbs steeply uphill to the right. Continue downhill. **Option**: You can lengthen the hike by taking the Alexander trail to the Waterfall trail. This optional route has one very steep up and down section.

2.9 Bridge and junction ❺. Head right on the Indian Valley FR.

3.3 Open space gate and junction. Continue straight.

3.5 IVC campus. Go past the circle and take the path along side the creek. **Option**: Tour the IVC campus.

3.8 Back at the parking area with no facilities.

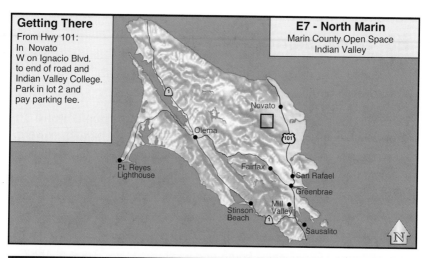

Getting There

From Hwy 101:
In Novato
W on Ignacio Blvd.
to end of road and
Indian Valley College.
Park in lot 2 and
pay parking fee.

E7 - North Marin
Marin County Open Space
Indian Valley

Novato

Olema

Pt. Reyes
Lighthouse

Fairfax

San Rafael

Greenbrae

Stinson
Beach

Mill
Valley

Sausalito

N

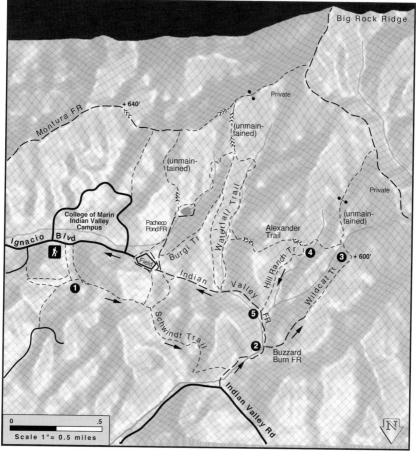

Big Rock Ridge

Private

Montura FR + 640'

(unmaintained)

(unmaintained)

(unmaintained)

Private

College of Marin
Indian Valley
Campus

Ignacio Blvd

Pacheco
Pond FR

Burgi Tr.

Waterfall Trail

Alexander
Trail

(unmaintained)

+ 600'

Field

Indian   Valley   FR

Hill Ranch Tr.

Wildcat Tr.

❶

❹

❸

❺

Schwindt Trail

❷

Buzzard
Burn FR

Indian Valley Rd

0   .5
Scale 1" = 0.5 miles

N

171

E8 Deer Island Loop Trail

Distance: 3.1 miles   Shaded: 60%
Elevation Change: 250'
Rating: Hiking - 7   Difficulty - 6   Moderately steep downhill.
When to Go: Good in winter for birds and spring for flowers.

A two-loop hike to explore 135 acre Deer Island lying in a floodplain east of Novato. Good views. Good flowers in rainy years.

0.0 Park in the small parking area and go through the open space gate. Take the trail right for 30', then go left uphill. The De Borba trail starts out in open grassland with oaks dotting the low-lying hillside.

0.3 Ridgetop. Good views south and west. Big Rock Ridge at 1887' dominates the southwestern skyline.

0.6 Knoll and junction ❶. A short, overgrown spur trail goes right. Take the main trail left downhill. The descent is moderately steep.

0.8 Junction ❷. Keep right at a Y and follow the Deer Island Loop trail to the right. The large pond on the left stores treated effluent from the Novato Sanitary treatment plant and is used to irrigate pasture lands. The smaller pond was created to support wildlife.

1.1 Viewpoint ❸. The view west of ponds, wetlands, creeks and shopping center represents a microcosm of the history of the bay. Deer Island was once a real island until the gold rush struck the Sierra and hydraulic mining washed million of tons of sediment into the bay, much of it deposited in the quieter areas of San Pablo Bay.

These shallow waters became mudflats and tidal marshes until 1890 when the railroad built a levee east of here. More dikes and fill turned some of the land into pasture, some into wetland. In 1990, more fill was added to create the Vintage Oaks shopping center due west.

2.0 Ranger residence and parking lot. The hike continues past the parking area to make another loop that explores the eastern side of the island. Up ahead, the trail enters a small forest of dense, skinny bay trees. Watch out for poison oak crowding the trail.

2.6 Junction ❹. An overgrown trail heads left and joins a road to the preserve boundary and private property. Continue straight. Look for some good displays of flowers here in spring, especially blue-eyed grass, buttercups and an unusually deep-purple vetch.

2.7 Junction ❷ again. Head right to climb to the hilltop and backtrack on the De Borba trail.

3.1 Back at the parking area. No facilities.

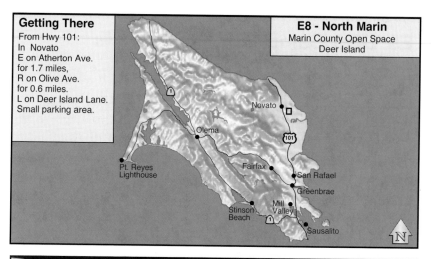

Getting There

From Hwy 101:
In Novato
E on Atherton Ave.
for 1.7 miles,
R on Olive Ave.
for 0.6 miles.
L on Deer Island Lane.
Small parking area.

E8 - North Marin
Marin County Open Space
Deer Island

Novato

Olema

Pt. Reyes
Lighthouse

Fairfax

San Rafael

Greenbrae

Stinson
Beach

Mill
Valley

Sausalito

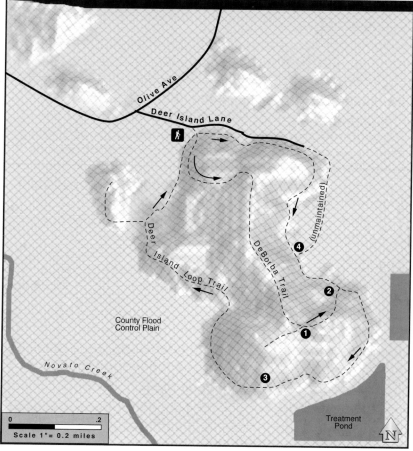

Olive Ave

Deer Island Lane

Deer Island Loop Trail

DeBorba Trail

(unmaintained)

County Flood
Control Plain

Novato Creek

❶

❷

❸

❹

Treatment
Pond

Scale 1"= 0.2 miles

0   .2

E9 Deer Camp - Big Trees Trails

Distance: 7.2 miles   Shaded: 80%
Elevation Change: 1300'   Some ruts. Can be muddy or dusty.
Rating: Hiking - 8   Difficulty - 5   Horses likely.
When to Go: Good anytime, best when not too wet or dry.

This hike climbs to one of the highest points in North Marin. It offers several groves of redwoods, great views and good spring flowers.

0.0 Park at the top of the hill just beyond the last house on Vineyard Rd. Head past the open space sign into grassland.

0.1 Junction ❶ and gate. Go through the cow gate and take the Upper Meadow trail to the right. Continue on this trail as it skirts the hillside above the stables and enters a canyon shaded by redwoods. **Note**: When the hillside is wet, this trail and the Deer Camp trail ahead can be muddy. If so, it may be best to stay on the Big Trees trail.

0.7 Junction ❷. Take the Deer Camp trail (a FR here) left. At the top of the canyon, bear left to follow the signed Deer Camp trail uphill.

2.1 Junction. Take the Big Trees trail right uphill.

2.5 Junction ❸ with Ship's Mast trail. Stay on the Big Trees trail.

2.9 Double junction ❹. It's well worth exploring the surrounding area. Take the road right and head west uphill into a grove of redwoods.

3.0 Fence and gate. The open space ends at the fence. Backtrack 100' and take the narrow trail right onto a hilltop offering good views south to Mt. Tam. When ready, backtrack to junction ❹.

3.1 Double junction ❹ again. Continue to the Y in the road and head right to another viewpoint and a grove of redwoods.

3.2 Redwood grove. The largest tree in this grove is called Indian Tree, Big Tree or Ship's Mast. Years ago, the tree had a narrow hollow on the south side. One story told about an Indian living there, hence the name. As the tree has grown, the entrance has closed. The tree used to be a Novato landmark, but surrounding trees have grown and diminished its prominence.

When ready, backtrack down to the Y in the road and head right on Indian Tree FR, which follows a fenceline down the ridge.

3.9 Junction ❺. Take the Ship's Mast trail left.

4.8 Junction ❸ again. Go right on the Big Trees trail.

5.2 Junction with Deer Camp trail. Stay right on the Big Trees trail.

7.2 Back at the parking area with no facilities.

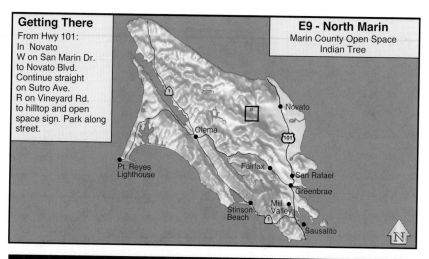

Getting There

From Hwy 101:
In Novato
W on San Marin Dr.
to Novato Blvd.
Continue straight
on Sutro Ave.
R on Vineyard Rd.
to hilltop and open
space sign. Park along
street.

E9 - North Marin
Marin County Open Space
Indian Tree

Novato

101

Olema

Pt. Reyes
Lighthouse

Fairfax

San Rafael

Greenbrae

Stinson
Beach

Mill
Valley

Sausalito

N

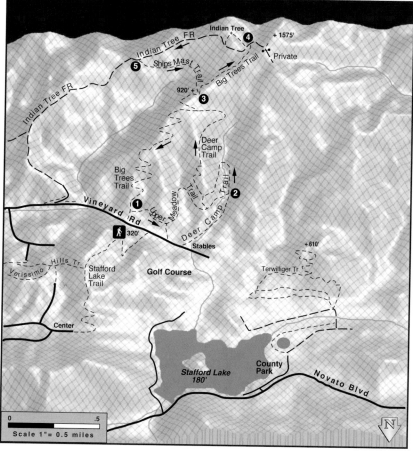

Indian Tree FR

Indian Tree

4

+ 1575'

Private

Ships Mast Trail

5

Big Trees Trail

Indian Tree FR

920' +

3

Deer
Camp
Trail

Big
Trees
Trail

Trail

Deer Camp Trail

1

2

Upper Meadow Trail

Vineyard Rd

320'

Stables

+ 610'

Verissimo Hills Tr.

Stafford
Lake
Trail

Golf Course

Terwilliger Tr.

Center

Stafford Lake
180'

County
Park

Novato Blvd

0   .5
Scale 1" = 0.5 miles

N

E10 Stafford Lake County Park

Distance: 2.0 miles   Shaded: 30%
Elevation Change: 400'   Some poison oak crowds the trail.
Rating: Hiking - 7   Difficulty - 6   Can be overgrown (See Note).
When to Go: Best in March and April for flowers and green hills.

Stafford Lake is a good place for a group or family hike followed by a picnic. The hike offers scenic views of the lake and local hills.

Note: At times, the trail will be overgrown with grasses. We have described an alternate start that is usually easier to follow.

0.0 When you enter the park, ask for the nature trail handout at the toll booth, then head right. The hike begins at the far end of the parking area. Follow the sign that directs you towards the frisbee course on the dirt road instead of the trail.

0.3 Picnic area, bridge and marsh. Just past a small picnic area, go left across a bridge. Continue on the road instead of following the trail marked to the right. After 100 yds., cross another bridge. The frisbee course is straight ahead, but head right towards the corner of the field.

The hike crosses a marshy section of Novato Creek. Water from this creek is stored in Stafford Lake. In the 1950s, it was the primary water source for Novato with enough water to supply about 15,000 people a year. Now, a much larger Novato also requires Russian River water.

0.4 Junction ❶. Just before a gate, head left up the Terwilliger trail.

0.6 Junction ❷. At the Loop Trail sign (lower loop), go to the right.

0.8 Junction ❸ and stairs. Go right on the upper loop trail.

0.9 Hilltop, bench and viewpoint. The tallest peak to the west is Black Mountain, which lies just east of Point Reyes Station. If it's not too overgrown, continue heading east along the fence on the upper loop.

1.0 Junction ❸ again. Continue downhill.

1.4 Junction ❷ again. Go left to retrace your steps. **Option**: Continue straight on the loop trail, which is often overgrown and hard to follow. The trail stays along a contour at about 400' for 0.2 miles, then drops into the frisbee course, where the object of the game is to toss a frisbee into the hole (a chain metal dish). The trail may be hard to follow as other trails from the frisbee course intersect the hiking trail. Also, if the frisbee course is being used, watch out for flying disks.

1.6 Junction ❶ again. Go right on the road.

2.0 Back at the parking area with full picnic facilities.

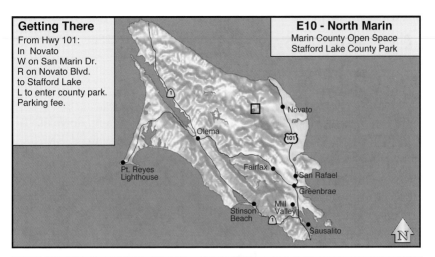

Getting There

From Hwy 101:
In Novato
W on San Marin Dr.
R on Novato Blvd.
to Stafford Lake
L to enter county park.
Parking fee.

E10 - North Marin
Marin County Open Space
Stafford Lake County Park

Novato

Olema

Pt. Reyes
Lighthouse

Fairfax

San Rafael

Greenbrae

Mill
Valley

Stinson
Beach

Sausalito

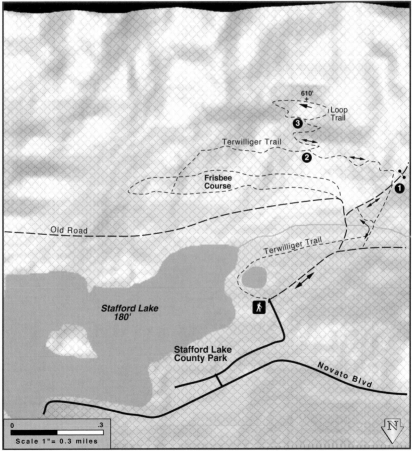

610'
±

Loop
Trail

Terwilliger Trail

**Frisbee
Course**

Old Road

Terwilliger Trail

*Stafford Lake
180'*

**Stafford Lake
County Park**

Novato Blvd

0   .3

Scale 1"= 0.3 miles

E11 Fieldstone - Simmons Trails

Distance: 2.7 miles   Shaded: 40%
Elevation Change: 600'   Can be overgrown in places.
Rating: Hiking - 7   Difficulty - 6   Moderately steep downhill.
When to Go: Good in late fall and winter, best in spring.
This hike climbs the south flank of Mt. Burdell into a fieldstone quarry.
It offers great oaks, good views south and spring flowers.

0.0 Park at the end of Simmons Lane and go through the open space gate. Head right on the road, which starts out level. In April, look for blue dicks and purple vetch on the grassy hills.

0.2 Gate and street. Take Butterfield Drive for 100 yds., then go left on Fieldstone Drive.

0.3 Junction ❶. Go through the open space gate and head uphill on the signed Fieldstone trail. Up ahead, the trail crosses a small wooden bridge, then zig-zags up the hill.

0.9 Junction. Although the trail right to the rock slide looks inviting, continue on the main trail. It offers a more interesting hike through the quarry. Up ahead, mosses, shrubs and oaks are slowly transforming the mining scars into a rock garden.

1.2 Junction ❷. Take the road left.

1.3 Junction. Go through the gate and continue straight on the Middle Burdell FR. Five of California's nine species of tree oaks are found on Mt. Burdell. These include the coast live, valley, black, blue, and garry (or Oregon) oak. Coast live oak is the only evergreen oak on the list and dominates the rolling hills of Mt. Burdell. This abundance of oak trees

Coast live oak on Mt. Burdell

is one reason the Miwoks thrived at Olompali on the north side of the mountain. One large oak can provide hundreds of pounds of acorns.

1.7 Junction ❸. Take the San Carlos FR left, down through the gate.

2.0 Junction. Take the Salt Lick FR left. Ahead, good views south.

2.2 Junction ❹. Take the San Marin FR right, which heads downhill.

2.5 Junction. Take the signed Simmons trail left down through the gate.

2.7 Back at the parking area. No facilities.

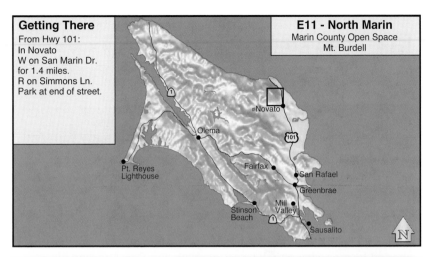

Getting There

From Hwy 101:
In Novato
W on San Marin Dr.
for 1.4 miles.
R on Simmons Ln.
Park at end of street.

E11 - North Marin
Marin County Open Space
Mt. Burdell

Pt. Reyes
Lighthouse

Olema

Novato

Fairfax

San Rafael

Greenbrae

Stinson
Beach

Mill
Valley

Sausalito

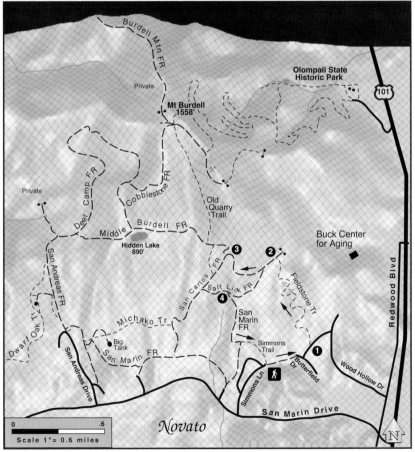

Burdell Mtn FR

Private

Olompali State
Historic Park

101

Mt Burdell
1558'

Deer Camp FR

Private

Cobblestone FR

Old
Quarry
Trail

Middle Burdell FR

Hidden Lake
890'

Buck Center
for Aging

San Andreas FR

San Carlos FR

Salt Lick FR

3

2

4

Fieldstone Tr

Dwarf Oak Tr

Michako Tr

San Marin
FR

San Andreas Drive

Big
Tank

San Marin FR

Simmons
Trail

1

Butterfield Dr

Wood Hollow Dr

Redwood Blvd

Simmons Ln

San Marin Drive

Novato

0   .6
Scale 1"= 0.6 miles

N

E12 West Flank of Mt. Burdell

Distance: 4.7 miles   Shaded: 20%
Elevation Change: 800'   Bicycles possible.
Rating: Hiking - 7   Difficulty - 5   Rocky in places.
When to Go: Best when the hills are vibrant green, usually early April.

This hike explores the west flank of Mt. Burdell. It offers fine specimens of oak and buckeye trees. Good views south and west.

0.0 Park near the end of San Andreas Drive. Go through the open space gate and take the road uphill.

0.1 Junction. Take the trail left through the fence gate. The trail, shaded by magnificent oak trees, parallels the San Andreas FR.

0.2 Junction. Take the road left towards a water tank.

0.3 Junction and water tank. Continue past the junction and take the small trail to the left of the water tank.

0.4 Lookout point and junction ❶. An open area provides good views down to Novato. Make a sharp right to take the Dwarf Oak trail back past the other side of the water tank. Watch for poison oak.

0.6 Cowgate and junction. Take the San Andreas FR left, to the north.

0.8 Junction. Continue straight on the Middle Burdell FR.

0.9 Junction ❷. Take the signed Deer Camp FR left. Up ahead, look for grand old buckeye trees with gnarled, twisted trunks.

1.8 Slopes of Mt. Burdell. The smooth, grassy slopes of Mt. Burdell rise above the trail, providing a peaceful calm. Mt. Burdell was named after Dr. Galen Burdell, San Francisco's first dentist, who arrived during the gold rush in 1849. Later, he married Mary Black and the couple received Olompali ranch, 800 cattle and Mt. Burdell as a wedding present from the Black family. Parts of the Burdell adobe mansion can be seen at Olompali. See Hike E14.

2.5 Junction ❸. This is the highest point of the hike at 1080'. Head right downhill on the rocky Cobblestone trail.

2.8 Junction and Hidden Lake. At one time, locals used to come here to swim in the lake. Now, it has become a marsh. Head left.

3.3 Junction ❹. Take the Old Quarry trail right downhill.

3.5 Junction. Take the San Carlos FR right.

3.9 Junction. Take the Michako trail right and continue west on the trail, crossing the Big Tank FR and then joining the San Marin FR.

4.7 Back at the parking area. No facilities.

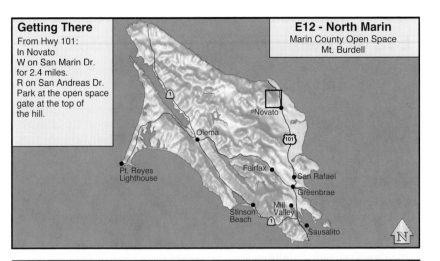

Getting There

From Hwy 101:
In Novato
W on San Marin Dr.
for 2.4 miles.
R on San Andreas Dr.
Park at the open space
gate at the top of
the hill.

E12 - North Marin
Marin County Open Space
Mt. Burdell

Pt. Reyes
Lighthouse

Olema

Novato

Fairfax

San Rafael

Greenbrae

Stinson
Beach

Mill
Valley

Sausalito

N

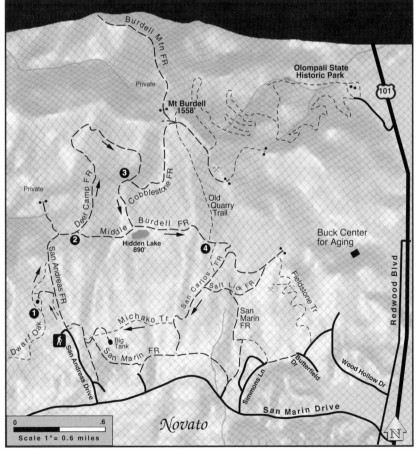

Burdell Mtn FR

Private

**Olompali State
Historic Park**

101

**Mt Burdell
1558'**

Private

3

Deer Camp FR

Cobblestone FR

Old
Quarry
Trail

Buck Center
for Aging

2

Middle   **Burdell   FR**

Hidden Lake
890'

4

San Carlos FR

Salt Lick FR

Fieldstone Tr

San Andreas FR

Michako Tr

San
Marin
FR

Redwood Blvd

1

Dwarf Oak

Big
Tank

San Marin   FR

Butterfield Dr

Wood Hollow Dr

San Andreas Drive

Simmons Ln

Novato

San Marin Drive

0   .6

Scale 1"= 0.6 miles

N

E13 Old Quarry Trail to Mt. Burdell

Distance: 5.5 miles   Shaded: 10%
Elevation Change: 1400'   Bicycles possible. Overgrown in places.
Rating: Hiking - 8   Difficulty - 8   Steep and rocky in places.
When to Go: In spring when the hills are green. Dusty in fall.

This is the best hike for exploring Mt. Burdell. It offers magnificent oak trees, good wildflowers, great views and a visit to a rock quarry.

0.0 Park near the end of San Andreas Drive. Go through the open space gate and take the trail right, which starts out level and soon joins the San Marin FR. Ahead, a trail parallels the road, which can be muddy when wet. In spring, look for a display of blue dicks.

0.4 Junction. Take the signed Michako trail left. Good views south.

0.9 Junction ❶. Take the San Carlos FR left. Notice the large oaks. Mt. Burdell has the best examples of oak savannah in Marin.

1.3 Junction. Take the signed Old Quarry trail left towards the gate.

1.5 Junction ❷. Take the road left 100' and then continue uphill on the Old Quarry trail, which climbs steeply into a large ravine.

2.4 Junction ❸. Head right on the Burdell Mountain FR. to explore the mountain top and enjoy some well-earned views.

2.6 Junction ❹ with dirt road. Continue on the Burdell Mountain FR.

2.7 Quarry, view and turnaround point. A small lookout point offers great views south and west. Opposite the viewpoint, a short, narrow spur trail leads 100' into a quarry, where cobblestones were mined to pave the streets of San Francisco in the 1870s. Return to junction ❹.

2.8 Junction ❹ again. Take the dirt road right 200 yds. up past a rock wall and the Olompali State Park boundary. This hilltop offers good views east to the Petaluma River, the bay and Mt. Diablo.

3.0 Junction ❸ again. Head right uphill on the trail. The rock walls were built in the 1870s by Chinese laborers who came here after completing work on the transcontinental railroad.

3.1 Mt. Burdell at 1558'. This is the highest point in north Marin and offers great views north. You can see Mt. St. Helena in the distance.

3.2 Junction ❸ again. Take the rocky Cobblestone FR downhill.

4.3 Junction and Hidden Lake. Head right on the Middle Burdell FR.

4.9 Junction ❺. Take the San Andreas FR left.

5.5 Back at the parking area. No facilities.

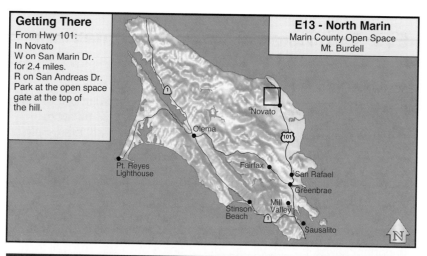

Getting There

From Hwy 101:
In Novato
W on San Marin Dr.
for 2.4 miles.
R on San Andreas Dr.
Park at the open space
gate at the top of
the hill.

E13 - North Marin
Marin County Open Space
Mt. Burdell

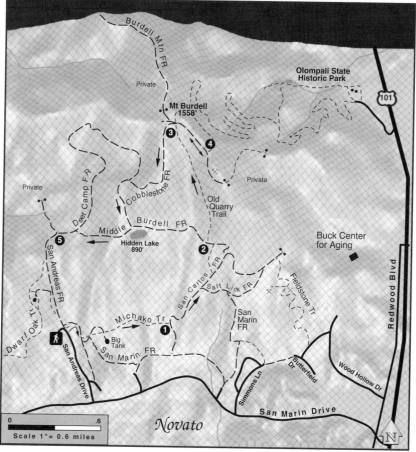

E14 Two Hikes at Olompali State Park

Distance: 2.7 and 10.3 miles   Shaded: 70% and 80%
Elevation Change: See below.   Grass crowds trail in places.
Rating: Hiking - 9 and 7   Difficulty - 6 and 7   Some rocks.
When to Go: Best in early March for wildflowers. Open 10am-6pm.

These 2 hikes on the north slopes of Mt. Burdell offer great views, spectacular wildflowers and a glimpse of early California history.

Lower Loop Trail - 2.7 miles and 700' Change

0.0 From the parking area, go north towards the buildings. A signpost offers historical information describing Olompali, which was an important Miwok trading village for hundreds of years. The trail then passes by the remains of the Burdell mansion, which is enclosed in a structure to protect its adobe walls. The hike starts on a dirt road just north of the buildings and heads west towards the barns.

0.3 Junction ❶. A sign marks the start of the Loop trail. Continue straight up the oak-bay covered hills. Ahead, the hike crosses a creek, then climbs past a small Miwok village, which is being reconstructed by volunteers and local Miwok descendants.

0.6 Fence and pond. Continue up the ravine.

0.7 Junction. The road right deadends. Go left.

1.2 Junction ❷. Continue straight on the Loop trail or go right to climb Mt. Burdell as described below. Good spring flowers ahead.

2.7 Back at the parking lot. Picnic area and restrooms available.

Upper Mt. Burdell Trail - 10.3 total miles and 1500' Change

1.2 Bench and junction ❷. Go right to begin a long, gradual climb.

4.6 Rock wall and junction ❸. After passing through a rock wall built by Chinese workers, head left on the Burdell Mtn. FR.

4.7 Rock quarry and view site. Opposite a splendid viewpoint, a short spur trail enters a quarry, where cobblestones were mined in the 1870s. Now, retrace your steps, back on the Burdell Mtn. FR.

5.0 Junction with Cobblestone FR. Take the unofficial trail right uphill.

5.1 Mt. Burdell at 1558' and good views to the north. When ready, retrace your steps back to junction ❸.

5.4 Junction ❸ again. Head back down the trail for a long descent.

8.8 Junction ❷. Take the Loop trail right. Good spring flowers ahead. The trail may be overgrown with grasses in places.

10.3 Back at the parking lot. Picnic area and restrooms available.

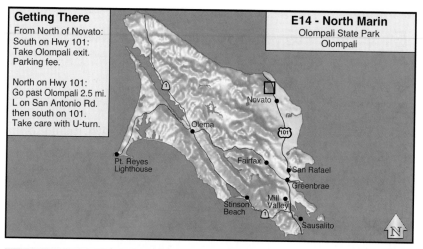

Getting There

From North of Novato:
South on Hwy 101:
Take Olompali exit.
Parking fee.

North on Hwy 101:
Go past Olompali 2.5 mi.
L on San Antonio Rd.
then south on 101.
Take care with U-turn.

Novato

101

Olema

Pt. Reyes
Lighthouse

Fairfax

San Rafael

Greenbrae

Stinson
Beach

Mill
Valley

Sausalito

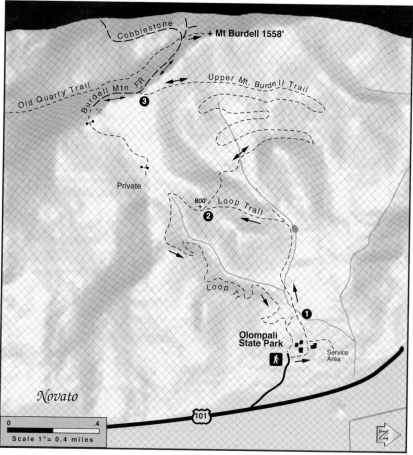

Cobblestone

+ Mt Burdell 1558'

Old Quarry Trail

Burdell Mtn FR

Upper Mt. Burdell Trail

3

Private

800'
+

Loop Trail

2

Loop Tr.

1

Olompali
State Park

Service
Area

Novato

0   .4
Scale 1"= 0.4 miles

101

F - Point Reyes South - 18 Hikes

Starting from Bear Valley at 105'
F1   Bear Valley Interpretive Trails 0.6, 0.7 and 0.8
F2   Bear Valley - Meadow - Horse Trails 6.1
F3   Bear Valley - Old Pine - Mt. Wittenberg Trails 7.3
F4   Bear Valley Trail to Arch Rock 8.4
F5   Bear Valley - Mt. Wittenberg - Sky Trails 10.9
F6   Bear Valley - Glen Camp Loop - Coast Trails 11.2
F7   Bear Valley - Sky - Woodward Valley - Coast 13.0

Starting from Five Brooks at 240'
F8   Five Brooks Trailhead to Bear Valley 4.4*
F9   Olema Valley - Bolema - Stewart Trails 6.3
F10 Stewart - Greenpicker Trails 7.5
F11 Greenpicker - Glen - Coast - Stewart Trails 12.0

Starting from along Highway 1 in Olema Valley
F12 Randall - Olema Valley - Bolema - Ridge Trails 9.8
F13 Olema Valley Trailhead to Five Brooks 5.5*

Starting from the roads between Hwy 1 and Palomarin
F14 Lagoon, Preserve, and Creek Trails 1.1, 1.2 and 2.4

Starting from PRBO or Palomarin Trailhead at 260'
F15 PRBO and Palomarin Beach Trails 0.5 and 1.6
F16 Ridge - Lake Ranch - Coast Trails 11.2
F17 Coast Trail to Wildcat Camp 11.0

Starting from Audubon Canyon Ranch at 30'
F18 Griffin Loop - Bird Overlook Trails 2.9

Notes
* Shuttle Hike
Dogs are not allowed on any hikes.
To download a hike, go to www.marintrails.com
The password for this region is f8ms2ac

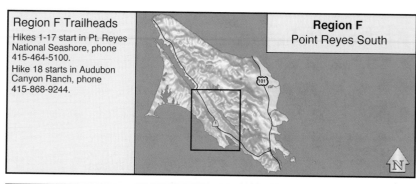

Region F Trailheads

Hikes 1-17 start in Pt. Reyes National Seashore, phone 415-464-5100.

Hike 18 starts in Audubon Canyon Ranch, phone 415-868-9244.

Region F
Point Reyes South

N

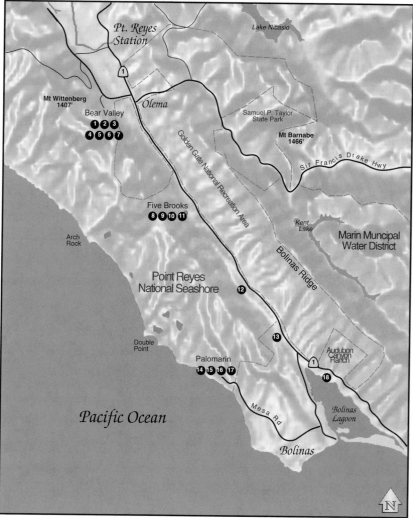

Pt. Reyes Station

Lake Nicasio

Mt Wittenberg 1407'

Olema

Samuel P. Taylor State Park

Mt Barnabe 1466'

Bear Valley
1 2 3
4 5 6 7

Golden Gate National Recreation Area

Sir Francis Drake Hwy

Five Brooks
8 9 10 11

Kent Lake

Marin Municpal Water District

Arch Rock

Point Reyes National Seashore

12

Bolinas Ridge

Double Point

13

Audubon Canyon Ranch

Palomarin
14 15 16 17

1

18

Pacific Ocean

Mesa Rd

Bolinas Lagoon

Bolinas

N

F1 Bear Valley Interpretive Trails

Distance: 0.6, 0.7 and 0.8 miles   Shaded: 70%
Elevation Change: See below.
Rating: Hiking - 10   Difficulty - 1, 2 and 3
When to Go: Excellent anytime, best in spring.

These 3 interpretive trails all have information signs explaining the geology, natural history or Miwok culture of Point Reyes.

Earthquake Trail - 0.6 miles and 100' Change
0.0 This trailhead is located east of the Visitor Center next to the picnic area. The trail is paved and is wheelchair accessible. The trail has signs and exhibits explaining the great earthquake of 1906, a 250 mile long rupture along the San Andreas fault.

0.3 Earthquake motion. The maximum motion occurred here, when the Pacific plate slipped 16-20' northward relative to the North American plate as shown by the fence display.

0.6 Back at the trailhead next to the restroom.

*Acorn Woodpecker
Found on all
3 hikes.*

Kule Loklo Trail - 0.7 miles and 50' Change
0.0 This trail starts about 100 yds. north of the Visitor Center and climbs slightly to a grove of eucalyptus. Notice the woodpecker holes drilled in dead snags for storing acorns.

0.3 Kule Loklo village. This reconstruction of a Coast Miwok village was started in 1976 and continues today. Cultural demonstrations, work parties and festivals are held here every year. Check the Visitor Center for a schedule of events.

0.4 Restroom and junction. For a longer way back, you can bear right to pick up the Horse trail as it circles the pasture adding 0.5 miles to the hike. Otherwise, head left and retrace your steps.

0.7 Back at the trailhead north of the Visitor Center.

Woodpecker - Morgan Trails - 0.8 miles and 150' Change
0.0 Start between the two signs at the Bear Valley trailhead and take the Woodpecker trail uphill. Ahead, look for the holes in the Douglas fir trees where woodpeckers store acorns for the winter.

0.7 Junction and museum. For an interesting side trip, you can tour the museum that explains the history and workings of the Morgan horse ranch. After that, head down the paved road to the start.
Option: To extend the hike, take the Morgan trail towards Kule Loklo.

0.8 Back at the Bear Valley trailhead.

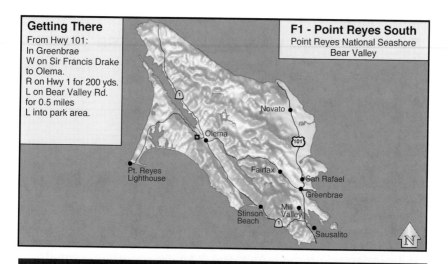

Getting There

From Hwy 101:
In Greenbrae
W on Sir Francis Drake
to Olema.
R on Hwy 1 for 200 yds.
L on Bear Valley Rd.
for 0.5 miles
L into park area.

F1 - Point Reyes South
Point Reyes National Seashore
Bear Valley

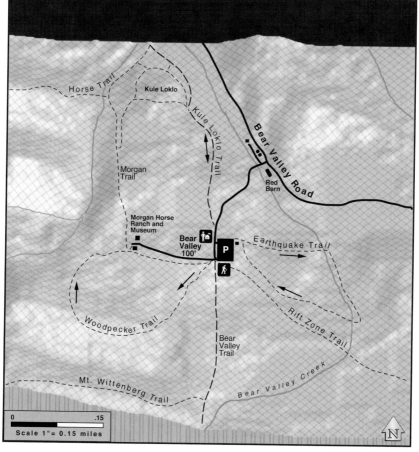

189

F2 Bear Valley - Meadow - Horse Trails

Distance: 6.1 miles   Shaded: 70%
Elevation Change: 1300'   Can be muddy in winter or dusty in fall.
Rating: Hiking - 9   Difficulty - 7   Steep in parts.
When to Go: Good anytime, best on clear days in spring.

This hike makes a round trip to the top of Mt. Wittenberg and back. Great views when clear and good wildflowers in May and June.

0.0 Start at the Bear Valley trailhead south of the parking area.

0.8 Junction ❶ with the Meadow trail. Cross the bridge to the right and notice the fallen bay tree on the left. The bay, or California laurel, is very adaptable. It can grow in sun or shade and, when downed, often starts new shoots. Although there are occasional bay trees here, this is primarily a Douglas fir forest, with some big ones ahead.

1.5 The meadow of the Meadow trail. On the right, you can see the deer-graze line about three feet up on the fir trees. At the north end of the meadow, look for fir tree cones, which provide food for squirrels and seeds for new trees. Douglas fir seeds germinate and survive only when they root in mineral soil and receive direct sunlight. These conditions often occur following a fire. Deer, which are common here, munch new seedlings and help maintain the meadow.

Mule Deer

The trail reenters the forest and circles a huge bowl-shaped canyon on the left. The understory is lush with huckleberry, sword fern, tanoak and elderberry.

2.3 Two junctions ❷. Head right on the Mt. Wittenberg trail. At this point, the trail leaves the forest and enters an open hillside. Up ahead, the trail provides great views of Drakes Bay and the Point Reyes headlands. You can also see evidence of the 1995 fire.

2.7 Junction ❸. Take the trail uphill to the top of Mt. Wittenberg.

2.9 Mt. Wittenberg. The hilltop used to be bare, offering great views. Now, it is beginning to look like a forest with lots of young Douglas fir.

3.1 Junction ❸ again. Take the Z Ranch trail right.

3.8 Junction. Take the Horse trail right downhill.

5.6 Junction ❹. Go left 100 yds., then right into Kule Loklo. Head for the large mound and the road through the eucalyptus.

6.1 Bear Valley trailhead. Water and restrooms.

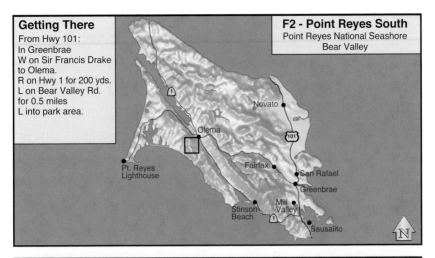

Getting There

From Hwy 101:
In Greenbrae
W on Sir Francis Drake
to Olema.
R on Hwy 1 for 200 yds.
L on Bear Valley Rd.
for 0.5 miles
L into park area.

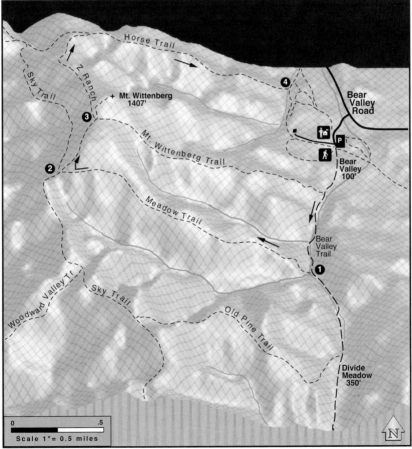

F3 Bear Valley - Old Pine - Mt. Wittenberg

Distance: 7.3 miles   Shaded: 80%
Elevation Change: 1300'
Rating: Hiking - 10   Difficulty - 7   Steep downhill.
When to Go: Excellent anytime, best from March to June.

This is the best and easiest hike to Inverness Ridge. It provides great views, forest vegetation, good berries and spring wildflowers.

0.0 Start at the Bear Valley trailhead at the south end of the parking area and head into the meadow. Most of the grasses are non-native, imported from Mediterranean countries to feed livestock.

0.8 Junction with the Meadow trail. There are two interesting plants growing along the left bank near here, trillium and wild ginger. Trillium has three symmetrical leaves and in late February and March, produces a beautiful flower with three white petals. Ginger has a dark-green, heart-shaped leaf, and from March to June produces deep-purple flowers that are hidden beneath the leaves. Up ahead, several trees are down, from the El Nino winter storms of 1998.

Wild Ginger

1.6 Divide Meadow and junction ❶. Take the Old Pine trail right, which provides the easiest climb to the crest of Inverness Ridge. Although called "Old Pine Trail," the trail passes through a magnificent Douglas fir forest.

2.5 Huckleberry lane. Winter rains and summer fog create a luxurious understory, dominated by tall huckleberry shrubs. The small black, edible berries are ripe for picking in August and September.

3.5 Junction ❷ with the Sky trail. Head right, to the north.

3.8 Junction with the Woodward Valley trail. In spring, this verdant meadow, edged with firs offers a peaceful rest stop and picnic area.

4.5 Two junctions ❸. The trail leaves the forest here. Continue straight on the Mt. Wittenberg trail.

4.9 Junction ❹ with the Z Ranch trail. Head uphill to Mt. Wittenberg.

5.1 Mt. Wittenberg, at 1407'. Fifty years ago, the entire hilltop was grass and cattle grazed here. Now, Douglas fir trees are moving in.

5.3 Junction ❹. Take the Mt. Wittenberg trail left downhill. **Option:** An unofficial trail heads south about 200 yds. for great views.

7.3 Back at the Bear Valley trailhead. Water and restrooms.

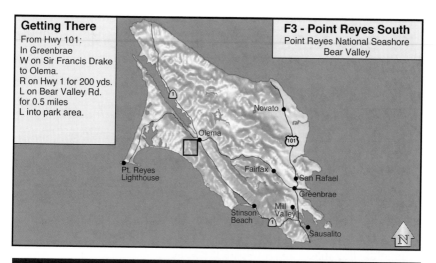

Getting There

From Hwy 101:
In Greenbrae
W on Sir Francis Drake
to Olema.
R on Hwy 1 for 200 yds.
L on Bear Valley Rd.
for 0.5 miles
L into park area.

F3 - Point Reyes South
Point Reyes National Seashore
Bear Valley

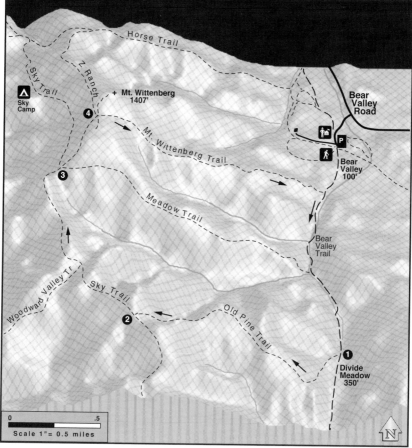

F4 Bear Valley Trail to Arch Rock

Distance: 8.4 miles   Shaded: 70%
Elevation Change: 400'   Bicycles allowed part way.
Rating: Hiking - 10   Difficulty - 3
When to Go: Excellent anytime. Best when the coast is clear.

This is the most popular hike on Point Reyes. It is an out and back hike, so you can turn around anytime. Great views at Arch Rock.

0.0 Start at the main trailhead south of the parking area. Head out into the meadow and imagine a time when wildlife was abundant. Grizzly bears, brown bears, tule elk, deer, coyotes and an occasional mountain lion made this a wildlife paradise.

1.6 Junction ❶ at Divide Meadow. In the early 1890s, the Pacific Union Club of San Francisco built a sportsman's lodge here with 35 rooms, stables and kennels. The original plans included a golf course, tennis courts and swimming pool. Fortunately, the entire resort was never built. The lodge building deteriorated and was removed in 1950. You might be able to discover its location on the east side of the meadow hilltop. Look for amaryllis and other plantings nearby.

Bear Valley Country Club c. 1895

3.2 Junction ❷ with the Glen and Baldy trails. Bicycles must stop here. Continue hiking towards the ocean.

4.0 Junction with the Coast trail. Head left along the Coast trail for 200 yds. and then continue straight on the trail to Arch Rock.

4.2 Arch Rock overlook with great views of the coast. To the south, you can see along Wildcat Beach to Double Point. To the north, you can see Drakes Bay and the Point Reyes headlands. Out to sea, you have sea stacks close in and the Farallone Islands on the horizon.

When ready, head back along the creek. **Option**: Take the Coast trail south over the bridge for 0.2 miles to another viewpoint, Millers Point, which was named after Representative Clem Miller, whose district included West Marin and who was instrumental in getting Congress to create Point Reyes National Seashore.

8.4 Bear Valley trailhead and Visitor Center.

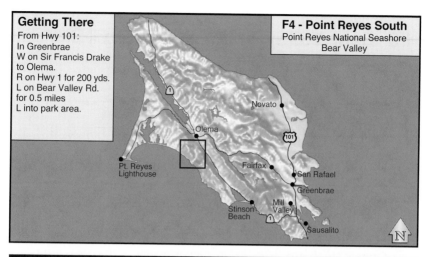

Getting There

From Hwy 101:
In Greenbrae
W on Sir Francis Drake
to Olema.
R on Hwy 1 for 200 yds.
L on Bear Valley Rd.
for 0.5 miles
L into park area.

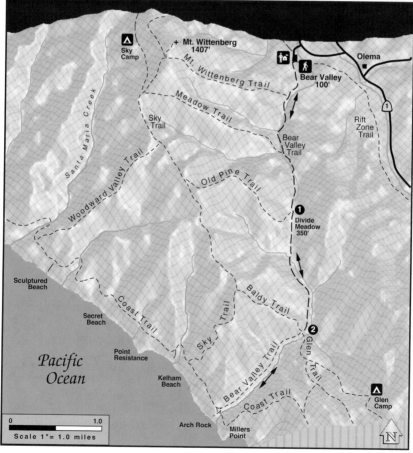

195

F5 Bear Valley - Mt. Wittenberg - Sky

Distance: 10.9 miles   Shaded: 60%
Elevation Change: 1600'   Some mud possible on the ridge.
Rating: Hiking - 9   Difficulty - 7   Steep in places.
When to Go: Excellent anytime, best in May.

This hike takes the steepest route to the Inverness Ridge and then follows the ridge to the coast. Great views and magnificent forests.

0.0 Start at the Bear Valley trailhead, south of the parking area.

0.2 Junction ❶ with the Mt. Wittenberg trail, which is guarded by a large bay tree. Turn right and set a slow steady pace to climb the moderately steep trail to the ridge. Occasionally, in the open areas, stop and enjoy the views back east across Olema Valley.

1.6 Junction ❷. The trail crests Inverness Ridge at 1250' offering spectacular views of Drakes Bay and the headlands with Sky Camp below in the foreground. For a side trip, you can climb to the top of Mt. Wittenberg. Otherwise, head left on the Mt. Wittenberg trail.

2.4 Two junctions. Head south on the Sky trail as it enters a dramatic Douglas fir forest kept refreshingly moist by winter rains and summer fog. The luxuriant understory is filled with ferns, elderberry, hedge nettle and huckleberry.

3.2 Junction ❸ with the Woodward Valley trail. Continue south on the Sky trail past this picturesque meadow edged with Douglas fir. Over the next half-mile, look for gooseberry, elderberry, huckleberry and thimbleberry.

Coyote Bush

4.9 Junction ❹ with the Baldy trail. Continue straight. Before the 1995 fire, this area produced some of the densest stands of coyote bush on Point Reyes. Coyote bush, called "fuzzy wuzzy" because of the white fluff produced on the seeds of the female plant in early summer, dominates the coastal scrub community. Other plants in this "soft chaparral" community include coffeeberry, blackberry, poison oak and sword fern. This is a good place to find brush rabbits, wrentits and the white-crowned sparrow. Ahead, down near the coast, look for views of Point Resistance.

6.2 Junction ❺. Take the Coast trail left.

6.9 Junction ❻. Head right to explore Arch Rock. (See Hike F4 for details.) The hike continues left on the Bear Valley trail.

10.9 Bear Valley trailhead with full facilities.

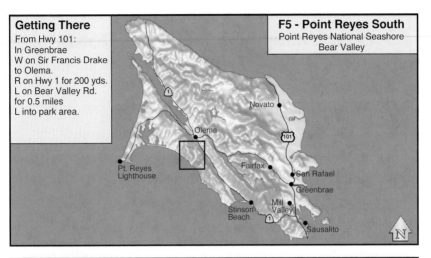

Getting There

From Hwy 101:
In Greenbrae
W on Sir Francis Drake
to Olema.
R on Hwy 1 for 200 yds.
L on Bear Valley Rd.
for 0.5 miles
L into park area.

F5 - Point Reyes South
Point Reyes National Seashore
Bear Valley

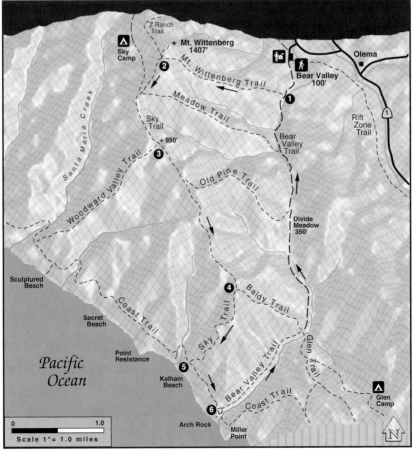

197

F6 Bear Valley - Glen Camp - Coast

Distance: 11.2 miles   Shaded: 70%
Elevation Change: 1400'   Can be wet.
Rating: Hiking - 10   Difficulty - 6
When to Go: Excellent anytime, best when calm and clear.

This is one of the premier hikes on Point Reyes that includes a riparian corridor, lush forest, breathtaking views and spring flowers.

0.0 Start at the Bear Valley trailhead, south of the parking area.

0.5 Floods and alders. People still talk about the storm of 1982. Bear Valley was completely blocked by flood debris and over one-half of the trail was destroyed. One of the few remaining signs of the flood are groves of young, red alders that seeded the following spring. Now, these alders are much larger, once again shading the trail.

3.2 Junction ❶ with Glen trail. Take the Glen trail left across the creek and head uphill out of the lush riparian corridor of alder, elderberry, ferns and mosses and into firs, bays, hazelnut, and forget-me-nots.

3.8 Junction ❷. Take the Glen Camp Loop trail left.

4.7 Glen Camp with tables, no water. This is the prettiest of the backpacking camps, nestled in a small meadow surrounded by oaks and firs. Look for iris under the oaks in spring. Campers will find lots of wildlife, especially at dusk. The trail continues from the west side of the meadow where it begins a moderately steep climb to the ridge.

5.2 Two junctions. Cross the Glen trail and take the signed Coast/Glen spur trail west towards the ocean.

5.5 Junction ❸ with Coast trail. Bear right. The trail heads north across open coastal grasslands. Watch for deer.

6.1 Junction and seasonal pond. Continue left on the Coast trail.

6.3 Outcropping, wildflowers, picnic spot and viewpoints. As you look north along Drakes Bay, the largest prominence is Point Resistance. Further down the trail by the bluffs, be sure to take two spur trails left, 50-200'. The 1st left goes to a plaque honoring Congressman Clem Miller. The 2nd left explores the cliff edge. Both trails offer magnificent views of the coast, especially south to Double Point and Alamere Falls.

6.9 Junction ❹ with Arch Rock trail. Head left to explore Arch Rock.

7.0 Arch Rock. (See Hike F4 for details.) To return, follow the signs back along the Bear Valley trail.

11.2 Bear Valley trailhead and Visitor Center.

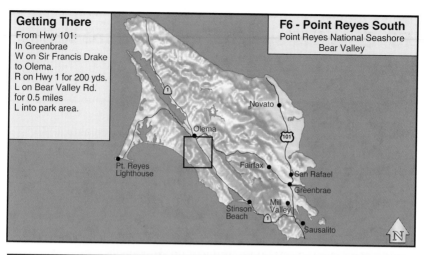

Getting There

From Hwy 101:
In Greenbrae
W on Sir Francis Drake
to Olema.
R on Hwy 1 for 200 yds.
L on Bear Valley Rd.
for 0.5 miles
L into park area.

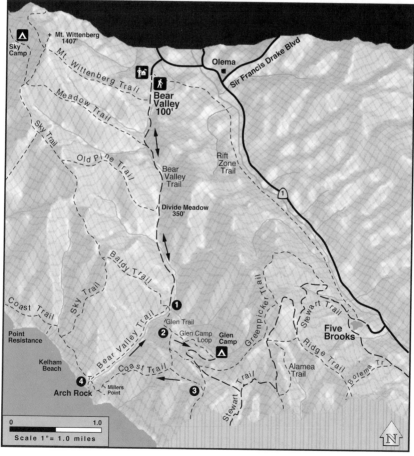

Scale 1"= 1.0 miles

0   1.0

F7 Bear Valley - Sky - Woodward Valley

Distance: 13.0 miles   Shaded: 60%
Elevation Change: 1700'   Can be overgrown. Can be windy.
Rating: Hiking - 10   Difficulty - 7   Steep in places.
When to Go: Excellent anytime, best when clear and calm.

This hike has it all! Meadows, forests, creeks, beaches, rolling hills, wildflowers and panoramic views, all await the vigorous hiker.

0.0 Start at the Bear Valley trailhead at the south end of the parking area. Look for deer in the meadow, especially in the early morning.

0.2 Junction ❶ with the Mt. Wittenberg trail. Head right and start a moderately steep climb under tanoak and Douglas fir.

2.0 Junction ❷. The trail crests Inverness Ridge offering dramatic views over Sky Camp to Drakes Bay and the headlands. If the weather is clear, you can take a short side trip and climb 300' to the top of Mt. Wittenberg. Otherwise, head left on the Mt. Wittenberg trail.

2.4 Two junctions. Head south on the Sky trail as it enters a dense Douglas fir forest. In the understory, lush, light-green elderberry presents a striking contrast to the tall, dark fir canopy.

3.2 Junction ❸ with Woodward Valley trail. Turn right and head west to follow the trail as it rolls downhill through meadow, forest and open coastal ridges. Tall grass crowds the trail in summer.

4.1 Ocean views. The trail levels off along a rocky outcrop above the ocean. This scenic viewpoint offers a panoramic sweep from the Point Reyes headlands to Double Point.

5.2 Junction ❹ with Coast trail. Bear left and head south.

7.7 Kelham Beach access trail. Continue south on the Coast trail. **Option:** At tides below plus one foot, the adventurous hiker can walk along Kelham Beach and view the sea tunnel up to Arch Rock.

8.7 Junction ❺ with Arch Rock trail. Head right.

8.9 Arch Rock. More great views, including Point Resistance, jutting out from the coast to the north. To complete the hike, follow the Bear Valley trail inland as it parallels the creek.

9.2 Buckeye trees. Two large, gnarled buckeyes with twisted trunks stand guard along the right of the trail. Buckeyes produce fragrant flowers in late spring, then soon after, in early summer, begin losing their leaves. The nut is large, brown and shiny like a buck's eye.

13.0 Bear Valley trailhead. Visitor Center, water and restrooms.

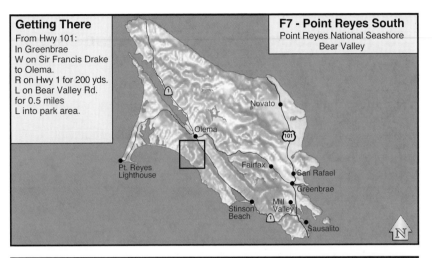

Getting There

From Hwy 101:
In Greenbrae
W on Sir Francis Drake
to Olema.
R on Hwy 1 for 200 yds.
L on Bear Valley Rd.
for 0.5 miles
L into park area.

F7 - Point Reyes South
Point Reyes National Seashore
Bear Valley

Novato

Olema

Pt. Reyes
Lighthouse

Fairfax

San Rafael

Greenbrae

Stinson
Beach

Mill
Valley

Sausalito

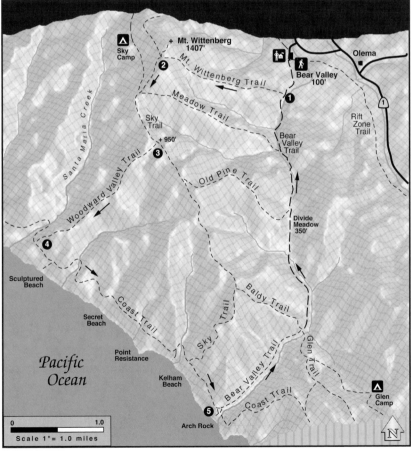

Sky
Camp

+ Mt. Wittenberg
1407'

Olema

Bear Valley
100'

Mt. Wittenberg Trail

Meadow Trail

Sky
Trail

+ 950'

Bear
Valley
Trail

Rift
Zone
Trail

Santa Maria Creek

Woodward Valley Trail

Old Pine Trail

Divide
Meadow
350'

Sculptured
Beach

Coast Trail

Secret
Beach

Baldy Trail

Point
Resistance

Sky Trail

Pacific
Ocean

Kelham
Beach

Bear Valley Trail

Glen Trail

Glen
Camp

Coast Trail

Arch Rock

0   1.0

Scale 1"= 1.0 miles

F8 Five Brooks Trailhead to Bear Valley*

Distance: 4.4 miles   Shaded: 50%
Elevation Change: 350'   Trail can be quite muddy or dusty.
Rating: Hiking - 8   Difficulty - 3   Some ruts.
When to Go: Best in winter and spring, but not when real wet.

This one-way hike explores the terrain of the San Andreas rift zone. Vegetation includes forest, meadow, pasture and wildflowers.

*Shuttle Hike. Leave pickup cars at Bear Valley and shuttle all hikers to the Five Brooks parking area and trailhead.

0.0 Go through the gate and head west towards Inverness Ridge.

0.1 Junction. Continue past the Rift Zone trail.

0.2 Junction ❶. Take the Stewart trail right towards the north.

0.3 Junction. Go through the metal gate and head downhill. California hazelnut dominates the understory here. At the bottom of the hill continue straight past the bathhouse, cross a small creek, and go straight into the meadow and campground. Then, veer left.

0.4 Creek. At the creek, take the signed Rift Zone trail left.

1.4 Private property. A sign indicates that the trail is now crossing land owned by the Vedanta Society, a religious retreat organization.

3.0 Junction ❷. Go through the gate, head right 100' and then left across the pasture. Up ahead, look for a glimpse of the Vedanta retreat house about one-half mile on your left. This magnificent old Victorian, called "The Oaks," was solidly built out of redwood by James Shafter in 1869 and easily survived the 1906 earthquake. James Shafter, and his brother, Oscar, two lawyers from Vermont, at one time owned most of the Point Reyes peninsula.

The Oaks c. 1920

3.8 Road. The hike passes through two gates and crosses the main road to the Vedanta house. The area before the gates can be very muddy if cows have churned up the soil. After passing through the second gate, the trail skirts a marshy area, climbs a knoll, then drops into a meadow leading to Bear Valley.

4.4 Bear Valley trailhead with full facilities.

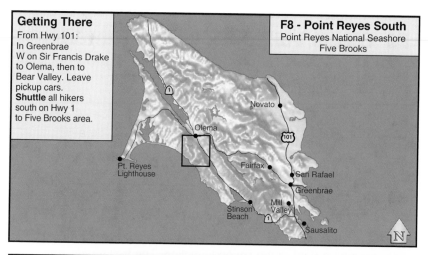

Getting There

From Hwy 101:
In Greenbrae
W on Sir Francis Drake
to Olema, then to
Bear Valley. Leave
pickup cars.
Shuttle all hikers
south on Hwy 1
to Five Brooks area.

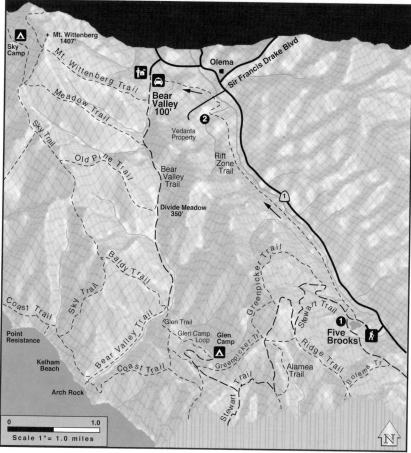

F9 Olema Valley - Bolema - Stewart

Distance: 6.3 miles   Shaded: 90%
Elevation Change: 1100'   Bicycles possible. Horses likely.
Rating: Hiking - 7   Difficulty - 5   Can be dusty or muddy.
When to Go: Best in spring, good anytime.

This hike makes a loop around the eastern side of Inverness Ridge through a dense and luxuriant Douglas fir forest.

0.0 Start at the Five Brooks trailhead and take the main trail west past the old logging pond towards Inverness Ridge.

0.2 Junction ❶. Take the Olema Valley trail left around the pond 100 yds., then bear right at the second junction. The trail heads south through an enchanting forest of Douglas fir, bay and alder with a dense understory of ferns, hazelnut, ginger, nettles and blackberry. Up ahead, the trail crosses a bridge, then starts a moderately steep climb in more open forest.

1.4 Junction ❷. Head right on the Bolema trail and continue to climb. Farther up the trail, look for stands of Monterey pines that were seeded after logging operations in the late 1950s. Monterey pines are distinguished from Douglas fir by their much longer needles.

2.5 Junction ❸, and the highest point of the hike at 1130'. Head right on the Ridge trail. Occasionally, you get glimpses west to the ocean.

3.1 Forest and berries. The trail enters a dark Douglas fir forest with lots of huckleberries that ripen from July through September. The forest is often damp in the summertime due to heavy fog drip.

3.2 Junction ❹. The Ridge trail goes left. Continue straight here and right at the next junction 100 yds. ahead.

3.3 Junction. Take the Stewart trail downhill to the right. The old road bed was once paved and wide enough for two lanes of traffic. Watch for an occasional large, old-growth Douglas fir on the edge of the road bed. These trees were left by loggers to support the road and to provide seeds for future trees.

5.2 Junction ❺ with the Greenpicker trail. Continue downhill. Ahead, the trail makes a large hairpin turn in a steep canyon and creek. Look for five-finger ferns along the bank. In June, an aralia with large 12" leaves, and even larger flower stalks, blooms along the moist banks.

6.1 Junction ❶ and mill pond. Head left.

6.3 Trailhead with picnic tables, water and restrooms.

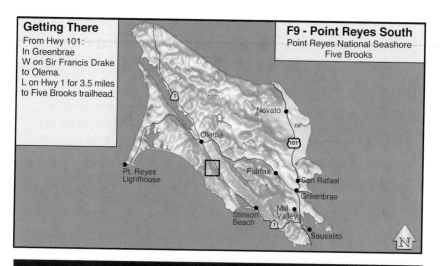

Getting There

From Hwy 101:
In Greenbrae
W on Sir Francis Drake
to Olema.
L on Hwy 1 for 3.5 miles
to Five Brooks trailhead.

F9 - Point Reyes South
Point Reyes National Seashore
Five Brooks

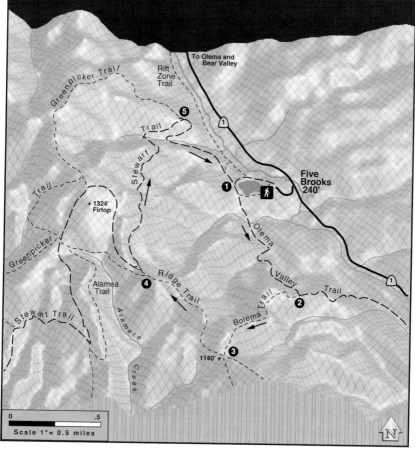

205

F10 Stewart - Greenpicker Trails

Distance: 7.5 miles   Shaded: 90%
Elevation Change: 1300'   Dusty when dry. Bicycles possible.
Rating: Hiking - 7   Difficulty - 7   Moderately steep in places.
When to Go: Good anytime, best in February and March.

This hike stays entirely in a scenic Douglas fir forest as it climbs the eastern slopes of Inverness Ridge.

0.0 Start at the Five Brooks parking area and head northwest through the gate. Circle the pond surrounded by willows and alders.

0.2 Junction ❶ with the Olema Valley and Stewart trails. Head right and follow the signs to Firtop. The Stewart trail is really a wide road that makes a moderate climb through a Douglas fir forest with occasional bay, alder and tanoak. Ferns and elderberry dominate the understory.

Five-finger Fern

0.7 Hairpin turn. Just past the turn, look for four different ferns on the steep bank: lady fern, sword fern, five-finger fern and chain fern.

1.1 Junction with the Greenpicker trail. Continue left towards Firtop. Up ahead, you'll find stumps of Douglas fir, remnants of the logging operations that ended in the early 1960s.

3.0 Junction ❷ with the Ridge trail. Continue on the Stewart trail.

3.8 Junction and Firtop at 1324'. The small meadow at Firtop is surrounded by firs, blocking what were once magnificent views. You can cut the hike short by returning on the Greenpicker trail. Otherwise, continue across the meadow and head downhill.

4.2 Two junctions ❸. Go right about 100' on the spur trail and pick up the Greenpicker trail to head back towards Five Brooks. The trail first makes a moderate descent for 0.3 miles, then climbs steeply through a very dense forest back up to Firtop.

4.9 Junction ❹ with the spur trail to Stewart trail. Continue left on the Greenpicker trail. This part of the hike borders the private property of the Vedanta Society. Up ahead, the terrain becomes more difficult as the trail leaves the road to enter an old growth Douglas fir forest with lots of huckleberries and sword ferns in the understory.

6.4 Junction. Head left, downhill on the Stewart trail.

7.5 Five Brooks trailhead with water and restrooms.

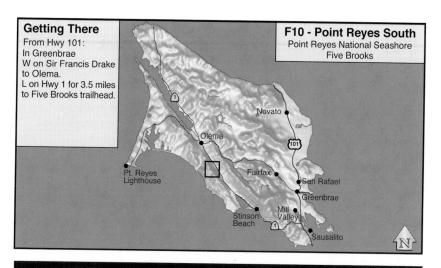

Getting There

From Hwy 101:
In Greenbrae
W on Sir Francis Drake
to Olema.
L on Hwy 1 for 3.5 miles
to Five Brooks trailhead.

F10 - Point Reyes South
Point Reyes National Seashore
Five Brooks

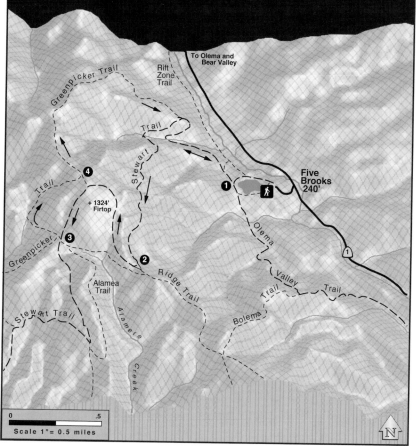

To Olema and
Bear Valley

Greenpicker Trail

Rift
Zone
Trail

Trail

Stewart

Trail

Greenpicker

❹

+ 1324'
Firtop

❸

❷

Greenpicker

Alamea
Trail

Ridge Trail

Stewart Trail

Alamere Creek

❶

Five
Brooks
240'

Olema

Valley

Trail

Bolema

Trail

1

Scale 1"= 0.5 miles

0   .5

N

207

F11 Greenpicker - Coast - Stewart Trails

Distance: 12.0 miles   Shaded: 80%
Elevation Change: 1900'   Bicycles possible. Mud possible.
Rating: Hiking - 8   Difficulty - 7   Poison oak may crowd trail.
When to Go: Good anytime, best when clear.

This is a rugged hike that makes a moderately steep climb through dense forest, then provides dramatic views along the coast.

0.0 From the Five Brooks parking area, head out past the pond.

0.2 Junction ❶. Go right on the Stewart trail.

1.1 Junction ❷. Take the Greenpicker trail right as it heads uphill, then skirts the private Vedanta property. The trail climbs through rugged terrain that supports a luxuriant Douglas fir forest. The tall canopy allows light for a dense growth of ferns and huckleberry.

2.6 Junction with trail to Firtop. Continue right on the Greenpicker trail.

3.3 Junction ❸ with spur to Stewart trail. Continue on the Greenpicker trail as it goes right downhill. Watch for poison oak.

4.3 Junction ❹ with Glen trail. Go left down the road.

4.4 Two junctions. Take the second right, the Coast/Glen Spur trail.

4.8 Junction with Coast trail. Head left.

5.3 Two viewpoints. This is one of the premier viewing spots on Point Reyes. To the northwest, you can see Drakes Bay and the Marin headlands. To the southeast, you can see Wildcat Lake and Double Point jutting out into the ocean. Look for Alamere Falls just below Double Point. The second viewpoint is down the trail and overlooks Wildcat Camp. The jumbled hills from Wildcat Camp to Double Point are mostly the result of massive landslides, which also created the lakes.

5.7 Junction ❺ with the Stewart trail. Bear left. **Option**: Head right for a side trip to Wildcat Camp and the beach.

6.2 Junction with Glen trail. Stay right on the Stewart trail.

6.7 Junction. Take the Old Out Road right. **Option**: If trails are muddy, it might be best to stay on the Stewart trail. On weekends, watch for bicycles on the Stewart trail, or horses on the Old Out Rd/Alamea trail.

7.0 Junction. Take the Alamea trail left up through a Douglas fir forest.

8.4 Junction. Take the Ridge trail right to circle Firtop.

9.0 Junction ❻. Go left 200', right 200', then down the Stewart trail.

12.0 Five Brooks trailhead with water and restrooms.

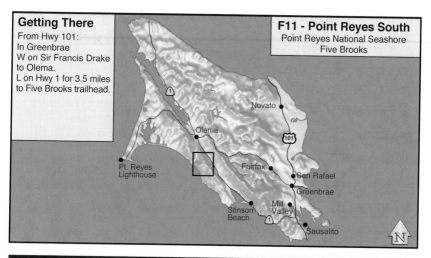

Getting There

From Hwy 101:
In Greenbrae
W on Sir Francis Drake
to Olema.
L on Hwy 1 for 3.5 miles
to Five Brooks trailhead.

F11 - Point Reyes South
Point Reyes National Seashore
Five Brooks

209

F12 Randall - Olema Valley - Bolema

Distance: 9.8 miles   Shaded: 70%
Elevation Change: 1200'   Steep in places. May be overgrown.
Rating: Hiking - 7   Difficulty - 7   Poison oak possible
When to Go: Best in April and May after the ground dries a bit.

This loop hike follows the earthquake terrain of Olema Valley, then climbs to travel along the heavily forested Inverness Ridge.

Note: See the note for Hike F13 about the Olema Valley trail, which can have standing water and a creek crossing.

0.0 Start at the Randall trailhead located near milepost 20.53 on Highway 1. Take the Randall Spur trail west along a bank of willows heading towards Inverness Ridge. Look for warblers in the willows.

0.4 Junction ❶. Head right on the Olema Valley trail and start a gentle climb through a mixture of open grassland and oak, bay, and fir trees. The trail can be muddy or dusty depending on the season.

Occasionally, look back to view the jumbled topography of the San Andreas rift zone. It is estimated that the Inverness Ridge to the west is moving 1.3" per year relative to the Bolinas Ridge to the east. This motion adds up to more than 1000' over the last 10,000 years, a very short time on the geologic time scale.

1.7 Junction ❷ with the Bolema trail. Head left to climb the old ranch road towards the ridge. This is mostly Douglas fir forest with ferns, hazelnut, hedge nettle and thimbleberries in the understory.

2.8 Junction ❸. Take the Ridge trail left and head south on the ridge.

3.1 Tree stumps and succession. Clearcut logging along the ridge in the late 1950s opened the way for manzanita to establish itself. Now, the second generation firs have formed a dense canopy shading out the manzanita and causing dieback.

5.3 Junction ❹. Take the Teixeira trail left. Watch for stinging nettles.

6.0 Junction with the Pablo Point trail. Continue downhill on the Teixeira trail. Ahead, the trail has been rerouted to avoid an old section of trail with deep ruts, exposed roots and jagged rocks.

7.1 Junction ❺. The trail crosses a bog right before the junction. (A bypass trail can be taken around the bog 0.1 mile before the junction.) Head left on the Olema Valley trail through an open meadow.

9.4 Junction. Take the Randall Spur trail east.

9.8 Back at the trailhead. If grass crowded the trail, check for ticks.

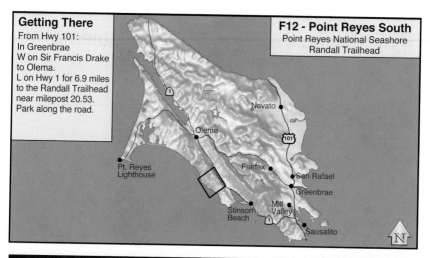

Getting There

From Hwy 101:
In Greenbrae
W on Sir Francis Drake
to Olema.
L on Hwy 1 for 6.9 miles
to the Randall Trailhead
near milepost 20.53.
Park along the road.

F12 - Point Reyes South
Point Reyes National Seashore
Randall Trailhead

Novato

Olema

Fairfax

Pt. Reyes
Lighthouse

San Rafael

Greenbrae

Stinson
Beach

Mill
Valley

Sausalito

N

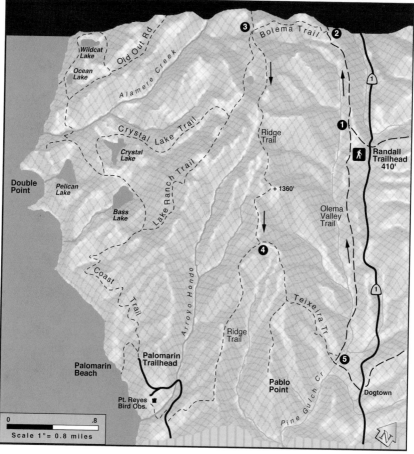

Wildcat
Lake

Ocean
Lake

Old Out Rd

Alamere Creek

Bolema Trail

③

②

①

Randall
Trailhead
410'

Crystal Lake Trail

Crystal
Lake

Ridge
Trail

Double
Point

Pelican
Lake

Lake Ranch Trail

+ 1360'

Olema
Valley
Trail

Bass
Lake

④

Coast
Trail

Arroyo Hondo

Ridge
Trail

Teixeira Tr.

⑤

Palomarin
Trailhead

Palomarin
Beach

Pablo
Point

Pine Gulch Cr.

Dogtown

Pt. Reyes
Bird Obs.

0   .8
Scale 1"= 0.8 miles

N

F13 Olema Valley to Five Brooks*

Distance: 5.5 miles   Shaded: 30%
Elevation Change: 600'   Trail can be impassable. See note.
Rating: Hiking - 9   Difficulty - 8   Moderately steep.
When to Go: Excellent anytime, best when the hills are green.

This one-way hike meanders, like the local creeks, through a mixture of vegetation along the San Andreas fault zone.

*Shuttle Hike. Leave pickup cars at Five Brooks and shuttle all hikers to the Olema Valley trailhead at milepost 18.17, north of Dogtown.

Note: The trail passes through a marshy area that can have 2-4" of standing water in winter and spring. Also, there are many deep holes along the trail created by horses' hooves sinking into soft mud. Within the first mile, the trail crosses a creek that can be 3-6" deep. The trail is scheduled for repair and a bridge is planned over the creek.

0.0 The trail starts in a meadow and heads northwest with good views to Inverness Ridge to the west.

0.4 Junction ❶ with the Teixeira trail. Continue north through the marsh area, past grasses and tall, poison hemlock.

0.8 Creek crossings. The trail crosses Pine Gulch Creek which follows an old faultline on its way to Bolinas Lagoon.

1.6 Earthquake country. Rolling hills, sag ponds, small scarps (slides) and slumps provide topographic evidence of the thousands of earthquakes that have formed the Olema Valley rift zone.

This variety of terrain supports a variety of vegetation. Alders line the creeks. Douglas fir and bay trees compete for light along the moist hillsides. Meadows, dotted with coyote bush and coffeeberry, offer good views to the surrounding hills.

2.7 Junction ❷ with a spur trail to the highway and the Randall trail. Continue north. If the trail is damp, look for animal tracks.

4.0 Junction ❸ with the Bolema trail. This is the highest point on the hike at 700'. Bear right and start a moderately steep descent through dense cover of Douglas fir with ferns, hazelnut, vines and nettles.

4.8 Small bridge. Up ahead, the creek widens into a broad, flat streambed shaded by a thicket of alders and bays.

5.2 Junction. The trail right heads to the stables. Continue left.

5.3 Junction ❹. Bear right to skirt the lake back to the trailhead.

5.5 Five Brooks trailhead. Pickup cars, tables, water and restrooms.

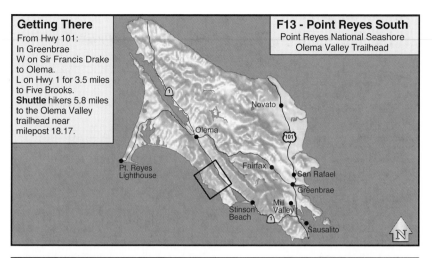

Getting There

From Hwy 101:
In Greenbrae
W on Sir Francis Drake
to Olema.
L on Hwy 1 for 3.5 miles
to Five Brooks.
Shuttle hikers 5.8 miles
to the Olema Valley
trailhead near
milepost 18.17.

F13 - Point Reyes South
Point Reyes National Seashore
Olema Valley Trailhead

Novato
Olema
Pt. Reyes
Lighthouse
Fairfax
San Rafael
Greenbrae
Stinson
Beach
Mill
Valley
Sausalito

N

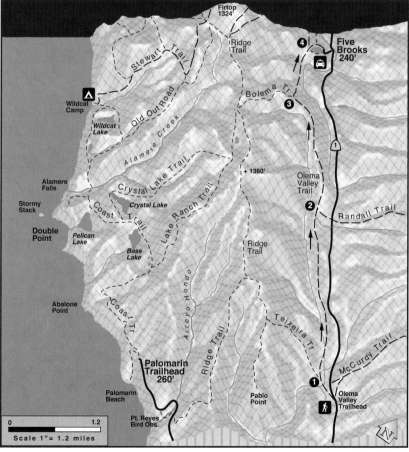

Firtop
1324

Ridge
Trail

Stewart Trail

④
Five
Brooks
240'

Wildcat
Camp

Old Out Road

Bolema Tr.

③

Wildcat
Lake

Alamere Creek

Crystal Lake Trail

+ 1360'

Olema
Valley
Trail

Alamere
Falls

②

Randall Trail

Stormy
Stack

Coast Trail

Crystal Lake

Lake Ranch Trail

Double
Point

Pelican
Lake

Bass
Lake

Ridge
Trail

Abalone
Point

Coast Tr.

Arroyo Hondo

Teixeira Tr.

McCurdy Trail

Palomarin
Trailhead
260'

Ridge Trail

①

Olema
Valley
Trailhead

Palomarin
Beach

Pablo
Point

Pt. Reyes
Bird Obs.

0   1.2
Scale 1"= 1.2 miles

N

F14 Lagoon, Preserve, and Creek Trails

Distance: 1.1, 1.2 and 2.4 miles   Shaded: 60%, 0% and 90%
Elevation Change: See below.   Duxbury hike can be muddy.
Rating: Hiking - 10   Difficulty - 4, 7 and 3
When to Go: Excellent anytime. Duxbury trail can be windy.

The first and third hikes feature birds in a lush riparian corridor. The second hike goes out to a bluff with great views of Palomarin beach.

Bolinas Lagoon Open Space - 1.1 miles and 0' Change
0.0 Park at the bend in the road, just before the stop sign at the nursery and junction of the Olema-Bolinas Rd and Horseshoe Hill Rd. At the open space sign, take the Bob Stewart trail into the small forest that borders Pine Gulch creek. Ahead, the trail joins the creek.

0.2 Junction and marsh. Continue right and cross the bridge. You can see Audubon Canyon Ranch across the lagoon.

0.4 Junction ❶ and driftwood (with Kent Island Nature Preserve written on it). Take the trail right, back into the forest.

0.5 Junction and small meadow. Head left back out to the lagoon.
1.1 Back at the parking area with no facilities.

Duxbury Reef Preserve Trail - 1.2 miles and 50' (See Map F15)
0.0 Start past the Commonweal entrance, down by the eucalyptus grove, and head through the gate. Go out along the power lines towards the ocean. If it's too wet, circle above the gully.

0.2 The trail passes under the power lines and crosses the gully, then continues towards the ocean.

0.6 Bluffs. At the cliffs edge, go left uphill 100' to get great views north along Palomarin Beach, which is part of the Duxbury Reef Preserve. The views are best at low tide. When ready, turn back.

Arroyo Hondo Creek Fire Road - 2.4 miles and 150' (See Map F15)
0.0 Park on Mesa Rd, just before the sign "No Parking - Fire Lane" at a turnout located 0.2 miles before PRBO. Go through the gate to follow the fire road along the creek. This lush riparian corridor is similar to Bear Valley, but with more birds in the trees.

Look for ferns, elderberries, nettles, horsetail and morning glory under the canopy of Douglas fir, bay and buckeye trees.

1.2 Dam and turnaround point. The road ends next to a small dam that supplies water for PRBO. From here, retrace your steps.

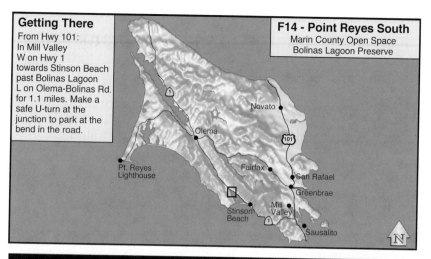

Getting There

From Hwy 101:
In Mill Valley
W on Hwy 1
towards Stinson Beach
past Bolinas Lagoon
L on Olema-Bolinas Rd.
for 1.1 miles. Make a
safe U-turn at the
junction to park at the
bend in the road.

F14 - Point Reyes South
Marin County Open Space
Bolinas Lagoon Preserve

Novato

Olema

Pt. Reyes
Lighthouse

Fairfax

San Rafael

Greenbrae

Stinson
Beach

Mill
Valley

Sausalito

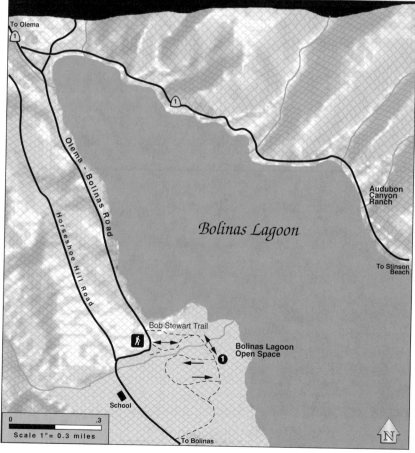

To Olema

Olema - Bolinas Road

Horseshoe Hill Road

Bolinas Lagoon

Audubon
Canyon
Ranch

To Stinson
Beach

Bob Stewart Trail

**Bolinas Lagoon
Open Space**

①

School

Scale 1"= 0.3 miles

0   .3

To Bolinas

215

F15 PRBO and Palomarin Beach Trails

Distance: 0.5 and 1.6 miles   Shaded: 60% and 20%
Elevation Change: See below.   Both trails can be overgrown.
Rating: Hiking - 9   Difficulty - 7, 4   Short steep section PRBO.
When to Go: Excellent anytime, best from December to July.

The Point Reyes Bird Observatory Nature trail explores a magnificent small canyon. The Palomarin Beach trail is best at low tides.

Point Reyes Bird Observatory Nature Trail - 0.5 miles and 50'
0.0 Start at the PRBO parking lot and take the signed Nature trail south past coyote bush and wind-pruned fir trees. Up ahead, the trail heads steeply down into Fern Canyon guarded by twisted buckeye trees covered with old man's beard, a grey-green lichen hanging in the branches. This little canyon provides a rain forest habitat of robust flora and noisy birds. Look for several kinds of ferns and berries – sword fern, five-finger fern, chain fern, blackberries and thimbleberries – under a canopy of buckeye trees.

0.1 The trail crosses the creek and climbs up the other side, where a multi-trunked buckeye stands over patches of low-growing Solomon's seal. Continue across the bluff to a 4-way junction marked by three poles on your left. If the trail is not overgrown, head left through the poles to the road. Otherwise retrace your steps.

0.3 Road. Go left past the exposed shale cliffs. **Option**: To extend the hike, go into Arroyo Hondo canyon just ahead. (See Hike F14)

0.5 Entrance to PRBO.

Palomarin Beach Trail - 1.6 miles and 260' Change
0.0 Start at 260' at the Palomarin parking area. Take the dirt road up towards the eucalyptus grove. In spring, look for lupine, cow parsnip, Indian paintbrush, iris, wild cucumber and poppies.

0.1 Junction ❶. Just past a park sign and massive eucalyptus, take the signed trail left past another large eucalyptus.

0.2 Overlook. At a viewpoint, the trail veers left down into a ravine. Below, grasses and thistles may crowd the trail.

0.8 Palomarin Beach with marine terraces exposed at low tides. These terraces were created by wave action eroding and leveling cliffs. Here, the tide pools are only fair, not as good as Duxbury Point. **Note**: The beach can not be walked at high tide.

1.6 Back at the parking area with restrooms.

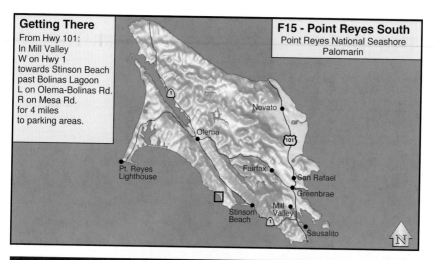

Getting There

From Hwy 101:
In Mill Valley
W on Hwy 1
towards Stinson Beach
past Bolinas Lagoon
L on Olema-Bolinas Rd.
R on Mesa Rd.
for 4 miles
to parking areas.

F15 - Point Reyes South
Point Reyes National Seashore
Palomarin

Novato

Olema

Pt. Reyes
Lighthouse

Fairfax

San Rafael

Greenbrae

Mill
Valley

Stinson
Beach

Sausalito

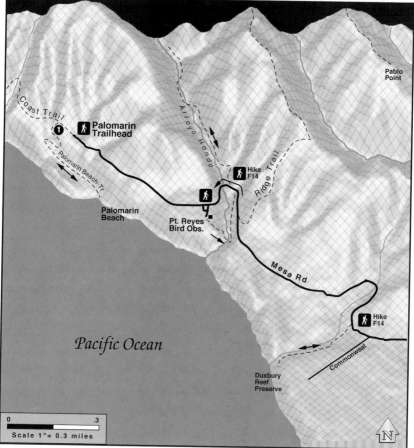

Pablo
Point

Coast Trail

Palomarin
Trailhead

Arroyo Hondo

Hike
F14

Ridge Trail

Palomarin Beach Tr

Palomarin
Beach

Pt. Reyes
Bird Obs.

Mesa Rd

Hike
F14

Pacific Ocean

Commonweal

Duxbury
Reef
Preserve

0   .3
Scale 1" = 0.3 miles

217

F16 Ridge - Lake Ranch - Coast Trails

Distance: 11.2 miles   Shaded: 70%
Elevation Change: 1700'   Overgrown in places. Some poison oak.
Rating: Hiking - 9   Difficulty - 6   Some ruts.
When to Go: Excellent anytime, best in spring when clear.

This hike climbs the southern end of Inverness Ridge into a magnificent fir forest, then drops through a massive landslide area.

0.0 Park in the Point Reyes Bird Observatory parking lot. Take the signed Nature trail down into a small canyon featuring luxuriant growth and striking buckeye trees. Cross the creek and immediately head up the other side. Follow the trail across the plateau to a four-way junction marked by three short poles on your left. Head left past the poles and through shrubbery towards the road.

0.3 Junction with Mesa Rd. Head right down the dirt road.

0.4 Junction ❶ with the Ridge trail. Turn left and start a moderate climb through coastal scrub dotted with Douglas fir. The trail may be overgrown in places. Watch out for poison oak.

1.6 Views. Good views east to Pablo Point and beyond to Bolinas Ridge and south to Bolinas Lagoon.

Up ahead, the trail enters a dense conifer forest that covers the Inverness Ridge from here to Point Reyes Hill ten miles north.

2.7 Junction ❷ with the Teixeira trail. Continue north on the ridge.

3.6 Mountain top at 1360'. A large, moss-covered Douglas fir stands at the highest point on the southern ridge. This area was heavily logged in the late '50s. Now, sword ferns and dense stands of huckleberries thrive under the shade of the second-growth fir trees.

5.2 Junction ❸. Take the Lake Ranch trail to the left. Up ahead, Mud Lake provides a home for red-winged blackbirds.

6.0 Junction with Crystal Lake trail. Continue on the Lake Ranch trail.

7.1 Views and landslides. The trail heads south into dense shrubs, with good views of the coast below and of the headlands north. On your left, look for evidence of the massive slides that reshaped the landscape and created a series of ponds and lakes below. For the next mile, try to imagine how these slides took place.

8.3 Junction ❹. Head left on the Coast trail.

10.5 Palomarin trailhead ❺. Continue on the road south.

11.2 PRBO parking area. No facilities.

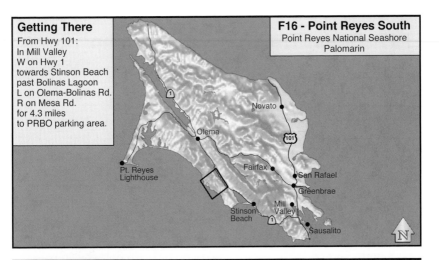

Getting There

From Hwy 101:
In Mill Valley
W on Hwy 1
towards Stinson Beach
past Bolinas Lagoon
L on Olema-Bolinas Rd.
R on Mesa Rd.
for 4.3 miles
to PRBO parking area.

F16 - Point Reyes South
Point Reyes National Seashore
Palomarin

Novato
Olema
Pt. Reyes
Lighthouse
Fairfax
San Rafael
Greenbrae
Stinson
Beach
Mill
Valley
Sausalito

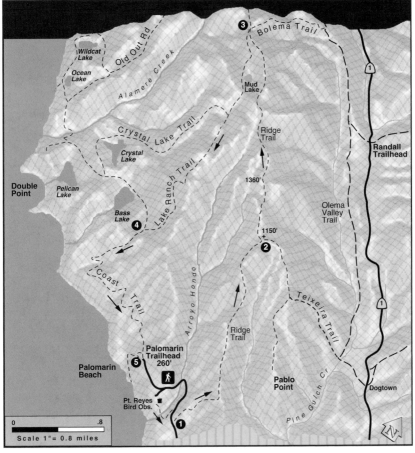

Wildcat
Lake
Ocean
Lake
Old Out Rd.
Alamere Creek
Bolema Trail
Mud
Lake
Crystal Lake Trail
Crystal
Lake
Ridge
Trail
Randall
Trailhead
Double
Point
Pelican
Lake
Lake Ranch Trail
1360'
Bass
Lake
Olema
Valley
Trail
Coast Trail
1150'
Teixeira Trail
Ridge
Trail
Palomarin
Trailhead
260'
Palomarin
Beach
Pablo
Point
Pt. Reyes
Bird Obs.
Pine Gulch Cr
Dogtown
Arroyo Hondo

0 .8
Scale 1"= 0.8 miles

F17 Coast Trail to Wildcat Camp

Distance: 11.0 miles   Shaded: 20%
Elevation Change: 1700'   Rocky and rutted in places.
Rating: Hiking - 9   Difficulty - 6   Poison oak possible.
When to Go: Good anytime, best in April and May.

This hike follows the Coast trail past ponds and lakes to Wildcat Camp where you can make a side trip to Alamere Falls. Good views.

0.0 Start at 260' at the Palomarin parking area. Take the Coast trail up past non-native French broom towards the eucalyptus grove.

0.6 Coastal views. The trail skirts the cliff offering dramatic views both north and south. In spring, the green hills are dotted with blue lupine, white cow parsnip and the red or yellow Indian paintbrush. Other spring wildflowers include iris, wild cucumber and poppy.

2.2 Junction ❶ with Lake Ranch trail. Continue left. Up ahead, the trail passes several small ponds formed by slumping soil. All of the ponds and lakes in this area were formed thousands of years ago by massive landslides that blocked normal creek drainage.

2.7 Bass Lake. Coastal scrub edges the southern shore of Point Reyes' most picturesque lake while Douglas fir frames the north side. Up ahead, a short spur trail left allows access to Bass Lake, where swimming is possible, but not easy.

Bass Lake

3.3 Pelican Lake. Across the lake, a small notch between Double Point allows an overflow in wet years.

3.6 Old junctions. There are two unmaintained trails here, 50 yds. apart - first to Double Point, then Alamere Falls. Both are overgrown.

4.2 Junction ❷ with Ocean Lake Loop. Head left. Good views ahead.

5.3 Junction ❸ with the Coast trail. Head left down to Wildcat Camp.

5.5 Wildcat Camp. Restrooms available. Be sure to go down the ravine to the beach for a view south to Alamere Falls. **Option:** If the tide is out, walk south along the beach 1.1 miles to the 40' Alamere Falls. Alamere Creek flows all year, but is most spectacular in the spring and after heavy rains. For the return trip, take the Coast trail south back to Palomarin, where restrooms are available.

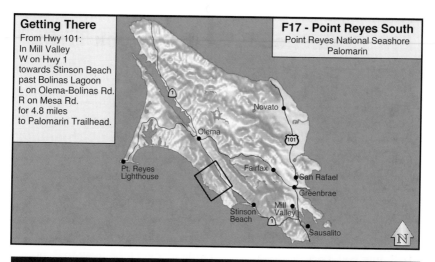

Getting There

From Hwy 101:
In Mill Valley
W on Hwy 1
towards Stinson Beach
past Bolinas Lagoon
L on Olema-Bolinas Rd.
R on Mesa Rd.
for 4.8 miles
to Palomarin Trailhead.

Pt. Reyes Lighthouse

Olema

Novato

101

Fairfax

San Rafael

Greenbrae

Stinson Beach

Mill Valley

1

Sausalito

N

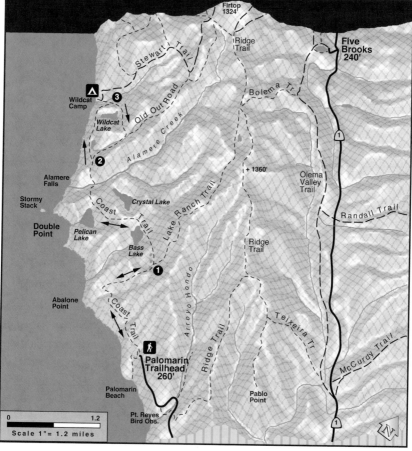

Firtop 1324'

Five Brooks 240'

Stewart Trail

Ridge Trail

Bolema Tr.

Wildcat Camp

3

Old Out Road

Wildcat Lake

Alamere Creek

1

2

Alamere Falls

+ 1360'

Olema Valley Trail

Stormy Stack

Crystal Lake

Lake Ranch Trail

Randall Trail

Double Point

Coast Trail

Pelican Lake

Bass Lake

1

Ridge Trail

Abalone Point

Coast Trail

Arroyo Hondo

Teixeira Tr.

Palomarin Trailhead 260'

Ridge Trail

McCurdy Trail

Palomarin Beach

Pt. Reyes Bird Obs.

Pablo Point

1

0   1.2

Scale 1"= 1.2 miles

N

F18 Griffin Loop - Bird Overlook Trails

Distance: 2.9 miles   Shaded: 70%
Elevation Change: 800'   Call 415-868-9244 for information.
Rating: Hiking - 9   Difficulty - 7   Moderately steep.
When to Go: Open mid-March to mid-July, weekends 10-4.

This hike leads to an overlook that offers a rare and unforgettable view of great blue herons and egrets in their tree-top colonies.

0.0 Park at the Audubon Canyon Ranch parking area. Before beginning, register at the welcoming table and pick up brochures that describe the preserve. The hike starts out on the Griffin Loop trail.

0.1 Junction, bench and Clem Miller Overlook. Good view to Bolinas Lagoon. Continue towards the Overlook.

0.3 Junction. A connecting trail heads left. Continue right.

0.5 Junction ❶. Take the trail right to the Overlook.

0.5 Henderson Overlook, benches and spotting scopes. Audubon volunteers with telescopes show visitors the herons and egrets in their nesting sites in the tops of redwood trees. Both herons and egrets display elaborate courtship rituals at the beginning of nesting season. Both species lay two to five eggs that take about four weeks to hatch. Young egret chicks start flying at about seven weeks of age; the young heron chicks at nine weeks. Typically, there are about 60-100 egret nests and 7-15 heron nests. One year, raccoons and an eagle raided the nests, significantly reducing the population.

Around the turn of the century, great egrets were nearly hunted to extinction for their courting plumes or feathers. The Audubon Society in the United States was first formed to stop their decimation.

0.6 Junction ❶. The hike continues by heading up the ridge on the Griffin Loop trail. (Some signs may call it the Canyon trail).

1.3 Junction ❷. Take the Griffin Loop trail right, which circles above Audubon Canyon in a redwood forest. **Option:** The North Loop (Zumie's Loop) trail heads left. It offers a more riparian, more diverse hike and is best in March and April. Both routes present great views.

2.9 Back at the Ranch with water, restrooms and a very agreeable picnic area. Be sure to visit the bookstore and exhibit hall. Also, a bird hide located next to the picnic area lets you watch birds feeding.

Option: If you would like more hiking. Take the Harwell Nature trail which makes a pleasant 0.8 mile loop into Garden Club Canyon. In early June, look for sweet-smelling buckeye trees and tiger lilies.

Getting There

From Hwy 101:
In Mill Valley
W on Hwy 1
to Audubon Canyon
located 3.8 miles
North of Stinson Beach
on Hwy 1. Good
parking on the ranch.
Donations requested.

F18 - Point Reyes South
Audubon Canyon Ranch
Bolinas Lagoon Preserve

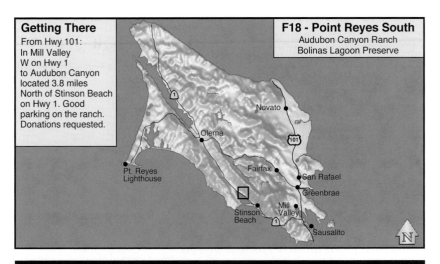

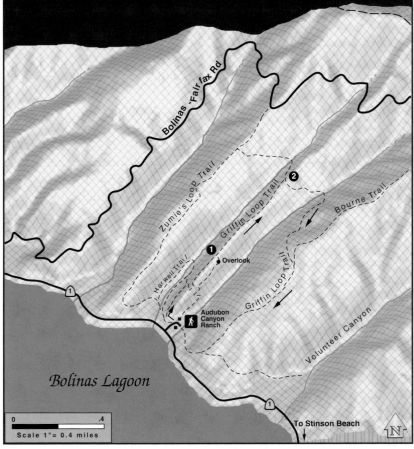

0   .4

Scale 1"= 0.4 miles

223

G - Point Reyes North - 19 Hikes

Starting from Sky Trailhead at 680'
G1   Sky - Horse - Z Ranch Trails 4.6
G2   Sky - Fire Lane - Laguna Trails 6.2
G3   Sky Trailhead to Bear Valley 7.3*
G4   Sky - Woodward Valley - Coast - Fire Lane Trails 9.3

Starting from Bayview Trailhead at 720'
G5   Bayview - Muddy Hollow - Laguna Trails 4.6
G6   Inverness Ridge - Bucklin - Bayview Trials 7.9

Starting from Muddy Hollow at 160'
G7   Coast - Beach - Muddy Hollow Trails 6.8
G8   Muddy Hollow Rd. - Estero Trails 4.4 or 8.7

Starting from Limantour Beach at 40'
G9   Limantour Spit - Beach Trails 2.0
G10 Beach Trail to Sculptured Beach at Low Tide 5.4

Starting from along Sir Francis Drake Hwy
G11 Estero - Drakes Head Trails 8.8
G12 Drakes Beach Trail 2.6
G13 PR Lighthouse and Chimney Rock Trails 1.0, 0.4 and 1.8

Starting from Tomales State Park
G14 Johnstone - Jepson Trails 4.5
G15 Pierce Point Road to Shell Beach 5.6*

Starting from along Pierce Point Road
G16 Beach and Lagoon Trails 3.0, 1.2 and 0.8
G17 Kehoe Beach Trailhead to Abbotts Lagoon 5.1*
G18 Tomales Point Trail 9.4

Starting from Tomales Bay State Park along Hwy 1
G19 Tomales Bay Trail and Millerton Point Loop 2.2 and 1.2

Notes
* Shuttle Hike
Dogs allowed on hike G16, Kehoe Beach trail only.
To download a hike, go to www.marintrails.com
The password for this region is g9bp2kv

Region G Trailheads

Hikes 1-13 and 16-18 start in Pt. Reyes National Seashore, phone 415-464-5100.

Hikes 14, 15 and 19 start in Tomales Bay State Park, phone 415-669-1140.

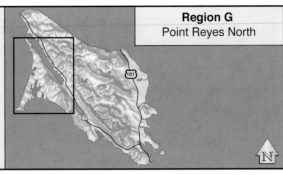

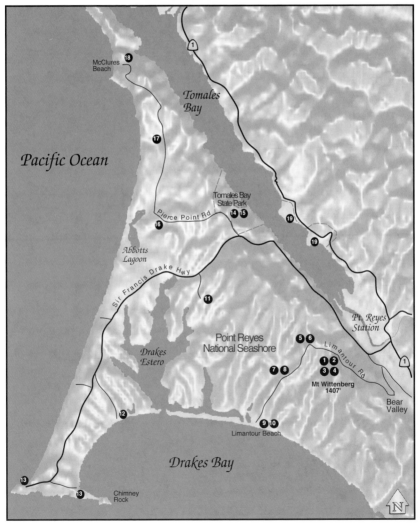

G1 Sky - Horse - Z Ranch Trails

Distance: 4.6 miles   Shaded: 50%
Elevation Change: 750'
Rating: Hiking - 10   Difficulty - 5   Can be muddy.
When to Go: Excellent anytime, best in late spring.

This is the easiest hike to the top of Mt. Wittenberg. When clear, the hike provides great views in all directions. Good wildflowers in May.

0.0 Start at the Sky trailhead about 3.5 miles out the Limantour Road. The trail is an old ranch road that climbs south through a mostly Douglas fir forest lush with berries, nettles and ferns.

0.7 Junction ❶. Take the Horse trail left. At the start of the trail, notice the large patch of salal with bright green, shiny leaves. Up ahead, the trail circles a steep canyon bare of conifers. The canyon's bowl shape suggests that a large slide occurred. In winter, water from a spring seeps out of the hillside, and may cause further soil erosion.

1.1 Junction ❷. The vegetation opens up to provide good views north. The large flat mountain due north is Point Reyes Hill at 1336'. Turn right and head uphill on the Z Ranch trail.

1.2 More evidence of slides. The trail doubles back above the large canyon. Here is where the slide must have started. Notice the large firs above the trail. Also, notice there is much less seepage. Up ahead, the view north gets better. You can just get a glimpse of Mt. St. Helena 40 miles northeast in Sonoma County.

1.8 Junction ❸ and more views. Drakes Bay and the Point Reyes headlands provide a nice background to the grassy slopes of Mt. Wittenberg and Sky Camp below. Take the spur trail up to the top of Mt. Wittenberg. Look for tidy tips and lupine in May and June.

2.0 Mt. Wittenberg at 1407'. This is the highest point on Point Reyes. The views are gone as Douglas fir trees have taken over the hilltop.

2.2 Junction ❸ again. Take the Mt. Wittenberg trail south along the ridge. **Option**: Take a short unmaintained trail left 170 yds. for views.

2.8 Two junctions ❹. Take the Sky trail right towards Sky Camp.

3.3 Sky Camp and spring. To explore the spring take the short spur trail to the left. When done, continue down the road past the restroom.

3.8 Junction ❶ and rock exposure. Just before the junction, slabs of sedimentary rock, called Monterey shale, lie exposed along the trail.

4.6 Back at the trailhead. No facilities.

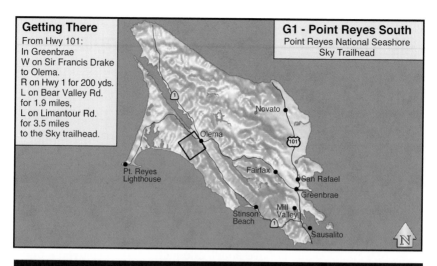

Getting There

From Hwy 101:
In Greenbrae
W on Sir Francis Drake
to Olema.
R on Hwy 1 for 200 yds.
L on Bear Valley Rd.
for 1.9 miles,
L on Limantour Rd.
for 3.5 miles
to the Sky trailhead.

G1 - Point Reyes South
Point Reyes National Seashore
Sky Trailhead

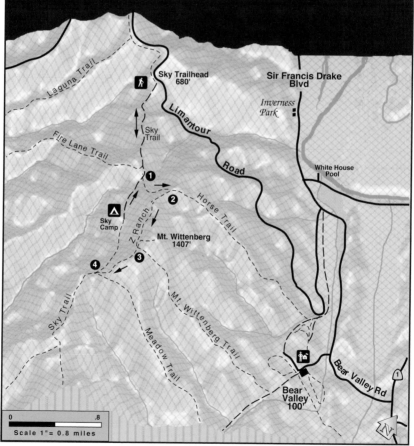

G2 Sky - Fire Lane - Laguna Trails

Distance: 6.2 miles   Shaded: 60%
Elevation Change: 850'   Can be wet.
Rating: Hiking - 9   Difficulty - 6   Moderately steep in places.
When to Go: Good anytime. Try early morning in winter for views.

This trail provides interesting terrain as it rolls down a ridgeline from Mt. Wittenberg. Early morning sunshine makes the headlands glow.

0.0   Start at the Sky trailhead and head uphill on the road. About 200 yds. up the trail, where it breaks into the open, look for Bishop pine to the right of the trail. This is a good hike for comparing Douglas fir and Bishop pine. Douglas fir have small, one-inch needles splayed around a stem. Bishop Pine have two needles per bunch, each three inches long. The cones of the Bishop pine are bigger, harder and heavier.

Most of this hike takes place in a transition zone between Douglas fir and Bishop pine communities.

Bishop Pine   *Douglas Fir*

0.8   Junction ❶ with Fire Lane trail. Take a right and follow the trail as it skirts the hilltop. The trail climbs slightly to 1090' then starts a moderate descent towards the ocean.

1.0   Great views. The trail descends through a mixture of dead trees, forest and coastal scrub. The dead trees are from the Mt. Vision fire. In open areas, look for great views of the rolling hills, Drakes Bay and the Farallon Islands.

2.0   The trail is deceptive. You expect it to be all downhill, but it climbs several knolls, each one bringing different views.

3.1   Junction ❷. Often, you can hear frogs in a marsh 300 yds. to the south. Take the Laguna trail north here. After heavy rains, there may be standing water up ahead. In some places, the trail consists of fine, sandy soil. When the trail is wet, look for animal tracks. **Option**: For a side trip, continue to Coast Camp and the ocean.

3.9   Junction ❸ with the road and the ranger residence at 140'. Stay on the Laguna trail as it heads uphill to the right. Notice the large, old buckeye trees with their multiple trunks covered with moss and lichen.

4.2   Junction with the Hidden Valley trail. Continue straight. At the end of the grassy meadow, the trail starts a moderate climb northeast.

5.5   Junction ❹ with the Bayview trail. Turn right and head southeast.

6.2   Sky trailhead. No facilities.

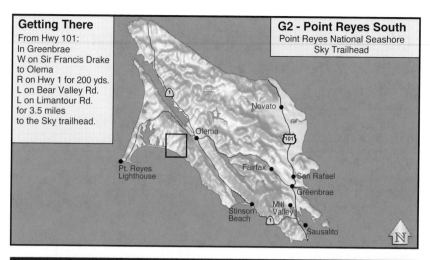

Getting There

From Hwy 101:
In Greenbrae
W on Sir Francis Drake
to Olema
R on Hwy 1 for 200 yds.
L on Bear Valley Rd.
L on Limantour Rd.
for 3.5 miles
to the Sky trailhead.

G2 - Point Reyes South
Point Reyes National Seashore
Sky Trailhead

229

G3 Sky Trailhead to Bear Valley*

Distance: 7.3 miles   Shaded: 80%
Elevation Change: 750' up and 1300' down
Rating: Hiking - 10   Difficulty - 5   Can be slightly muddy.
When to Go: Excellent anytime, best when clear.

This is the easiest and best all-around hike for exploring the forested Inverness Ridge and Bear Valley. Good views too.

*Shuttle Hike. Leave pickup cars at Bear Valley and shuttle all hikers to the Sky trailhead about 3.5 miles along the Limantour Road.

0.0 The Sky trail starts by heading south up an old ranch road. There's not much evidence left of the bulldozing that cleared the understory west of the trail for a fire break in the big fire of 1995.

0.8 Junction ❶. Take the Horse trail left through dense vegetation along the moist, north-facing slope of Mt. Wittenberg. Up ahead, the trail circles a landslide that occurred in 1982.

1.2 Junction. Turn right and head uphill on the Z Ranch trail.

1.9 Junction ❷ and more views. The grassy slopes of Mt. Wittenberg and Sky Camp below provide a picturesque foreground to Drakes Bay and the Point Reyes headlands. Take the spur trail left up to the top.

2.1 Mt. Wittenberg at 1407' is the highest spot on Point Reyes. Retrace your steps down the mountain when ready to continue.

2.3 Junction. Take the Mt. Wittenberg trail south along the ridge line.

2.7 Two junctions. Continue south on the Sky trail, which now enters a magnificent forest of Douglas fir towering over a smaller forest of elderberry. In early spring, the light-green leaves of the elderberry provide a striking contrast to the darker colors of the fir. Later in spring, cream-colored blossoms and inedible red berries create changing patterns in this woodsy setting.

Red Elderberry

3.5 Junction ❸ and meadow. The Woodward Valley trail heads right through a beautiful meadow, ideal for picnics. Continue straight.

3.8 Junction ❹. Take the Old Pine trail left as it leaves the Inverness Ridge and makes a long, gradual descent down to Bear Valley.

5.7 Junction ❺ and Divide Meadow. Head downhill to the left.

7.3 Bear Valley trailhead with water, restrooms and pickup cars.

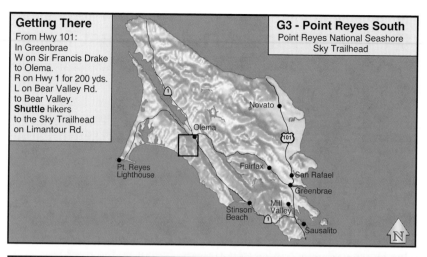

Getting There

From Hwy 101:
In Greenbrae
W on Sir Francis Drake
to Olema.
R on Hwy 1 for 200 yds.
L on Bear Valley Rd.
to Bear Valley.
Shuttle hikers
to the Sky Trailhead
on Limantour Rd.

G3 - Point Reyes South
Point Reyes National Seashore
Sky Trailhead

Novato

Olema

Pt. Reyes
Lighthouse

Fairfax

San Rafael

Greenbrae

Stinson
Beach

Mill
Valley

Sausalito

N

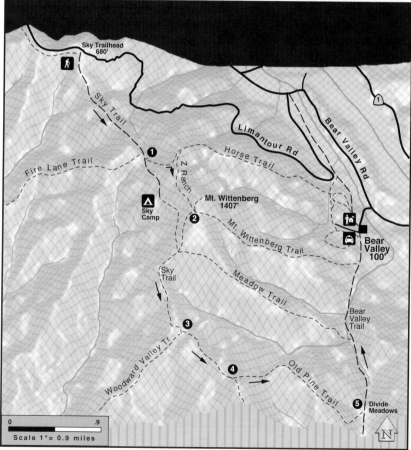

Sky Trailhead
680'

Sky Trail

Fire Lane Trail

1

Z Ranch

Horse Trail

Limantour Rd

Bear Valley Rd

1

Sky
Camp

Mt. Wittenberg
1407'

2

Mt. Wittenberg Trail

Bear
Valley
100'

Sky
Trail

Meadow Trail

3

Woodward Valley Tr

4

Old Pine Trail

Bear
Valley
Trail

5 Divide
Meadows

0   .9

Scale 1"= 0.9 miles

N

231

G4 Sky - Woodward Valley - Coast Trails

Distance: 9.3 miles   Shaded: 50%
Elevation Change: 1600'   Wet in winter, overgrown in summer.
Rating: Hiking - 9   Difficulty - 7   Moderately steep downhill.
When to Go: Excellent anytime, best when clear and calm.

This hike explores the western slopes of Mt. Wittenberg down to the ocean. It offers a variety of terrain and views, and beach access.

0.0 Start at the Sky trailhead located 3.5 miles out the Limantour Road and take the trail south as it climbs towards Sky Camp.

0.7 Two junctions ❶. Continue uphill past both the Fire Lane trail and the Horse trail, which is located 100 yds. farther up the road.

1.2 Sky Camp. Near the restroom, you can climb a small knoll to the right to get good views of Drakes Bay. The trail continues south.

1.8 Two junctions ❷. Bear right and head south past the Meadow trail. The Sky trail rolls downhill along the Inverness Ridge and enters a magnificent Douglas fir forest. Huckleberry, elderberry, ferns and nettles make up the lush understory.

2.6 Junction ❸ and meadow. Take the Woodward Valley trail as it heads down through the oval-shaped meadow.

4.3 View point. The trail levels off along a rocky outcrop offering commanding views of the coastline. To the south, you can see all the way to Double Point and just below it, Alamere Falls. To the north, you see the sweeping arc of Drakes Bay culminating in the Point Reyes headlands and Chimney Rock.

4.6 Junction. Take the Coast trail north. Up ahead, the trail turns inland to cross Santa Maria Creek, then returns to the coast. Look for a large, granite outcropping high above the trail.

5.3 Coast Camp. Water, restrooms and beach access. **Option**: Take the trail west along the creek to explore the beach.

5.4 Junction ❹. Take the Fire Lane trail to the right and start a moderate climb through open grassland. Up ahead, the trail passes a marshy area where you may hear frogs croaking.

6.5 Junction ❺. Continue straight on the Laguna trail, which can have standing water in winter.

7.3 Junction ❻. Head right, staying on the Laguna trail.

8.6 Junction. Take the Bayview trail right climbing through the fire area.

9.3 Back at the Sky trailhead. No facilities.

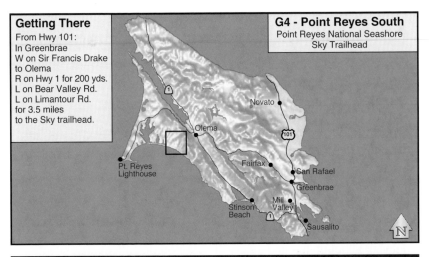

Getting There

From Hwy 101:
In Greenbrae
W on Sir Francis Drake
to Olema
R on Hwy 1 for 200 yds.
L on Bear Valley Rd.
L on Limantour Rd.
for 3.5 miles
to the Sky trailhead.

G4 - Point Reyes South
Point Reyes National Seashore
Sky Trailhead

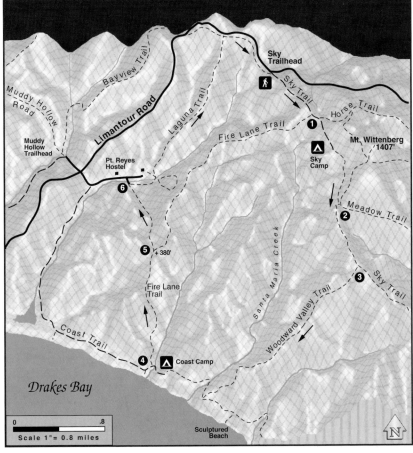

233

G5 Bayview - Muddy Hollow - Laguna

Distance: 4.6 miles   Shaded: 50%
Elevation Change: 600'   Trail can be wet in winter.
Rating: Hiking - 9   Difficulty - 5   Some poison oak.
When to Go: Excellent anytime, best in April and May.

This hike descends the slope of Inverness Ridge offering great views to the west, then enters a lush riparian corridor.

0.0 Start at the Bayview trailhead and take Bayview trail west. The hike starts in what was once a mixture of Bishop pine and coastal scrub. Most of the pine burned in the fire of 1995 (See Hike G6 for details), although the understory of huckleberry, coffeeberry, coyote bush, ferns and blackberry returned quickly. Good views to the ocean.

1.4 The trail drops down into a scenic canyon and riparian corridor dominated by red alder, which is prone to wind damage. Nettles, miner's lettuce, sedges and cow parsnip provide a lush, green understory. In the spring, the succulent leaves and stems of miner's lettuce, also known as Indian lettuce, provided a nourishing treat for Native Americans and early settlers.

1.6 Junction with Drakes View trail. A bench provides a chance to rest and admire the bridge design. Continue left. Up ahead, the trail crosses a wooden plank bridge, then passes through a small marshy area. Farther ahead, majestic old buckeyes, their contorted branches covered with lichens, overhang the trail.

Miner's Lettuce

2.1 Junction ❶ with the Muddy Hollow road. Head left and watch for birds along the creek and in the marsh.

2.4 Junction with Limantour Road. Cross the road and continue along the pavement past the Pt. Reyes Youth Hostel. Follow the signs to the Laguna trailhead.

2.8 Junction ❷ with the Laguna trail. Just past the residence, take the Laguna trail left. Up ahead, the trail enters an open, grassy meadow. The Clem Miller Environmental Center can be seen on the left. A short loop trail up Hidden Valley takes off on the right.

At the end of the meadow, the trail, which was once the main road to the beach, starts a moderate climb up the slopes of Inverness Ridge.

4.1 Junction ❸ with the Bayview trail. Head left.

4.6 Bayview trailhead. No facilities.

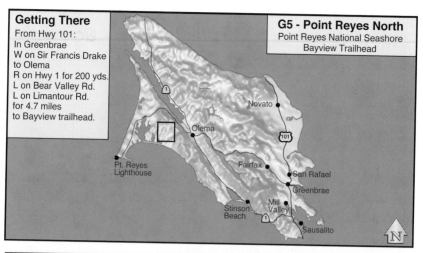

Getting There

From Hwy 101:
In Greenbrae
W on Sir Francis Drake
to Olema
R on Hwy 1 for 200 yds.
L on Bear Valley Rd.
L on Limantour Rd.
for 4.7 miles
to Bayview trailhead.

G5 - Point Reyes North
Point Reyes National Seashore
Bayview Trailhead

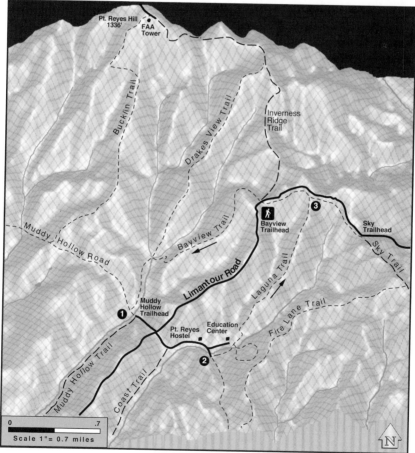

G6 Inverness Ridge - Bucklin - Bayview

Distance: 7.9 miles   Shaded: 40%
Elevation Change: 1400'   Rocky in places.
Rating: Hiking - 8   Difficulty - 7   Moderately steep.
When to Go: Good when clear, best in spring.

This is the best hike for exploring the Bishop pine forest and fire zone along Inverness Ridge. It also offers great views, both east and west.

0.0 From the Bayview trailhead, take the signed Inverness Ridge trail north down the dirt road.

0.7 Gate. Go 100 yds. past the gate and up the paved road to pick up the trail left, which climbs steeply.

1.3 Junction ❶. Continue straight. The first edition of this book described this area as a "luxuriant mix of forest and coastal scrub that includes ceanothus, coyote bush, manzanita, oak, madrone, blackberry, coffeeberry, bracken fern, salal, monkeyflower and Bishop pine." Now, after the fire, ceanothus is the dominant shrub. However, ceanothus is a short-lived plant with a lifetime of 5-10 years. It will be interesting to see the succession of plant communities.

Mt. Vision Fire of 1995

In October 1995, an illegal campfire on Mt. Vision, fanned by strong winds, started a major fire on Pt. Reyes that lasted 4 days. The fire burned over 12,000 acres and destroyed 45 homes on nearby private land.

The Bishop pine forest suffered the most damage with about 90% of the trees in the fire zone destroyed. However, Bishop pine requires periodic fire for regeneration and survival. Fire is a part of the forest's natural life cycle.

2.1 Good views. After crossing an open saddle, the trail heads steeply uphill through coastal scrub and grasses that occasionally crowd the narrow rutted path. Great views to Tomales Bay.

2.6 FAA Station and junction ❷ on Point Reyes Hill at 1336'. Continue along the paved road about 100 yds. to pick up the Bucklin trail which follows the fence west, then heads downhill. The hike now rolls down a ridgeline offering great views of Drakes Bay and the headlands. In the spring, look for the white, hairy star tulip.

5.0 Junction ❸ with the Muddy Hollow Road. Head left.

5.8 Junction ❹ with the Bayview trail. Head left and start the long easy climb towards Inverness Ridge.

7.9 Back at the trailhead. No facilities.

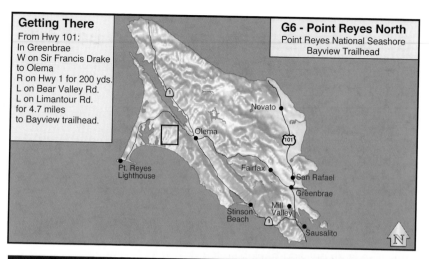

Getting There

From Hwy 101:
In Greenbrae
W on Sir Francis Drake
to Olema
R on Hwy 1 for 200 yds.
L on Bear Valley Rd.
L on Limantour Rd.
for 4.7 miles
to Bayview trailhead.

G6 - Point Reyes North
Point Reyes National Seashore
Bayview Trailhead

Novato

Pt. Reyes
Lighthouse

Olema

Fairfax

San Rafael

Greenbrae

Stinson
Beach

Mill
Valley

Sausalito

N

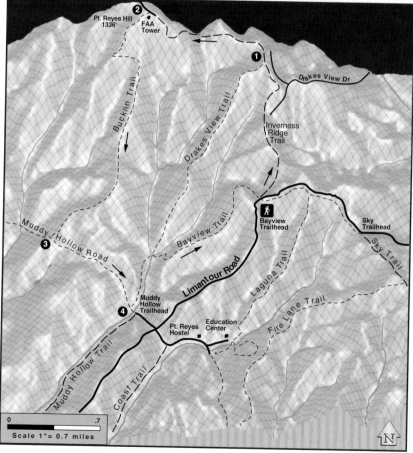

Pt. Reyes Hill
1336'

FAA
Tower

Bucklin Trail

Drakes View Dr

Drakes View Trail

Inverness
Ridge
Trail

Muddy Hollow Road

Bayview Trail

Bayview
Trailhead

Sky
Trailhead

Limantour Road

Laguna Trail

Sky Trail

Muddy
Hollow
Trailhead

Pt. Reyes
Hostel

Education
Center

Fire Lane Trail

Muddy Hollow Trail

Coast Trail

0   .7
Scale 1"= 0.7 miles

N

237

G7 Coast - Beach - Muddy Hollow Trails

Distance: 6.8 miles - See Note below.   Shaded: 0%
Elevation Change: 200'
Rating: Hiking - 9   Difficulty - 3
When to Go: Best in fall and winter for birds.

This hike travels along creeks, fresh and saltwater marshes, and the ocean to offer a variety of habitats and good birding locations.

Note: The Muddy Hollow trail is closed! Short sections of the Muddy Hollow trail are under 5-20" of water. The trail is also overgrown in places. Eventually, the trail will be rerouted and reopened. Until then, this hike is an out-and-back hike to junction ❹ below.

0.0 Park at the Muddy Hollow parking area 0.2 mile north of the Limantour Road. The hike starts by heading back up toward the road.

0.2 Limantour Road. Continue across the road towards the hostel.

0.4 Junction ❶. Before reaching the hostel, take the Coast trail south towards Drakes Bay. The Coast trail parallels a riparian corridor following a small creek into Limantour Marsh. In the early morning, the chatter of birds fills the air.

Brown Pelican

1.3 Creek crossing and alders. Up ahead, the trail skirts the marsh, then doglegs to the right towards the ocean.

2.1 Junction ❷ with the beach. Take the signed trail 30' through the dunes and head right along the beach. If it's not too windy, this can be an exhilarating walk with views of Drakes Bay, pounding surf and much beach activity. Watch for pelicans, willets and plovers.

2.9 Trail inland ❸. Look for the greatest concentration of people or a break in the dunes and head inland towards the Limantour parking area.

Willet

3.0 Junction, water and restroom. At the restroom, head left to pick up the Muddy Hollow trail. Look for sandpipers, willets, egrets and herons in Limantour Estero to the west.

3.4 Junction ❹ with the Estero trail. The trail is closed beyond here. Retrace your steps. **Option**: Explore Limantour Spit - see Hike G9.

6.8 Back at the Muddy Hollow parking area. No facilities.

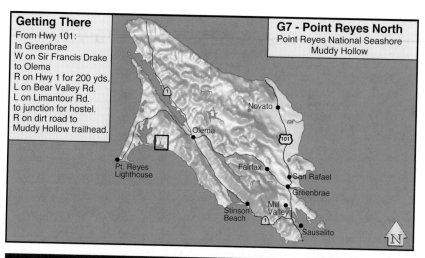

Getting There

From Hwy 101:
In Greenbrae
W on Sir Francis Drake
to Olema
R on Hwy 1 for 200 yds.
L on Bear Valley Rd.
L on Limantour Rd.
to junction for hostel.
R on dirt road to
Muddy Hollow trailhead.

G7 - Point Reyes North
Point Reyes National Seashore
Muddy Hollow

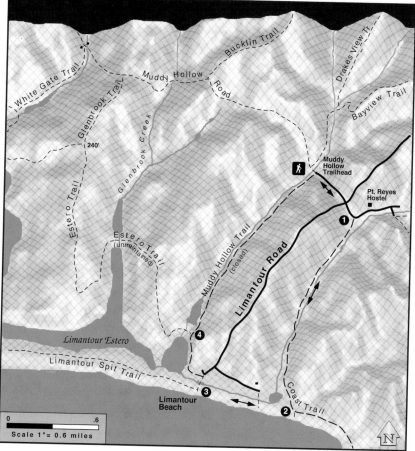

239

G8 Muddy Hollow Rd - Estero Trail

Distance: 4.4 or 8.7 miles (See Option below)   Shaded: 10%
Elevation Change: 450'   Some poison oak and nettles.
Rating: Hiking - 7   Difficulty - 4 or 8 (depending on Option below)
When to Go: Good when clear skies, best in spring, but not too wet.

This hike traverses open coastal hills offering excellent views of Drakes Bay and Limantour Estero, then returns via the same route.

Note: The Estero trail is scheduled for a major rerouting in 2006/2007.

0.0 Start at the Muddy Hollow trailhead located 0.2 mile north of Limantour Road. Take the dirt road northeast through the gate.

0.1 Junction. Continue past the Bayview trail and the site of the old Muddy Hollow ranch, which was located near the cypress trees. If the road is wet, look for deer tracks in the wet sandy soil.

0.9 Junction ❶ with the Bucklin trail. Continue straight and follow the trail as it heads down into the Glenbrook Creek drainage basin.

1.5 Junction ❷. Take the Glenbrook trail left and make a short climb to a rise offering great views of the coast.

2.2 Junction ❸ with the Estero trail. Retrace your steps back to the start.

Option: The Estero trail is unmaintained and overgrown, but passable at the time of this writing. If you choose this option, head south towards the ocean. Continue at your own risk and be ready to backtrack.

3.7 Bridge. As you head inland, the trail drops down past eucalyptus trees. The first dairy on Point Reyes was established here in 1857 by the Steele brothers. Up ahead, the trail crosses a bridge on Glenbrook Creek. This section of trail can be muddy and overgrown with stinging nettles. After crossing the bridge, the trail makes a short climb up to a ridge.

5.2 Dam. The last section of Estero trail drops down a rutted bank to a pond, then crosses a dam (to be removed during trail rerouting).

5.3 Junction ❹. Go right towards the beach, then down to the beach.

5.8 Beach. Head left. Keep an eye on the dunes and look for an opening 0.7 miles away. There is also a Douglas fir tree next to the opening, the only tree in this area. Head up through the opening.

6.5 Junction ❺. Take the Coast trail left.

8.3 Junction with the Hostel road. Head left. Cross the Limantour Rd.

8.7 Back at the Muddy Hollow trailhead. No facilities.

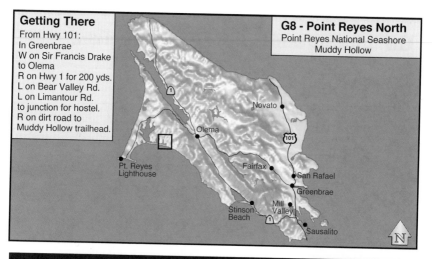

Getting There

From Hwy 101:
In Greenbrae
W on Sir Francis Drake
to Olema
R on Hwy 1 for 200 yds.
L on Bear Valley Rd.
L on Limantour Rd.
to junction for hostel.
R on dirt road to
Muddy Hollow trailhead.

G8 - Point Reyes North
Point Reyes National Seashore
Muddy Hollow

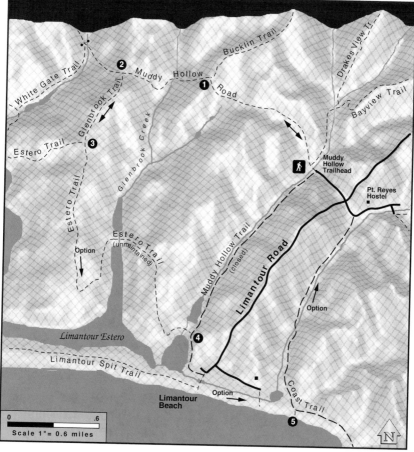

Scale 1" = 0.6 miles

G9 Limantour Spit - Beach Trails

Distance: 2.0 miles   Shaded: 0%
Elevation Change: less than 100'
Rating: Hiking - 8   Difficulty - 2   Can be windy.
When to Go: Anytime, best when calm and clear.

This refreshing hike along the dunes and beach provides good views, lots of birds and a reminder of the historic struggle to create a park.

0.0 Start at the Limantour parking area and head down past the restroom towards the ocean. Just after passing the marsh area, turn right and head north along the trail in the dunes.

This trail was once called Limantour Drive, which led into a subdivision called Drakes Bay Estates. This area of the development had been divided into over one hundred lots. When the National Seashore formed in 1962, six of the lots already had homes built! As you walk along, you'll see an occasional pipe or concrete pad, reminders of what might have been and of the heroic efforts of the early conservationists to create a new park.

Modern landowners were not the first to use this spit. Before the developers moved in, archeologists had uncovered three middens or shell mounds that were garbage dumps of the Coastal Miwoks. Not only did the middens contain shells, but archeologists also found dozens of pieces of Chinese Ming porcelain and other artifacts that indicate that the Spaniard, Cermeno, may have camped on the spit after the shipwreck of the San Agustin in 1595.

Harbor Seal

0.5 Birds of the estero. Look for egrets, herons, willets, and plovers, especially in winter.

1.0 End of the road. Head out across the dunes to the beach, then go left again. **Option**: To add to the hike, continue northwest 1.8 miles to the end of the spit. (You might see an old shipwreck about 1.5 miles out.)

1.5 Harbor seal or sea lion? The two most common marine mammals at Point Reyes are harbor seals and sea lions. Harbor seals are smaller and have a mottled coat. They have large eyes and no ears. When they go under,

Sea Lion

they often sink straight down, while sea lions tend to dive forward.

2.0 Limantour parking area, restrooms and water.

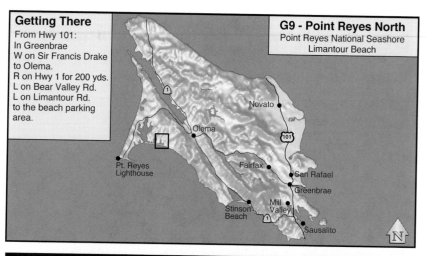

Getting There

From Hwy 101:
In Greenbrae
W on Sir Francis Drake
to Olema.
R on Hwy 1 for 200 yds.
L on Bear Valley Rd.
L on Limantour Rd.
to the beach parking
area.

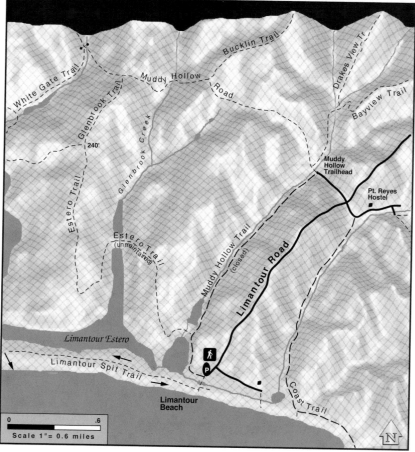

243

G10 Beach Trail to Sculptured Beach

Distance: 5.4 miles   Shaded: 0%
Elevation Change: 50'   Check tide tables before taking this hike.
Rating: Hiking - 7   Difficulty - 2 to 5 (See text below.)
When to Go: Best at low tide in the summer and fall.

This hike explores the interesting rock formations and tidepools on the beaches south of Limantour. Conditions vary with beach level.

0.0 Park in the auxiliary parking area south of the main parking lot at Limantour Beach. Take the trail across the dunes to the beach and head south. Before leaving the dunes, look back and note the trees and ranger residence, which provide a landmark for returning.

1.4 Creek, Coast Camp and junction ❶. Continue along the beach.

1.8 Santa Maria Creek and Sculptured Beach. The sandy beach here changes with storm activity. During some winters, large wave action moves sand offshore lowering the level of the beach and making travel over the rocky terraces difficult. Later in the year, smaller wave action usually brings the sand back ashore, making it easier to walk along here and explore the rocks and tidepools.

2.5 Junction ❷. You can climb up to a small rocky terrace and scan the beach south to Pt. Resistance and Arch Rock. Usually, this is as far as you can go. When done exploring, retrace your steps.

Option: If the beach sand level is high enough and there is a minus tide, you may be able to explore the beach south. You will probably have to climb down off the terrace 4-6 feet to reach the beach. If you can safely do this, there are interesting caves and tunnels ahead. (This is not an approved park trail. Hike at your own risk and be sure to watch the tide!)

Low Tide

Low tide at Point Reyes occurs 35-40 minutes earlier than Golden Gate low tide, which is usually given in the tide tables.

Also, the tide comes in slowly at first, then rises more quickly about two hours after the minimum. You should plan to have a clear, safe route off any beach by this time.

3.6 Junction ❶ and Coast Camp. Head inland, veer left and follow the Coast trail towards Limantour Beach.

4.8 Junction ❸. Leave the Coast trail and take the beach north.

5.3 Junction. Look for the trees and residence and head inland again.

5.4 Parking area. Restrooms and water at the main parking area.

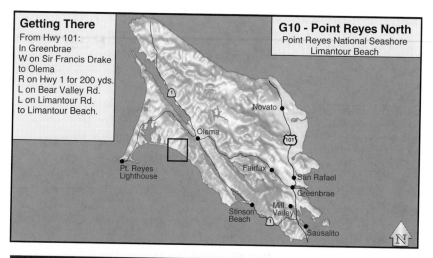

Getting There

From Hwy 101:
In Greenbrae
W on Sir Francis Drake
to Olema
R on Hwy 1 for 200 yds.
L on Bear Valley Rd.
L on Limantour Rd.
to Limantour Beach.

G10 - Point Reyes North
Point Reyes National Seashore
Limantour Beach

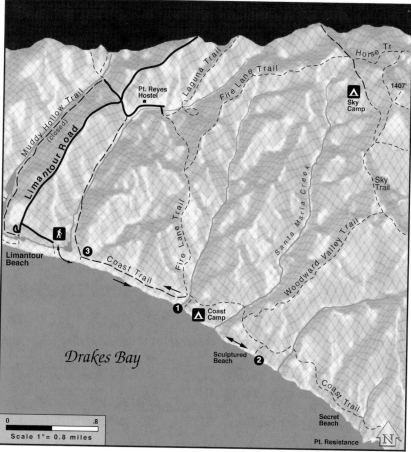

245

G11 Estero - Drakes Head Trails

Distance: 8.8 miles   Shaded: 0%
Elevation Change: 750'   Can be overgrown in places.
Rating: Hiking - 8   Difficulty - 4   Trail can be muddy in parts.
When to Go: Best in late fall and winter when calm and clear.

This is an out and back hike through rolling pastureland to the best viewpoint on Point Reyes. A good hike to see birds and mammals.

0.0 From the parking area, take the Estero trail south towards the pine forest. This rangeland is part of Home Ranch, which has been grazed since the 1850s. In spring, patches of blue iris dot the hillsides.

1.0 Dam and bridge at point ❶. Notice the Home Ranch farm buildings to the east. James Shafter's ranch, started in 1857, is the oldest surviving ranch on Point Reyes. Also, see if you can spot the massive slide caused by rains from El Nino 1998. Over 200' of hill slid down towards the bay. The trail now heads uphill. Watch for wildlife along the way: deer, rabbits, coyote, osprey, ducks and egrets.

1.5 Plateau and view of Drakes Estero. The point across the water was one of two schooner landing sites. The estero and bay were deeper in earlier days allowing small schooners, like the *Point Reyes*, to deliver highly-prized butter to San Francisco. Johnson's Oyster Farm now uses the shallower estero waters.

Schooner Point Reyes

2.4 Junction ❷ with the Sunset Beach trail. Bear left and head uphill.

3.0 Junction ❸ and corral. Turn right and follow the signed Drakes Head trail towards the ocean.

4.0 Water tank and trees. This is the site of the Drakes Head Ranch, which operated from the 1850s to 1960. Keep to the right.

4.4 Drakes Head. On a clear day this is the best view spot on all of Point Reyes! It offers a panoramic sweep of Drakes Bay from the headlands to Double Point. Look for harbor seals sunning at the end of the spit. When ready to return, retrace your steps. **Caution:** The cliff edge may be unstable.

8.8 Back at the parking lot. Restrooms available.

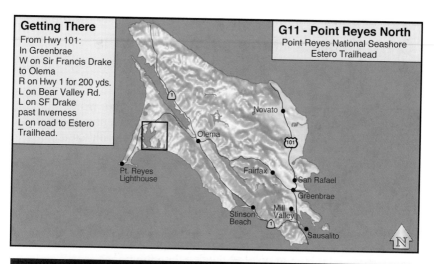

Getting There

From Hwy 101:
In Greenbrae
W on Sir Francis Drake
to Olema
R on Hwy 1 for 200 yds.
L on Bear Valley Rd.
L on SF Drake
past Inverness
L on road to Estero
Trailhead.

G11 - Point Reyes North
Point Reyes National Seashore
Estero Trailhead

Novato

Olema

Pt. Reyes
Lighthouse

Fairfax

San Rafael

Greenbrae

Stinson
Beach

Mill
Valley

Sausalito

N

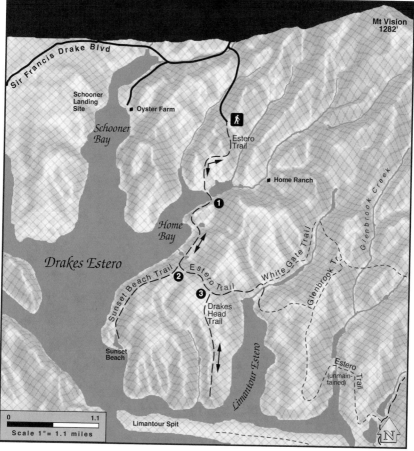

Mt Vision
1282'

Sir Francis Drake Blvd

Schooner
Landing
Site

■ Oyster Farm

Schooner
Bay

Estero
Trail

■ Home Ranch

Glenbrook Creek

❶

Home
Bay

Drakes Estero

Sunset Beach Trail

Estero Trail

White Gate Trail

Glenbrook Tr.

❷

❸

Drakes
Head
Trail

Sunset
Beach

Limantour Estero

Estero
Trail
(unmaintained)

Limantour Spit

0   1.1
Scale 1"= 1.1 miles

N

G12 Drakes Beach Trail

Distance: 2.6 miles   Shaded: 0%
Elevation Change: 10'   May not be passable. See Note.
Rating: Hiking - 8   Difficulty - 2   Trail overgrown near monument.
When to Go: Low tide required. Best in spring for wildlife.

This hike explores the beach and historic plaque marking Drake's landing. Estero views, harbor seals and nesting egrets are possible.

Note: In some years, winter storms remove beach sand, and then this hike can only be done at tides of one foot or lower.

0.0 Start at the Ken Patrick Visitor Center picnic area and head to your left down the beach. As you walk along the beach, see if you can spot fault lines in the cliff above. These show up as shifts in the horizontal lines. These light-colored cliffs reminded Drake of the "white cliffs of Dover" and are strong evidence that Drake beached his ship here. He named this land, Nova Albion, meaning New England.

0.5 Horseshoe Pond. **Option 1**: An unmaintained trail climbs up to the bluffs from here offering great views of the estero. The trail can be difficult to access during heavy water runoff from the pond. **Note**: The bluffs can also be accessed at the end of the beach. See Option 2.

1.2 Dunes and Drakes Estero. Either cross the dunes or circle them to head inland towards the cliff and trees. If harbor seals are basking in the estero, continue quietly for they spook easily, and if agitated, may abandon their pups.

1.3 Drake Monument. Look for the pole and monument about 50' inland. Most experts believe that this is the spot where Drake careened the Golden Hinde for repairs in 1579. When ready retrace your steps.

Option 2: Continue through the gate and up the unmaintained road to the bluffs. Note that the road may be overgrown with shrubs, including poison oak.

2.6 Back at the Visitor Center with restrooms, museum and snack bar.

*Monument to
Sir Francis Drake*

Option 3: There is another monument to Drake located opposite the bus parking area, just west of the road entering the parking lot. There is also a short trail to the Peter Behr Overlook opposite the Visitor Center. Both are worth doing.

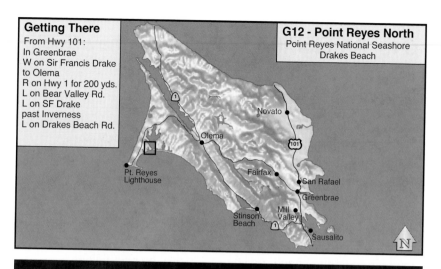

Getting There

From Hwy 101:
In Greenbrae
W on Sir Francis Drake
to Olema
R on Hwy 1 for 200 yds.
L on Bear Valley Rd.
L on SF Drake
past Inverness
L on Drakes Beach Rd.

G12 - Point Reyes North
Point Reyes National Seashore
Drakes Beach

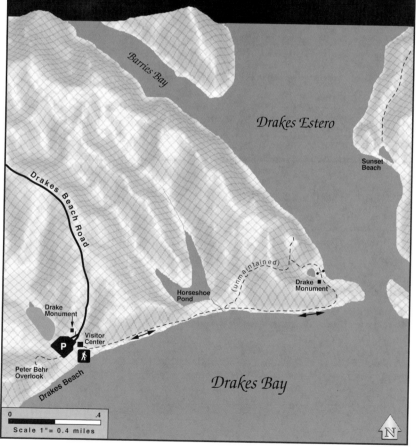

G13 PR Lighthouse and Chimney Rock

Distance: 1.0, 0.4 and 1.8 miles   Shaded: 0%
Elevation Change: See below.
Rating: Hiking - 10   Difficulty - 2, 3 and 4   Wind and fog likely.
When to Go: Best in early January and again in March-April.

These are three exhilarating hikes. The lighthouse offers whale watching. Chimney Rock has elephant seals and great wildflowers.

Note: During peak visitor times, usually December to April, the park service restricts traffic to the lighthouse and Chimney Rock, and runs a weekend bus shuttle from the Drakes Beach parking lot during the hours from 9 am to 3 pm. Call 415-464-5100 for information.

To Lighthouse Visitor Center and Back – 1.0 miles and 100' Change.
0.0 Start at the lighthouse parking lot and head uphill past the gate. The view north along Point Reyes Beach (also known as the "Great Beach"), which runs 11 miles, offers a classic picture-taking spot.

0.5 Visitor Center. The center is open Thursday to Monday, 10 am to 5 pm. The lighthouse stairs, all 308 of them, are open from 10 am to 4:30 pm Th-M, weather permitting. Check the Visitor Center for tours of the lighthouse itself. The lighthouse platform is the best place in Marin to watch grey whales migrating between Alaska and Baja California.

To Elephant Seal Overlook and Back – 0.4 miles and 50' Change
0.0 From the Chimney Rock trailhead, head downhill on the paved road 50' and pick up the trail heading towards Drakes Beach.

0.2 Overlook. On weekends, docents may be available to describe elephant seal breeding habits. Bring binoculars.

To Chimney Rock and Back – 1.8 miles and 100' Change.
0.0 From the Chimney Rock trailhead, follow the trail as it skirts the hillside above the cypress trees and ranger residence.

0.3 Junction with Underhill road. Continue straight. The US Coast Guard Lifeboat Station, below, operated between 1927 and 1968. Dozens of people were saved after shipwrecks near here.

0.5 Junction ❶. An unmaintained trail goes right to an overlook offering spectacular coastline scenery. However, the entire cliff area is dangerous and unstable due to several slides in recent years.

0.9 Chimney Rock, viewpoint and flowers. Expert observers have counted over 60 species of spring wildflowers including pussy-ears and iris. When ready, head back.

Pussy-ears

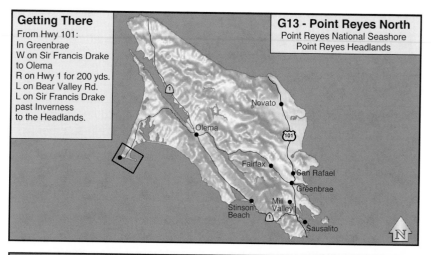

Getting There

From Hwy 101:
In Greenbrae
W on Sir Francis Drake
to Olema
R on Hwy 1 for 200 yds.
L on Bear Valley Rd.
L on Sir Francis Drake
past Inverness
to the Headlands.

Novato

Olema

Fairfax

San Rafael

Greenbrae

Mill Valley

Stinson Beach

Sausalito

N

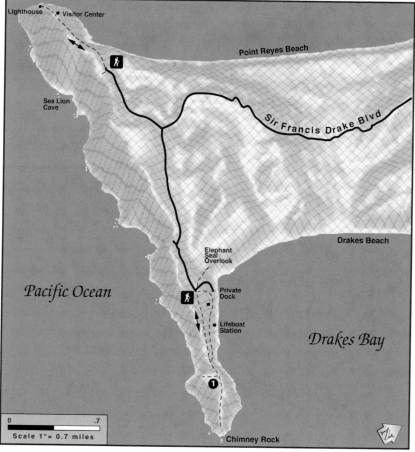

Lighthouse   ■ Visitor Center

Point Reyes Beach

Sea Lion Cave

Sir Francis Drake Blvd

Drakes Beach

Elephant Seal Overlook

Private Dock

Lifeboat Station

Pacific Ocean

Drakes Bay

①

| 0 | .7 |

Scale 1"= 0.7 miles

Chimney Rock

251

G14 Johnstone - Jepson Trails

Distance: 4.5 miles   Shaded: 80%
Elevation Change: 500'
Rating: Hiking - 10   Difficulty - 4   Can be muddy in winter.
When to Go: Great anytime. Birds in winter, beaches in summer.

This is a magnificent hike through Tomales Bay State Park. It features a luxuriant Bishop pine forest, Indian Nature trail and three beaches.

Option: If you want to picnic or wade in the bay after the hike, you might drive into the park (pay fee) and start the hike at mile 2.1 below.

0.0 Start at the small parking area located one mile out Pierce Point Rd. and two-tenths of a mile before the entrance to Tomales Bay State Park. Take the signed Jepson trail uphill into Bishop pine forest.

0.1 Junction. Head right towards signed Shell Beach.

0.3 Junction ❶. Take the Johnstone trail left towards Pebble Beach. Up ahead, after crossing the road again, the trail enters a luxuriant Bishop pine forest produced by winter rain and summer fog drip.

1.6 Junction ❷. Continue right past the restroom to delightful Pebble Beach. When ready to continue, return to junction ❷ and take the trail towards Heart's Desire Beach. Up ahead, toyon and huckleberry shrubs are almost twice their normal size in this lush rain forest.

2.0 Junction. A trail leads left to the parking circle. Continue straight towards Heart's Desire. Great views of the bay.

2.1 Heart's Desire Beach. Continue across the beach, past the restroom and take the signed Indian Nature trail to Indian Beach.

2.3 Junction ❸ with the Loop trail. Keep to the right.

2.6 Bridge and Indian Beach. Head down the beach towards the Indian kotchas. The hike continues on the road that circles the marsh.

3.2 Junction. Leave the road and take the loop trail left.

3.3 Junction ❸ again. Head right.

3.5 Heart's Desire Beach. Cross the beach and take the Johnstone trail along the shoreline.

3.6 Junction. Head right up to the parking lot, then circle around counterclockwise on the paved street.

3.7 Junction. Take the signed Jepson trail uphill.

4.4 Junction with the trail to Shell Beach. Stay right.

4.5 Back at the parking area. No facilities.

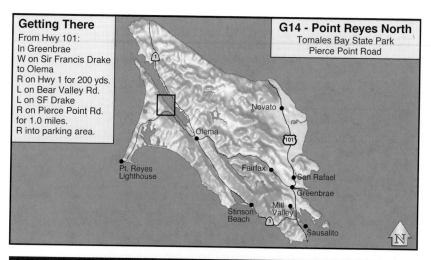

Getting There

From Hwy 101:
In Greenbrae
W on Sir Francis Drake
to Olema
R on Hwy 1 for 200 yds.
L on Bear Valley Rd.
L on SF Drake
R on Pierce Point Rd.
for 1.0 miles.
R into parking area.

G14 - Point Reyes North
Tomales Bay State Park
Pierce Point Road

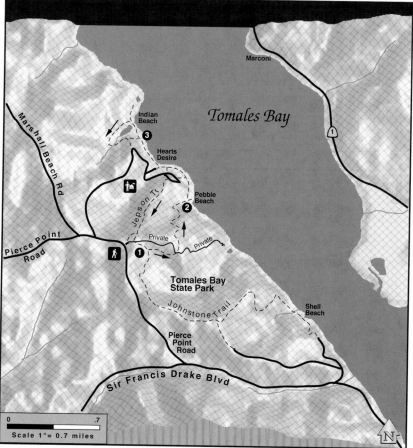

253

G15 Pierce Point Road to Shell Beach*

Distance: 5.6 or 3.1 miles (See Option below)   Shaded: 90%
Elevation Change: 1100' down, 600' up.   Poison oak possible.
Rating: Hiking - 9   Difficulty - 5   Beaches crowded in summer.
When to Go: Great anytime. Best early fall for swimming and berries.

This one-way hike in Tomales Bay State Park makes a loop down to Heart's Desire Beach, then heads towards Shell Beach.

*Shuttle Hike. Leave pickup cars in the parking area in Tomales Bay State Park at the end of Camino Del Mar. Shuttle all hikers to the small parking area located one mile out Pierce Point Rd.

0.0 Take the signed Jepson trail uphill into Bishop pine forest.

0.1 Junction. Head left towards signed Heart's Desire Beach. Ahead, the trail enters the Jepson Memorial Grove, one of the finest groves of Bishop pine in California. Bishop pine are smaller than most pines. They have two needles per bunch, each about 3" long. Cones are tightly bound to branches.

Bishop Pine

Option: You can cut the hike short by 2.5 miles and save 500' of climbing by heading right towards Shell Beach (switch to jct ❸ below).

0.8 Parking lot. Head left around the parking circle to find the trail.

0.9 Junction ❶ with the Johnstone trail. Head left.

1.0 Heart's Desire Beach. Return to junction ❶.

1.1 Continue on the signed Johnstone trail towards Pebble Beach.

1.5 Junction ❷. Head left past the restroom to Pebble Beach. Return here to continue the hike towards Shell Beach.

2.8 Junction ❸. Head left on the Johnstone trail to Shell Beach. Down below, the trail crosses the upper end of a lush ravine.

Huckleberry

3.3 Bench and viewpoint. Good views east to Tomales Bay. **Caution**: Poison oak crowds the trail, but it is sometimes difficult to spot. Up ahead, good huckleberries in the fall.

4.0 Junction ❹. Continue left to start a long gradual descent.

5.3 Shell Beach and restroom. This small sandy beach offers good picnicking and swimming. Continue the hike across the beach.

5.6 Beach. Continue across the beach to the parking area and car.

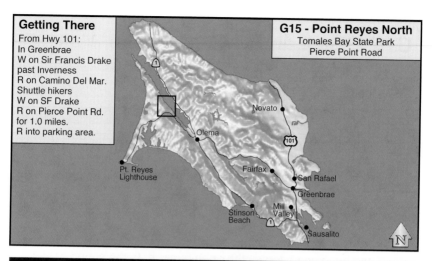

Getting There

From Hwy 101:
In Greenbrae
W on Sir Francis Drake
past Inverness
R on Camino Del Mar.
Shuttle hikers
W on SF Drake
R on Pierce Point Rd.
for 1.0 miles.
R into parking area.

G15 - Point Reyes North
Tomales Bay State Park
Pierce Point Road

Novato

Olema

Pt. Reyes
Lighthouse

Fairfax

San Rafael

Greenbrae

Stinson
Beach

Mill
Valley

Sausalito

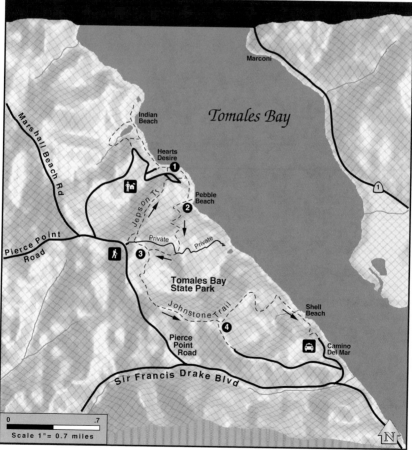

Marconi

Indian
Beach

Tomales Bay

Hearts
Desire

1

Pebble
Beach

2

Jepson Tr.

Private

Private

3

Tomales Bay
State Park

Johnstone Trail

Shell
Beach

4

Pierce
Point
Road

Camino
Del Mar

Marshall Beach Rd

Pierce Point
Road

Sir Francis Drake Blvd

0	.7

Scale 1" = 0.7 miles

255

G16 Beach and Lagoon Trails

Distance: 3.0, 1.2 and 0.8 miles   Shaded: 0%
Elevation Change: See below.
Rating: Hiking - 8   Difficulty - 3, 3 and 5   Kehoe trail can be wet.
When to Go: Best weather in fall and winter, best flowers in spring.

All three of these trails provide access to ocean beaches on the northern end of Point Reyes. Good birding at Abbotts Lagoon.

Note: Dangerous surf! Do not swim or wade in the ocean here.

Abbotts Lagoon Trail - 3.0 miles and 100' Change
0.0 Start at the trailhead located 3.4 miles along the Pierce Point Road and head west across the open pasture. In the spring of wet years, these fields are aglow with yellow poppies and fiddleneck.

1.1 Bridge, lagoon, wildflowers and birds. Yellow goldfields cover the hill on the left, while the bridge offers a good view spot for shore birds. Cross the bridge and follow the edge of the lagoon to the ocean.

1.5 Point Reyes Beach is also called Ten-mile Beach and Great Beach. This beach is a nesting area for the snowy plover. From April to June, you may see hatching enclosures that protect the plovers nest from predators, mainly crows that eat the eggs. These enclosures have increased chick survival rates from 3% to 60%.

Kehoe Beach Trail - 1.2 miles and 100' Change
0.0 Start at the trailhead 5.5 miles along the Pierce Point Road. This is a level trail that parallels Kehoe Marsh out to the beach. Good birding in the winter and abundant wildflowers in the spring.

0.6 Beach and wildflowers. The cliffs on the right are often covered in goldfields, poppies, lupine and baby blue eyes in April and May. There are good tidepools to the far right during very low tides.

McClures Beach Trail - 0.8 miles and 300' Change (See Map G18)
0.0 The trailhead is located at the end of the Pierce Point Road, 9.5 miles from the Sir Francis Drake Hwy. junction. The trail follows a ravine as it descends 300' to the ocean.

On the way down, notice the occasional erosion on the hillside. This is caused by herds of tule elk that range at this end of Tomales Point.

0.4 Beach. This is the most picturesque of the ocean beaches. During super-low tides, there are great tidepools at the south end of the beach. Be sure to check the tide tables and plan your return while the tide is still low.

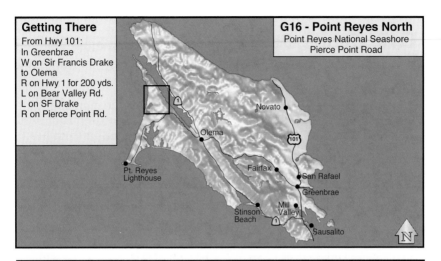

Getting There

From Hwy 101:
In Greenbrae
W on Sir Francis Drake
to Olema
R on Hwy 1 for 200 yds.
L on Bear Valley Rd.
L on SF Drake
R on Pierce Point Rd.

G16 - Point Reyes North
Point Reyes National Seashore
Pierce Point Road

Novato

Olema

Pt. Reyes
Lighthouse

Fairfax

San Rafael

Greenbrae

Stinson
Beach

Mill
Valley

Sausalito

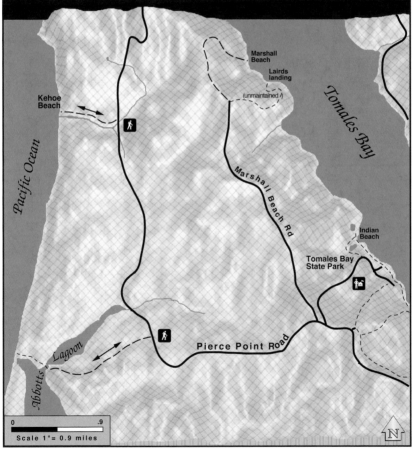

Marshall
Beach

Lairds
landing

(unmaintained /)

Kehoe
Beach

Pacific Ocean

Tomales Bay

Marshall Beach Rd

Indian
Beach

Tomales Bay
State Park

Abbotts *Lagoon*

Pierce Point Road

0   .9

Scale 1"= 0.9 miles

257

G17 Kehoe Beach to Abbotts Lagoon*

Distance: 5.1 miles   Shaded: 0%
Elevation Change: 100'   Trail can be wet near the marsh.
Rating: Hiking - 7   Difficulty - 3   Includes 2 miles on beach.
When to Go: Best in April and May when not too windy.

This one-way trail and beach hike is one of the three best wildflower hikes on Point Reyes. Go in the morning before winds get too strong.

*Shuttle Hike. Leave pickup cars at Abbotts Lagoon trailhead, 3.4 miles along the Pierce Point Road and shuttle hikers another 2.1 miles north to the Kehoe Beach trailhead.

0.0 The trail starts next to an exposed slab of Monterey shale on the northern hillside and follows a mostly level path through sandy soil to the beach. On the left, Kehoe Marsh provides freshwater habitat for sedges, reeds and birds. In spring, the grassy hills on the right are dotted with fragrant bush lupine and occasional patches of iris.

0.5 Dunes, cliffs and wildflowers. Take the narrow path towards the right along the exposed cliff to view gold fields, poppies, tidy tips, baby blue eyes and blue lupine.

Goldfields

At the beach, head down by the water and hike along the wet sand south towards Abbotts Lagoon.

3.1 Abbotts Lagoon. You should be able to spot the lagoon from the beach by looking for a low-lying opening in the dunes. The lagoon is close to the ocean and low enough in elevation that heavy breakers enter it at high tide to create brackish water. Follow the northern edge of the lagoon inland. Look for the yellow flowers of lizard tail along the way.

3.6 Bridge and wildflowers. Cross the bridge and enjoy another hillside covered in gold. Just like Chimney Rock and Kehoe Beach, the best wildflower displays often appear in the most hostile environments. Up ahead, notice the wind-pruned coastal scrub on the hillside opposite the lagoon. Also, keep an eye out for birds.

Continue following the trail as it heads inland to the east. After crossing a small swale, the trail passes through fields of poppies, lupine, mustard and orange fiddleneck.

5.1 Abbotts Lagoon trailhead with pickup cars and restrooms.

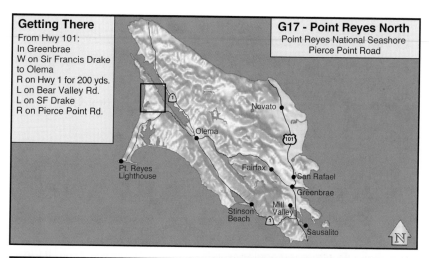

Getting There

From Hwy 101:
In Greenbrae
W on Sir Francis Drake
to Olema
R on Hwy 1 for 200 yds.
L on Bear Valley Rd.
L on SF Drake
R on Pierce Point Rd.

G17 - Point Reyes North
Point Reyes National Seashore
Pierce Point Road

Novato

Olema

Pt. Reyes
Lighthouse

Fairfax

San Rafael

Greenbrae

Stinson
Beach

Mill
Valley

Sausalito

N

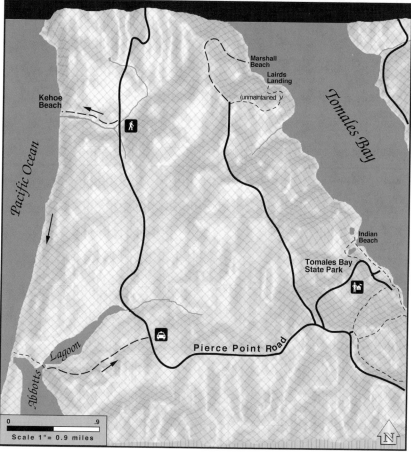

Marshall
Beach

Lairds
Landing

(unmaintained)

Tomales Bay

Kehoe
Beach

Pacific Ocean

Indian
Beach

Tomales Bay
State Park

Lagoon

Abbotts

Pierce Point Road

Scale 1"= 0.9 miles

0

.9

N

G18 Tomales Point Trail

Distance: 9.4 miles   Shaded: 0%
Elevation Change: 1000'   Can be very windy and/or foggy.
Rating: Hiking - 9   Difficulty - 4
When to Go: Winter is good; best flowers in April and May.

This hike along an open, exposed ridge can be spectacular or
miserable depending on the weather. Carry ponchos in case of fog.

0.0 Start at the parking lot at the end of Pierce Point Road. Follow
the signs around the old dairy ranch. If fog cuts your hike short, you
can tour the ranch when you get back.

0.8 Point ❶ with spectacular coastal views. Just before the trail turns
inland, you can see the dramatic coastal cliffs to the north rising over
400' above the ocean. In spring, this spot also provides a great
wildflower display with yellow gold fields, tidy tips, buttercups, sun
cups, poppies, lupine and wild strawberries.

1.0 The trail heads inland offering a view east down White Gulch to
Hog Island in Tomales Bay.

Watch for Tule elk and for their large
V-shaped tracks on the trail.

2.5 Highest point at 471'. As you
climb to the highest spot on Pierce
Point, you can see across Bodega
Bay to the Bodega headlands and
the Sonoma coast. On clear days,
look for the jutting profile of Mt. St.
Helena 30 miles northeast.

Tule Elk

3.3 Lower Pierce Ranch site and
unmarked junction ❷. At the ravine, near the cypress trees, a small
trail heads down the right side of the ravine to a beach on Tomales
Bay. Continue on the main trail.

4.0 Bird Rock viewpoint. If the tide is right, you can see a blowhole
on the left side of the rock. From here, the trail climbs through a
sandy area and dunes.

4.7 Tomales Point. In 1852, the English merchant ship, *Oxford*,
mistaking Tomales Bay for San Francisco Bay, came full sail into the
bay until she ran permanently aground just before Hog Island. After
enjoying the view, retrace your steps back south.

9.4 Back at the Pierce Point trailhead. Restrooms available.

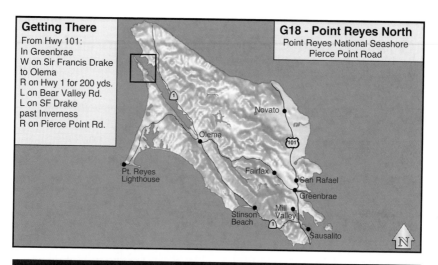

Getting There
From Hwy 101:
In Greenbrae
W on Sir Francis Drake
to Olema
R on Hwy 1 for 200 yds.
L on Bear Valley Rd.
L on SF Drake
past Inverness
R on Pierce Point Rd.

G18 - Point Reyes North
Point Reyes National Seashore
Pierce Point Road

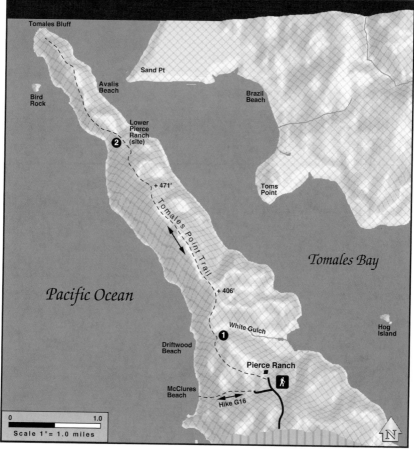

Tomales Bluff

Sand Pt

Avalis
Beach

Bird
Rock

Brazil
Beach

Lower
Pierce
Ranch
(site)

❷

+ 471'

Tomales Point Trail

Toms
Point

Tomales Bay

+ 406'

Pacific Ocean

White Gulch

❶

Hog
Island

Driftwood
Beach

Pierce Ranch

McClures
Beach

Hike G16

| 0 | | 1.0 |
Scale 1"= 1.0 miles

G19 Tomales Bay and Millerton Point

Distance: 2.2 and 1.2 miles   Shaded: 0%
Elevation Change: See below.   Strong winds possible.
Rating: Hiking - 6   Difficulty - 3   Can be muddy.
When to Go: Best in winter for birds and spring for green hills.

These are fairly level hikes through pastureland out to bluffs overlooking Tomales Bay. Osprey nest at Millerton Point.

Tomales Bay Trail - 2.2 miles and 100' Change

0.0 Park at the signed Tomales Bay Trailhead 1.5 miles north of Point Reyes Station on Hwy 1. The hike starts by passing through a gate into a pasture that may have cows grazing in it.

0.3 Junction ❶. Three trails join here. Head to the right for an out-and-back hike to a bluff that provides a good view of the mudflats of Tomales Bay and also shore birds. The levee running north was the bed of the North Pacific Coast Railroad originally built to haul lumber from the Russian River and West Marin to San Francisco.

0.5 Junction ❶. Go right, down to the dam and up to the next bluff.

1.0 Junction ❷. There are two out-and-back trails from here. The right trail heads to another viewpoint of the bay. Continue straight to go down by the water and to follow the old railroad bed. When done exploring, head back to the parking area. No facilities.

Millerton Point Loop - 1.2 miles and 50' Change

0.0 Park at the signed Millerton Point area located about 5 miles north of Point Reyes Station. The picnic area is on the left. The hike starts by heading uphill along the fence towards the knoll.

A sign at the trailhead describes an osprey nest that was relocated from a PG&E utility pole to a new non-electrical pole. This nest is one of 10-20 nests on Tomales Bay (depending on the year). Usually, about twice as many nests are located along Kent Lake, making this area one of the most important osprey nesting regions on the west coast.

0.1 Junction ❶. At the top of the knoll, head right to parallel the highway north. This knoll offers good views across the bay to the Inverness Yacht Club and to the heavily forested Inverness Ridge.

0.4 Clifftop ❷. The edge of the cliff provides a nice view north up Tomales Bay. The white stakes mark the position of oyster beds.

0.7 Junction ❸. Head to the parking area. **Option:** At low tide, it is possible to walk down to the beach, then north towards the oyster beds.

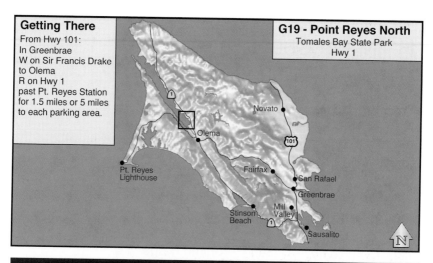

Getting There

From Hwy 101:
In Greenbrae
W on Sir Francis Drake
to Olema
R on Hwy 1
past Pt. Reyes Station
for 1.5 miles or 5 miles
to each parking area.

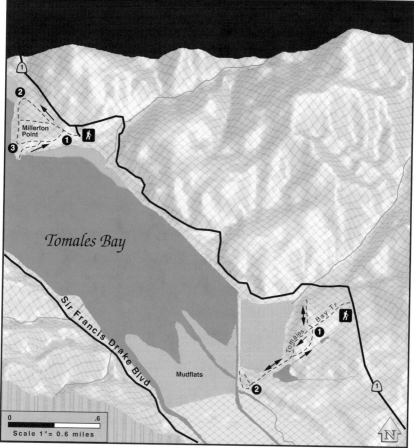

263

H - Marin County - 12 Hikes

Starting in Southern Marin
H1   Tennessee Valley to Muir Beach Loop 7.3
H2   Camino Alto FR - Alto Bowl 4.4

Starting on Mt. Tamalpais - Southern Side
H3   Dipsea - Sun - Tenderfoot Trails 6.6
H4   Dipsea - Coast View - Heather Cutoff Trails 7.6

Starting in Central Marin
H5   Sorich Ranch and Terra Linda Ridge 2.5 and 3.5
H6   Evans Canyon - San Geronimo Ridge 5.6
H7   Kent Lake - San Geronimo Ridge 6.6
H8   Samuel P. Taylor State Park to Bolinas Ridge 10.2

Starting in North Marin
H9   Pinheiro FR at Rush Creek 4.6
H10 Kaehler, Dwarf Oak and Little Mountain 1.4, 3.6 and 4.4

Starting at Point Reyes North
H11 Bull Point and South Beach Trails 4.0 and 2.0
H12 Marshall Beach Trail 2.6

Notes
Dogs are allowed on hikes H2, H5, H6, H7, H9 and H10.
To download a hike, go to www.marintrails.com
The password for this region is h2sn2wr

Notes about hikes for the 2nd Edition
All of the hikes in Region H are new. All of the other hikes in
this 2nd edition are the same as hikes in the 1st edition with the
following exceptions:

Minor route changes: B1, B2, B10, C14, C19, E4, E10, F6, F11,
F14, G4, G12, G19

Major route changes: A6, B13, C3, C10, D1, D3, E12, E14,
G11, G13

All hike descriptions and maps have been checked and
updated. For additional information, including temporary trail
closures, check our website at www.marintrails.com

Region H Trailheads
New Hikes for 2nd Edition

Hike 1 starts in GGNRA, phone 415-331-1540.

Hikes 2, 5-7, 9, 10 start in Marin County Open Space, phone 415-499-6387.

Hike 3 starts in Old Mill Park in Mill Valley, then enters Mt. Tamalpais State Park, phone 415-388-2070.

Hike 4 starts in Mt. Tamalpais State Park, phone 415-388-2070.

Hike 8 starts in Samuel P. Taylor State Park, phone 415-488-9897.

Hikes 11 and 12 start in Point Reyes National Seashore, phone 415-464-5100.

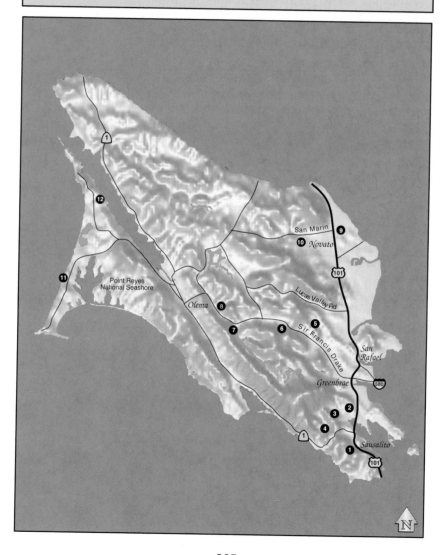

H1 Tennessee Valley to Muir Beach Loop

Distance: 7.3 miles   Shaded: 0%
Elevation Change: 1900'   Bicycles likely.
Rating: Hiking - 9   Difficulty - 8   Trail can be wet or muddy.
When to Go: Best when clear, calm and cool. Winter can be great.

This hike travels over rolling hills to the most remote area of the Marin Headlands, offering great views of the coast and ocean.

0.0 From the parking area, go through the gate heading towards the ocean on the Tennessee Valley trail.

0.7 Junction. Leave the paved road and continue straight.

1.0 Junction. Continue on the upper Tennessee Valley trail right.

1.3 Junction ❶. Take the Coastal trail right uphill.

2.0 Knoll and junction ❷. Good coastal views. Take the Pirates Cove trail left downhill. (May be signed Coastal trail.) This remote trail drops down near the ocean and provides wonderful views along the way.

3.2 Junction with the Coastal FR. Stay on a trail heading left up to a knoll and viewpoint.

3.3 Knoll. More great views along the coast. To the north beyond Muir Beach, lie Bolinas Head and the Point Reyes Headlands. Continue downhill to rejoin the Coastal Trail, heading for Muir Beach.

Tennessee Valley from Coast Trail

3.6 Junction ❸. Take the Middle Green Gulch trail right. **Option**: Head left for 0.2 miles to visit Muir Beach.

3.8 Junction and fence. Go left along the tall fence for 200', then right through the gate into Green Gulch Farm, a non-profit, organic farm and Zen center, that offers training in Zen meditation and farming.

4.3 Junction ❹. Near the end of the growing fields, take the signed Middle Green Gulch trail right 100' and go through a gate.

5.6 Junction ❺. Take the Coyote Ridge trail right. Great views east to the Tiburon peninsula with Mt. Diablo in the background.

5.8 Two junctions. Go left 100 yds. to take the Fox trail downhill.

7.0 Junction. Take the Tennessee Valley trail left.

7.3 Back at the parking area with restrooms and picnic area.

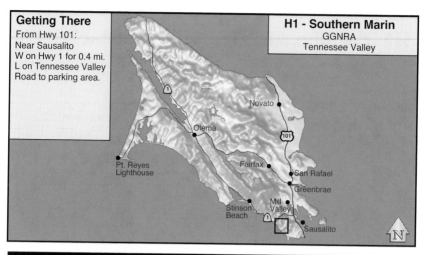

Getting There
From Hwy 101:
Near Sausalito
W on Hwy 1 for 0.4 mi.
L on Tennessee Valley
Road to parking area.

H1 - Southern Marin
GGNRA
Tennessee Valley

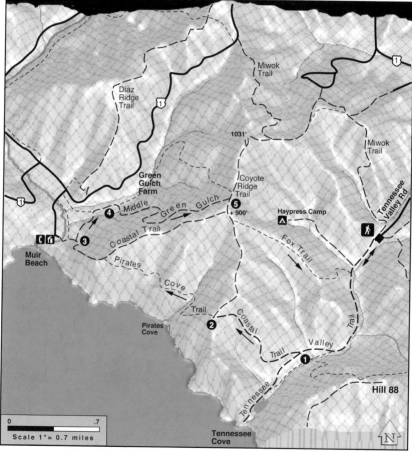

267

H2 Camino Alto FR - Alto Bowl

Distance: 4.4 miles   Shaded: 40%
Elevation Change: 600'   One short steep section.
Rating: Hiking - 7   Difficulty - 7   Can be muddy in winter.
When to Go: Good anytime.

This is mostly an out-and-back hike that explores the area around Alto Bowl and Horse Hill. Good local views.

0.0 Take the Escalon FR north past the gate and into open space.

0.1 Junction ❶. Keep right and head uphill on the Camino Alto FR. Ahead, there are good views of Alto Bowl to the east.

0.5 Fence, water tank and junctions. Continue on the FR. Over the next 200 yds., look for 3 small trails heading left (for use later).

0.7 Street and junction ❷. Go right down the street 50 yds., then take the Bob Middagh trail left. Notice the hilltop with eucalyptus trees on the left, once the property of rock promoter Bill Graham.

1.1 Junction ❸. After crossing a seasonal stream, take the FR right down to the street.

1.2 Gate, street and junction. At the street, head left to make a steep climb on an old dirt road under the power lines.

1.4 Junction ❹. At the saddle, go right on the Horse Hill trail. The trail skirts the ridgeline and heads out to a knoll overlooking Hwy 101.

1.8 Horse Hill, viewpoint and turnaround point. This hilltop under the power line poles offers great views. Horse Hill was named for the grazing horses that can usually be seen by people driving on the freeway. In 1982, developers planned to build 61 homes on these hills, but a Save Horse Hill group formed and successfully preserved it for open space. When ready to continue, backtrack.

2.2 Junction ❹ again. Head left downhill to return the way you came.

2.9 Junction ❷ again. Go right 50 yds., then take the FR left uphill.

3.0 Junction. About 100' past a landing with a power pole at one end, take the unofficial trail right, which heads downhill into a small forest. Watch out for poison oak. **Option**: Continue to backtrack.

3.4 Junction. The trail enters a large junction, called the "octopus." Take the first left, the Escalon FR.

3.9 Junction ❶. Continue straight for 0.2 miles to a knoll and viewpoint. When ready, return to Jct. ❶ and go right.

4.4 Back at the parking area. No facilities.

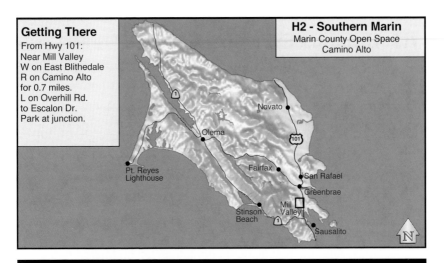

Getting There

From Hwy 101:
Near Mill Valley
W on East Blithedale
R on Camino Alto
for 0.7 miles.
L on Overhill Rd.
to Escalon Dr.
Park at junction.

H2 - Southern Marin
Marin County Open Space
Camino Alto

Novato

Olema

Pt. Reyes
Lighthouse

Fairfax

San Rafael

Greenbrae

Stinson
Beach

Mill
Valley

Sausalito

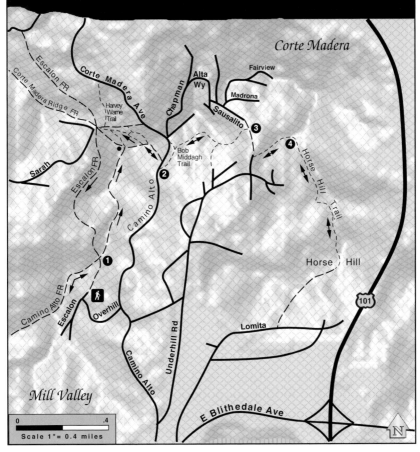

Corte Madera

Fairview

Escalon FR

Corte Madera Ridge FR

Corte Madera Ave

Chapman

Alta
Wy

Madrona

Sausalito

Harvey
Warne
Trail

Sarah

Escalon FR

Bob
Middagh
Trail

Camino Alto

Horse Hill Trail

Horse Hill

Camino Alto FR

Escalon

Overhill

Camino Alto

Underhill Rd

Lomita

101

Mill Valley

E Blithedale Ave

0   .4

Scale 1" = 0.4 miles

269

H3 Dipsea - Sun - Tenderfoot Trails

Distance: 6.6 miles   Shaded: 70%
Elevation Change: 1100'   Includes 2 miles on streets.
Rating: Hiking - 9   Difficulty - 6   Over 600 stairs.
When to Go: Excellent anytime, best when creeks flow.

This hike climbs the famous Dipsea steps, circles the ridge above Muir Woods, then returns along creeks and waterfalls in Cascade Canyon.

0.0 Take Cascade Dr. into Old Mill Park, cross the bridge, then cross the street and go up Cascade Way 200' to the start of the Dipsea stairs. The Dipsea race, held in June, begins by climbing 672 steps in three flights. After the first flight, go right, then left on Marion Ave to the 2nd flight of stairs. At the next street, go left on Hazel, then right up the 3rd flight of stairs.

0.5 Junction. Go right on the path along side of Sequoia Valley Rd.

0.7 Junction ❶. Go past the gate to the street and right up Walsh Drive to enter the Flying Y Ranch housing development.

1.0 Junction. Go right, 100' up Panoramic Hwy, then left on the trail.

1.1 Junction ❷. Leave the Dipsea trail and take the Sun trail right. The hillside has been burned repeatedly to remove French broom.

1.8 Junction. Go 50 yds. to continue on the Redwood trail, which passes above the Tourist Club. Refreshments may be available on weekends at the Tourist Club, a European hiking club with a chapter that started here in 1912.

2.6 Junction. Take the Panoramic trail north, then continue on the paved Camp Eastwood Rd.

3.1 Junction ❸. Take the Trestle trail right up to the Mountain Home Inn. Pick up Edgewood Rd. on the other side of the inn.

3.6 Junction. Just before the paved road ends, at a fire hydrant, take the Tenderfoot trail left, downhill past a carport. Bicycles likely.

4.8 Junction. Take Cascade Drive left. Watch for 2-way traffic.

5.0 Junction ❹. Take Lovell Ave right to just past house #766.

5.5 Junction ❺. Take the Three Wells trail right down into a ravine.

5.6 Junction. Go left for a view of the falls and the 3 inkwells. Then, take a short loop trail over the bridge for more views of the falls.

5.7 Junction. Cross Cascade Drive for a short trail along the creek. Then continue on Cascade Drive to Old Mill Park.

6.6 Back at Old Mill Park. Restrooms, water and picnic facilities.

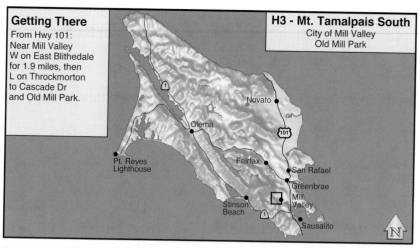

Getting There

From Hwy 101:
Near Mill Valley
W on East Blithedale
for 1.9 miles, then
L on Throckmorton
to Cascade Dr
and Old Mill Park.

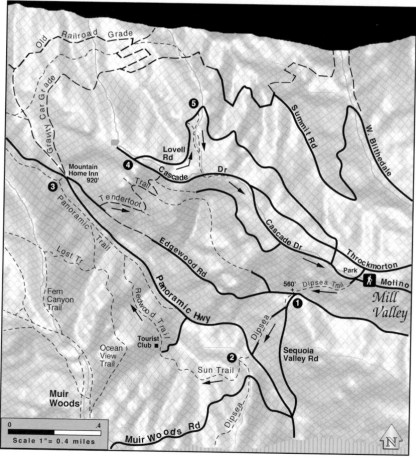

Scale 1" = 0.4 miles

H4 Dipsea - Coast View Trails

Distance: 7.6 miles   Shaded: 30%
Elevation Change: 1400'   Overgrown in places. Bicycles likely.
Rating: Hiking - 9   Difficulty - 7   Can be muddy.
When to Go: Great whenever cool and not too windy or foggy.

This hike explores the coastal ridges below Pantoll offering great views when it is clear. Good spring flowers on Heather Cutoff Trail.

0.0 Go through the gate and take the Deer Park FR uphill towards Pantoll and the Dipsea trail. The hike starts out in coastal scrub, mostly grass and coyote bush, with some oaks and Douglas fir.

0.5 Junction ❶. If you want more shade and it's not too wet, take the Dipsea trail which parallels the fire road in several places. Grasses may crowd the trail. This description follows the Dipsea Trail.

1.9 Junction with the Ben Johnson trail. Continue straight.

2.0 Junction. Continue uphill on the Deer Park FR.

2.1 Junction. Take the Dipsea trail right to climb "Cardiac Hill" as it is known to the 1500 Dipsea runners, who run here each June.

2.2 Junction with the TCC trail. Keep left and keep climbing.

2.3 Junction ❷ and the top of Cardiac. Take the Coastal FR left. **Option**: Go right 0.6 miles to Pantoll for tables, water and restrooms.

2.4 Junction with the Deer Park FR. Head down the Coast View trail. This new, multi-use trail, opened in 2005, replaces the old Coastal FR and makes a gradual, graceful descent down the open hillside.

Ahead, the views keep getting better. The bay and Mt. Diablo can be seen to the east, the Marin Headlands and San Francisco can be seen to the south and the coast and ocean lie to the west.

4.8 Gate and junction ❸. Take the Heather Cutoff trail left, which makes a long zig-zag descent to the valley. **Option**: It's worth continuing down to Hwy 1 for views along the immediate coast.

5.0 Rock garden. This trail offers luxuriant growth and a wide variety of great spring flowers. It may also be heavily overgrown at times.

6.1 Junction ❹. If possible, go right past the horse arena towards the group area. Cross the bridge, then go left to cross Muir Woods Road. Take the Heather Cutoff Spur trail. Otherwise, go left out to the road and go right along the road for 0.2 miles to the Heather Cutoff Spur.

6.2 Junction. Take the Redwood Creek trail left. It may be overgrown.

7.6 Back at the parking area. No facilities.

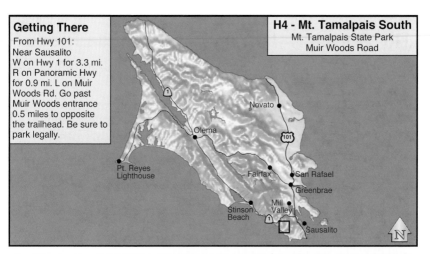

Getting There
From Hwy 101:
Near Sausalito
W on Hwy 1 for 3.3 mi.
R on Panoramic Hwy
for 0.9 mi. L on Muir
Woods Rd. Go past
Muir Woods entrance
0.5 miles to opposite
the trailhead. Be sure to
park legally.

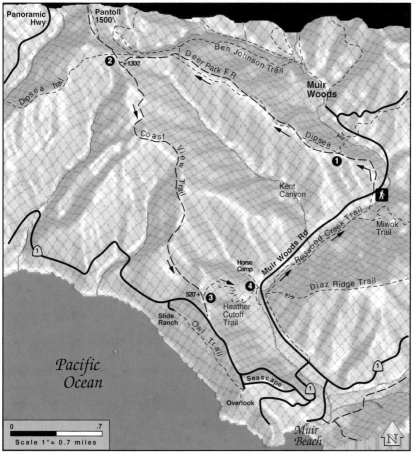

273

H5 Sorich Ranch and Terra Linda Ridge

Distance: 2.5 and 3.5 miles   Shaded: 50%
Elevation Change: 600'   Steep in places.
Rating: Hiking - 7   Difficulty - 7   Can be muddy in places.
When to Go: Excellent anytime, best in April and May.

These two hikes explore the same area, a ridge dividing San Anselmo and Terra Linda. Each hike starts from a different street.

Sorich Ranch - Terra Linda Ridge - 2.5 miles and 600' Change

0.0 From the parking area at Sorich Ranch, head into the canyon to pick up the trail, which starts out under eucalyptus trees. Up ahead, you may still see evidence of a fire that swept through here in 1976.

0.4 Junction with Cemetery FR. Head left uphill.

0.9 Water tank and double junction ❶. At the 2nd junction, take the Ridgewood FR to the left. It offers the best views, including Big Rock Ridge to the north and the Marin Civic Center to the east.

1.6 Junction ❷. Take the road left, which heads steeply downhill.
Option: For a longer hike, take the road right out to the street and on to the Fox Lane trail, where there is more open space. See Hike E1.

1.8 Junction ❸ at a saddle. Continue uphill to a viewpoint.

1.9 Hilltop, rock and view point. When done retrace your steps.

2.0 Junction ❸ again. Head right for a moderately steep downhill.

2.4 Stairs and street. Head left on the street.

2.5 Back at the parking area. No facilities.

Cemetery FR - Terra Linda Ridge - 3.5 miles and 500' Change

0.0 **Note**: Cemetery gate hours are from 8 am-5 pm daily. If closed, take the trail by the school (return route). From the end of 5th Ave in San Rafael, go through the cemetery gate 10', then head right along the fence to pick up a paved road with a public access easement.

0.3 Junction. Continue uphill on Cemetery FR to the water tank.

0.8 Double junction ❶ and water tank. At the first junction, the Sun Valley trail right is the return route. For now, continue to the ridgetop and head left on the Ridgewood FR.

1.5 Junction ❷. Head left, steeply downhill. **Option**: See above.

1.8 Junction ❸. Continue uphill to a viewpoint. When ready, retrace your steps back to junction ❶, then take the trail downhill to 5th Ave.

3.5 Back at the parking area. No facilities.

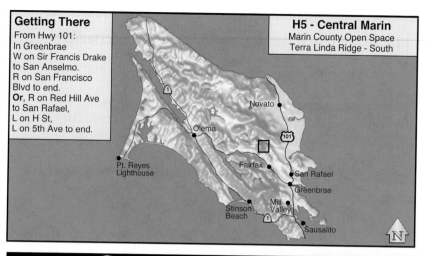

Getting There

From Hwy 101:
In Greenbrae
W on Sir Francis Drake
to San Anselmo.
R on San Francisco
Blvd to end.
Or, R on Red Hill Ave
to San Rafael,
L on H St,
L on 5th Ave to end.

H5 - Central Marin
Marin County Open Space
Terra Linda Ridge - South

Novato

Olema

Pt. Reyes
Lighthouse

Fairfax

San Rafael

Greenbrae

Stinson
Beach

Mill
Valley

Sausalito

N

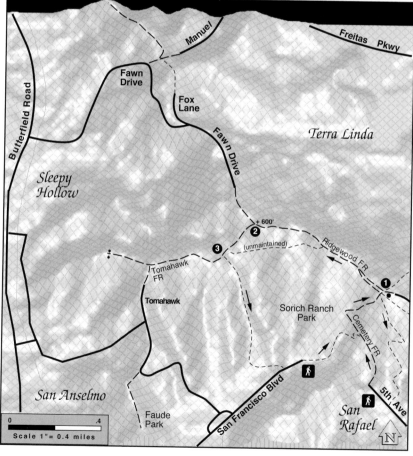

Manuel

Freitas   Pkwy

Butterfield Road

**Fawn
Drive**

**Fox
Lane**

Fawn Drive

Terra Linda

*Sleepy
Hollow*

+ 600'

❷

Ridgewood F.R.

(unmaintained)

❸

❶

*Tomahawk
FR*

Tomahawk

Sorich Ranch
Park

Cemetery F.R.

San Anselmo

San Francisco Blvd

5th Ave

*San
Rafael*

*Faude
Park*

0   .4

Scale 1" = 0.4 miles

N

275

H6 Evans Canyon - San Geronimo Ridge

Distance: 5.6 miles   Shaded: 50%
Elevation Change: 1400'   Can be muddy. Bicycles on weekends.
Rating: Hiking - 8   Difficulty - 7   Moderately steep fire roads.
When to Go: Good anytime when cool, clear and calm.

This hike in the Giacomini Open Space area starts in a redwood ravine, then climbs up to San Geronimo Ridge offering great views.

0.0 Go through the open space gate on Redwood Canyon Drive and take the Willis Evans Canyon trail into a redwood forest. (Originally, the trail was called the Bates Canyon trail.) Ahead, before the bridge, stay left and start climbing on the fire road.

0.3 Mud. A small section of road can get very muddy in winter. Watch out for poison oak on the side of the road.

0.6 Junction ❶. Continue straight past the gate and take Conifer Way right past a couple of houses. Ahead, the trail passes another gate.

0.9 Water tank and junction. Take the fire road right uphill. Ahead, the road enters grassland, offering good views of the hills.

1.5 Saddle. The trail reaches a saddle offering views east to Mt. Barnabe, identified by the fire station at the top.

1.7 Triangular junction ❷. Go right 200 yds., then right again onto the San Geronimo Ridge FR. Up ahead, just past the power lines, the road enters a Sargent cypress forest. These trees are native to California and mostly grow on serpentine soil. Notice that mature trees range in height from 5' to 30', depending on soil conditions.

2.7 Junction. The road left goes down alongside Kent Lake. The road right goes to Forest Knolls. Continue straight to climb Green Hill.

2.9 Green Hill and viewpoint. Around the high point, you can see, from left to right, Kent Lake with Bolinas Ridge behind it, and behind that, Inverness Ridge, a glimpse of Tomales Bay, then Mt. Barnabe with the fire lookout station on top and behind that, Black Mountain.

3.5 Junction ❸. Take the Hunt Camp FR right. This side of Green Hill has much more luxuriant growth, redwoods and huckleberries.

3.7 Horse camp and picnic tables. Continue on the road.

3.9 Junction. Take the Sylvestris FR left downhill. At the open space gate, continue downhill. Take care walking the narrow streets.

5.1 Junction. Take San Geronimo Valley Drive right to the east.

5.6 Back at the parking area. No facilities.

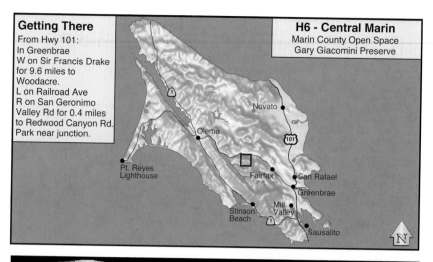

Getting There

From Hwy 101:
In Greenbrae
W on Sir Francis Drake
for 9.6 miles to
Woodacre.
L on Railroad Ave
R on San Geronimo
Valley Rd for 0.4 miles
to Redwood Canyon Rd.
Park near junction.

H6 - Central Marin
Marin County Open Space
Gary Giacomini Preserve

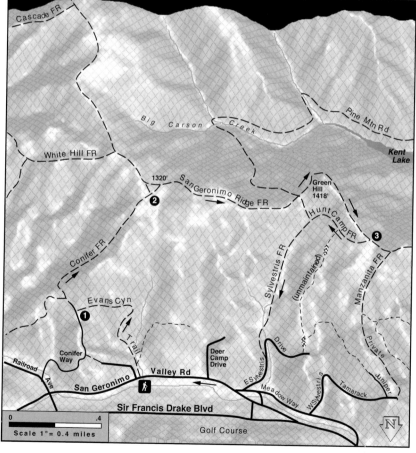

H7 Kent Lake - San Geronimo Ridge

Distance: 6.6 miles   Shaded: 60%
Elevation Change: 1300'   Some bicycles on weekends.
Rating: Hiking - 8   Difficulty - 6   Moderately steep fire roads.
When to Go: Best in late winter and early spring for water runoff.

This hike, all on fire roads, circles above Peters Dam to explore Kent Lake and San Geronimo Ridge. Good local views, some spring flowers.

0.0 Walk back along Sir Francis Drake Hwy towards Shafter Bridge. Be careful as this is a narrow section of road with lots of traffic.

0.2 Bridge and junction. Go over the bridge, then carefully cross the highway to head up the left side of the Lagunitas Creek. Look for salmon spawning in the creek after the first heavy rains in winter.

0.4 Two junctions ❶. Go right, then left to stay on the paved road.

1.0 Top of Peters Dam. Go right 100 yds. to view the new spillway, which is 40' higher than the old spillway (downhill to the right). The dam itself is the tallest of the 4 dams in the Lagunitas drainage basin, which consists of Lagunitas, Bon Tempe, Alpine and Kent Lakes.

Most of the water used by southern and central Marin comes from these lakes, over 1 million gallons per hour in summer. When ready, go across the dam and head right.

1.9 Junction ❷. At a Y-junction, continue straight and downhill. MMWD will be closing the left road, the lower section of Grassy Slope FR.

2.2 Junction ❸. Head left uphill **Option**: Head right downhill to a peaceful spot to view Kent Lake and watch for ospreys.

3.0 Junction ❹. Take the San Geronimo Ridge FR right.

4.0 Hilltop and turnaround point ❺. An unofficial trail goes right 50', then down 30' offering good views of the lake. Pine Mountain Ridge and Bolinas Ridge lie behind the lake, with Bolinas Ridge farther away and to the right. When ready, head back. **Option**: There is another viewpoint at the next hilltop 0.1 miles ahead.

5.0 Junction ❹ again. Go right to begin an easy descent in a heavily forested area with lots of ferns on the hillside. Look for trillium in March.

6.2 Junction ❶ again. Head right out to the highway.

6.4 Sir Francis Drake Hwy. Carefully cross the road, then go right 30' to check the new bridge over the "Inkwells" on San Geronimo Creek. The bridge was opened in 2004. When ready, walk back to the car.

6.6 Roadside parking area. No facilities.

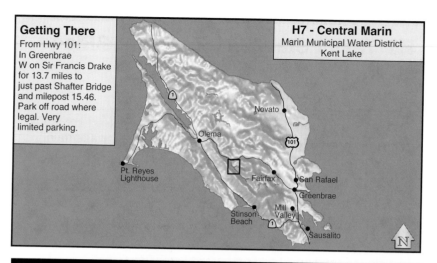

Getting There

From Hwy 101:
In Greenbrae
W on Sir Francis Drake
for 13.7 miles to
just past Shafter Bridge
and milepost 15.46.
Park off road where
legal. Very
limited parking.

H7 - Central Marin
Marin Municipal Water District
Kent Lake

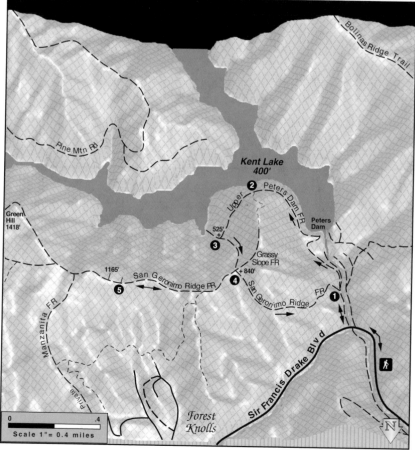

Scale 1" = 0.4 miles

H8 Taylor State Park to Bolinas Ridge

Distance: 10.2 miles   Shaded: 60%
Elevation Change: 1300'   Lots of bicycles on weekends.
Rating: Hiking - 8   Difficulty - 7   Moderately steep uphill.
When to Go: Best when clear and calm. Salmon runs after rain.

This hike climbs out of SP Taylor Park to Bolinas Ridge, heads north for 4 miles offering great views, then loops back down to the park.

0.0 From the picnic area, head into the park along the creek, then take the bridge left over the creek. Go left again on the bike path.

1.0 Junction. Cross Drake Hwy on the overpass and continue straight.

1.8 Inkwells footbridge and highway crossing. If you're lucky, you may see coho salmon navigating the "Inkwells" on San Geronimo Creek in winter. Then, carefully cross the highway and head up the right side of Lagunitas Creek, passing through the small parking lot. Again, look for salmon, usually from November to January. These two creeks are major spawning grounds for coho salmon.

1.9 Junction ❶. Take the paved road steeply uphill.

2.1 Landing and junction. Cross the landing and continue uphill.

3.4 Junction ❷ with Bolinas Ridge. The forest ends at the ridgeline and open hillsides now provide good views south and west. Up ahead, the hike passes through several gates, part of fences used to control grazing cattle. Be sure to close gates.

5.0 A knoll provides spectacular views east to Mt. Barnabe, north to Black Mountain and Tomales Bay, and west to Mt. Wittenberg.

You can get a feeling for three of Marin's largest geological features here, Bolinas Ridge, Olema Valley and Inverness Ridge. It's also interesting to note that the shady slopes of Bolinas Ridge are forested with redwoods, while three miles away, the shady slopes of Inverness Ridge contain only Douglas fir and Bishop pine.

7.5 Junction ❸. Take the Jewell trail right downhill.

8.5 Gate and bike path. Head right on the bike path.

9.3 Bridge, swimming hole and junction. Continue on the bike path.

9.4 Historical marker and two junctions ❹. A plaque marks the site of the first papermill on the West Coast. At this point, you have three choices for continuing. The Ox trail on the right is the most secluded. The Creek trail offers a riparian setting. The bike path is easiest.

10.2 Bridge and junction at Camp Taylor. Water and restrooms.

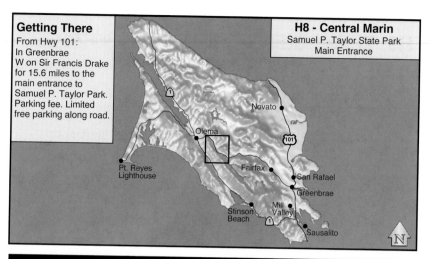

Getting There

From Hwy 101:
In Greenbrae
W on Sir Francis Drake
for 15.6 miles to the
main entrance to
Samuel P. Taylor Park.
Parking fee. Limited
free parking along road.

H8 - Central Marin
Samuel P. Taylor State Park
Main Entrance

Novato

Olema

Pt. Reyes
Lighthouse

Fairfax

San Rafael

Greenbrae

Stinson
Beach

Mill
Valley

Sausalito

N

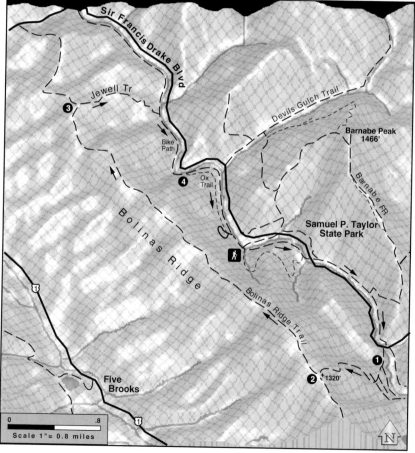

Sir Francis Drake Blvd

Jewell Tr

3

Devils Gulch Trail

**Barnabe Peak
1466'**

Bike
Path

4

Ox
Trail

Barnabe FR

**Samuel P. Taylor
State Park**

Bolinas Ridge

Bolinas Ridge Trail

1

1

**Five
Brooks**

2 1320'

1

0   .8

Scale 1"= 0.8 miles

N

281

H9 Pinheiro FR at Rush Creek

Distance: 4.6 miles   Shaded: 10%
Elevation Change: 100'   Bicycles possible.
Rating: Hiking - 7   Difficulty - 3   Can be muddy.
When to Go: Good in winter for birds and spring for flowers.

This is an easy out-and-back hike that skirts a tidal marsh offering spectacular shorebirds in winter and colorful wildflowers in spring.

Note 1: Views of the marsh are best at high tide, which occurs about 2 hours later than times shown in tide tables for the Golden Gate.

Note 2: An old road lies along the ridgeline offering good views, oaks and wildflowers. However, as yet, there are no official access trails. There is an unofficial path up the grassy hillside 150 yds. along the trail to Atherton Ave. The map shows parts of the ridge trail. The best time to hike the ridge is when the grasses are still green.

0.0 Head through the open space gate on the Pinheiro FR. Tall reeds along the marsh provide cover and allow you to ease up closer to see fall and winter shorebirds, egrets, pelicans and ducks.

Mt. Burdell looms up across the freeway. In the center of the mountain, you can see the Buck Center for the Aging.

1.2 Junction ❶. In the middle of a small grove of bay and oak trees, a trail leads down and across a low-lying levee, cutting off a small inlet. Continue on the FR, which may be overgrown at times. (This trail provides an optional return route).

Mt. Burdell from Rush Creek

1.7 Junction ❷ and two bridges. The Pinheiro FR right provides a loop back along the street. Continue straight on the Rush Creek FR.

2.3 Double junction ❸. The road right climbs up to the ridge. The middle road continues along the marsh for about 0.6 miles. The road left leads 100 yds. to the 2nd junction. Take the road left to the 2nd junction and turnaround point. When ready, head back.

Option 1: Take the trail along the levee back to junction ❶.

Option 2: Go back 100 yds. and take the middle FR along the marsh.

Option 3: Go back to junction ❷ and take the FR out to the street, then take the path that parallels the street back to the parking area.

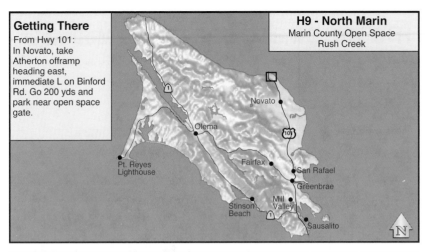

Getting There

From Hwy 101:
In Novato, take
Atherton offramp
heading east,
immediate L on Binford
Rd. Go 200 yds and
park near open space
gate.

H9 - North Marin
Marin County Open Space
Rush Creek

Novato

Olema

Pt. Reyes
Lighthouse

Fairfax

San Rafael

Greenbrae

Stinson
Beach

Mill
Valley

Sausalito

N

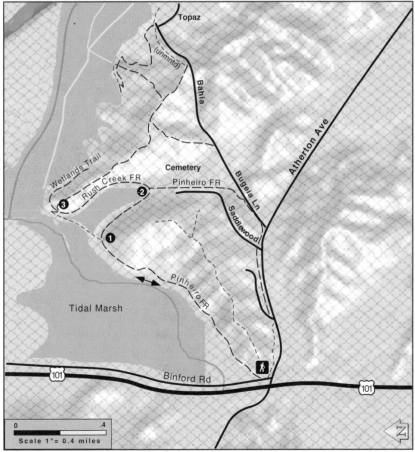

Topaz

(unmntd)

Bahia

Atherton Ave

Wetlands Trail

Rush Creek FR

Cemetery

Pinheiro FR

Bugeia Ln

Saddlewood

❸

❷

❶

Pinheiro FR

Tidal Marsh

101

Binford Rd

101

0   .4
Scale 1"= 0.4 miles

N

H10 RK, Dwarf Oak and Little Mountain

Distance: 1.4, 3.6 and 4.4 miles   Shaded: 80%, 20% and 30%
Elevation Change: See below.
Rating: Hiking - 6, 8 and 6   Difficulty - 2, 4 and 5
When to Go: Best in spring for green hills and wildflowers.

These three out-and-back hikes explore the area surrounding O'Hair Park in Novato. The two longer hikes are mostly on grassy hills.

Reuben Kaehler (RK) Trail - 1.4 miles and 50' Change
Note: Horses likely. Trail can be very muddy in winter, dusty in fall.

0.0 Take the RK trail into the park and along the creek.

0.1 Junction with Little Mountain trail. Go right. Up ahead, the trail divides into two parallel tracks. Take the left trail along the hillside. This is a pleasant area with ferns and trillium under bay and oak.

0.7 End of loop and turnaround point ❶. Take the lower trail back.

Dwarf Oak Trail - 3.6 miles and 400' Change
Note: An alternate start is on Novato Blvd (See Note above).

0.0 Take the RK trail into the park and along the creek. Continue past the Little Mountain trail.

0.2 Junction. Leave the RK Trail and go right out to bridge and street.

0.4 Junction with Novato Blvd. Go right along the street 200 yds., then cross the street and take the Dwarf Oak trail, located between the fenced power station and the school. The trail climbs past a new development and circles the hillside. Look for white milkmaids, pink shooting star, blue brodeia and yellow buttercups in spring.

1.8 Junction ❷. Dwarf oaks, a water tank and good views down to Novato, mark the turnaround point. When ready, head back.

Little Mountain Trail - 4.4 miles and 600' Change
0.0 Take the RK trail into the park and along the creek.

0.1 Junction. Take the Little Mountain trail left, which begins an easy climb in the shade, then circles the mountain to join the Doe Hill FR.

1.3 Fence and street. Cross the FR to take the Stafford Lake trail.

1.7 Junction. The trail divides into an upper and lower trail. Take the upper trail left for great hilltop views, then return on the lower trail.

1.9 Junction with Verissimo Hills trail. Continue the hilltop tour.

2.1 Gate and junction. After the gate, take the lower trail.

2.2 A fence, switchback and view mark turnaround point ❸.

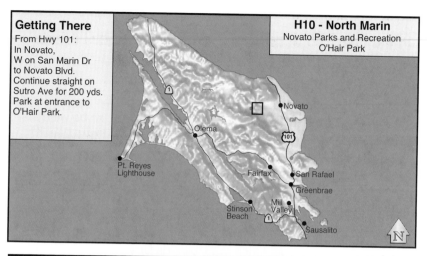

Getting There

From Hwy 101:
In Novato,
W on San Marin Dr
to Novato Blvd.
Continue straight on
Sutro Ave for 200 yds.
Park at entrance to
O'Hair Park.

H10 - North Marin
Novato Parks and Recreation
O'Hair Park

Pt. Reyes
Lighthouse

Olema

Novato

101

Fairfax

San Rafael

Greenbrae

Stinson
Beach

Mill
Valley

Sausalito

N

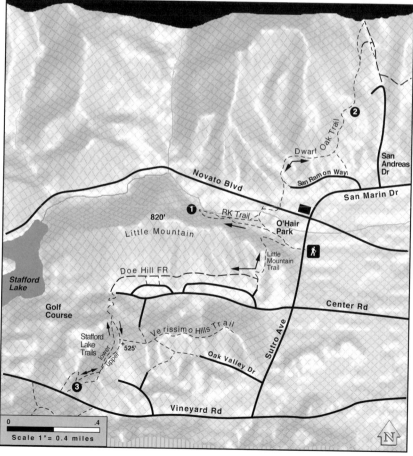

Dwarf Oak Trail

San Andreas Dr

San Ramon Way

Novato Blvd

San Marin Dr

RK Trail

O'Hair Park

820'

Little Mountain

Little Mountain Trail

Doe Hill FR

Stafford Lake

Golf Course

Center Rd

Verissimo Hills Trail

Stafford Lake Trails

lower

upper

525'

Oak Valley Dr

Sutro Ave

Vineyard Rd

0   .4

Scale 1" = 0.4 miles

N

285

H11 Bull Point and South Beach Trails

Distance: 4.0 and 2.0 miles   Shaded: 0%
Elevation Change: See below.   Can be muddy. Can be overgrown.
Rating: Hiking - 6 and 6   Difficulty - 5 and 2   Can be windy.
When to Go: In spring to Bull Point. Fall and winter on the beach.

One hike leads through flowers and pasture to a great view of Drakes Estero, while the other hike explores the ocean beach.

Bull Point Trail out and back - 4.0 miles and 150' Change

0.0 Park at the signed Bull Point trailhead just past the AT&T antenna farm on Sir Francis Drake Blvd. The hike passes through a fence and follows an old ranch road towards Drakes Estero. The large group of cypress trees to the north was the site of F Ranch established in 1852. The first post office on Point Reyes was housed in a small room off the kitchen.

0.8 Spring and moist area. A spring on the left provides water for cows and moisture for the tall evergreen shrub, wax myrtle. On the right, you may see pilings at the end of Creamery Bay. This was one of several schooner landings on Point Reyes. Schooners delivered dairy products to San Francisco and brought supplies to the ranches.

1.9 Estero and junction ❶. The trail ends at a cliff overlooking the estero. Look for oyster beds in the water. **Option:** At low tide, go 100 yds. to the right for beach access and a driftwood bench. When ready, head back.

South Beach Trail out and back - 2.0 miles and Flat

0.0 Park at the end of the South Beach parking lot. The hike starts by heading south along the beach with views towards the Point Reyes Headlands. The lighthouse light can be seen flashing at the edge of the cliff, but the lighthouse itself can not

*Life Saving Station
Operated from 1890-1927*

be seen. Lots of driftwood washes ashore at this end of the beach. **Note:** Dangerous surf! Do not swim or wade in the ocean.

1.0 Coast Guard Life-Saving Station. The buildings (private property) on the cliff were part of the life-saving station that later moved to Drakes Bay. At least 38 shipwrecks occurred at Point Reyes. When ready, retrace your steps to the parking area.

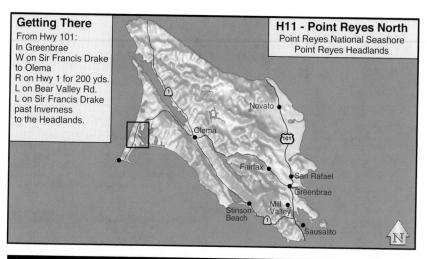

Getting There

From Hwy 101:
In Greenbrae
W on Sir Francis Drake
to Olema
R on Hwy 1 for 200 yds.
L on Bear Valley Rd.
L on Sir Francis Drake
past Inverness
to the Headlands.

H11 - Point Reyes North
Point Reyes National Seashore
Point Reyes Headlands

Novato

Olema

101

Fairfax

San Rafael

Greenbrae

Stinson
Beach

Mill
Valley

Sausalito

N

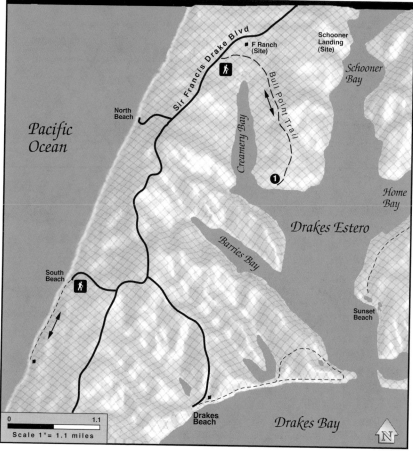

Sir Francis Drake Blvd

F Ranch
(Site)

Schooner
Landing
(Site)

Schooner
Bay

North
Beach

Creamery Bay

Bull Point Trail

①

Pacific
Ocean

Home
Bay

Drakes Estero

Barries Bay

South
Beach

Sunset
Beach

Drakes
Beach

Drakes Bay

0   1.1
Scale 1"= 1.1 miles

N

287

H12 Marshall Beach Trail

Distance: 2.6 miles   Shaded: 10%
Elevation Change: 360'
Rating: Hiking - 8   Difficulty - 5   Can be windy at the start.
When to Go: Best weather in fall and winter, best flowers in spring.

This hike starts on the ridge and hikes down to Tomales Bay. It offers great views of the bay, spring flowers and local history.

Marshall Beach Trail - 2.6 miles and 360' Change

0.0 From the Marshall Beach parking area, head north and take the trail through pasture, then down towards a cypress grove. In the spring, look for a small white Calochortus, called pussy ears.

1.2 Cove and beach. This picturesque beach offers sunbathing, picnicking, wading and views across Tomales Bay to the town of Marshall. In 1875, Marshall was a stop on the North Pacific Coast Railroad. It was also the site of the west coast's first wireless communications system. Today, it supports oyster farms and Tomales Bay's only remaining boatyard.

Look for a shell midden along the north end of the beach.

Marshall Beach as seen from the trail to Lairds Landing

Option: Lairds Landing Trail - 2.4 miles and 360' Change

0.0 From the Marshall Beach parking area, head east through the gate and down the paved road. Note that this is an unmaintained trail, not part of the official trail system. Use at your own risk.

1.2 At Lairds Landing, you may find several interesting old structures where artist Clayton Lewis lived from the 1960s until he died in 1995. One of the buildings is very small and seems like a cross between a doll house and a guest cottage. Most of these buildings are scheduled for removal.

Note: At tides below +1.0', it is possible to get from Lairds Landing to Marshall Beach (and beyond) by scrambling along a rocky beach, thus making a loop trip. However, the rocks are slippery and the 200 yd. trip requires a small amount of climbing. Low tide occurs here almost one and one-half hours later than times given for the Golden Gate.

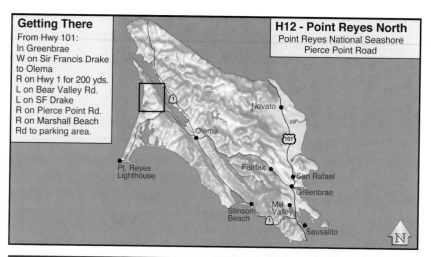

Getting There

From Hwy 101:
In Greenbrae
W on Sir Francis Drake
to Olema
R on Hwy 1 for 200 yds.
L on Bear Valley Rd.
L on SF Drake
R on Pierce Point Rd.
R on Marshall Beach
Rd to parking area.

Novato

Olema

Pt. Reyes
Lighthouse

Fairfax

San Rafael

Greenbrae

Stinson
Beach

Mill
Valley

Sausalito

N

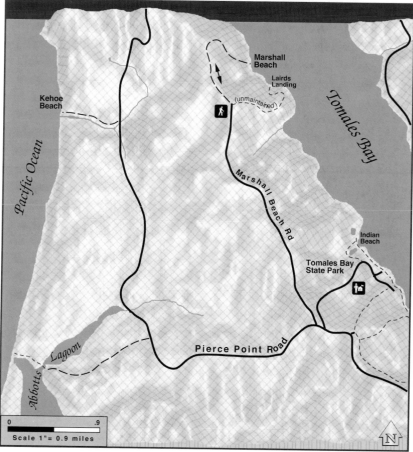

Marshall
Beach

Lairds
Landing

Kehoe
Beach

(unmaintained)

Tomales Bay

Pacific Ocean

Marshall Beach Rd

Indian
Beach

Tomales Bay
State Park

Pierce Point Road

Lagoon

Abbotts

| 0 | | .9 |

Scale 1"= 0.9 miles

N

J - Marin County - 9 Hikes

Starting in Southern Marin
J1 Hiking the Tiburon Peninsula* 6.3
J2 Old St. Hilarys and Uplands Preserve 3.4 and 0.7

Starting on Mt. Tamalpais - Southern Side
J3 Homestead Valley Loop 3.4
J4 Gravity Car - Vic Haun and Temelpa 3.6 and 7.8
J5 Three Hikes at Stinson Beach 2.6, 4.8 and 6.5

Starting in Central Marin
J6 Gold Hill - San Pedro Ridge - Aquinas FR 5.5
J7 Thorner Ridge and French Ranch 2.8 and 4.6

Starting in North Marin
J8 Loma Alta and Big Rock Ridge Trail 4.2 and 7.2
J9 Wetlands Trail at Rush Creek 2.0

Notes
* Shuttle Hike
Dogs are allowed on all hikes, except J4 and J5.
To download a hike, go to www.marintrails.com
The password for this region is j9km2ak

Notes about hikes for the 3rd Edition
All of the hikes in Region J are new (note that there is no
Region I). All of the other hikes in this 3rd edition are the same
as hikes in the 2nd edition with the following exceptions:

Minor route or description changes: 62 hikes

Major route changes: A12, A15, B7, B21, C8, C9, C10, C18,
C19, D5, E9, E14, F14, F15, G7, G8, H4, H12

For additional information, including temporary trail closures,
check our website at www.marintrails.com.

Region J Trailheads
New Hikes for 3rd Edition

Hike 1 starts in City of Tiburon Open Space, phone 415-435-7390.

Hike 2 starts in Marin County Open Space, phone 415-499-6387.

Hike 3 starts in Homestead Valley Land Trust, phone 415-383-5874.

Hike 4 starts in Marin Municipal Water District, phone 415-945-1181.

Hike 5 starts in Mt. Tamalpais State Park, phone 415-388-2070.

Hikes 6-9 start in Marin County Open Space, phone 415-499-6387.

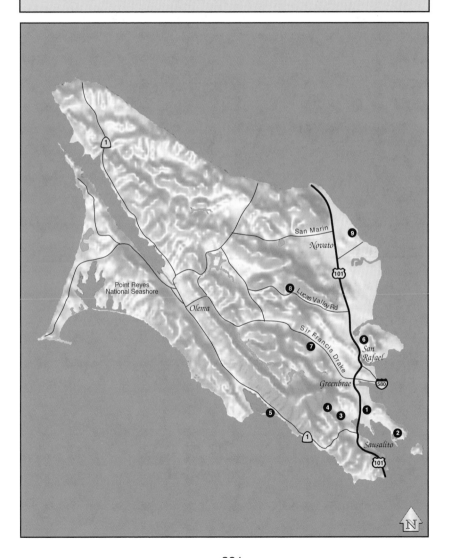

J1 Hiking the Tiburon Peninsula*

Distance: 6.3 miles   Shaded: 10%
Elevation Change: 1400'   Lots of walking on quiet streets.
Rating: Hiking - 10   Difficulty - 7   Rocky downhill section. Stairs.
When to Go: Best when clear and calm in the spring.

This is a spectacular hike along the entire Tiburon Ridge with magnificent views, luxurious houses and great spring wildflowers.

*Shuttle Hike. Leave pickup cars at the parking lot in downtown Tiburon and shuttle hikers to the start at Blackfield and Karen.

0.0 Just past Karen, take Via Los Altos left uphill. Near the top, just past the roundabout, head left at the Y-junction and look for the stairs.

0.5 Junction. Take the stairs uphill, then continue right to join the FR.

1.4 Junction ❶ with Phyllis Ellman trail. Continue straight. **Option**: It's worth exploring this area. See Hike A11 for details.

1.6 Junction. A road goes north to houses. Continue straight.

1.7 Junction. Head right downhill. **Option**: Continue straight to explore the top of Ring Mtn. with great views and great flowers in April.

2.4 Junction with the church parking area. Head downhill.

2.5 Junction ❷. Go left on Trestle Glen. Watch for cars.

2.6 Junction. Carefully cross Trestle Glen and take Hacienda uphill. Up ahead, the street becomes private property, but with a trail easement.

3.5 Junction. Go through the gate onto open space. Ahead, continue straight towards the houses. **Option**: It's worth a side trip right, down the road, then out to a lookout point under a large eucalyptus tree.

3.8 Junction ❸ with the street. Go left on Gilmartin.

4.0 End of street. Take the trail east and follow the Tiburon Ridge signs.

4.1 Water tank. After passing the tank, look for a post across the street signed Tiburon Ridge trail. It points the way up Mt. Tiburon Rd.

4.2 Post and stairs. Climb the 150 stairs and follow the trail to Place Moulin. Continue to Sugarloaf. This is the highest point on the peninsula with interesting houses and great views. Continue down.

4.7 Junction. Go left on Heathcliff to Old St. Hilary open space.

4.8 Junction ❹. Take the Lyford FR right to Lyford and head downhill.

5.2 Junction. Go left on Vistazo and then down to Old St. Hilarys church. Continue down Esperanza, then Beach Rd. See Map J2.

6.3 Junction with Tiburon Blvd. Go right to parking lot.

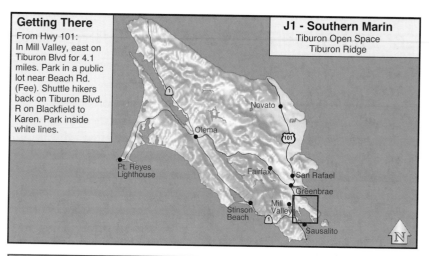

Getting There

From Hwy 101:
In Mill Valley, east on Tiburon Blvd for 4.1 miles. Park in a public lot near Beach Rd. (Fee). Shuttle hikers back on Tiburon Blvd. R on Blackfield to Karen. Park inside white lines.

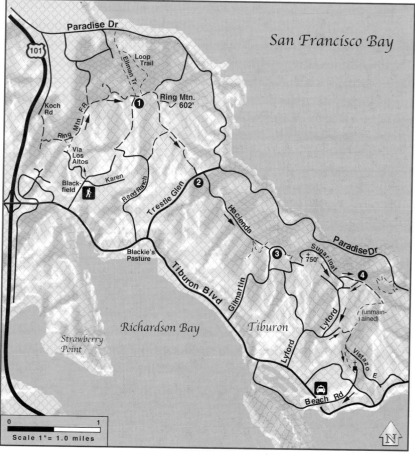

San Francisco Bay

Paradise Dr

Loop Trail

Elman Tr

Ring Mtn. FR.

Koch Rd

Ring Mtn

① Ring Mtn. 602'

Via Los Altos

Blackfield

Karen

Reed Ranch

Trestle Glen

② Hacienda

Blackie's Pasture

Paradise Dr

Sugar loaf + 750'

③

④

Tiburon Blvd

Gilmartin

Lyford

(unmaintained)

Tiburon

Richardson Bay

Strawberry Point

Lyford

Lyford

Vistazo E

Beach Rd

0   1

Scale 1"= 1.0 miles

293

J2 Old St. Hilarys and Uplands Preserve

Distance: 3.4 and 0.7 miles   Shaded: 0% and 70%
Elevation Change: See below.   Part of 1st hike on streets.
Rating: Hiking - 8 and 7   Difficulty - 4 and 6
When to Go: Good when cool and clear. Good flowers in spring.

The first hike explores one of Marin's historical treasures, then climbs to the ridge offering great views. The 2nd hike loops through forest.

Old St. Hilary Open Space - 3.4 miles and 500' Change

0.0 From the corner of Esperanza and Centro West, walk up Esperanza towards Old St. Hilarys Church. This redwood church was built in 1888 on land donated by pioneer John Reed and used until 1954. It is now owned by the Tiburon Landmarks Society.

0.1 Walkway. Just before the church, take the stone and concrete walkway left. After exploring the church area, continue to follow the walkway and trail as it gradually climbs to meet Vistazo FR.

0.3 Junction. Continue left on Vistazo FR.

0.4 Junction ❶. An unofficial trail goes up along the ravine. Continue west on Vistazo FR. **Note**: Old St. Hilarys Open Space has two official trails, Vistazo FR here and Heathcliff FR up on the ridge. This unofficial trail connects the two, but is not recommended. If you do take it, it is better to go up than down, because the 0.3 mile trail is moderately steep and rocky in places.

0.5 Gate and junction with the street Vistazo West. Continue west.

0.7 Junction ❷ with Lyford Dr. Head right uphill. Watch for traffic.

1.1 Junction ❸ with Sugarloaf Dr. Go left to Heathcliff, then right.

1.3 Open Space gate. Follow Heathcliff FR along the ridgetops with great views in all directions. Up ahead, the high point is at 640'.

1.7 Open Space sign, old fence, and junction ❹ with the unofficial trail. When ready, backtrack on Heathcliff FR and Heathcliff Drive.

3.4 Back at the parking area. No facilities.

Tiburon Uplands Preserve - 0.7 miles and 200' Change

0.0 Park opposite the Romberg Tiburon Center located 6.8 miles from Hwy 101 out Tiburon Blvd, which turns into Paradise Dr. Walk back 200' to the stairs to start the hike. At the top of the stairs, head right.

0.3 Bench and junction ❺. An unofficial trail climbs steeply up to the ridge and Heathcliff FR. Continue straight and enjoy the views east.

0.7 Back at the stairs and car. No facilities.

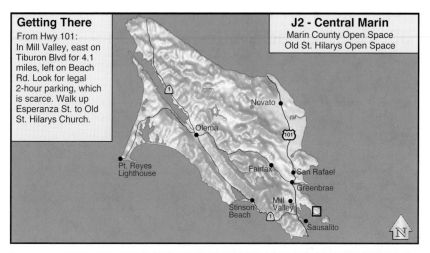

Getting There

From Hwy 101:
In Mill Valley, east on
Tiburon Blvd for 4.1
miles, left on Beach
Rd. Look for legal
2-hour parking, which
is scarce. Walk up
Esperanza St. to Old
St. Hilarys Church.

J2 - Central Marin
Marin County Open Space
Old St. Hilarys Open Space

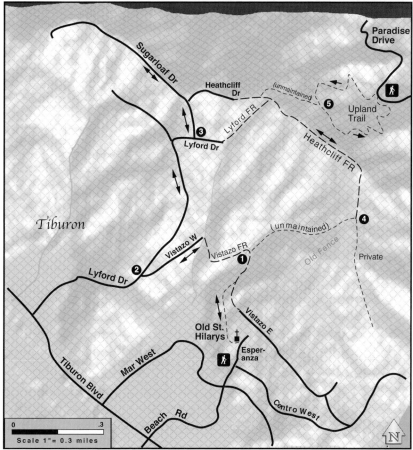

295

J3 Homestead Valley Loop

Distance: 3.4 miles   Shaded: 50%
Elevation Change: 1000'   Trail overgrown in places.
Rating: Hiking - 8   Difficulty - 8   Poison oak in places.
When to Go: Good anytime when not too wet.

This hike explores Homestead Valley and its redwood groves, then climbs to the ridge at Four Corners providing views. Good flowers.

0.0 From the parking area under the eucalyptus trees, take the private drive at #361 Ridgewood uphill to the open space gate. Go through the gate and continue climbing.

0.2 Junction ❶. Take the signed Homestead trail right. There are lots of trails here. In most cases, stay on the most heavily traveled trail.

0.4 Junction ❷. Take the signed Eagle trail, which starts downhill.

0.5 Junction. The Ridgewood trail goes left, head right on the Eagle trail towards Stolte grove. Stay on the main trail towards the redwoods.

0.8 Junction ❸ and Stolte Grove. After exploring Stolte Grove (water, restroom and tables), go left to the end of Tamalpais. Cross the bridge and head up the stairs. Then, cross a second bridge to more stairs.

1.1 Junction and post. Go right towards Cowboy Rock, named by the Stolte children in the 1920s as they played "cowboys and Indians."

1.2 Cowboy Rock and bench. When ready, backtrack.

1.3 Junction. Continue on Ridgewood trail. After descending into and crossing a redwood ravine, the trail zig-zags up to a level trail. Go left.

1.5 Junction ❹. Fifty yards after crossing another redwood ravine, bear right and stay on the main trail uphill (other trails lead off).

1.7 Junction and street. Head up Amaranth 200' to a small yellow fire hydrant where the street turns sharp right. Head left uphill.

1.9 Junction near Four Corners. Continue straight and onto the FR.

2.2 Junction ❺ atop Homestead Hill. Good views all around, but especially to the east. When ready, go downhill on the FR. Ahead, the FR veers right and joins another FR heading towards Waterview.

2.5 Junction ❻. About 200 yds. before the street, head left downhill.

2.6 Junction. Left on the Homestead trail. Ahead, low-hanging bay trees.

2.9 Junction with trail to Madrone Park and bench. Continue straight.

3.2 Junction ❶ again. Head right towards Ridgewood Avenue.

3.4 Back at the parking area. No facilities.

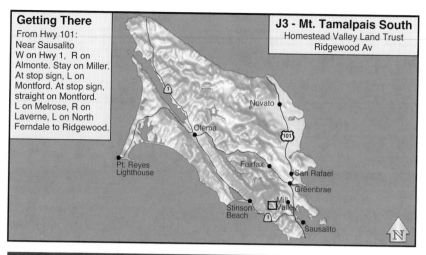

Getting There

From Hwy 101:
Near Sausalito
W on Hwy 1, R on
Almonte. Stay on Miller.
At stop sign, L on
Montford. At stop sign,
straight on Montford.
L on Melrose, R on
Laverne, L on North
Ferndale to Ridgewood.

J3 - Mt. Tamalpais South
Homestead Valley Land Trust
Ridgewood Av

Novato

Olema

Pt. Reyes
Lighthouse

Fairfax

San Rafael

Greenbrae

Stinson
Beach

Mill
Valley

Sausalito

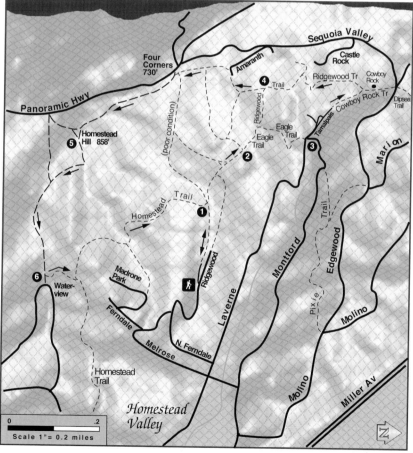

Sequoia Valley

Four
Corners
730'

Amaranth

Castle
Rock

Ridgewood Tr

Cowboy
Rock

Panoramic Hwy

Trail

Cowboy Rock Tr

Dipsea
Trail

(poor condition)

Ridgewood

Eagle
Trail

Tamalpais

Marion

Homestead
Hill 858'

Eagle
Trail

Trail

Homestead   Trail

Montford

Edgewood

Molino

Water-
view

Madrone
Park

Ridgewood

Laverne

Pixie

Ferndale

Melrose

N. Ferndale

Molino

Miller Av

Homestead
Trail

Homestead
Valley

Scale 1" = 0.2 miles

0   .2

297

J4 Gravity Car - Vic Haun and Temelpa

Distance: 3.6 and 7.8 miles   Shaded: 60% and 30%
Elevation Change: See below.   Wheeler trail steep in places.
Rating: Hiking - 9   Difficulty - 6 and 9   2nd hike rocky in places.
When to Go: Best when cool and clear.

The first hike visits two of Mt. Tam's special places. The second hike continues on up to East Peak offering a steep climb and great views.

Gravity Car - Vic Haun Trails - 3.6 miles and 700' Change

0.0   From the parking lot, cross the road and take the Gravity Car FR right as it starts downhill, then gradually climbs.

1.0   Junction. Take the Old Railroad Grade left.

1.3   Junction ❶ with Hoo-Koo-E-Koo FR. Take the Vic Haun trail, which heads up a few stairs, then enters a narrow alley of chaparral.

1.6   Unmaintained trail. A path leads down a creek bed 200' to a few remnants of a navy plane that crashed here in 1944, killing 8 crew members. The site is at 37° 55.376N and 122° 34.433W. Note that it is illegal to remove historical artifacts from district lands.

1.8   Junction ❷ with the Temelpa trail. Go right downhill 70' to a large boulder with a small plaque embedded. The environmental statement was made by the Sioux Indian Chief Sitting Bull in 1877. When ready, head back to the start or continue the hike as described below.

3.6   Back at Mtn. Home Inn. Restrooms and water available.

Temelpa - Eldridge - Wheeler Trails - 7.8 miles and 1500' Change

1.8   From junction ❷ of the Vic Haun and Temelpa trails, take the Temelpa trail (western-most trail) as it climbs to East Peak. Stay on the newly improved Temelpa trail as it switchbacks up the slope. Avoid unofficial trails. Enjoy the great views from east to west.

2.8   Junction ❸. Take the paved Verna Dunshee trail left or right.

3.1   East Peak (See Hike B20 for details including hiking to the top.) Take the paved trail on the south side of the parking area to the west.

3.4   Junction ❹. Take Eldridge Grade right. The upper section is rocky.

5.2   Junction ❺. At a hairpin turn, take the Wheeler trail straight ahead. This trail starts out level, but soon becomes very steep and rocky.

5.7   Junction. Take the Hoo-Koo-E-Koo FR right.

6.5   Junction ❶ again. Head left down the Old RR Grade, then on Gravity Car to return to the parking area.

7.8   Back at Mtn. Home Inn. Restrooms and water available.

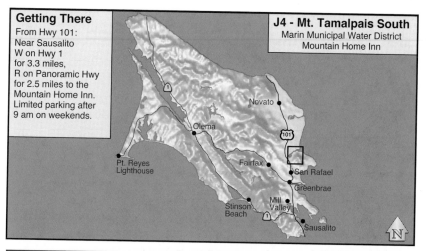

Getting There

From Hwy 101:
Near Sausalito
W on Hwy 1
for 3.3 miles,
R on Panoramic Hwy
for 2.5 miles to the
Mountain Home Inn.
Limited parking after
9 am on weekends.

J4 - Mt. Tamalpais South
Marin Municipal Water District
Mountain Home Inn

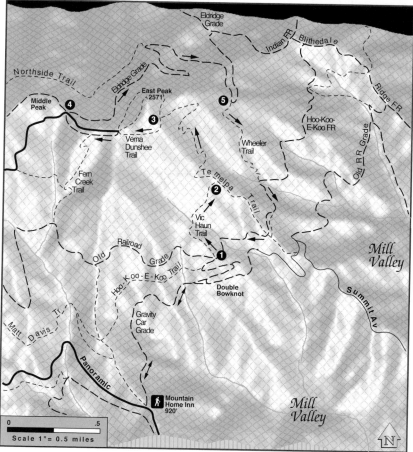

J5 Three Hikes at Stinson Beach

Distance: 2.6, 4.8 and 6.5 miles   Shaded: 20%, 0% and 30%
Elevation Change: See below.   Grasses can crowd some trails.
Rating: Hiking - 9   Difficulty - 4, 2 and 7   Steep down in places.
When to Go: Good anytime when not too foggy or windy.

These 3 hikes provide a great introduction to the beach, hills and mountains around Stinson Beach. Spectacular views in clear weather.

Note: See Hike B16 for another hike out of Stinson Beach.

South to the "moors" and back - 2.6 miles and 580' Change
0.0 From the beach, go out the gate to the Parkside Cafe and head south along Arenal Street to Shoreline Hwy (Hwy 1).

0.2 Shoreline Hwy. Cross the road and take the famed Dipsea trail uphill to cross Panoramic Hwy. Continue up towards Pantoll. Ahead, the open, undulating land is poorly drained in areas, like a moor.

1.0 Junction. After some steps, take the FR right. Near the large eucalyptus, head right uphill to an old military bunker and viewpoint.

1.3 Viewpoint ❶. When ready, head back to Stinson Beach.

North along the beach and back - 4.8 miles and 0' Change
0.0 From the beach opposite the Parkside Cafe, head north. The hike soon leaves public land and passes along the Seadrift community, where public access is restricted to below the mean high-tide line.

2.4 The north end of the beach, Pt. ❷, lies at the inlet to Bolinas Lagoon, which is too deep to cross. When ready, return.

Matt Davis - Coastal - Willow Camp FR - 6.5 miles and 1900'
0.0 From the beach, go out the gate to the Parkside Cafe and head south along Arenal Street to Shoreline Hwy. Go left 200' to Belvedere, then up Belvedere to the signed Matt Davis trail, which starts at a bridge. Up ahead, a trail joins from the right. Continue straight.

0.7 Bridge and junction ❸. Just past the bridge, go right on the trail for a long steady climb. Up ahead, check the view at Table Rock.

2.8 Junction ❹. Head left on the Coastal trail with great views.

4.2 Junction ❺. Take the Willow Camp FR left for a long downhill.

6.0 Gate and junction ❻. Take the public street, Avenida Farralone downhill and continue L on Belvedere, R on Lincoln, R on Buena Vista, R on Calle del Mar. Watch for cars on the narrow streets.

6.5 Back at the state park with cafe, restrooms and picnic areas.

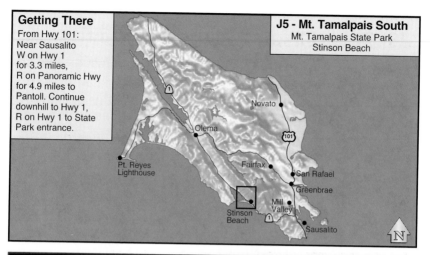

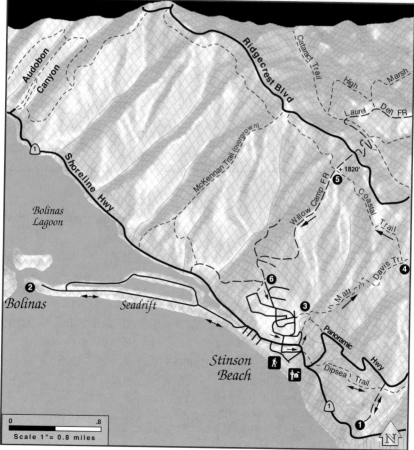

Getting There

From Hwy 101:
Near Sausalito
W on Hwy 1
for 3.3 miles,
R on Panoramic Hwy
for 4.9 miles to
Pantoll. Continue
downhill to Hwy 1,
R on Hwy 1 to State
Park entrance.

Novato

Olema

Pt. Reyes
Lighthouse

Fairfax

San Rafael

Greenbrae

Mill
Valley

Stinson
Beach

Sausalito

N

Audobon
Canyon

Ridgecrest Blvd

Cataract Trail

High

Marsh

Laurel   Dell   FR

Shoreline Hwy

McKennan Trail (overgrown)

+1820'   **5**

Coastal

Trail

Bolinas
Lagoon

Willow Camp FR

Davis Trl

4

6

2

Bolinas

Seadrift

3

Matt

Panoramic

Hwy

*Stinson
Beach*

Dipsea   Trail

1

0   .8
Scale 1"= 0.8 miles

N

J6 Gold Hill - San Pedro Ridge FR

Distance: 5.5 miles   Shaded: 50%
Elevation Change: 1100'   Hike includes 1.5 miles on quiet streets.
Rating: Hiking - 7   Difficulty - 7   Lots of bicycles on weekends.
When to Go: Good anytime, best when cool and clear.

This hike climbs up a fire road behind Dominican College to the ridge above China Camp offering great views.

0.0 Start by passing through the Gold Hill FR gate and head uphill into non-native eucalyptus. You can see the negative aspects of these trees here: debris, falling limbs, fire hazard, crowding of natives.

0.1 Junction with fire road. Head left on a more level road.

0.3 Clearing and bench. The clearing at the end of the eucalyptus grove offers views across the canyon to the return route.

1.0 Hairpin turn. Two metal posts from an old sign mark the start of an unofficial trail, now often used by bicyclists.

1.3 Junction ❶ with paved road. Head left. **Option**: Go right for about 200 yds. to explore a fenced area surrounding a microwave antenna.

1.4 Junction ❷ with Bay Hills FR. Take the dirt fire road downhill right for some great views south. Ahead, at a Y, head right to the power pole.

1.5 Viewpoint and turnaround point. When done, head back.

1.6 Junction ❷ again. Take the paved road right.

2.2 Junction with FR into China Camp State Park. Continue left.

Nike missile radar platform

2.4 Nike missile radar site, viewpoint and picnic area.

2.5 Junction ❸. Leave the paved road and head left through the gate onto the San Pedro Ridge FR.

3.7 Junction ❹. Take the Aquinas FR left. It gets steep in places.

4.2 Water tank and street. Continue downhill on Aquinas Dr., then left on Dominican Dr. for 0.3 miles, then left on Sienna Way.

4.7 Junction. Take Mountain View right, then left on Grand, left on Locust, all the way to the start, which becomes Gold Hill Grade.

5.5 Back at the start with no facilities.

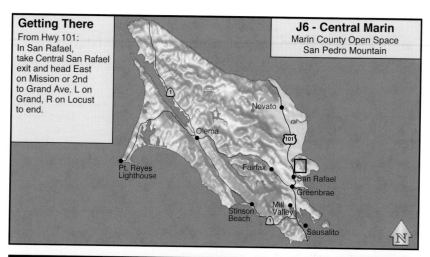

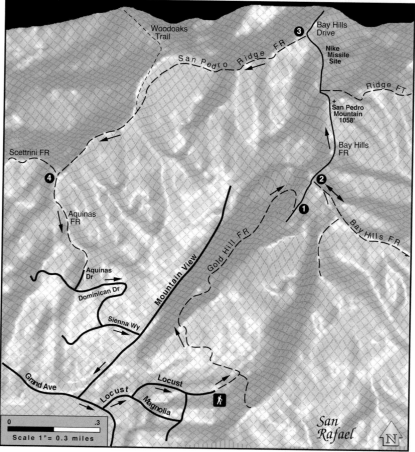

J7 Thorner Ridge and French Ranch

Distance: 2.8 and 4.6 miles   Shaded: 60%
Elevation Change: See below.   Quite muddy in winter.
Rating: Hiking - 8   Difficulty - 3 and 6   Moderately steep FR.
When to Go: Best when cool and not too wet.

The first hike loops around the golf course, then up Thorner Ridge. The second hike climbs to a forested ridge, then returns. Good local views.

W. Nicasio Rd. - Thorner Ridge Trail - 2.8 miles and 200' Change
0.0 From the parking area on Nicasio Valley Rd., take the trail through the gate heading west.

0.1 Junction with the street, W. Nicasio Rd. Head right to parallel the golf course and head towards the houses.

0.6 End of paved street and junction ❶. Continue on the trail, bearing right at a Y-junction to follow the golf course as it doglegs right.

1.1 Junction with French Ranch FR. Go left downhill.

1.5 Junction ❷ with School trail. Go left to parallel Sir Francis Drake.

1.6 Junction with Lagunitas School Rd. Head left to go to the end of the road and the school parking area.

2.0 Junction ❸. Take the Thorner Ridge trail left zig-zagging uphill.

2.7 Bridge and junction. Cross Nicasio Valley Rd on the bridge, then go left on the trail.

2.8 Back at the parking area. No facilities.

French Ranch FR - 4.6 miles and 1000' Change
0.0 You can park on school grounds on weekends, otherwise look for safe off-street parking. This hike starts at the corner of Lagunitas School Rd and Sir Francis Drake Blvd. Take the School trail heading east and paralleling Sir Francis Drake Blvd.

0.1 Junction ❷. Take the French Ranch FR north between fences to parallel the golf course. Ahead, look for blackberries in summer.

0.4 Metal posts and junction. Just past the metal posts, a small trail heads right downhill. Continue climbing on the FR.

1.4 Junction ❹ with Barnabe FR. Head left.

2.3 Turnaround point ❺. A "No Trespassing" sign on a tree signals the end of the Open Space area. **Note**: The Barnabe FR continues on private land to connect to Devils Gulch and Mt. Barnabe.

4.6 Back at the parking area. No facilities.

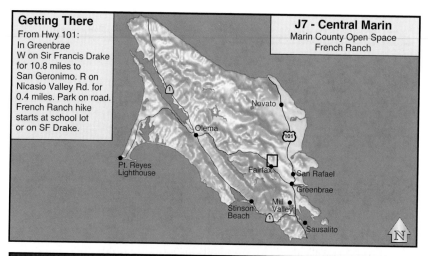

Getting There

From Hwy 101:
In Greenbrae
W on Sir Francis Drake
for 10.8 miles to
San Geronimo. R on
Nicasio Valley Rd. for
0.4 miles. Park on road.
French Ranch hike
starts at school lot
or on SF Drake.

J7 - Central Marin
Marin County Open Space
French Ranch

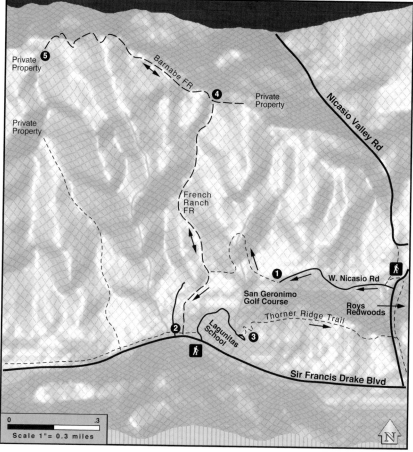

J8 Loma Alta and Big Rock Ridge

Distance: 4.2 and 7.2 miles   Shaded: 0% and 20%
Elevation Change: See below.   Bicycles on weekends.
Rating: Hiking - 7 and 9   Difficulty - 5 and 6   Can be windy.
When to Go: Good when calm, cool and clear. Best in early April.

These two hikes explore opposite sides of Lucas Valley. Both hikes climb to a peak offering specacular views. Good spring flowers.

Loma Alta out and back - 4.2 miles and 1100' Change
Note: MCOSD is working on a public easement that will connect Loma Alta with Terra Linda Ridge. This will allow a good shuttle hike.

0.0 From Lucas Valley Rd, go south through the gate and head uphill on the Loma Alta FR. Look for masses of yellow buttercups in spring.

0.7 Junction ❶ with a FR and gate on the right. Continue uphill.

1.5 Junction ❷. Another FR leads off to the right. Continue uphill.

2.1 Loma Alta peak and junction ❸ with great views. Big Rock Ridge dominates to the north. Mt. Tam is seen south, Mt. Diablo to the east. No peaks dominate to the west, but you can just see the fire lookout station atop Mt. Barnabe and the knuckle-like top of Black Mtn. When ready, return the way you came. **Option**: Continue down to the right and loop back on the lower FR to junction ❷.

4.2 Back at the parking area with no facilities.

Big Rock Ridge out and back - 7.2 miles and 1500' Change
Note: You can do a shuttle hike from here to the Luiz or Queenstone FR. However, the out and back trail is easier and more interesting.

0.0 From the parking area, carefully cross the road and take the Big Rock trail past the 30' tall rock, which gave the ridge and trail its name.

1.3 Fence and gate. Just ahead, good views down to the Lucasfilm lake and buildings. Spring flowers include blue-eyed grass, purple filaree, pink checkerbloom, buttercup and the small white popcorn flower.

2.5 Junction ❹. Take the Big Rock Ridge FR right uphill. Great views.

3.1 Junction ❺. The FR continues left. Take the bypass trail right.

3.3 Junction. The trail rejoins the road on the ridgetop offering great views north and east. Continue a little farther towards the towers, which are the distinctive landmarks of Big Rock Ridge.

3.6 Turnaround point ❻. Just past the second tower, a clear spot provides the best viewing. When ready, retrace your steps.

7.2 Back at the parking area. No facilities. Use caution exiting.

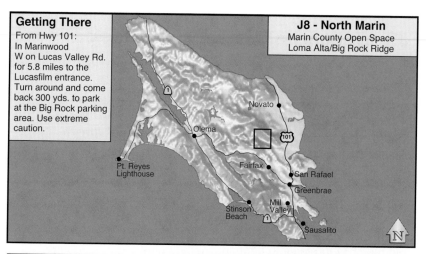

Getting There

From Hwy 101:
In Marinwood
W on Lucas Valley Rd.
for 5.8 miles to the
Lucasfilm entrance.
Turn around and come
back 300 yds. to park
at the Big Rock parking
area. Use extreme
caution.

J8 - North Marin
Marin County Open Space
Loma Alta/Big Rock Ridge

Novato

Pt. Reyes
Lighthouse

Olema

Fairfax

San Rafael

Greenbrae

Stinson
Beach

Mill
Valley

Sausalito

N

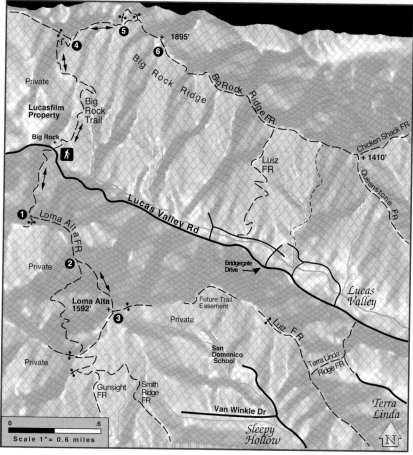

5

+ 1895'

4

6

Private

Big
Rock
Ridge

Big
Rock
Trail

Lucasfilm
Property

Big
Rock
Ridge FR

Chicken Shack FR

Big Rock
+

Luiz
FR

+ 1410'

Queenstone FR

1

Loma Alta FR

Lucas Valley Rd

Private

2

Bridgegate
Drive

Lucas
Valley

Loma Alta
1592'
+

3

Future Trail
Easement

Luiz FR

Private

Private

San
Domenico
School

Terra Linda
Ridge FR

Gunsight
FR

Smith
Ridge
FR

Van Winkle Dr

Terra
Linda

Sleepy
Hollow

N

0		.6

Scale 1" = 0.6 miles

307

J9 Wetlands Trail at Rush Creek

Distance: 2.0 miles   Shaded: 80%
Elevation Change: 300'   Trails are still under construction.
Rating: Hiking - 7   Difficulty - 6   Can be muddy.
When to Go: Good in winter for birds and spring for flowers.

This hike skirts a tidal marsh with shorebirds in winter and wildflowers in spring, then climbs to explore the surrounding ridge.

0.0 Head through the open space gate onto the Wetlands trail, which is the main trail around the marsh. Other trails go down to the levee or come down from the ridge. Ahead, the trail curves inland where the old marsh is turning into a meadow after being diked years ago.

0.5 Junction ❶ with an unofficial trail that crosses. Good views north to twin peaks of Mt. Diablo and the Hwy 37 bridge. Continue straight.

0.7 Junction and post. Head left, and continue around the marsh until the trail runs out or disappears under water, then return. **Option:** Continue on an unofficial bypass trail that skirts the marsh.

0.9 Junction and post again. Continue on the lower trail which goes past a levee (good birding spot), then climbs 10' to a small ridge.

1.0 Small ridge and junction. Take the unofficial trail right up a rocky, moderately steep slope.

1.1 Junction ❶ again. Continue to climb up through the oaks to the ridgetop. This is the largest blue oak forest in Marin. They are more common in the hot, dry California foothills. Blue oaks are short trees, about 30' tall, with an open canopy. Leaves are blue-green on top and yellow-green underneath. Also, the blue oak does not appear susceptible to Sudden Oak Death.

1.3 Knoll and junction ❷. Head right along the ridge FR.

1.4 Junction ❸ and turn-around point. The FR ahead continues down to the marsh. The FR left drops steeply down to Bugeia Lane.

1.5 Junction ❷ again. Continue along the ridge.

1.7 Viewpoint. Notice the boat docks behind the houses at Bahia. Over the last 20 years, the channel has severely silted in. Permits to dredge have been denied for various reasons, including the discovery of the endangered California clapper rail. Continue down to the gate and take the street back to the start. **Option:** An unofficial trail parallels the street, but may be overgrown and rocky in places.

2.0 Back at the parking area with no facilities.

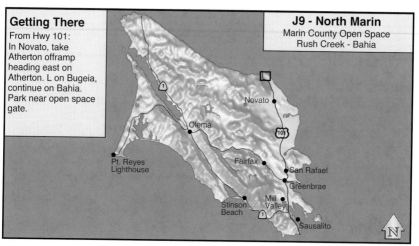

Getting There

From Hwy 101:
In Novato, take
Atherton offramp
heading east on
Atherton. L on Bugeia,
continue on Bahia.
Park near open space
gate.

J9 - North Marin
Marin County Open Space
Rush Creek - Bahia

Novato

Olema

Pt. Reyes
Lighthouse

Fairfax

San Rafael

Greenbrae

Stinson
Beach

Mill
Valley

Sausalito

N

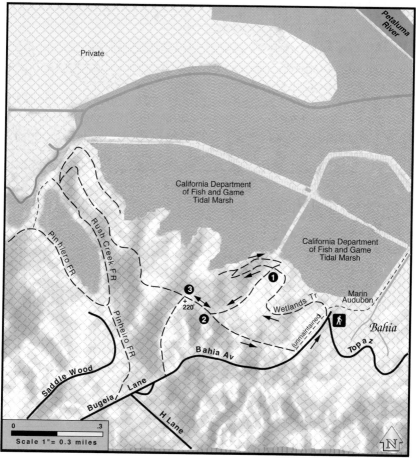

Petaluma
River

Private

California Department
of Fish and Game
Tidal Marsh

California Department
of Fish and Game
Tidal Marsh

Pinheiro FR

Rush Creek FR

Pinheiro FR

3

+220'

2

1

Wetlands Tr

(unmaintained)

Marin
Audubon

Bahia

Topaz

Saddle Wood

Bahia Av

Bugeia Lane

H Lane

0   .3

Scale 1"= 0.3 miles

N

309

1 A Trail For All Seasons

December - January
The sun is at its lowest angle of the year and it's often cold and wet or foggy. This is the rainiest period in Marin County with rainfall averaging 20 inches on the wettest areas of Mt. Tamalpais. But you can beat the indoor blues by getting out and looking for views, coastal hills and beaches, creeks, waterfalls, mosses and lichens, whales, wintering birds and southern exposures. Here are a few suggestions:

Southern Marin - Hikes A2, A4, A7, A10, A15, H1, J2
Mt. Tamalpais South - Hikes B1, B4, B8, B10, B14, B20, J4
Mt. Tamalpais North - Hikes C3, C4, C8, C10, C11, C12, C16
Central Marin - Hikes D2, D3, D5, D9, D12
North Marin - Hikes E1, E2, E4, E5, E8, E11, E13, J9
Point Reyes South - Hikes F7, F14, F15
Point Reyes North - Hikes G6, G10, G11, G12, G13

February - March
This is the premier hiking time of the year. Even though rainfall averages 16 inches in the wettest areas, the weather is getting better, and water runoff is high. Trillium, milkmaids and hound's tongue start the wildflower parade. All the hikes are at their best.

Southern Marin - Hikes A3, A5, A11, A12, A14, A15, J1, J2
Mt. Tamalpais South - Hikes B2, B4, B9, B12, B14, B15, B16, B18, H3
Mt. Tamalpais North - Hikes C2, C8, C9, C11, C17
Central Marin - Hikes D2, D4, D10, D11, D13, H7
North Marin - Hikes E3, E6, E8, E10, E11, E14, H9
Point Reyes South - Hikes F3, F6, F7, F14, F17
Point Reyes North - Hikes G1, G2, G11, G12, G13, G17, G18

April - May
More great hiking time. The weather is at its best, the hills are green and the late wildflowers reach their peak. Be sure to visit the rolling hills around Pt. Reyes, Mt. Burdell and the MMWD lakes area. Look for iris peaking in April. All the hikes are great.

Southern Marin - Hikes A3, A5, A6, A11, A12, J1, J2
Mt. Tamalpais South - Hikes B14, B15, B16, B17, B19, B21, H3
Mt. Tamalpais North - Hikes C1, C3, C4, C5, C7, C10, C12, C17
Central Marin - Hikes D3, D5, D11, D12, D14
North Marin - Hikes E1, E6, E7, E9, E10, E11, E12, E13, H10, J8
Point Reyes South - Hikes F4, F6, F8, F13, F16, F18
Point Reyes North - Hikes G2, G4, G5, G6, G8, G11, G12, G13, G17

June - July

While much of Marin is hot and dry, Marin Headlands, Muir Woods, Steep Ravine and the Pt. Reyes coast are often cool and foggy as the Bay Area air-conditioning system runs full blast. Some summer wildflowers, yellow mariposa lily, monkeyflower, poppy, yarrow and clarkia hang on while the hills turn brown.

Southern Marin - Hikes A4, A5, A6, A7, A8, A10, A11, A12, H1
Mt. Tamalpais South - Hikes B4, B16
Mt. Tamalpais North - Hikes C2, C14
Central Marin - Hikes D7, D15
Point Reyes South - Hikes F4, F14, F15, F16, F17, F18, H11
Point Reyes North - Hikes G5, G6, G7, G8, G9, G10

August - September

Now is the time to avoid the dry, dusty roads. Head for the coast and beaches, north-facing trails, creeks, conifer forests and ripe huckleberries. Try an early morning hike. Caution: During hot, dry and windy days, fire danger is high. Avoid Mt. Tamalpais and the ridges of central and north Marin.

Southern Marin - Hikes A2, A4, A5, A10, A13
Mt. Tamalpais South - Hikes B4, B14, J5
Mt. Tamalpais North - Hike C17
Central Marin - Hikes D11, D13, D14, D15
North Marin - Hike E2
Point Reyes South - Hikes F5, F7, F10, F15
Point Reyes North - Hikes G4, G6, G10, G14, G15

October - November

Look for fall red color from poison oak, and yellow and brown colors from big-leaf maple and deciduous oaks. First winter storms arrive. Rainfall, averaging 8 inches around Mt. Tamalpais, settles the dust and brings out mushrooms. This is great weather time with gusty winds, clear days and marvelous views. It's a good time to head for the coast, south-facing trails and the oak-bay woodlands in central Marin and around the lakes.

Southern Marin - Hikes A2, A4, A5, A9, A10, A12
Mt. Tamalpais South - Hikes B1, B2, B8, B10, B12, B14, B16, J4, J5
Mt. Tamalpais North - Hikes C3, C4, C13, C16, C18
Central Marin - Hikes D5, D11, D12, D13
North Marin - Hikes E1, E4, E5, E8, E9, E12, E13
Point Reyes South - Hikes F2, F4, F6, F11, F16, F17
Point Reyes North - Hikes G1, G4, G5, G6, G9, G10, G14, H12

2 A Selection Of Best Trails

Not sure where to go? Here is our selection of best trails. Remember that the season and weather influence trail conditions.

Where to See Waterfalls

Marin County is blessed with an amazing number of waterfalls. The best time to visit these falls is in winter and early spring. Here's a list with our favorites near the top.

Cascade Falls

1. Cataract Creek - Scenery from Hawaii - Hike C11
2. Steep Ravine - Falls under the redwoods - Hikes B14 and B16
3. Cascade Falls - An easy hike, but difficult parking - Hikes D2 and D3
4. Little Carson Falls - Over 100' total drop - Hikes C8 and C9
5. Alamere Falls - Can only be seen from the beach - Hike F17
6. Dawn Falls - Easy hike to Baltimore Canyon - Hike A15
7. Redwood Creek - Start in Muir Woods and climb - Hike B6
8. Tucker Trail - Several small cascades - Hike C5
9. Loma Alta Falls - You'd never expect falls like this here - Hike D5
10. Stairstep Falls - Samuel P. Taylor Park - Hike D10
11. Troop 80 Trail - South side of Mt. Tamalpais - Hike B9
12. Indian Valley Falls - Only after rains - Hike E6
13. Warner Canyon Falls - Small, but nice - Hike A14
14. Several small, unnamed falls - Hike C18

Great Views from High Up

Every once in a while, maybe two or three times a year, the air gets crystal clear with visibility over 50 miles. When that happens, drop everything and head for the peaks.

1. East Peak - On top of the mountain - Hikes B8, B20, C19, J4
2. Mt. Livermore on Angel Island - Best Bay Area location - Hike A12
3. Big Rock Ridge - Marin's second tallest peak - Hikes E4, J8
4. Old Mine Trail - More Tamalpais views - Hikes B13, B15
5. Coastal Trail - Marin Headlands - Hike A3
6. China Camp Nike Missile Site - Hike D12
7. Ring Mountain - Tiburon Peninsula - Hikes A11, J1
8. Hawk Hill - Marin Headlands - Hike A2
9. Mt. Barnabe - Samuel P. Taylor Park - Hikes D9 and D11
10. Blithedale Ridge - Mill Valley - Hike B1

11. Mt. Burdell - Verdant rolling hills - Hikes E13, E14
12. Bald Hill - Near San Anselmo - Hike C3
13. Bolinas Ridge - Fault zone and Tomales Bay - Hike H8
14. Loma Alta - Views from Mt. Tam to Big Rock - Hikes D5, J8

Looking for Local Views

Not all views require hiking to the top of a mountain. Marin offers lots of great views of hills, valleys and spectacular coastline. In fact, there are too many to list them all. Here are some of the best.

Drakes Bay

1. Estero Trail - Tremendous view of coast and beaches - Hike G11
2. Northside trails - Views north from Mt. Tamalpais - Hikes B21 and C18
3. Matt Davis Trail - Above Stinson Beach - Hikes B16, J5
4. Tomales Point Trail - Coastline, hills and elk - Hike G18
5. Coast Trail - Marin Headlands - Hikes A5, A10 and H1
6. Drakes Bay - White cliffs of Marin - Hike G12
7. Double Point - Spectacular views at Pt. Reyes - Hike F15
8. Coastal Trail - More coastal views on Pt. Reyes - Hike F6
9. Kent Trail - Views of Alpine Lake - Hike C14
10. Chimney Rock, Pt. Reyes Lighthouse - Glorious - Hike G13
11. Mt. Wittenberg - Views of Pt. Reyes - Hike F2, F3 and G1

The Best Wildflower Trails

There are many kinds of wildflower hikes. Some hikes, like Chimney Rock, provide a splendid variety of flowers. Other hikes visit areas with great abundance, or carpets of wildflowers. Many hikes lead to old-time favorites like trillium or iris. And a few hikes offer the discovery of rare jewels like the lovely calypso orchid or the Tiburon Calochortus.

1. Chimney Rock - One of the best wildflower hikes on the west coast - Hike G13
2. Tiburon Ridge and Ring Mtn. - Variety, abundance and the rare Tiburon Calochortus - Hike A11, J1, J2
3. Coastal Trail - Marin Headlands in March for variety - Hike A3
4. Benstein Trail - Mar-Apr for rare calypso orchid - Hike B18
5. Baltimore Canyon - March for trillium - Hike A15
6. Olompali - March for early spring flowers - Hike E14
7. Tomales Pt. - Mar-Apr for possible carpets - Hike G18
8. Cascade Canyon - March for great spring flowers - Hike D2

Best Wildflower Trails (continued)

9. Yolanda Trail, both north and south - Hikes C4 and C6
10. Pumpkin Ridge Trail - April for iris - Hike C17
11. Big Rock Ridge - March-April for variety - Hike J8
12. Kehoe Beach and Abbotts Lagoon - Carpets - Hikes G16, G17
13. Wolf Ridge - Marin Headlands March-May for variety - Hike A5
14. Loma Alta - April for carpets - Hike J8
15. Coastal Trail - Mt. Tamalpais in April for variety - Hike B15

Best Birding Trails

Marin County is one of the premier birding areas on the west coast. Of the almost 1000 species of birds in the United States, more than 180 have been spotted at Las Gallinas, more than 300 on Mt. Tamalpais and over 450 species have been counted on Pt. Reyes. Birding locations that are good for experienced birders are not always best for beginners. Here's where we suggest beginners go. Winter is usually the best time unless otherwise indicated. Bring binoculars.

1. Hawk Hill - Sept-Oct migration reaches 2000 per day - Hike A2
2. Las Gallinas Wildlife Ponds - Many birds year-round - Hike E2
3. Pt. Reyes Bird Observatory - May see banding - Hike F14
4. Audubon Canyon Ranch - Open March-July weekends - Hike F18
5. Muddy Hollow at Pt. Reyes - Both shore and land birds - Hikes G5 and G7
6. Limantour Spit at Pt. Reyes - Hike G9
7. Rodeo Lagoon at Marin Headlands - Lots of shore birds - Hike A4
8. Lake Lagunitas - Hike C15
9. Simmons Trail on Mt. Tamalpais - Hike B17
10. Bon Tempe Lake Trail - Hike C13
11. Rush Creek - Hikes H9, J9

Great Blue Heron

Hiking on the Beach

Like to walk on the beach? All of these hikes start on or lead to a sandy beach. All are great year-round, except when too foggy or windy. Bring a picnic in the fall when weather is often best. Listings are by area rather than ranking.

1. Kirby Cove - Good views to San Francisco - Hike A2
2. Rodeo Beach - Look for semi-precious stones - Hike A3
3. Tennessee Cove - Easy hike, but dangerous surf - Hike A7
4. Muir Beach - Start at the beach - Hike A10
5. Stinson Beach - Several options - Hikes B16, J5
6. China Camp Village - Swimming and picnicking - Hike D13
7. Palomarin Beach - South Pt. Reyes - Hike F14

8. Wildcat Beach and Alamere Falls - Twelve mile hike - Hike F17
9. Limantour Beach - Wading possible - Hike G9
10. Sculptured Beach - Long beach hike. Best at low tide - Hike G10
11. Drakes Beach - Best beach on Pt. Reyes. Wading - Hike G12
12. Kehoe and McClures Beach - Dangerous surf - Hike G16
13. Kehoe Beach to Abbotts Lagoon - Long beach hike - Hike G17
14. Tomales Bay beaches - Good swimming - Hikes G14 and G15
15. South Beach - Wild, ocean beach at Pt. Reyes - Hike H11

Historical Hikes

Marin County has a rich human history that began with Native Americans over 7000 years ago. And long before the pilgrims landed at Plymouth Rock, Drake and Cermano both beached at Drakes Bay. Some hikes, especially those that include a Visitor Center, provide a glimpse of that history.

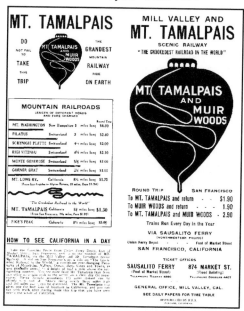

Old Railroad Ad

1. Miwok Village - Kule Loklo Trail at Pt. Reyes - Hike F1
2. Francis Drake - Pt. Reyes Visitor Center and Hikes G12 and G13
3. Olompali - Miwoks and early Marinites - Hike E14
4. China Camp Village - Old buildings and Museum - Hike D13
5. Military fortifications - Headlands Visitor Center and Hike A4
6. Shipwrecks on the coast - Tennessee Valley - Hike A7
7. Crookedest Railroad in the World - Mt. Tam - Hikes B2 and B10
8. Mountain Theater - Outdoor amphitheater - Hikes B12 and B13
9. Pioneer cabin - Phoenix Lake - Hike C1
10. The first papermill - SP Taylor State Park - Hike D7
11. Historical dairy ranch - Tomales Point - Museum and Hike G18
12. Earthquake evidence - Pt. Reyes - Visitor Center and Hike F1
13. East Peak Museum - Weekends on Mt. Tam - Hikes B20 and B21
14. Angel Island - Military History - Museum and Hike A12
15. Pt. Reyes Lighthouse - Museum and Hike G13
16. Tomales Bay State Park - Indian Nature Trail - Hike G14

3 Plant Communities

Marin County offers a magnificent diversity of plant life that can be described by several plant communities.

Redwood Forest

The mature redwood forest is one of nature's masterpieces as a visit to Muir Woods will attest. Branches of redwoods form flat sprays with dark, shiny green, one-inch pointed needles. The cones are small, from 1-2 inches long. Redwoods have a shallow root system spreading out from the base and in severe winters, a few trees will topple.

Redwood

Redwoods form a dense canopy that shades and restricts growth on the forest floor. Decomposition of its needles produces a rich humus that favors acid-loving plants like redwood sorrel, trillium, clintonia and several species of ferns. Other plants in the understory include hazelnut, huckleberry, tanoak and occasionally bay trees.

Redwoods need winter rain and summer moisture (from streams or fog), conditions that are found in Muir Woods, Samuel P. Taylor State Park, Baltimore Canyon and many of the smaller canyons around Mt. Tamalpais and in central and north Marin.

Douglas Fir Forest

The Douglas fir is a majestic tree that can reach heights of 200' with a pyramid shaped crown. The one-inch needles are sprayed out at various angles and the 2-3 inch cones have bracts that resemble mouse tails. These characteristics clearly distinguish Douglas fir trees from other conifers.

Douglas Fir

Elderberry, huckleberry and ferns comprise most of the understory in the Douglas fir forest. The Douglas fir forest dominates the more moist ridges, canyons and valleys of the southern half of the Point Reyes peninsula. You can get a good feel for the forest by hiking any of the trails out of Bear Valley and Five Brooks. Smaller stands of Douglas fir can be found on the north slopes of Mt. Tamalpais.

Bishop Pine Forest

North of the Douglas fir forest on Point Reyes, on slightly drier slopes, the Bishop pine forest grows on the exposed granite of Inverness

Ridge. Bishop pine grow to about 70' in height and are similar in shape to Monterey pines. The needles of the Bishop pine are 2-4 inches long and come two to a bunch. (Monterey pines have slightly longer needles, three to a bunch.) The asymmetrical cones are tight swirls 3-5 inches in size that open to release seeds in hot weather or after fires. About half of the Bishop pine forest on Point Reyes burned in the Mt. Vision fire of 1995. However, Bishop pine is a fire-adapted species that need fire to regenerate the forest. Thousands of new seedlings have started since the fire.

Bishop Pine

Other plants found in the Bishop pine understory include coffeeberry, huckleberry, salal and in drier areas, manzanita and ceanothus.

A good place to see a new Bishop pine forest is on Inverness Ridge, north of Limantour Road. An old Bishop pine forest can be seen in Tomales Bay State Park.

The Oak - Bay Hardwood Forest

The oak-bay hardwood community, composed primarily of oaks and bay, is also referred to as the broadleaf evergreen community. Several oaks grow in this community with the coast live oak, the most common. It is a large 30-75 foot tree with a broad round crown and 1-2 inch oval, cup-shaped leaves. The acorns are slender, pointed and mature in one season.

Coast Live Oak

Other oaks include the evergreen canyon live oak (or goldcup oak) and chaparral oak, the deciduous blue oak and California black oak.

California bay or laurel, has a dark green, lance shaped leaf with a distinctive odor when crushed.

Two common, evergreen members of this community are the madrone, with its distinctive smooth red bark, and the tanoak, which ranges in size from a small 3' shrub to a tall 100' tree.

California Bay

Many shrubs, herbs and grasses are found in the understory of the hardwood forest, including coffeeberry, California hazel, ocean spray, poison oak, bracken fern and wood rose.

The oak-bay hardwood forest can best be seen around the lakes in the Marin Municipal Water District.

Since 1995, large numbers of tanoaks, coast live oaks and black oaks have been found dying in Marin, an epidemic labeled, "Sudden Oak Death." It has since been found elsewhere and in other species. It is believed to be caused by a fungus-like organism.

The Mixed Forest Communities

Most of the communities listed above are small and often intermixed. Thus, you may find Douglas fir in an oak-bay community or conversely, oaks and bay mixed into a Douglas fir forest. Likewise, it is common to find redwoods and Douglas fir mixed together around Mt. Tamalpais (not Point Reyes - redwoods do not appear to grow on the Point Reyes peninsula because of soil conditions).

The Oak Woodland and Oak Savannah Communities

Mt. Burdell, in northern Marin provides a striking example of the oak woodland community that features majestic oaks standing in a sea of grasses. Five of the nine species of oaks in California are found at Mt. Burdell with valley oak being the most common.

Oak woodland has a tree cover of more than 30%, while the oak savannah consists of more widely spaced trees and a tree cover of less than 30%. Northern Marin offers fine examples of each community.

Chaparral Community

The chaparral community, comprised mostly of chamise, manzanita, ceanothus and oaks, are dense, drought resistant shrubs. Most of them have small, evergreen leaves with a waxy, shiny or hairy covering to prevent water loss and long roots to tap moisture from surrounding soil.

Chamise

Chamise is the most common shrub of the chaparral community. It is a member of the rose family and ranges in height from 3-10 feet with tiny, needle-like leaves and small white flowers that start blooming in May. In the fall, the flowers dry to a reddish-brown color and give Mt. Tamalpais its characteristic autumn hue.

There are several species of manzanita found in Marin. They range from 3-10 feet tall with simple, oval-shaped leaves and small, urn-shaped, waxy flowers that start blooming in December. The trunks of manzanita shrubs are very distinctive with a smooth, deep reddish-brown bark that resembles the madrone tree. However, the bark of the madrone tree is a much lighter, tan color.

Manzanita

Several species of ceanothus, or California lilac, are found in Marin. Their appearance varies from prostrate ground cover to erect shrubs, ranging in size from 1-15 feet. They have shiny leaves, often with 3 veins diverging from the base. The fragrant flower clusters vary from white to blue to purple and blooming begins in February.

Four species of oaks are found in the chaparral community in Marin. These are the leather oak, chaparral oak, canyon live oak and scrub oak. The leather oak, *Quercus durata*, is restricted to serpentine soil. Surprisingly, the canyon live oak is the same species that becomes a majestic 50-foot hilltop oak under better conditions.

Other common chaparral plants include toyon, bush monkeyflower, yerba santa, chaparral pea, huckleberry, tree poppy, poison oak, pitcher sage and Indian paintbrush.

The largest chaparral stands in Marin County are located high on the south-facing slopes of Mt. Tamalpais. Although the chaparral communities of

Ceanothus

Mt. Tamalpais are healthy, they are decreasing in area, especially at lower elevations. Because there has not been a large fire on the mountain in a long time, oak-bay hardwoods and Douglas fir trees have invaded many chaparral areas where soil and moisture conditions are adequate.

Coastal Scrub

Coyote bush is the dominant shrub in the coastal scrub community. It consists primarily of 4-6' shrubs that range from impenetrable thickets to isolated shrubs dotting grassy hillsides. Coyote bush, also called "fuzzy wuzzy," is a nondescript shrub that forms white flowers in summer.

Coyote Bush

Joining the coyote bush in this community are sword fern, bracken fern, coffeeberry, bush lupine, monkeyflower and poison oak. California sagebrush with grey-green, needle-like leaves can also be found on drier slopes.

The best place to see this community is on the the Sky trail on Inverness Ridge at Point Reyes.

Grass, Prairie and Pastureland

The largest area of Marin, including about 50% of Point Reyes, is covered with grasses. Historically, much of this land has been used for dairy and cattle grazing and many of the native, perennial bunch grasses have been replaced with non-native, annual grasses like wild oats.

Other Communities

Other plant communities in Marin include the salt marsh, sand dune, riparian and freshwater marsh. Each has its own environmental conditions and distinctive plants.

4 Animals and Animal Tracks

In the days before the Europeans came, the San Francisco bay area and Marin County were rich in wild life. Among the large animals, there were grizzly and black bear, mountain lions, coyotes, tule elk and deer. Today, the bear are gone, although one was spotted for a short time in 2004. Coyotes and mountain lion have recently returned. Tule elk were reintroduced to Point Reyes in 1978 and are thriving.

Mule Deer

The only large mammal to continuously inhabit the land is the mule deer.

Mule Deer

The black-tailed or mule deer are abundant in Marin. They are most noticeable on the hills throughout Marin and on the coast. Males begin rutting in fall and should be considered dangerous. Antlers are shed in the winter. Females usually give birth to two fawns in the spring.

There are two non-native deer at Point Reyes. Axis deer can be identified by their brown coloring with spotted sides. Fallow deer have palmated antlers and their color ranges from black to solid white.

Smaller Animals

There are dozens of smaller animals living in Marin. These include squirrels, chipmunks, possums, shrews, weasels, moles, skunks, jack rabbits, raccoons, rats, feral pigs, bats, foxes and bobcats.

Grey Fox

The pigs are non-native, introduced elsewhere for hunting. In the 1980s, there were as many as 200 wild pigs on Mt. Tamalpais causing considerable damage digging roots and bulbs. By the 1990s, their numbers were reduced significantly by traps and hunters.

The grey fox can sometimes be seen in oak-bay woodland hills and in the coastal grasslands. They often have a reddish hue on the front flanks and can be identified by their black-tipped tail.

Bobcats are common in Marin, but probably seen less often than foxes. They can be found in coastal canyons, oak-woodland hills and along the edges of meadows. They are slightly larger than a domestic cat and are identified by their short ears and stubby tail.

Bobcat

Animal Tracks

Most animals are not easily seen. They are wary of open areas and many only appear at dusk or at night. Their footprints are the primary evidence we see during the daytime. The first thing to check when looking at animal tracks is the number of toes. Deer have two toes. Coyotes, dogs, foxes, cats, mountain lions, bobcats and rabbits have four toes. Raccoons, weasels and skunks have five toes.

Track size depends on several factors, the size and age of the animal, whether it's the front or hind foot, condition of the ground and whether the animal is walking or running. The tracks shown here are about 3/4 actual size for an adult animal.

Raccoon 2-3"

Bobcat 1.5-2"

Skunk 1-1.5"

Grey Fox 1.5-2"

Coyote 2.5"

Mountain Lion 3-4"

Running Deer 2-3"

5 Jurisdictions and Resources

Angel Island State Park
Facilities include Visitor Center, Museum, snack bar, picnic areas and camping*. Fee for ferry.

Angel Island Park Headquarters 415-435-1915
Angel Island Association 415-435-3522
Tiburon Ferry Information 415-435-2131

China Camp State Park
Facilities include Ranger Station, Museum, snack bar, picnic areas and camping*. Day use parking fee for most areas.

China Camp Park Headquarters 415-456-0766

Golden Gate National Recreation Area (GGNRA)
Facilities include Visitor Center, historical forts, Marine Mammal Center, picnic areas and camping*.

Marin Headlands Visitor Center 415-331-1540
Hostel information 415-331-2777
Stinson Beach Information 415-868-1922
Golden Gate National Parks Conservancy 415-561-3000

Marin County Open Space District (MCOSD)
No facilities. Hiking, biking and picnicking only.

Marin County Open Space District Office 415-499-6387
Volunteer Program 415-499-3778

Marin Municipal Water District (MMWD)
No facilities. Hiking, biking, fishing and picnicking only. No swimming in the lakes. Entrance fee for main lakes area.

Sky Oaks Ranger Station 415-945-1181

Mt. Tamalpais State Park
Facilities include Ranger Station, Museum, outdoor theater, snack bar, picnic areas and camping. Parking fee for some areas.

Pantoll Ranger Station and Campground* 415-388-2070
East Peak Visitor Center - Hours 10-4 on weekends
East Peak Snack Bar - Usually 10-4 summer and winter weekends
Steep Ravine Cabins and Campground* - www.reserveamerica.com
Mt. Tamalpais Interpretive Association - Weekly hikes 415-388-2070
Mountain Play Association - Plays in May and June, 415-383-1100
Tamalpais Conservation Club - PO Box 2272, Mill Valley, CA 94942
Mt. Tamalpais History Project - c/o Mill Valley Public Library

Muir Woods National Monument

Facilities include Visitor Center, gift shop and snack bar. No biking or picnicking allowed. Entrance fee.

Muir Woods Park Headquarters 415-388-2595

Olompali State Historic Park

Facilities include a historical display area and picnicking. Parking fee.

Olompali Park Headquarters 415-892-3383
The Olompali People - Volunteer group 415-892-3383

Point Reyes National Seashore (PRNS)

Facilities include three Visitor Centers, gift shop and snack bar. First-time visitors should stop at the main Visitor Center at Bear Valley to view exhibits and pick up information about a wide variety of ranger-led activities and hikes.

Bear Valley Visitor Center 415-464-5100. Main Visitor Center.
Lighthouse Visitor Center 415-669-1534. Check hours.
Drakes Beach Visitor Center 415-669-1250. A cafe is located here.
Hostel information 415-663-8811 early morning and evenings only.
Backpacking Reservations* 415-663-8054
Recorded Weather and Whale Information 415-464-5100
Point Reyes Field Seminars 415-663-1200

Samuel P. Taylor State Park

Facilities include Ranger Station, historical display area, picnic areas and camping*. Entrance fee to main area.

Samuel P. Taylor Park Headquarters 415-488-9897

Tomales Bay State Park

Facilities include Ranger Station, swimming area and picnic areas. Entrance fee to main area.

Tomales Bay Park Headquarters 415-669-1140.

Related organizations include:

Sierra Club - Weekly hikes, 6014 College, Oakland 94618
Tamalpa Runners - PO Box 701, Corte Madera 94925
Olema Ranch Campground* www.olemaranch.com, 1-800-655-2267
Bicycle Trails Council of Marin - PO Box 494, Fairfax 94978
California Native Plant Society - 1 Harrison Ave, Sausalito 94965
Marin County Fire Department "Red Flag Days" 415-499-7191

*Camping in most areas is limited. Call before planning a trip.
All state parks use www.reserveamerica.com, 1-800-444-7275

6 Index of Names

Trails and Roads - All trails and fire roads that are hiked are listed in the index by hike number.

Place Names, Mountains and Lakes - These are listed in the index if they are on the map and the hike visits the place or area.

Burdell Mountain FR E13, E14
Buzzard Burn FR E7
Camino Alto FR H2
Camp Alice Eastwood B4, B7
Camp Eastwood Rd B7, B9
Camp Reynolds (West Garrison) A12, A13
Canyon Trail C7
Cardiac Hill B6, B11, H4
Carey Camp Trail D2
Carson Falls C9
Cascade Canyon Open Space D2
Cascade Falls D2, D3
Cascade Peak D4
Cataract Trail B15, B17, B19, C11
Cavallo Pt A1
Cedar FR D1
Chicken Shack FR E5
Chimney Rock G13
China Camp Historic Area D13
China Camp State Park D12-D15
Coast Camp G4, G10
Coast Trail (Point Reyes) F5-F7, F11, F15-F17, G4, G7, G10
Coastal Trail (GGNRA) A1, A3, A8, A10, B15, H1, J5
Coast View Trail H4
Cobblestone FR E12, E13
Colier Spring B21, C18,
Colier Trail C18
Concrete Pipe FR C7, C12
Conifer FR H6
Corte Madera Ridge FR A14
Corte Madera Trail B1
County View Trail A8
Cowboy Rock Trail J3
Coyote Ridge Trail A8, A10, H1
Creamery Bay H11
Cross Country Boys Trail C18
Cross Marin Trail D7-D9
Crown Road C5
Dawn Falls Trail A15
DeBorba Trail E8
Deer Camp FR (Indian Tree) E9
Deer Camp FR (Mt. Burdell) E12

Deer Camp FR (San Geronimo Ridge) H6
Deer Camp Trail E9
Deer Island Loop Trail E8
Deer Park C6, C7
Deer Park FR (Fairfax) C6, C7
Deer Park FR (Mt. Tamalpais) B6, H4
Devils Gulch Trail D10, D11
Diaz Ridge Trail A9
Dipsea Trail B6, B11, B14, B16, H3, H4, J5
Discovery Museum A1
Divide Meadow F3-F7, G3
Doe Hill FR H10
Double Bowknot B2
Double Point F15
Drake Memorial G12
Drakes Beach G12
Drakes Estero G11, G12, H11
Duxbury Reef Preserve F14
Dwarf Oak Trail E12, H10
Eagle Trail J3
Earthquake Trail F1
East Fort Baker A1
East Peak B8, B20, B21, C19
Easy Grade Trail B13
Eldridge Grade B21, C5, C19, J4
Elliott Trail C12
Escalon FR H2
Estero Trail G8, G11
Evans Canyon Trail H6
F Ranch (Site) H11
Fern Canyon Trail B4, B7
Fern Creek Trail B8
Fieldstone Trail E11
Fire Lane Trail G2
Firtop F10, F11
Five Brooks Trailhead F8-F11
Five Corners C7, C12
Fort Barry A4
Fort Cronkhite A5
Fort McDowell (East Garrison) A13
Foul Pool C11, C14
Four Corners J3
Fox Trail H1
French Ranch FR J7

About the Authors

Kay Martin is retired from the California Academy of Sciences where she was managing editor for scientific publications. She works as a volunteer docent for Bay Shore Studies and is active with the California Native Plant Society and the Marin Master Gardener Program. In training for five marathons, she has logged several thousand miles running the trails of Marin County.

Don Martin is retired from the College of Marin where he taught physics and computer science. While Kay runs, Don hikes and occasionally rides his mountain bike.

The Martins have lived in San Anselmo since 1965. They are members of the Sierra Club, Tamalpa Runners, Audubon Society and St. Anselm's Church. They have four grown children and four soon-to-be-hiking grandchildren.

Bob Johnson is a well-known Sonoma and Marin County illustrator. He has illustrated and designed dozens of books. In recent years, he has become very active in the wine industry, designing labels and packaging for many Sonoma and Napa wineries.

You can contact the Martins by writing:
Martin Press LLC
P.O. Box 2109
San Anselmo, CA 94979

or email:
book@marintrails.com